Kingdom in crisis

War, Armed Forces and Society

General Editor: Ian F. W. Beckett

John Laband

Kingdom in crisis

The Zulu response to the British invasion of 1879

Manchester University Press
Manchester and New York
Distributed exclusively in the USA and Canada by St. Martin's Press

Published by Manchester University Press
Oxford Road, Manchester M13 9PL, UK
and Room 400, 175 Fifth Avenue, New York, NY 10010, USA

Distributed exclusively in the USA and Canada
by St. Martin's Press, Inc., 175 Fifth Avenue, New York,
NY 10010, USA

British Library Cataloguing-in-Publication Data

A catalogue record for this book is available from the British Library

Library of Congress Cataloging-in-Publication Data applied for

ISBN 0 7190 3582–1 *hardback*

Photoset in Linotron Sabon
by Northern Phototypesetting Co. Ltd, Bolton

Printed in Great Britain
by Biddles Ltd, Guildford and King's Lynn

Contents

List of maps

Acknowledgements

Work towards this investigation into the Zulu dimension to the Anglo–Zulu War began in 1984 when, with the help of grants from the Human Sciences Research Council and the University of Natal, I conducted research in Britain. There, and in South Africa, the staffs of the many archives and libraries I visited always did their best to smooth my path as a researcher. I have been fortunate also in the way in which colleagues and experts in the field of the Anglo–Zulu War have helped and encouraged me through discussion, positive criticism and comradeship. In particular, I must thank Dr Paul Thompson, who in 1978 first inspanned me to research into the Anglo–Zulu War, and with whom I still continue to plough the field; Professor Colin Webb and Professor Bill Guest, who gave unstintingly of their considerable knowledge but limited spare time to supervise this work in its original form as a doctoral dissertation; and Dr Jeff Mathews, with whom I am currently engaged on several Anglo–Zulu War projects. Professor John Wright and Adrian Koopman have done their best to ensure that my spelling of Zulu names conformed with modern orthographic practice.

My grateful memories go also to the late Frank Emery of St Peter's College, Oxford, who arranged with Dr G. K. Woodgate that I should have access to the important Woodgate Papers, and was my host when researching in Oxford. Others joined in succouring me when far from home, in particular Jane and Jonathan Ruffer, who provided my comfortable and welcoming research-base in London, and Gail and Jeremy Andrew of Johannesburg.

Dr Ian Beckett, general editor of the War, Armed Forces and Society series, first encouraged me to consider turning my dissertation into a book. I am extremely grateful for the considerable forbearance both he and Jane Carpenter of Manchester University Press have since exercised in expertly managing the transformation.

Helena Margeot and Raymond Poonsamy have, as so often in the past, changed my inept drafts into elegant maps.

Finally, I can only thank my wife, Fenella, and my two children, Felix and Zoë, for their patience and understanding over the long period during which this work has been in gestation, and for accepting my long absences, both physical and mental, in its thrall.

J.P.C.L.
Department of Historical Studies
University of Natal, Pietermaritzburg

List of abbreviations

AC	Alison Collection, papers in the Brenthurst Library, Parktown, Johannesburg
AAG	Assistant Adjutant-General
AG	Adjutant-General
ASNA	Acting Secretary for Native Affairs, Natal
AU	Argief Utrecht, papers in Transvaal Archives Depot, Pretoria
BPP	*British Parliamentary Papers*
CO	Colonial Office, London
CP	Chelmsford Papers, National Army Museum, Chelsea, London
CSO	Colonial Secretary's Office, Natal, papers in Natal Archives Depot, Pietermaritzburg
DAG	Deputy Adjutant-General
FC	Fannin Collection, papers in Natal Archives Depot, Pietermaritzburg
GH	Government House, Natal, papers in Natal Archives Depot, Pietermaritzburg
JSA	Webb, C. de B. and Wright, J. B. (eds. and trs.) *The James Stuart Archive of Recorded Oral evidence relating to the History of the Zulu and Neighbouring Peoples*, Pietermaritzburg and Durban, 1976, 1979, 1982, 1986, vols. 1–4
KCAL	Killie Campbell Africana Library, Durban
NAD	Natal Archives Depot, Pietermaritzburg
RM	Resident Magistrate
SNA	Secretary for Native Affairs, Natal, papers in Natal Archives Depot, Pietermaritzburg
SS	Staatsekretaris, Transvaal, papers in Transvaal Archives Depot, Pretoria

TS	Sir Theophilus Shepstone Papers, Natal Archives Depot, Pietermaritzburg
WC	Sir Evelyn Wood Collection, Natal Archives Depot, Pietermaritzburg
WO	War Office, papers in Public Record Office, Kew, London
ZA	Zululand Archives, papers in Natal Archives Depot, Pietermaritzburg

Thou great and mighty chief

Thou great and mighty Chief!
Thou who hast an army
The son of Sogica [Sir T. Shepstone] sent his forces:
(*Chorus*) We destroyed them.
The Amasoja [soldiers] came:
(*Chorus*) We destroyed them.
The mounted soldiers came:
(*Chorus*) We destroyed them.
The Amalenja [Volunteers] came:
(*Chorus*) We destroyed them.
The Nonqai [Mounted Police] came:
(*Chorus*) We destroyed them.
Thou the Great Chief!
Thou who hast an army;
When will they dare to repeat their attack?

(CSO 1927, no. 2451/1879: Fannin to Colonial Secretary, 12 May 1879: Natal Border Police report of praises sung in honour of King Cetshwayo and his army during a celebration at an *umuzi* on the Zulu banks of the Thukela River, opposite the eMthanjeni Drift. Interpolations in brackets by J. E. Fannin, Special Border Agent, Umvoti County, Colony of Natal.)

Introduction: The stakes of war

For historians to ask new questions has the important effect of alerting them to unfamiliar aspects of familiar problems, and to unsuspected data in well worked sources. So it is with the Anglo–Zulu War of 1879, where the field has apparently been thoroughly traversed.[1] Yet, until recently, the war has been treated from the standpoint of the invading British, and in the manner traditional to Victorian colonial campaigns. The Zulu dimension to the struggle, which should embrace not only an appreciation of Zulu military capability and planning, but also an understanding of the structure of Zulu society and the functioning of the Zulu state, has consequently suffered neglect. Clearly, though, any attempt to comprehend the efforts of the Zulu kingdom to meet the challenge of invasion by a well equipped, professional British army must take into account the interrelationship of all these elements.

It is true that the traditional handling of the war from the purely military perspective of the British (an approach best exemplified by Donald Morris in *The Washing of the Spears*[2]) has begun increasingly to give way to scholarly concern with the Zulu role in the conflict. Yet the pioneering work of Anglo–Zulu War historians F. W. D. Jackson, Jeff Mathews and Paul Thompson still retains a eurocentric slant.[3] Even Ian Knight, whose recent popular synthesis, *Brave Men's Blood*,[4] conscientiously attempts a balanced assessment of the opposing sides, neglects Zulu political and strategic options. Robert Edgerton, who set out in *Like Lions They Fought*[5] deliberately to investigate the part the Zulu played in the war, is not entirely successful either. By confining himself to examining how the Zulu, within the constraints of their particular culture, responded to the stresses of combat, he failed to satisfy the historian endeavouring to understand the workings of the Zulu polity and its ultimate military and political failure.

Rather, the examination of the Zulu kingdom in its moment of crisis in 1879 should be approached through the medium of war and society studies. This school, which has only comparatively recently received common scholarly recognition, emerged in reaction to the circumscribed work of traditional campaign-conscious historians, which has tended to extract war from the wider social and historical contexts which should give it meaning. By contrast, war and society studies (or the 'new military history' as it is also known) stress the interrelationship between the nature and structure of society, the condition of the economy, the functioning of the state, military capability and planning, and actual performance in battle.

Since the theme of this study is war, and whatever light its investigation throws upon those societies waging it, it is essential to understand what is meant by it here. Theories on wars and their causes can only too often reflect abstract preoccupations, though in this case the thought of von Clausewitz has proved illuminating. 'War,' he declared, 'is a clash between major interests that is resolved by bloodshed – that is the only way in which it differs from other conflicts.'[6] In other words, it is a drastic means of testing a power relationship. When one side in a conflict admits it is defeated, agreement is reached and peace, based on a new relationship, becomes possible. War, therefore, is of a reciprocal nature, and the aggressor's assumptions of relative advantage are matched by others on the part of the prospective victim. If the latter contemplates resistance, it is because he has a perception of a hostile power which threatens the restriction (if not extinction) of the state over which he rules. Naturally, the forms resistance might take are conditioned by a state's internal economic, social, political and ideological condition – let alone its military capability. And at the moment of crisis the victim does have the option of submitting peacefully, of accepting the aggressor's own perception of his superior power. When he does not, it shows that he calculates that more is to be gained by fighting than through capitulation – even if it is only to salvage honour in the face of hopeless odds. Clearly, wars can only endure so long as the antagonists persist in thinking it more worthwhile to fight than to negotiate or submit. But determination to persevere with a war, even in the most contrary circumstances, should not be considered remarkable when the stakes can be, in Raymond Aron's words, 'the existence, the creation and the elimination of states'.[7]

This reflection is particularly apposite in the case of the Zulu kingdom. For as William McNeill has shown, when a state is confronted by a better equipped and organized armed force against which it finds it difficult to protect itself with success, it is in danger of losing not only its autonomy, but its corporate identity as well.[8] Such indeed was the prospect facing the Zulu in 1878 as they contemplated the British troops concentrating along the borders of their kingdom.

Notes

1 See, for example, the bibliography in J. P. C Laband and P. S. Thompson, *Field Guide to the War in Zululand and the Defence of Natal 1879*, Pietermaritzburg, 1987, pp. 118–20, 124.

2 D. R. Morris, *The Washing of the Spears: A History of the Rise of the Zulu Nation under Shaka and its Fall in the Zulu War of 1879*, London, 1966.

3 This is not the case with Jeff Guy, but he is primarily concerned with the civil war which destroyed Zululand after 1879, rather than with the war itself. Consult the bibliography for publications by these authors.

4 I. J. Knight, *Brave Men's Blood: The Epic of the Zulu War, 1879*, London, 1990.

5 R. B. Edgerton, *Like Lions They Fought: The Zulu War and the Last Black Empire in South Africa*, Great Britain, 1988.

6 C. von Clausewitz (eds. M. Howard and P. Paret), *On War*, Princeton, 1976, p. 149.

7 R. Aron, *Peace and War: A Theory of International Relations*, London, 1966, p. 7.

8 W. H. McNeill, *The Pursuit of Power*, Oxford, 1983, p. viii.

1

Grounds for aggression

It is a common historical assumption that nations go to war over their perceived 'vital interests'. In fact, these may be less than objectively 'vital', nor completely susceptible to rational political and economic analysis. The sweeping search for security in the future, for example, can justify present policies of aggression and annexation, and the rejection of another state's legitimate interests.[1] Such a situation pertained on 11 December 1878, when the representatives of Sir Bartle Frere, the British High Commissioner in South Africa, presented his ultimatum to the emissaries of the Zulu king, Cetshwayo kaMpande. Of course, the British had explicable motives for risking war with the Zulu to impose their will. If these were not always justifiable, they must nevertheless be extracted from the distorting context of the subsequent cruel military campaign and disastrous political settlement, and be understood in terms of the men who conceived of them.

Perhaps it is inevitable that modern historians should be at variance when attempting to interpret British motives, though the events themselves leading up to the Anglo–Zulu War are well enough established. Essential to an understanding of what was at issue is some familiarity with the concept of the 'frontier', which in the South African context may be defined as a zone of interpenetration between two previously distinct societies. The frontier opens when the first white settlers, representatives of an intrusive society, arrive, and closes when a single political authority has eventually established its hegemony over the indigenous peoples, normally through force. In the late 1870s the frontiers were closing abruptly in the Transkei, Transvaal and Zululand as policy-makers in London exerted their inherently superior power in the region to safeguard British interests.[2]

Scholars perceive these interests in different ways. One approach is to argue that British policy in southern Africa in the 1870s must be seen in the context of the transformation of the local economy by the mineral revolution. With the development of both mining and capitalist agriculture came increasing pressures for labour and land, a stimulated local market economy, and closer links with the capitalist economy of Europe. Therefore, the schemes of the British to consolidate their hold in the sub-continent are seen as arising out of a desire to create a settled environment for economic integration and progress.[3] In this vein, Norman Etherington has shown how vital in the case of Zululand were the ambitions of Natal commercial interests to secure an orderly supply of labour for their concerns.[4] Similarly, Jeff Guy, in his influential work on the Zulu kingdom, has explained the British invasion of pre-capitalist Zululand as essential in order to open the anachronistic kingdom to the developing capitalistic economy of the region, and to unlock a supply of wage-labourers.[5]

Yet if political considerations were inevitably linked with economic transformations and the material forces at play, difficulties still remain in accounting for the British invasion of Zululand in terms of the advance of capitalistic production. It is surely myopic to perceive war simply as part of the 'superstructure', determined by the socio-economic 'base'. For war is a crisis in relations between states, and while foreign policy is inevitably influenced by internal conditions, these cannot usefully be elevated to sole primacy. Colin Webb has emphatically made this point when interpreting the origins of the Anglo–Zulu War. Particular events demand particular explanations. In turn, these require an understanding within a specific historical context of the prevailing values and assumptions of the participants, as well as a grasp of their conscious motives and intentions.[6]

Every war has an ideological quality, in that the belligerents justify their participation by appealing to general principles. The Anglo–Zulu War was no exception. By the 1870s imperial policy-makers in Britain were looking to consolidate, rather than extend, the empire. India, so vital to Britains commercial interests and her status as an imperial power, remained the key. India's security depended on control of the routes to the east through the Suez Canal and around the Cape, and these required that Britain remain the supreme power in Egypt and southern Africa for essentially strategic, rather than commercial, reasons. The difficulty in maintaining Britain's traditional paramountcy of the African sub-continent lay not so much with the ambitions of rival colonial powers as with the politically and economically fragmented nature of the region itself. The unco-ordinated activities of British colonies, Voortrekker republics and the surviving independent black polities made for inefficient and incomplete management. Lord Carnarvon, who became Colonial Secretary in 1874, saw in the concept of confederation an answer to this problem. He began obsessively to pursue the chimera of a confederation of the white-ruled states of the region. Ideally, such a confederation would bear the costs of its own administration and internal security, possibly be a base from which to extend British paramountcy north over much of the rest of Africa, and at the same time provide a firmer link in the British route to India.[7]

The solving of the 'native question', however, was the key to the success of the project. What complicated relations with blacks living in the white states was the presence of independent black neighbours, whom whites perceived as constituting a serious and common danger. Confederation, it was supposed, by creating a stable political structure for the region and effectively closing the frontier, would diminish the opportunity for costly and undesired wars between the white colonies and their black neighbours. The Cape Colony, however, as the weightiest member of any proposed union, presented a problem, for it feared that it would have to bear the responsibility for coping with the threat posed by independent black neighbours. Consequently, it was reluctant to become involved unless Britain continued to provide military protection (which obligation confederation was designed to diminish), or until the black polities along its own eastern borders and those adjoining the Transvaal and Natal had been subdued.[8]

Thus it was the Transvaal Republic's unsuccessful struggle between May 1876 and February 1877 against Sekhukhune's Pedi that brought direct imperial intervention to that region. In January 1877 Theophilus Shepstone set about the process of annexing the Transvaal to Britain both to placate the Cape and to overcome the Boers' resistance to confederation. Annexation would transfer the responsibility for the Pedi war to the British military, who expected to make short work of it.

Meanwhile, Carnarvon was encouraged by Shepstone's success in the Transvaal to entrust his plans to a statesman capable of carrying them into effect. The instrument he selected was Sir Bartle Frere, the great Indian administrator. Frere departed for South Africa in March

1877 as Governor of the Cape, High Commissioner of South Africa and commander-in-chief of the British forces. With these very considerable powers he was expected to complete confederation and then to stay on as the first governor-general of the new South African dominion – an architect of empire in the mould of a Lord Durham.[9]

Frere is the key figure in the prelude to the Anglo–Zulu War, for British diplomatic relations with the Zulu kingdom were conducted through his agency. Though he was influenced by local statesmen, notably Theophilus Shepstone and Sir Henry Bulwer, the Lieutenant-Governor of Natal, the great decisions of war and peace were nevertheless his alone. It is essential, therefore, to understand the mainsprings of his actions, especially since of late he has been severely handled by some historians.[10]

Frere conceived of his mission in Carnarvon's terms, and therefore it was a great blow to him when his patron resigned in February 1878. Nevertheless, Frere stayed on, determined to implement confederation. The new Colonial Secretary, Sir Michael Hicks Beach, was so engrossed in crises elsewhere that he was inclined to leave the revered and vigorous elder statesman in South Africa to his own devices.

Frere was an administrator reared in the Indian school, who brought his methods and principles intact to the South African situation. A committed evangelical and trained to act vigorously on his own initiative, he considered that it was Britain's high mission to spread the civilizing influence of Christian government and to eradicate barbarous institutions. By extending British rule over blacks, he believed, it would be possible to guide them up the ladder of evolution and improve their standards of living through good administration and economic prosperity.[11] He envisaged putting them to 'civilized' labour for wages, so they could spend their earnings on European manufactured goods to the benefit of white colonists, and to their own advantage.[12]

When Frere arrived in South Africa in late March 1877, Shepstone was on the verge of consummating the annexation of the Transvaal, thus securing the northern component of the budding confederation. The High Commissioner thus turned his attention to closing the Cape eastern frontier, and during the course of the Ninth Frontier War of 1877–78 against the Ngqika-Gcaleka fitted the Transkei into his structure of confederation. His annexation of Walvis Bay in March 1878 and Port St John's in September helped secure the coast of southern Africa for Britain. However, some portions of the frontier remained obstinately open. The Mpondo continued a source of unresolved difficulty, as did the Griqua of Griqualand East. The Pedi of the north-eastern Transvaal were proving much more difficult to overcome than had been anticipated, and their resistance posed a real threat to Shepstone's administration and to confederation as a whole.[13] But these problems were as nothing to that of the Zulu kingdom. Frere was convinced that until it had been neutralized a solution to the 'native question' could not be found, nor could confederation be fully realized.

Frere consequently employed a variety of arguments and capitalized on every incident to convince his superiors in London that Zululand was a savage and barbaric state which, because it threatened the stability of the rest of southern Africa, had to be brought to heel.[14] In taking this approach he could always refer for verification to the dominant (though not unanimous) opinion of the white settlers, officials and missionaries, who lived in anticipation of a Zulu invasion abetted by a domestic black uprising, and who looked to the imperial government to turn the barbarous Zulu into docile and productive citizens. All characterized the Zulu kingdom as a bloodthirsty despotism where arbitrary executions were the order of the day,[15] and where missionary endeavour (so prized by Frere as the gateway to civilized life) was constantly thwarted.[16]

It was the Zulu 'military system', though, which, as an apparently perpetual menace to its neighbours, provided the best reason for action against the Zulu monarchy. No matter the military system's true nature, it was perceived as a 'frightfully efficient manslaying war-machine'.[17] Moreover, it was said to be in the hands of an 'unscrupulous and extremely ambitious savage',[18] commonly regarded in official, military and popular opinion as the inspiration of a black conspiracy long brewing to overthrow white supremacy in the sub-continent.

In consequence, Frere could always claim that any action he initiated against Zululand was morally justifiable and necessary for the safety of the white colonists.[19] Nevertheless, legitimate and 'legal' grounds were necessary before steps could actually be taken. These he found in the so-called 'coronation laws' of 1873, whose conditions Cetshwayo was apparently failing to keep.

The coronation laws were the consequence of Cetshwayo's efforts on the death of his father King Mpande to gain the support of the

Natal government against internal opposition among the great chiefs, and to find an ally in Zululand's long-standing territorial dispute with the Transvaal. Shepstone, on the other hand, who as Natal Secretary for Native Affairs 'crowned' Cetshwayo on 1 September 1873, hoped in return to extend Natal's political control over Zululand. What Shepstone saw as a mark of British suzerainty over Zululand Cetshwayo understood as a diplomatic success, and the laws – which forbade condemnation without open trial and executions without royal consent – as restricting the arbitrary powers of the great chiefs and strengthening his own.[20] Cetshwayo was consequently outraged when the Natal government perversely interpreted the laws as restricting his powers, and resisted its claims of authority over him.[21] Yet in insisting that Cetshwayo should abide by the laws, Frere found the 'legal' excuse – as well as the moral grounds – for interfering in Zululand's internal affairs.[22]

Such interference was made imperative by developments in the Transvaal, since April 1877 a British colony. Relations between the Zulu kingdom and the Transvaal had revolved since 1848 around their smouldering border dispute in the region of the Ncome (Blood) and Mzinyathi (Buffalo) rivers. Boer farmers were constantly encroaching deeper into territory claimed by the Zulu, and in 1864 and again in 1875 attempted to lay down boundary lines that alienated large tracts of Zululand. In 1876 open conflict between the two sides was averted only when the Boers backed down.[23] Shepstone, when Secretary for Native Affairs in Natal, had been inclined to side with the Zulu, if only because he saw Boer expansion into Zululand as threatening his grandiose plan to extend British influence to the north by creating a corridor which would carry labour and trade into the interior and cut the Boers off from the sea. But now, as Administrator of the Transvaal, he had to take the Boers' part. He was especially concerned to win over those unreconciled to loss of independence through a demonstration of the advantages of British paramountcy. Such a demonstration involved successfully subduing the Pedi claims to independence. Yet Shepstone believed Sekhukhune's obduracy to stem from the moral support and example of King Cetshwayo, the leader of the reputed 'black conspiracy'. A demonstration of imperial power over the boundary question was therefore necessary to humble Cetshwayo, bring Sekhukhune to his senses and mollify the Boers.[24]

Shepstone set about this objective. On 18 October 1877, after a series of incidents in the border area, he met a Zulu delegation at Conference Hill. The Zulu made it clear that they would never abandon their land claims.[25] Over the next few months further incidents and strained negotiations increased the chance of hostilities and gave substance to Shepstone's requests to Frere to be allowed to settle the whole issue by force. That solution seemed all the more tempting in that Shepstone did not consider it would take 'much trouble or much time' to put down the Zulu, whose defeat would eradicate the 'root of all evil' in South Africa.[26]

At this tense moment Bulwer intervened, so temporarily thwarting Frere's and Shepstone's plans. His fears of the implications for Natal of a full-scale war caused him to send word to Cetshwayo on 8 December 1877, offering to mediate in the dispute. The Zulu king accepted with relief, while Shepstone and the belligerent apostles of confederation could not but acquiesce. Bulwer's Boundary Commission, which was made up of Natal officials, began its sittings at Rorke's Drift on 17 March 1878. In June it handed its scrupulously completed work to Bulwer. Though it did not consider the disputed area north of the Phongolo River, it recognized the Transvaal's right to the land between the Mzinyathi and Ncome rivers, but not to the territory beyond the Ncome where some Boers had settled.[27]

When Frere received the Commission's report on 15 July 1878, he analysed it in terms of its likely effect on the Transvaal in particular, and on confederation in general. On both counts it was disastrous to his plans, and he was at a loss as to how best to respond.

Historians, notably Colin Webb, have criticized Frere for suppressing the report and delaying an award in terms of its recommendations in order to prepare the ground for war.[28] Yet Graham Dominy has shown that Frere's approach was not as Machiavellian as has been supposed. Frere passed the report around South Africa, soliciting advice on how best to act, and then pondered the alternatives.[29] He was loath to come to a decision without Shepstone's approval; while at the same time he was being harassed by Bulwer, who feared that delay in announcing an award would provoke the Zulu to war.[30]

Frere arrived in Pietermaritzburg on 28 September 1878 with the intention first of announcing the boundary award, and then of proceeding to the Transvaal to settle that increasingly reluctant colony's affairs.[31] There Shepstone had commenced operations in April 1878 against Sekhukhune, but despite a strong infusion of imperial troops the campaign was proving a disaster, and by the end of October the British would have to withdraw from Pedi territory.[32] In these negative circumstances, any award which failed to demonstrate Britain's determination to guarantee Boer security against the blacks could well lead to rebellion. Such an uprising might draw in the Dutch elsewhere in South Africa, and encourage the Zulu and their black allies to attack the whites. Frere began to envisage a dreadful scenario where the choice lay between risking a Zulu war at once, or bringing about a Zulu war a few months later, preceded by a Boer rebellion.[33]

While Frere pondered how best to act, a number of minor incidents occurred in the second half of 1878 along the Zulu border. They involved only insignificant violations of British territory and apparent threats to some white officials, traders and farmers. They were merely symptoms of a tense frontier and in no way a cause of war. Nevertheless, they were a godsend to Frere. Causing great alarm among white settlers, they provided an immediate excuse for taking action against the incorrigibly aggressive Zulu, as well as a vital justification to the Colonial Office for doing so.[34]

Frere's military and naval commanders had preceded him to Natal, and by September were preparing, on a contingency basis, for hostilities against Zululand. The movement earlier in the year of troops from the Cape had been to act against Sekhukhune and to guard against a Boer rebellion in the Transvaal, and the troops had been deployed accordingly. Between September and November troops were moved to the Zulu border in a steady trickle. By mid-November, Lieutenant-General Lord Chelmsford, the General Officer Commanding, considered events to be moving so rapidly that he was anxious that all available troops should reach the frontier as soon as possible.[35]

The British Cabinet was reluctant to send reinforcements and insisted that the troops be used only for the defence of Natal; while Bulwer deprecated the bellicosity of the military, which was undermining the negotiated settlement for which he had been striving.[36] But military and much colonial sentiment held increasingly strongly that a Zulu war neither could, nor should, be long delayed if the 'native question' were to be settled permanently.[37]

For Frere, it was daily more difficult 'to decline the contest'.[38] How, indeed, could he? He had come to South Africa to effect confederation, and to almost all white observers it was the savage

Cetshwayo who stood in the way. Morally and politically it was Frere's duty to proceed against him. Nevertheless, the decision to go to war is perhaps the weightiest a statesman can make. Was it not still possible to break Zulu power by diplomatic means? After all, when a policy-maker contemplates adopting violent rather than peaceful means to gain his objectives, a choice between alternatives is still involved. War is not the necessary Clausewitzian continuation of policy if political aims can still be gained otherwise.[39]

That was Frere's dilemma in the last months of 1878, and why the framing of his ultimatum to the Zulu king was so crucial. Its purpose was to precipitate a final and satisfactory solution to the Zulu problem, and at the same time to mollify Transvaal opinion. For these reasons the announcement of the boundary award was to be tied to a set of conditions which, if accepted, would neutralize the Zulu monarchy. Would the Zulu accede to such stringent terms? There was indeed a chance, though it should be emphasized that Frere was never very sanguine. For him, the ultimatum was primarily a means of forcing war on the Zulu, and only secondarily an instrument whereby the kingdom could be emasculated without a struggle.

In devising the ultimatum, Frere relied mainly upon Shepstone's advice.[40] Frere himself insisted, though, that the ultimatum be framed so that it was clear that the British had no quarrel with the Zulu nation, but with the 'tyrant' alone.[41] It was equally his concern that effective security should be required to ensure that Cetshwayo kept his coronation oaths as they were understood by the British. However, Frere realistically doubted whether any verbal undertaking extracted from Cetshwayo could be binding, especially if his military might was allowed to remain intact. Yet a large British force could hardly be maintained on the borders of Zululand to 'ensure performance' of whatever promises Cetshwayo might make. Besides, Frere was so conscious of having provoked the Zulu over the preceding months that he knew it would be an enormous risk to leave the issue unresolved. He consequently found himself where he had no choice but to 'draw the Monster's teeth and claws' by ensuring that his military capability was neutralized.[42]

Having at last received Shepstone's tardy comments on the draft ultimatum, Frere and Bulwer finalized the document at the end of November. They decided to present it as soon as possible so as to facilitate Chelmsford's military preparations.[43] The ultimatum, which was read to Cetshwayo's representative on 11 December

1878, fell into two parts. The first dealt with compensation for the recent, but minor, border incidents. The remaining demands were of far greater significance. A British Resident was to be stationed in Zululand; the Zulu army was to be disbanded; all the young warriors were to be granted permission to marry; the king was to observe his coronation oaths regarding the unjust shedding of blood; missionaries were to be readmitted to Zululand; and the king was to undertake not to make war without the consent of the Resident and his Council.[44]

To Bulwer, there was nothing excessive or unjust in these demands, despite the fact that their aim was to subvert the social, political and economic structure of the Zulu kingdom. For, ultimately, he considered them necessary to attain the better government of Zululand and the security of the adjoining British territories. Even Bishop Colenso, the 'ultra philo-Zulu',[45] approved of the terms, which he considered commensurate with Britain's 'civilizing mission' and the 'harbinger of better . . . days for Zululand'. His fear was simply that if it came to war the potentialities for improving 'the social and moral condition' of the Zulu might be negated.[46] Yet Bulwer did not seriously suppose that Cetshwayo would give up his sovereignty without a fight, and neither did Shepstone or Frere. The military certainly thought Cetshwayo had been left with no alternative but to fight. Accordingly, Chelmsford's preparations for the invasion of Zululand were complete by 13 December, and his troops positioned to strike into Zululand to enforce Frere's terms once the ultimatum expired on 11 January 1879.[47]

Yet why did the Colonial Office, which certainly had no intention of seeking a war in Zululand, and was increasingly doubtful of the wisdom of Frere's ambitious South African schemes, not step in to restrain him? In October, Hicks Beach, faced with a coming conflict in Afghanistan and anxious to avoid unnecessary entanglements, did instruct Frere to exercise forbearance, and to avert war.[48] But he was unable to reverse the drift of events. For in a crisis the Colonial Office had to depend on the judgement of the High Commissioner, whom it had entrusted with wide discretionary powers, and poor communications meant that reports and orders took weeks to arrive. Frere undoubtedly manipulated the situation to deceive Hicks Beach and to proceed with plans which he knew would not receive his sanction.[49]

Yet Frere suffered from no misgivings concerning his disingenuous conduct and its consequences. It was his intention, once the Zulu army was defeated, Cetshwayo's power broken and the military system dismantled, to ensure the future good government of Zululand according to his Indian principles. Zululand would not be annexed, but would be subjected to a system of indirect rule by compliant chiefs under a British agent. Thus the frontier would be closed, and a demilitarized Zululand would be slotted into its assigned place in the confederation rather like an Indian 'subject ally'.[50]

Ultimately, Frere's going to war with Zululand regardless of the wishes of his government might have been condoned had the campaign been swift, decisive and cheap, and successfully furthered the cause of confederation. As it was, instead of settling the regional problems of southern Africa for the price of a minor campaign, he committed Britain to a humiliating, extended and expensive war in Zululand, and sparked off the Transvaal rebellion two years later.

In pursuing his goal in Zululand, Frere miscalculated according to two of the most important factors which Blainey has isolated as influencing statesmen when assessing their ability to impose their will through war.[51] Firstly, he was confident that the military strength and skill at his disposal were sufficient for the task. Secondly, he supposed that the internal divisions in Zululand could be exploited to fragment resistance. It has often been colonial policy to foment such cleavages in the pre-conquest phase and in the closing of the frontier,[52] and Frere was persuaded by Shepstone that under the stress of war existing opposition to Cetshwayo would grow, and that political disarray, compounded by military defeat, would rapidly bring the Zulu kingdom to its knees.[53] These assumptions were to prove ill founded, and the British were to find that Zulu military ability and political cohesion were greater than they had presumed.

Notes

1 B. Brodie, *War and Politics*, London, 1974, pp. 342–9.

2 See H. Lamar and L. Thompson (eds.), *The Frontier in History: North America and Southern Africa Compared*, New Haven and London, 1981, pp. 7–10; and C. Saunders, 'Political processes in the South African frontier zones', in ibid., pp. 149–50, 164–5, 170–1.

3 See A. Atmore and S. Marks, 'The imperial factor in South Africa in the nineteenth century: towards a reassessment', *Journal of Imperial and Commonwealth History*, III, 1, 1974, pp. 121–7.

4 See especially N. Etherington, 'Labour supply and the genesis of South African confederation in the 1870s', *Journal of African History*, XX, 3, 1979, pp. 236–45.

5 Jeff Guy, *The Destruction of the Zulu Kingdom: The Civil War in Zululand, 1879–1884*, London, 1979, especially pp. 41–51.

6 C. de B. Webb, 'The origins of the Anglo–Zulu War: problems of interpretation', IN A. Duminy and C. Ballard (eds.), *The Anglo–Zulu War: New Perspectives*, Pietermaritzburg, 1981, p. 11.

7 C. F. Goodfellow, *Great Britain and South African Confederation*, Cape Town, 1966, pp. 208–9.

8 W. R. Guest, 'The war, Natal and confederation' in Duminy and Ballard, *New Perspectives*, p. 67.

9 J. A. Benyon, *Proconsul and Paramountcy in South Africa: The High Commission, British Supremacy and the Sub-continent, 1806–1910*, Pietermaritzburg, 1980, pp. 144–8.

10 See in particular N. Etherington, 'Anglo–Zulu relations, 1856–1878' in Duminy and Ballard, *New Perspectives*, pp. 13–14, in which Frere is described as 'a bully with a black hat . . . caught with a smoking gun in his hand.'

11 F. V. Emery, 'Geography and imperialism: the role of Sir Bartle Frere (1815–84)', *Geographical Journal*, 50, 3, November 1984, pp. 346–8.

12 CO 879/14: *African Confidential Print* 166, p. 5: notes by Frere, 3 February 1879.

13 Benyon, *Proconsul*, pp. 153, 161–2.

14 See *BPP* (C. 2222), enc. 1 in no. 42: memorandum by Frere, 6 December 1878, in which he sets out a comprehensive list of his official reasons for moving against Zululand.

15 As a good example of this viewpoint, see Sir H. Rider Haggard, *Cetywayo and his White Neighbours: or, Remarks on Recent Events in Zululand, Natal and the Transvaal*, London, 1888, pp. 16–19.

16 Missionaries were leading detractors of the Zulu monarchy and called vociferously for Cetshwayo's overthrow. The Revd R. Robertson of the Anglicans and the Revd O. Oftebro of the Norwegians were the most militant.

17 CO 879/14: *African Confidential Print* 166, p. 5: notes by Frere, 3 February 1879.

18 H. Hallam Parr, *A Sketch of the Kafir and Zulu Wars*, London, 1880, p. 125.

19 WC II/2/4: Frere to Wood, 25 March 1879.

20 R. L. Cope, 'Political power within the Zulu kingdom and the "Coronation Laws" of 1873', *Journal of Natal and Zulu History*, VIII, 1985, pp. 11–18.

21 'Do I come to Natal and dictate to him [the Lieutenant-Governor] about his laws?' (SNA 1/7/13, p. 17: message from the king, 2 November 1876).

22 TS 34: Frere to Shepstone, 15 November 1878.

23 For the Transvaal–Zululand boundary dispute, see J. P. C. Laband, 'Mbilini, Manyonyoba and the Phongolo River frontier: a neglected sector

of the Anglo–Zulu War of 1879', in J. Laband and P. Thompson, *Kingdom and Colony at War: Sixteen Studies on the Anglo–Zulu War of 1879*, Pietermaritzburg, 1990, pp. 184–5.

24 P. Delius, *The Land Belongs to Us: The Pedi Polity, the Boers and the British in the Nineteenth Century Transvaal*, Johannesburg, 1983, pp. 225–9.

25 R. L. Cope, 'Shepstone and Cetshwayo, 1873–1879', unpublished M.A. thesis, University of Natal, 1967, pp. 226–34, 237–9.

26 TS 68: Shepstone to Carnarvon, 11 December 1877; Shepstone to Frere, 18 December 1877.

27 C. de B. Webb and J. B. Wright, *A Zulu King Speaks: Statements made by Cetshwayo kaMpande on the History and Customs of his People*, Pietermaritzburg and Durban, 1978, pp. xiii–iv.

28 C. de B. Webb, 'Lines of power – the high commissioner, the telegraph and the war of 1879', *Natalia*, 8, December 1978, p. 34.

29 G. A. Dominy, 'Awarding a retrospective white hat? A reconsideration of the geopolitics of "Frere's War" of 1879', paper presented at a workshop on Natal in the Colonial Period, University of Natal, Pietermaritzburg, October 1984, pp. 10–11.

30 TS 34: Frere to T. Shepstone, 26 October 1878; 2 November 1878; 29 November 1878.

31 A Boer deputation had already gone to London to plead unsuccessfully for the restoration of the Transvaal's independence, and Frere knew that agitation could only increase.

32 Intelligence Branch of the War Office, *Narrative of the Field Operations Connected with the Zulu War of 1879*, London, 1881, pp. 6–10.

33 GH 600: Frere to Hicks Beach, 5 September 1878.

34 CO 874/14: *African Confidential Print* 162, no. 199: Frere to Hicks Beach, 10 September 1878.

35 TS 34: Thesiger to T. Shepstone, 17 November 1878 (private and confidential).

36 Bulwer Letters: Bulwer to Edward Bulwer, 8 December 1878.

37 Even the Colonial Office was inclined to agree that the root of all 'native difficulties' lay with Cetshwayo. See CO 879/14: *African Confidential Print* 164, p. 21: Confidential Memorandum on the Zulu Question by E. F. [Edward Fairfield], 19 March 1879.

38 J. Martineau, *The Life and Correspondence of the Right Hon. Sir Bartle Frere, Bart.*, London, 1895, vol. II, p. 253: Frere to Hicks Beach, 8 December 1878.

39 J. Lider, *On the Nature of War*, Farnborough, 1979, pp. 59–61.

40 TS 34: Frere to T. Shepstone, 7 November 1878.

41 See GH 601, no. 12A/79: Notification by His Excellency the High Commissioner, 4 January 1879, in which Frere calls on the Zulu to repudiate their ruler with the aid of the British.

42 TS 34: Frere to T. Shepstone, 30 November 1878.

43 WC II/2/2: Chelmsford to Wood, 10 December 1878.

44 SNA 1/6/3, n.n.: original draft of the ultimatum, signed by Bulwer on 4 December 1878.

45 Martineau, *Frere*, vol. II, p. 264: Frere to Hicks Beach, 23 December 1878.

46 Sir G. W. Cox, *The Life of J. W. Colenso*, London, 1888, pp. 496–7.

47 TS 35: Chelmsford to T. Shepstone, 13 December 1878.

48 *BPP* (C. 2220), no. 92A: Hicks Beach to Frere, 17 October 1878.

49 Webb, 'Lines of power', pp. 31–6. In 1878 it took five weeks for a despatch to travel between Frere and the Colonial Office, and telegrams had to come by steamer from the Cape Verde Islands, taking at least sixteen days. Not until late in 1879 was direct telegraphic communication established.

50 Martineau, *Frere*, vol. II, pp. 259–60: Frere to Hicks Beach, 28 October 1878; *BPP* (C. 2222), no. 54: Frere to Hicks Beach, 14 December 1878.

51 G. Blainey, *The Causes of War*, Melbourne, 1977, p. 270.

52 Saunders, 'Political processes', pp. 156, 168, 171; Blainey, *Causes of War*, pp. 70–1, 86.

53 J. P. C. Laband, 'The cohesion of the Zulu polity under the impact of the Anglo–Zulu War: a reassessment' in Laband and Thompson, *Kingdom and Colony*, p. 4.

2

The Zulu polity and the ultimatum crisis

Colonists habitually characterized Zulu government as despotic and arbitrary, based on the king's control of an aggressive military organization. Yet as Julian Cobbing has shown with the Nguni-speaking Ndebele, who shared certain common traditions and features with the Zulu 'military state', the army was but an organ within the state and subordinate to it. Indeed, the Ndebele 'military system' is best understood in terms of its political, social and economic functions.[1]

Likewise, the Zulu army was never a separate, professional institution like the British army, but was integrated into the whole fabric of the nation's life.[2] The military system was built upon the institution of age-set units, called *amabutho*, which seem to have developed from the ancient practice among the Natal Nguni of banding together youths of similar age in circumcision sets. By the early nineteenth century, in the area later to be dominated by the Zulu kingdom, the practice of forming *amabutho* was changing its function from that of assembling youths for initiation purposes into that of grouping them together for various forms of service, economic and military, that would facilitate more effective management of resources and of the reproductive processes on which the continuance of society depended. Shaka had brought this *amabutho* system to its fully articulated form and it endured, with modifications, until the destruction of the Zulu state.[3]

In Cetshwayo's time, Zulu boys between the ages of fourteen and eighteen would gather at military homesteads (*amakhanda*) which, as the focus of royal authority in the locality, were presided over by representatives of the king in the form of members of the royal family or trusted royal officers. There youths might serve for two to three years as cadets, herding cattle, working the fields and practising military skills. Once enough boys of an age-group were congregated

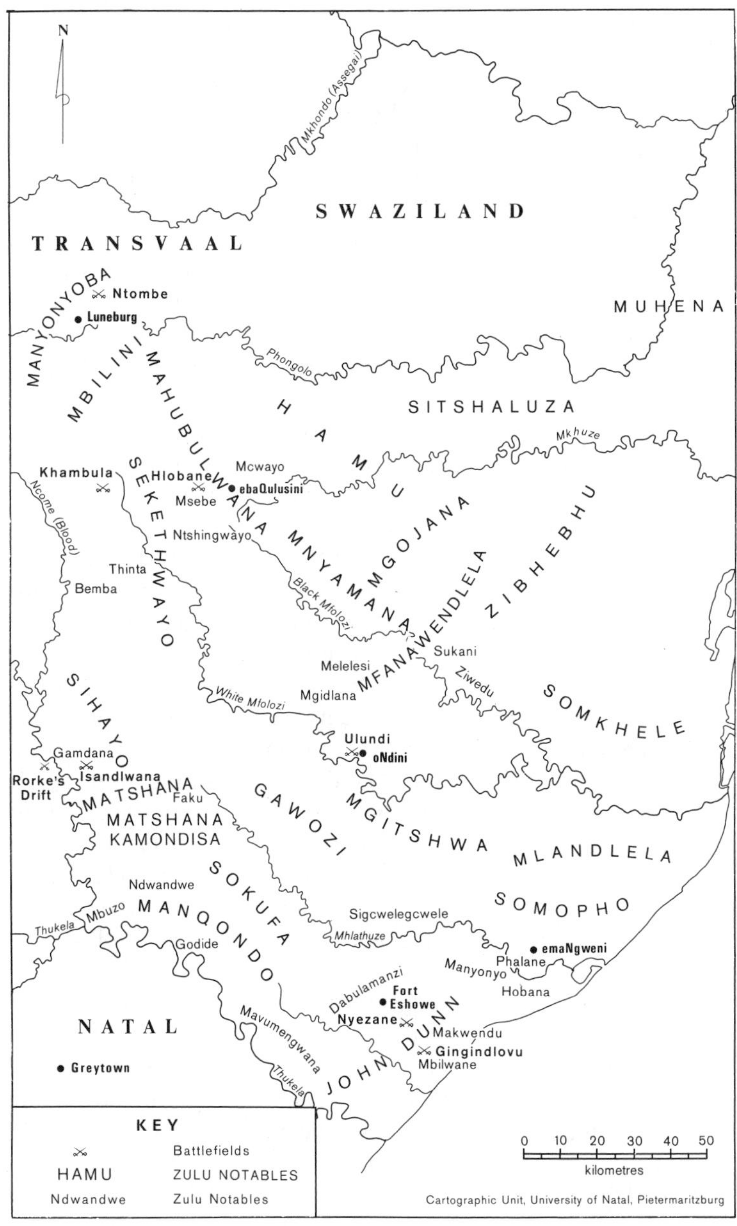

1 Zululand in 1879

at the various *amakhanda* around the country, they would all be brought before the king, usually at the annual first-fruits ceremony (*umKhosi*) held at his 'great place'. The king then formed them into an *ibutho* with orders to build a new *ikhanda*, often bearing the name the king had given the *ibutho*. Sometimes, as with the uVe in 1875, the new *ibutho* was incorporated into an old *ibutho* – in that case the iNgobamakhosi – whose strength the king had decided to maintain, and quartered with it in the old *ibutho's* existing *ikhanda*. Not all the *amabutho* were made up of elements from every district of the kingdom. The Qulusi, for example, who had developed out of an *ikhanda* founded by Shaka, formed a separate *ibutho* composed only of men living in the district of north-western Zululand which they had come to dominate.

Women were part of the military system in that they formed the major labour force in Zulu society and produced food to feed their male relatives serving in the army.[4] Girls in Zululand were formed into *amabutho* for the purpose of marriage, and at intervals the king gave the members of a female *ibutho* leave to be married, but only to suitors from those male *amabutho* which had received royal permission to put on the head-ring (*isicoco*), a privilege usually not granted men until about the age of thirty-five or forty. Each man paid *ilobolo* of up to three cattle for his bride. It seems likely that the custom of head-rings was a substitute for the defunct circumcision ceremony, which had marked the attainment of manhood and full incorporation into communal life. By withholding the headring until middle age, the king was prolonging the period in which the men of his *amabutho* would be regarded as youths in Zulu society, and consequently be more thoroughly under the authority of their elders and, through them, the king. Besides, he was also controlling the rate and direction of the establishment of new reproductive households in the kingdom.

There was apparently a considerable degree of flexibility in the *ibutho* system in Cetshwayo's time. Enrolment in an *ibutho* was no longer compulsory, and the possibility existed of putting on the *isicoco*, marrying and establishing a homestead without having first served the king – though not without being exposed to the scorn of the vast majority of men who continued to conform to the system.[5]

In 1879 there were twenty-seven *amakhanda* in Zululand, thirteen of them (including oNdini, Cetshwayo's 'great place') concentrated in the Mahlabathini plain and the emaKhosini valley to the south-west over the White Mfolozi.[6] On account of the nature of the materials used in their construction (primarily grass and wood), all these *amakhanda* have disappeared. However, contemporary descriptions and the archaeological evidence of clay and dung hut-floors baked in the conflagrations that usually destroyed them, as well as the evidence of refuse-dumps and the like, allow a reasonably comprehensive mental reconstruction.

Ondini, with its estimated 1 000 to 1 500 huts, was larger than most, but can serve as exemplar. Like all *amakhanda* it was modelled on the traditional circular or elliptical Zulu homestead (*umuzi*). At the upper end was the *isigodlo*, or royal enclosure, where the king lived with his wives and entourage. The king was the only male who slept in the *isigodlo* at night, and the whole area was treated with great reverence. From it on either side swept two wings of huts (the *uhlangoti*) housing the warriors, which surrounded the large parade ground. Here the king inspected his men and performed various ceremonies and rituals. At the upper end of the parade ground was a small cattle enclosure sacred to the king. Behind the *isigodlo* and outside the main complex stood two small homesteads where the royal women bore their children, and the king's grain and milch cattle were kept.[7]

The thirteen central *amakhanda* were occupied by unmarried *amabutho* for seven to eight months immediately after their formation, and thereafter for only a few months a year when they served the king; otherwise they were used by all *amabutho* when they gathered during the annual national ceremonies. The remaining fourteen *amakhanda* were widely dispersed and formed regional centres of royal influence and mobilization points for local elements of the *amabutho*. Young men gathered there as cadets before being formed into *amabutho*, and married men during service assembled there for short periods of two to five months, often with their wives.[8]

While serving at an *ikhanda* the members of an *ibutho* kept it in repair, attended the royal cattle attached to it and cultivated the king's land. Ostensibly maintained there at the king's expense, the men were actually dependent on food supplied from their own *imizi* by their women. There were dancing and praise-singing daily which effectively doubled as military exercises. Yet it must be emphasized that the king did not mobilize his *amabutho* only for the purpose of war. Sometimes he would call up a limited number of *amabutho* (perhaps only one or two) for special tasks – building him a new *ikhanda* or repairing an old one, participating in great hunts, supplying him with exotic foodstuffs (for example, bananas from the coast), or collecting tribute from outlying peoples such as the Tsonga. All the *amabutho* would be summoned annually to take part in the great national ceremonies when the king and the army were ritually strengthened, the ancestral spirits praised and the allegiance of the people renewed. The *amabutho* also served as a police force, collecting fines from offenders against the king or destroying their *imizi*. The cattle and commodities which the *amabutho* accumulated for the king on their forays, or as a result of their labour at the *amakhanda*, provided a vital source of royal power. By redistributing a portion of these fruits as rewards to royal functionaries and favoured *amabutho*, the king was able constantly to consolidate his position and ensure the loyalty of his subjects.[9]

The *ibutho* system, in other words, formed the basis of the king's power and authority. Through it he was theoretically able to exercise a real degree of social and economic control over his subjects, harness their productive and military potential to the service of the Zulu state, and to undermine the regional power-bases of overmighty subjects. Nevertheless, on the eve of the Anglo–Zulu War the Zulu kingdom was not as centralized, nor the king's power as effective, as was once supposed. Not only was the king constrained by traditional law and custom, but it seems that there remained considerable scope for independent action by the leading men of the kingdom. Forces of decentralization, which had always to a degree neutralized the political integration of the Zulu state, were distinctly in evidence.

Most fundamental in this regard was the basic social and economic unit of the kingdom, the *umuzi* itself.[10] The state depended on the homestead for part of its labour potential through the *ibutho* system, as well as upon its surplus production. Cattle, so central to Zululand's political economy, though in theory belonging to the nation and so, by extension, through the chiefs to the king (as did the land itself), were in reality part of the *umuzi* unit. Individuals' private control over ordinary cattle was almost complete, while even the king's own cattle, for reasons of pasture availability, were entrusted with right of usufruct to *amakhanda* or *imizi* through the custom of *ukusisa*. These realities were inevitably a force militating against political cohesion, for as large numbers of the Zulu people were not ultimately dependent on centralized authority for the economic functioning of their *imizi*,[11] their way of life was secure as long as the *umuzi* structure survived. And as the Anglo–Zulu War was to prove, this consideration all too frequently came before a commitment to the centralized political structure.

The patrilineal segmentary lineage system was the basis of Zulu social organization (as the *umuzi* unit was the basis of the economy), and with similar consequences to state integration. Lineage segmentation gave rise to clans in which there was a concentration of wealth in the dominant lineage. The clan formed part of a chiefdom, where political power was vested in the dominant lineage of the strongest clan. Such chiefdoms, where they had survived the Shakan 'revolution', were a force for decentralization which the Zulu kings had been unable to overcome. Despite centralizing institutions such as the *amabutho*, there was always the danger that members of a chiefdom would give their first loyalty to their hereditary chief and kinsman, rather than to the king. And far from countering this check to his authority, it would seem that a king such as Cetshwayo often recognized such traditional leaders as district chiefs, who were often consulted by the king, and whose views he was wise to take into account before adopting decisions that would affect their districts or the kingdom as a whole. Such consultation might take place on an individual basis, or in assemblies (known as *amabandla*), whose composition might vary depending upon the issue under consideration. Consequently, many subordinated pre-Shakan chiefdoms still maintained a measure of political cohesion and, through the territorial chiefs, who were too powerful for the king to disregard, exerted their influence in the highest councils of the land.[12]

In effect, this meant that the central state authority was in the habit of delegating powers to existing political hierarchies. This may have been unavoidable, considering problems of distance and communications and the lack of means to support a developed bureaucracy, but it had grave disadvantages. It placed in the hands of the great chiefs, already enjoying the advantages of a personal following and a developed power-base, additional authority vested in them through royal recognition.[13] This inevitably gave them considerable political power and the opportunity to amass wealth through tribute, fines and royal gifts. Similarly, *abantwana*, or princes of the royal clan, with whom the king could not avoid sharing a degree of power, and who possessed a status that was a reflection of his own, were naturally permitted to function as *izikhulu*, or high-ranking persons who, although holding no official position, were distinguished by birth or royal favour. They were consequently in a position to build up a regional following which, as with the great hereditary chiefs (some of whom might also be acknowledged as *izikhulu*), could serve as the basis of a movement towards regional autonomy, especially in those parts remote from the focus of authority in the Mahlabathini plain.

The *izinduna*, whom the king appointed to perform administrative functions – such as commanding the *amabutho*, or ruling over a district where they had no strong claims of hereditary power – were more tightly under his control, as were the collaterals of chiefly houses who, with royal support, had displaced the former ruling line, for they owed their elevation (or subsequent disgrace) to royal favour and not necessarily to illustrious lineage. They frequently joined great chiefs and *izikhulu* in the *amabandla* when they were consulted with them by the king on matters of policy.

By the time of Cetshwayo's reign the temptation among some members of this ruling elite towards local autonomy was accentuated by interaction with whites along Zululand's borders. Goods brought in by trade, especially firearms, were of considerable political value. The king was unable to retain a monopoly of this trade, and chiefs, through the status of possessing the desired articles, or through redistributing them as rewards to their adherents, were able to enhance their own prestige and power at the expense of the central authority.[14] Furthermore, it would seem that in some instances their political allegiance to the king was complicated by their connections with white traders. These men, once they had gained a chief's confidence, were inclined to use their influence and knowledge of the rivalries and tensions within the kingdom to their own advantage, and to promote a chief's ambitions towards autonomy and closer integration with the white economy, to the detriment of the integrated state and royal control.

Considering these fissures (both real and potential) in the structure of their polity, there was some room for uncertainty as to how the Zulu might respond to the British threat of invasion. Ultimately, options depended on perceptions of how best to preserve personal and national interests, and here opinion increasingly diverged. On the one hand, it was possible to accede to British demands or to fail to resist if invaded, thus pacifically conceding the destruction of the independent Zulu state, though possibly preserving some local autonomy. When the majority of Zulu resolved to reject these passive alternatives, they were consciously opting for a military solution. Yet wars require at least two willing belligerents, and only occur when the opposing parties accept that diplomatic means are no longer sufficient to resolve a dispute.[15]

The British were certainly prepared to risk war, and it can be questioned whether a viable alternative was ever open to Cetshwayo once he began to hear 'the whistling of winds'.[16] As early as July 1878 he was expecting to have to fight the British. Portents reinforced this foreboding. Towards the end of July an eagle flying above oNdini was attacked and driven off by four hawks, which the king's medicine-men interpreted as a sign that the states adjoining Zululand would combine to destroy him.[17]

The single issue in the brewing crisis which assumed major proportions in Zulu eyes was the demand that the leaders of those involved in a cross-border incident of 28 July 1878 be handed over to British justice. On that day Mehlokazulu, the son of Chief Sihayo kaXongo of the Qungebe, had raided Natal near Rorke's Drift with a party consisting of two of his brothers, an uncle and thirty armed men. The object was to apprehend and kill two of Sihayo's miscreant wives.[18] Cetshwayo's initial response was to minimize the culpability of 'rash boys' acting in 'zeal for their father's welfare', and he offered a fine of £50 sterling in restitution. The British response was to dismiss this 'ridiculously small sum' as adding insult to injury. Consequently, despite Cetshwayo's repeated deprecations of any quarrel with the British, and increasing alarm as British troop movements seemed calculated to hem him in, Bulwer sternly insisted at the end of September that the offenders be surrendered.[19]

Cetshwayo could not make decisions that involved the independent sovereignty of Zululand without prior consultation with the leading men of his kingdom. It is clear that an inner core of these, known as the *umkhandlu*, determined policy.[20] Between four and six of the most influential would typically hold a confidential conclave in the cattle enclosure to concert their plans before proceeding to consult the king. Only after the king had considered their proposals would other great men of the realm be summoned to hear the royal decision. An even larger meeting, which would include the *izinduna* of the *amakhanda*, might then be called to air the issue. But, in effect, the vital decision on how best to respond to British demands and threats was in the hands of Cetshwayo and his inner council, known to ordinary people as the *amanqe* (or vultures) from the grey military blankets they wore. At the time of the war, the most regular members of the conclave were Chief Mnyamana kaNgqengelele of the Buthelezi, Cetshwayo's chief *induna*, Chief Ntshingwayo kaMahole of the Khoza, Chief Godide kaNdlela of the Ntuli, Chief Sekethwayo kaNhlaka of the Mdlalose, Chief Mbopha kaWolizibi of the Hlabisa and Chief Mvundlana kaMenziwa of the Biyela. Prince Hamu kaNzibe and Chief Zibhebhu kaMaphitha of the Mandlakazi, though of the highest standing, were too young to be included.[21]

In one sense, therefore, Cetshwayo was not simply fobbing the British off when he repeatedly stated that he must wait for his council's decision before deciding on the fate of Sihayo's sons. Yet he was also being disingenuous. John Dunn had spoken privately to Bulwer's messengers in late August, warning them that they must never hope that Cetshwayo would ever consent to giving up the sons of Sihayo kaXongo, his favourite. For not only were there close connections between Sihayo's family and the Zulu royal house, but Sihayo had been the staunchest of Cetshwayo's supporters during the succession dispute of 1856 and the troubled years thereafter, and the king had rewarded his friend in 1872 by confirming him as chief of the Qungebe.[22] Thus it is clear that although a large majority in Cetshwayo's council were in favour of surrendering Sihayo's sons to placate the British, he was determined to thwart them. He therefore encouraged Sihayo's sons to flee for sanctuary to Mbilini kaMswati, a scion of the Swazi royal house on the north-western marches of the kingdom who owed allegiance to the Zulu king, and to remain with him until the war began, out of reach of those chiefs who wished to hand them over to the British.[23] These chiefs were in consequence greatly incensed, and were more determined than ever to undermine Sihayo's influence.

Meanwhile, Cetshwayo, who by September was feeling increasingly threatened by the British military build-up along his frontiers, was being left little alternative but to mobilize his people to withstand a possible invasion. When the Zulu king wished to mobilize his army, he sent out orders by runner to the *izinduna* commanding the various district *amakhanda* to collect the local contingents of the *amabutho*, and to proceed with them to the *amakhanda* clustered in the Mahlabathini plain.[24] If hostilities on a smaller scale or in a theatre far from oNdini were intended, the king might then order the local territorial chief or *induna* of the regional *ikhanda* to summon the warriors of the district to muster at and operate from his particular great place or military homestead.

The details of Zulu mobilization for the war of 1879 are often obscure, and doubtless for this reason have not been considered in the standard secondary sources. The problem lies with the nature of the evidence.[25] The statements of Zulu prisoners-of-war, including that of King Cetshwayo himself, while sometimes based on personal knowledge or observation, are as often founded on hearsay. Their reliability is also affected by being filtered through the medium of white interpreters, recorders or translators. By far the most copious source for the mustering of the Zulu army is the information which Natal Border Agents, stationed along the Thukela and Mzinyathi rivers, gleaned through their spies and border police; and that which Bishop Schreuder, positioned at his station of kwaNtumjambili, near Kranskop, learned through his Christian converts still in Zululand. Yet, as the military and colonial officials to whom this intelligence was transmitted recognized, it was often suspect (if not demonstrably inaccurate), and they frequently reprimanded the border officials for their apparently uncritical acceptance of every tale. In all fairness, however, the border officials spent much of their time trying to sift the 'contradictory and false reports being constantly circulated', and were aware that much of the intelligence they passed on was 'utterly unreliable'.[26] Nevertheless, it was all they had and, like them, it is for the modern historian to make the best of it.

The normal reasons for full or partial Zulu mobilization – war, service to the king or participation in the national rituals – must be borne in mind when trying to unravel the movements of the *amabutho* on the eve of the war.

In September Cetshwayo gave orders for a great hunt, to extend from the Ncome River down the Mzinyathi and Thukela to the sea, to be undertaken by the border population south of the Mhlatuze River. While the border people gathered, ostensibly to hunt, but really to keep watch on British movements, reports reached all the colonial border agents that Cetshwayo had at the same time ordered up the uMbonambi, uMcijo and iNgobamakhosi *amabutho* to oNdini for 'war talk' – which included manoeuvres and practice with guns – and to protect his person.[27] These *amabutho* were also evidently intended for a more obviously warlike and organized hunt along the border than the first local ones, for in late September some members moved close to the border carrying their war-shields, stabbing-spears and guns. Such a show of force was not normal for a hunting-party as regularly organized by the king, and could be construed as a hostile act by the British, especially since there was hardly sufficient game in the region of the lower Thukela to warrant such a concentration. The fact that the hunt was not supplying itself as was usual, but had its food carried by women and boys as on campaign, reinforced this impression. Similar 'hunting' took place at the same time along the Mzinyathi.

The king was aware that he was playing a provocative though necessary game to show that he was prepared to defend his frontiers, and at first officially denied all knowledge of the hunts. On being pressed, he tried to explain them away by saying that the usual annual hunts were bigger than normal because of the undeniable scarcity of food and lack of rain.[28] But there was no doubt that *amabutho* were being called up, if only to build new *amakhanda* (as was one of their routine functions). Yet to build a new *ikhanda* in the direction of St Lucia Bay – as the iNgobamakhosi were reported to have been sent to do – and thus to establish a military presence in the region was in itself a response to the threat the king perceived as coming from that direction. Reports filtering into Natal indicated that there was clearly much unease and movement of people about the kingdom, and that by the end of September the men of standing about the king were anxious concerning the consequences of assembling the *amabutho*, and wished to order them home in the interests of relations with Britain.

Cetshwayo bowed to the pressure, but ordered his *amabutho* to reassemble in a fortnight's time. In making this decision he was influenced not merely by the younger *amabutho*, who were clamouring for action against the British, but by a quite rational desire to be prepared against the British, who were persisting in their military preparations. In particular, the movement of British troops from Utrecht to Luneburg in the disputed territory on 19 October 1878, in order to protect the settlers from further raids by the obstreperous Mbilini, persuaded the king to take precautions. By the third week of October the British had learned from various sources that the Zulu were again mustering in their *amakhanda* on the king's orders, one concentration being at the kwaGingindlovu *ikhanda* to watch the south-eastern border, and another at kwaNodwengu in the Mahlabathini plain. Every *induna* had apparently received orders to provide ten cattle for the commissariat, and it seemed that the Zulu (especially the younger *amabutho*) were this time seriously preparing for war.[29] The response of the Natal authorities was to send a sharp message to Cetshwayo, insisting that British troop movements had been only in reaction to his hostile stance, and that aggression against the kingdom was not intended.[30] It seems that the king (influenced by John Dunn) had in any case begun to consider that he had been unduly alarmist, for by 28 October his *amabutho* were again beginning to disperse. And even if his younger *amabutho* were full of brave talk of how they would invade Natal, the king still hoped for a negotiated settlement of the crisis.[31]

Yet there was another pressing reason why it was necessary for the *amabutho* to return home. With the young men all called up, the women had been left alone on the land to take care of the cattle and the fields at the time of planting. It had been an exceptionally dry season, however. Mealies left over from the previous season were scarce, the young crops which had been planted at the normal time were ruined, and cattle were in poor condition for lack of pasture and were dying in large numbers. There was consequently a general lack of food and little surplus to send as provisions to the menfolk in their *amakhanda*. To feed them, and to keep them occupied, the king had to set them to cultivating the royal gardens and to hunting game near the confluence of the Black and White Mfolozi rivers. Hungry, and thwarted of their expectations of a campaign into Natal, many of the warriors were not waiting to be dismissed but were dispersing to their homes of their own accord. Though angered at their desertion, the king refrained from punishing them, as he could see how some were even dying of hunger at the *amakhanda*.[32] By the end of November the *amabutho* were all reported to have left the king, and to be back at their homes by early December.[33]

The lack of discipline among the *amabutho*, as well as the disaffection among many of his council regarding his protection of Sihayo and conduct of the crisis, had the potential to erode Cetshwayo's authority. By the end of October there were clear indications that a serious rift was opening up within the Zulu leadership, a development which did not go unnoticed by those planning the British invasion. On the one side stood Cetshwayo, who was apparently swayed by the younger *amabutho*, who were keen for a chance to prove themselves in war; while on the other were most of the king's brothers and the older men of status in the kingdom, who were beginning to constitute an appeasement, or pro-peace, party.[34]

Significantly, the three leaders of this faction, Mnyamana, Zibhebhu and Hamu, were among the most powerful *izikhulu* of the kingdom.

Since 1873 the politically astute and cautious Mnyamana had been Cetshwayo's chief *induna*. After the king, he was the most powerful man in Zululand and the richest in cattle. Born about 1813, tall and of slight build, with a dark complexion, now troubled with rheumatism and with his moustache and little peaked beard going grey, he had a resonant, deep voice and an imposing presence. His father, Ngqengelele, who had been King Shaka's chief *induna*, had been rewarded with the rich Buthelezi chiefdom in north-western Zululand. Soon after Mpande's succession, Mnyamana was recognized as chief of the Buthelezi and was created *induna* of the main section of the uThulwana *ibutho*. Eight of Mpande's sons were enrolled under him, and Mnyamana grew in influence, wealth and favour. He was respected for his wisdom, and though open to reasoned argument, could not easily be swayed from his viewpoint.[35]

Zibhebhu, who was born in 1841, was of royal blood, a cousin to the king. In 1872 he had succeeded his father Maphitha as chief of the Mandlakazi, a Zulu lineage, and was dominant in north-eastern Zululand, far from the centre of power. Also *induna* of the uDloko, he was recognized as the ablest general in Zululand. The British were always to recognize his intelligence, force of character and straightforwardness, which, coupled with his undoubted courage and reserved mien, earned their respect. Although he had been a vital supporter of Cetshwayo in the succession crisis of 1856, his trading interests and developed contacts with colonial Natal (whose Western technology he so admired), coupled with his known yearnings for greater political independence and his resistance to the exercise of royal authority in his chiefdom, had for some time made his loyalty to the king a matter of some uncertainty.

Yet it was Hamu's opposition to war with Britain which was most immediately dangerous to Cetshwayo. He was an *umntwana*, full and elder brother to Cetshwayo, though through the *ukuvuza* custom heir not to Mpande but to his father's deceased brother Nzibe, senior son of Senzangakhona, Shaka's father. *Induna* of the uThulwana, he was chief of the Ngenetsheni, a Zulu lineage, and as an *isikhulu* since the 1850s he had built up a strong personal following in north-western Zululand. Flabby, with immense thighs and impassive features, he was immoderately fond of gin and gaudy blankets. Despite a violent and overbearing manner with subordinates, he was the most popular of the *abantwana* and appreciated for his liberality and plain-spokenness. Like Zibhebhu, he was far from the focus of authority, and also had close trading connections with the colonial world. Through the influence of Herbert Nunn, a white trader who had resided in his district since the 1860s, and on whom he relied for advice and trading goods, the groundwork had been laid for future collaboration with the British. Furthermore, although he had aided Cetshwayo in the crisis of 1856, he had differed increasingly with him over the years about the way in which the king was handling the long-standing border dispute with the Transvaal. Since his territory was prey to Boer encroachments, any concessions to them were made at his expense. Besides which, he was acutely conscious of his status as a great *umntwana*, and at the time of Mpande's death in 1872 many in northern Zululand had favoured him as king in preference to Cetshwayo. Comporting himself as if he were Cetshwayo's equal, Hamu kept an *isigodlo* in royal style at kwaMfemfe, his great place, appointed his own *izinduna*, and brooked no interference from the king in the administration of his chiefdom.

Such a heady combination of high lineage, power, wealth and local interest predisposed Hamu to flout the king in great matters.[36] This had perhaps been most spectacularly apparent at the *umKhosi* festival on 25 December 1877, when Hamu's uThulwana fell upon the iNgobamakhosi, the king's most prized *ibutho*, commanded by Sigcwelegcwele kaMhlekehleke, an Ngadini lineage head and royal favourite. Whether or not Hamu deliberately fomented this fracas, it was nothing less than an assertion of his power and independence, and confirmed the king's suspicions that Hamu intended to usurp his throne.

Hamu retired to his district in consequence, and for fear of his life persistently refused the king's summons to oNdini. He only reappeared at the royal council called in November 1878. But he was already playing a double game. Clearly convinced as early as September that the British were determined on war against Zululand, he anticipated the consequences by initiating negotiations with them. Between early September and mid-November his *induna*, Ngwegwana, delivered a series of messages to British officials and officers along the north-western border of Zululand, undertaking in case of war to 'run over with all his people to the Government, if

Government [would] receive and protect him'.[37]

Because of Cetshwayo's determination to protect Sihayo's sons, and his precautionary partial mobilization of the *amabutho*, it should not be inferred that the king was a warmonger. Indeed, he continued to protest his peaceful desire 'to sit quietly'.[38] Nevertheless, there is every indication that when he sent out his placatory messages he did so under the influence of Hamu, Mnyamana and the other members of the peace party. What was significant was that the peace party began to risk its own initiatives. On 13 November messengers were sent across the lower Thukela by Mnyamana, Ntshingwayo, and Sitshaluza kaMamba, Chief of the eMgazini, to convey their disquiet with the shape of events and their desire for peace. Surprisingly, Sihayo was associated as one of the initiators of the message, and it is only possible to speculate on what pressure the others had brought to bear on him.[39]

It seems likely that these principal chiefs decided to take their potentially treasonable action only after a great assembly called by Cetshwayo about the second week of November to discuss the crisis. By all accounts, it was Hamu who led a determined attack on Sihayo, making it clear that his sons should be given up or put to death, rather than that Zululand should go to war on their account.[40] Sihayo was reportedly insulted and assaulted in council as the cause of the crisis by a son of Mnyamana and by Hayiyana kaMaphitha (Zibhebhu's brother), and spat upon and abused for the same reason by Hamu; but the king continued to stand by his favourite.[41] Indeed, to have abandoned him at this stage would have surely been an unacceptable blow to the king's authority and prestige.

Yet possibly, if surrendering Sihayo's sons could have deflected the British from their determination to emasculate Zululand, Cetshwayo would eventually have bowed to his council's wishes. However, mounting British military preparations during November doubtless made it clear to him that the unpalatable sacrifice would have little effect in staving off an invasion. Such conclusions received further confirmation when, towards the end of November, Bulwer sent to Cetshwayo notifying him that John Shepstone would meet the representatives of the Zulu nation at the lower Thukela drift to deliver Frere's boundary award and, sinisterly, 'other communications'.[42]

Bulwer's messengers did not actually see Cetshwayo, who was in seclusion after the recent death of one of his children, but conferred with him through Mnyamana. They also held discussions with Hamu, Dabulamanzi, Sihayo and five or six other principal chiefs of the inner circle. Every one of them expressed a strong desire to avoid war. It was obvious that Sihayo was out of favour with all – except the king – for bringing ruin on the country, and that John Dunn was universally blamed for not having warned the king sufficiently strongly of the danger in which the kingdom stood. Indeed, it was noticeable that all were in a state of great apprehension. There was consequently relief that the British still apparently wished to negotiate, and Cetshwayo decided to send a deputation of *izinduna* to the requested meeting. Only then did he summon an enlarged *ibandla* of the great men of the realm to report his decision.[43] But the council apparently broke up in confusion over the persistent issue of whether or not to deliver up Sihayo's sons, and many of the great chiefs were reported to have returned home angry with Cetshwayo for continuing against all advice in protecting them.[44]

When the Zulu deputation of forty members and about fifty attendants crossed the Thukela on 11 December to hear John Shepstone, the British were pleased to see that it was composed primarily of elderly and middle-aged men. Their maturity, it was presumed, would predispose them to avoid an open rupture with Britain. However, the British should not have concluded that they necessarily represented the peace party in the king's council. Prominent among them were Vumandaba kaNtati, a royal *induna* and principal *induna* of the uMcijo *ibutho*; Phalane kaMdinwa, *induna* of the Hlangezwa; Muwundula kaMamba, a royal *induna* and brother of the eMgazini chief; Mahubulwana kaDumisela, principal *induna* of the Qulusi; Gebula, an *induna* of the kwaGqikazi *ikhanda* and once a favoured messenger of Mpande; and Mbilwane kaMhlanganiso, *induna* of the kwaGingindlovu *ikhanda*.[45] In other words, although they were trusted elders of rank and distinction, not one was an *isikhulu* with a place on the king's inner council.[46] Rather, they were royal *izinduna*, functionaries raised up through the king's favour and committed to serving his interests. They were in fact typical of the personnel of a Zulu diplomatic mission, and had strict instructions regarding the limits of what they were permitted to discuss.[47] This was borne out by the professionally calm and diplomatic way in which, though obviously anxious and concerned, they responded to the devastating demands of the British ultimatum. Their mission was to convey the terms of the ultimatum to

Cetshwayo and his council for deliberation, and they made it clear that they understood and remembered all the points.[48] However, they did indicate that thirty days was insufficient time for discussion and decision, but their plea for an extension was refused. It was also clear that they were most reluctant to convey the very unpalatable terms to Cetshwayo, and feared his displeasure. They also hesitated to deliver the written terms of the ultimatum – set out in English and Zulu – as the British legalistically insisted.[49]

As the deputies had warned, no quick decision could be reached on the terms of the ultimatum. They delivered the written copies at Mangete, John Dunn's great place just north of the Thukela. Dunn, realizing that the reluctant deputies were travelling very slowly, sent a messenger in advance to the king with all the details. This messenger returned on 18 December, and Dunn forwarded Cetshwayo's initial response to Bulwer. The king agreed to surrender Sihayo's sons and pay the fine, but complained of the short time allowed for compliance and the need for discussion with his council on the more important issues.[50] Meanwhile, the deputies managed to make particularly heavy going of crossing the flooded rivers, and did not succeed in reporting to the king until about 22 December. Unaware that the king already knew the details, they did not disclose all the terms of the ultimatum at once, and at first suppressed the most unpalatable, thus delaying formal discussion in council.[51]

The Zulu leaders could risk no delays, however. For the British it was 'quite settled' that, unless Cetshwayo gave in punctually and completely to their demands, the troops would invade the moment the ultimatum expired.[52] Yet in this moment of crisis the Zulu were not sure how to respond. In order to save the kingdom from being 'spoiled by war', the king's inner council were reportedly prepared to acquiesce to all the terms of the ultimatum – except the fundamental ones relating to the abolition of the *ibutho* system. Both king and councillors were in agreement that those could never be conceded except at the point of the sword.[53] However, the hope remained that the British could still be placated by sufficient concession of the minor demands.

The king consequently proposed in council that all the chiefs subscribe a number of cattle to make up the number required to pay the cattle fines, but this they resisted. They strongly felt that Sihayo must first give up all his stock, and only then would they consent to make up any shortfall.[54] Cetshwayo accepted this decision, and in late December began to round up Sihayo's cattle and those of Qethuka kaManqondo of the Magwaza, whose adherents had been involved in a provocative border incident on 17 September, when they had assaulted two members of the Colonial Engineer's Department. Yet Cetshwayo evidently did not attach sufficient importance to collecting the cattle within the time the British had stipulated, and on 26 December his messengers arrived at the lower Thukela to plead for a further extension.[55] Perhaps this lack of enthusiasm can be explained by Cetshwayo's steadily diminishing faith in the purpose to be served by going through the motions of collecting the cattle fine, and it was increasingly apparent that he would renege on his private undertaking of 18 December to deliver up Sihayo's sons. Certainly, by the end of December he seems reluctantly to have decided that there was little alternative but to go to war. This was borne out by his increasingly truculent tone, even if his demeanour became daily more dejected and tearful at the prospect.[56]

With war now almost unavoidable, it was necessary once again to call up the long-suffering *amabutho*. This time their mustering coincided with the *umKhosi*, the annual first-fruits ceremony for which they habitually mustered, regardless of whether or not a campaign was in the offing. For weeks before the date set by the king for the 'big' *umKhosi*, which always took place at his kwaNodwengu *ikhanda* when the moon was at its full and about to wane in December–January, they gathered at their *amakhanda* to prepare for the festival.[57] As it so happened, the appointed day in 1879 was 8 January – just three days before the British ultimatum was due to expire. In normal times, when the kingdom was not on the brink of war, men and women from every part of the country attended, attired in all their finery. On such occasions the *amabutho* never mustered in their full strength. Rather, representatives of each attended the three days of ritual, but many men never went at all, and those that were there changed daily, coming and going.[58] However, the situation was not normal in 1879.

There was some reluctance to muster on account of the continuing scarcity of food, for although the rains had at last come and the people were everywhere taking advantage of the wet conditions to plant their crops, the season was inevitably going to be a late one. The mealie crop, which was later to prove splendid, could not be expected to be ripe until the end of February. Consequently, as in October–November, it would be difficult to feed the assembled *amabutho*, or to keep them together for any length of time without employment, such as sending them off on campaign.

The king clearly had this service in mind, for when he ordered his *amabutho* to assemble in the Mahlabathini plain it was, most significantly, to be without the ceremonial dress normal for the *umKhosi*. They were to leave their ornaments at home, and instead to come with their arms and ammunition prepared for immediate active service.[59] According to the adherents in western Zululand of Bemba (an *induna* of the Mdlalose chief), who by the third week of December were repairing on the king's orders to their district *amakhanda*, the king expected to have to fight when the new moon was 'still young', or early in January and close to the date set for the *umKhosi*.[60]

Bemba's adherents were not the only Zulu whom the king ordered to gather along the threatened frontiers and keep watch, rather than to go straight to Mahlabathini. The Qulusi, north-east of Bemba and also facing Wood's column concentrating at Utrecht, assembled at their district *ikhanda* to await his advance. Along the Mzinyathi, opposite the Centre Column at Rorke's Drift, Sihayo's adherents were assembled at Sokhexe (his principal *umuzi*) to oppose the British crossing. Elements of *amabutho* were also stationed initially along the Thukela, especially at the drifts.[61] By the date set for the *umKhosi*, however, most of the men initially guarding the frontier had orders to assemble with those already at the king's great place. These included those from the Phongolo valley and the majority from along the Thukela. The most obvious exceptions were the Qulusi, Sihayo's adherents, and Mavumengwana's Ntuli opposite the lower Thukela drifts where Pearson's column was massing, besides small parties elsewhere who remained on watch. The king ordered them not to resist the British should they advance, so that his last-ditch negotiations should not be jeopardized. His commands were obeyed, but cynically, for none seemed to feel that war could any longer be averted.[62]

Cetshwayo's inner council and the princes, meanwhile, were becoming increasingly dismayed with the drift of events, and continued to vent their frustrations on John Dunn, Cetshwayo's main (and obviously imperfect) channel of communication with Natal. Realizing that some were beginning to demand that he be put to death for his apparent treason, and knowing that his economic and political future in Zululand depended upon extricating himself from a war Britain was bound to win, Dunn began crossing over into Natal on 31 December 1878 with 2 000 adherents and 3 000 cattle, leaving his *imizi* to be looted and burned.[63] Thus Dunn, the king's white *induna*, who had been raised to his position of power in south-eastern Zululand solely through the king's favour, was, to the disgust of most Zulu, the first of the ruling elite to abandon him in order to seek his own interests. Intending initially to remain neutral, he was to be increasingly drawn into aiding the invaders and carving out a place for himself in post-war Zululand. His adherents were to be employed as scouts and spies, and he himself as political adviser to the British command.

Not that Hamu was far behind Dunn in preparing to desert the king. Lord Chelmsford, heartened by Hamu's November overtures, suggested in mid-December to Colonel Wood, who was in command of the troops massing at Utrecht, that direct negotiations be opened up with the prince through Nunn the trader. Hamu was to be assured that chiefs who collaborated with the British would be placed in the safety of a location in Natal for the duration of the conflict, and that afterwards they would be reinstated in their territory and recognized as independent under the British crown. Hamu's fears that in the event of war the Swazi might descend on his district gave Chelmsford an additional lever, for he declared that he would only be able to come to Hamu's aid if he openly aligned himself as an ally of the British.[64] Hamu was not yet prepared to go quite that far (if only for fear of Cetshwayo's wrath), but meanwhile entered into communication with the Swazi and, apparently unbeknown to Cetshwayo, assured them – as if he were an independent ruler – of his pacific intentions.[65] In all, Hamu's negotiations convinced the British by the end of December that once they invaded Zululand he, like Dunn before him, would abandon the Zulu cause.

The inner council continued to labour under the misplaced impression that if Sihayo's sons were surrendered the British would somehow be satisfied and drop their other demands. The king knew better, and perhaps for this reason resisted calling an assembly of all the great men of the kingdom to discuss the situation. His councillors did not take kindly to having their advice persistently ignored, and by early January there were signs that some wished to take it upon themselves to deliver Sihayo's sons to the British. In the end, they probably refrained because of the strong feeling in the country at large which, though unsettled and divided, generally supported the king's decision to resist rather than appease the British and succumb to unacceptable white rule.[66] Besides, the *amabutho* gathering in the Mahlabathini plain were adamant in their aggressive determination not to give in to white demands, and their obvious loyalty to the king made it increasingly risky for his councillors to act openly in opposition to his wishes.[67]

In the event, the *amabutho* mustered at oNdini that January did not participate in the true *umKhosi* festival, which after all did not take place that year on account of the impending hostilities.[68] Instead, they were 'doctored' for war in rituals that were effectively an abbreviated version of the *umKhosi*.[69] The Zulu believed in an overlap that existed between this world and the world of the spirits. This was expressed by a mystical force, *umnyama*, which was darkness, or evil influence, and was represented by the colour black. It reduced resistance to disease, created misfortune and, in its worst form, was contagious. Because such pollution was a mystical rather than organic illness, it could be cured only by symbolic medicines. Deaths by violence, expressed as *umkhokha*, were an especially virulent form of *umnyama*, as the killer himself was polluted. In consequence, warriors about to go to war were in particular danger of pollution, and needed to be purified of evil influences and strengthened against them through treatment by black medicines (which symbolically represented death) in a ritual context.[70]

On the first day of the essential rituals, the *amabutho*, who were mustered at their respective *amakhanda* in the Mahlabathini plain, collected great heaps of firewood and green mimosa. A black bull from the royal herds, upon which all the evil influences which had accumulated in the land were symbolically cast, was caught on the second day and killed bare-handed by a favoured *ibutho*. War-doctors cut strips of meat from the bull (*umbengo*), treated them with the black medicines intended to strengthen the warriors and bind them together in loyalty to their king, and then roasted them in a fire of the wood collected the previous day. They then threw the strips up into the air and the *amabutho*, who were drawn up in a great circle, caught and sucked them. Meanwhile, the war-doctors burned further medicines and made the warriors breathe in the smoke and sprinkled them with the cinders. Then, in order finally to expel all dangerous influences from the body, each warrior drank a mouthful from a pot of medicine, and a few at a time vomited the contents into a specially dug hole close by where the eNtukwini stream flows into the White Mfolozi. This ritual vomiting took all day to complete, and occurred when hostilities were supposed to be imminent. Its purpose was once again to bind all the people together in loyalty to their king, and some of the vomit was added to the great *inkatha* of the Zulu nation, the sacred grass coil which was the symbol of the nation's unity and strength. On the third day the warriors went down to any running stream to wash, but not to rub off the medicines with which they had been sprinkled. Once these rituals were completed, the warriors (who had undergone a symbolic death) withdrew from society and, like bereaved persons, abstained from all pleasurable experiences (*ukuzila*). They could no longer sleep at home or on their mats, nor could they have anything at all to do with girls or women. Not even the men who remained as bodyguards with the king could, for all who had participated in the rituals were now set aside from ordinary life and were in an intensified and contagious state of *umnyama*.[71]

It seems that two war-doctors were responsible for sprinkling the army, one of whom was a Sotho of special powers. He doctored the firearms with smoke to make the bullets go straight, and smeared *muthi* on the warriors' foreheads, promising that his magic had weakened the British bullets, so that they would be harmless.[72]

When ritually preparing for a campaign, the king would call a few favoured pairs of *amabutho* who were *uphalane* (or of nearly the same age and numbers, and who regularly accompanied each other into battle) into the cattle enclosure. There, in a ceremony that would continue until sunset, one individual after another would leap and *giya*, shouting ritual challenges to the rival *ibutho*, or responses to those hurled by its representative. His own *ibutho* would praise him all the while. The effect of the ritual harangues was to spur the rival *amabutho* on to outdo each other in deeds of valour during the coming war. During battle itself *izinduna* would remind their men of their rivals' challenge, and after the campaign there would be a close accounting. In January 1879 the king first called the uMcijo and iNgobamakhosi into the cattle enclosure to challenge each other. (The iNgobamakhosi was his favourite *ibutho*, and he considered it the bravest and the best.) Two or three days later the king called the uMbonambi and uNokhenke in their turn.[73]

It was also important that the spirits of the king's ancestors should approve of the decision to go to war. In January 1879 the assembled *amabutho* slept the night at the royal *ikhanda* of esiKlebheni, and the following day visited the graves of the Zulu kings in order formally to address them through the customary sacrifice of cattle and accompanying rituals. Moreover, cattle were sent to the spirits to ask them to go with the army when it set out, and they answered through the bellowing of the oxen late at night. Thus reassured, the king could issue his orders for the coming campaign.[74]

Yet, even at the eleventh hour, Cetshwayo seemed uncertain how best to act. He was under enormous pressure and felt himself deserted by those councillors on whose support he had hoped to rely. Although he appears to have accepted the inevitability of war, and summoned his *amabutho* with the intention of fighting, he nevertheless persisted in his negotiations with the British. The latter were not unnaturally convinced that these feelers were no more than a ploy to postpone hostilities until after the harvest was in, but it also seems that Cetshwayo had not quite given up hope of a diplomatic settlement. Thus on 11 January 1879, the very day the ultimatum expired, the British received yet another royal message – the sixth since the king's initial response to the ultimatum[75] – begging for more time to discuss the terms with the people gathered at oNdini for the *umKhosi*.[76] But it was too late. Bulwer replied that if Cetshwayo wished to communicate, it must in future be solely with Lord Chelmsford, whose forces were entering Zululand. Furthermore, no reply short of unconditional acceptance of all the conditions of the ultimatum could be entertained.[77] Zululand was at war with Britain, and no compromise settlement was any longer possible.

Notes

1 J. Cobbing, 'The evolution of the Ndebele amabutho', *Journal of African History*, XV, 4, 1974, pp. 607–31, passim.

2 For the *ibutho* system, see Laband and Thompson, *Field Guide*, pp. 3–4.

3 See Guy, *Zulu Kingdom*, pp. 28–9. Swaziland still exemplifies how in a conservative Nguni-speaking kingdom, closely allied in origin to the Zulu, the age-set system continues (despite modern challenges) to be fundamental to the functioning of society. See H. Kuper, *An African Aristocracy: Rank among the Swazi*, London, 1947, pp. 117–33, and A. Booth, *Swaziland: Tradition and Change in a Southern African Kingdom*, Boulder, Colorado, 1983, pp. 34–43.

4 However, men of lower rank might help their wives in hoeing and weeding, besides their normal tasks of clearing the ground for cultivating, building the homestead and herding cattle (Webb and Wright, *Zulu King Speaks*, pp. 73, 99).

5 Ibid., pp. 32–3, 70–1, 83, 95; C. Vijn (Bishop Colenso, tr. and ed.), *Cetshwayo's Dutchman: Being the Private Journal of a White Trader in Zululand during the British Invasion*, London, 1880, pp. 127, 189–90, 192: Colenso's notes; *JSA* I, p. 34: testimony of Baleni kaSilwana; ibid. IV, pp. 378–9: testimony of Ndukwana kaMbengwana; Guy, *Zulu Kingdom*, pp. 11–12.

6 Vijn, *Cetshwayo's Dutchman*, p. 70; *Times of Natal*, 25 June 1879. Archaeological evidence and local tradition support this figure.

7 This account is based on personal observation, on R. Rawlinson, 'Ondini: royal military homestead of King Cetshwayo kaMpande, 1872–1879', paper presented at the Conference on Natal and Zulu History, University of Natal, Durban, July 1985; and James Stuart's verbal reconstruction of life in emGungundlovu, based on the oral evidence he collected, in James Stuart Collection, file no. 83: MS translation by E. R. Dahle of J. Stuart, *uKulumetule*, London, 1925, chaps. 2–4. For a vivid, first-hand account of life in the *isigodlo*, see H. Filter (compiler) and S. Bourquin (tr. and ed.), *Paulina Dlamini: Servant of Two Kings*, Pietermaritzburg and Durban, 1986, pp. 32–4, 43–6.

8 Webb and Wright, *Zulu King Speaks*, pp. 93, 95.

9 Vijn, *Cetshwayo's Dutchman*, p. 191: Colenso's notes; Webb and Wright, *Zulu King Speaks*, p. 63; *JSA* I, pp. 63–4: testimony of Bikwayo kaNoziwana; ibid., p. 108: testimony of Dinya kaZokozwayo; ibid., pp. 304, 310, 323: testimony of Lunguza kaMpukane; Guy, *Zulu Kingdom*, pp. 10–12, 20–5.

10 The following discussion is based on M. Gluckman, 'The kingdom of the Zulu of South Africa' in M. Fortes and E. E. Evans-Pritchard (eds.), *African Political Systems*, London, 1940, pp. 28–55; H. C. Lugg, *Life under a Zulu Shield*, Pietermaritzburg, 1975, pp. 31–6; Guy, *Zulu Kingdom*, pp. 21–40; P. Colenbrander, 'The Zulu political economy on the eve of the war' in Duminy and Ballard, *New Perspectives*, pp. 78–97; J. Guy, 'Production and exchange in the Zulu kingdom', in J. B. Peires (ed.), *Before and after Shaka*, Grahamstown, 1981, pp. 33–48; and J. Wright, 'Control of women's labour in the Zulu kingdom', in ibid., pp. 82–99.

11 It seems probable, though, that some men were dependent on the monarchy, in that it was through service in the *amabutho* that poorer individuals were able to acquire some of the cattle necessary to marry and to set themselves up as young heads of households.

12 Webb and Wright, *Zulu King Speaks*, pp. 80–3, 93; R. Mael, 'The problem of political integration in the Zulu empire', unpublished Ph.D. thesis, University of California, Los Angeles, 1974, pp. 130–38. It was usual in Africa for kings to consult with a council of elders (L. Mair, *African Kingdoms*, Oxford, 1977, p. 106). Bishop Colenso aptly drew a comparison between King John constrained by his barons and Cetshwayo and his *izikhulu* (Colenso Collection 2: Letter Book, 1872–82, p. 236: Colenso to Frere, 14 January 1879).

13 For the tendency among chiefs to exercise power over life and death and to settle disputes over land without reference to the king, see Webb and Wright, *Zulu King Speaks*, pp. 80–2, 84, 94.

14 For the most useful discussion on this issue, see P. Colenbrander, 'External exchange and the Zulu kingdom: towards a reassessment', in B. Guest and J. Sellers (eds.), *Enterprise and Exploitation in a Victorian Colony: Aspects of the Economic and Social History of Colonial Natal*, Pietermaritzburg, 1985, pp. 99–119.

15 Blainey, *Causes of War*, pp. 55–6, 157–62.

16 SNA 1/4/2, confidential no. 91: message from Cetshwayo to Fynney, 28 November 1878.

17 *Natal Witness*, 7 August 1878.

18 See GH 501, no. G671a/79: Wolseley to Bulwer, 13 October 1879: the preparatory examination of Mehlokazulu.

19 GH 1399, pp. 105–7: message from Cetywayo to Bulwer, 30 August 1879; GH 1399, pp. 152–61: message from Cetywayo to Bulwer, written by Dunn, 20 September 1878; *BPP* (C. 2260), sub-enc. 29 in enc. 1 in no. 6: reply of Bulwer to messages from Cetywayo, 28 September 1878.

20 Lugg, *Zulu Shield*, pp. 32–3.

21 *JSA* IV, pp. 306–7, 318, 328: Ndukwana's testimony; ibid. III, p. 257: testimony of Mmemi kaNguluzane; ibid., p. 179: testimony of Mkando kaDhlova.

22 GH 1399, pp. 96–102: statement of Umlungu, Siguklu and Mabuna, taken by J. W. Shepstone, 9 September 1879; E. Unterhalter, 'Confronting imperialism: the people of Nquthu and the invasion of Zululand', in Duminy and Ballard, *New Perspectives*, p. 99.

23 GH 501, no. G67/a/79: declaration of Mehlokazulu in the Pietermaritzburg gaol, 18 September 1879.

24 F. Fynney, *The Zulu Army and Zulu Headmen*, Pietermaritzburg, 1879, p. 5.

25 For a detailed discussion on the faulty nature of evidence concerning Zulu activity during the Anglo–Zulu War, see J. P. C. Laband, 'The Zulu army in the war of 1879: some cautionary notes', in Laband and Thompson, *Kingdom and Colony*, especially pp. 34–5.

26 CSO 1925, no. 546/1879: Fannin to Colonial Secretary, 26 January 1879; SNA 1/1/33, no. 122: Fynney to ASNA, 31 March 1879.

27 See in particular SNA 1/4/2, no. 30: statement of Ndabinjani, taken by Fynn, 4 November 1878; and SNA 1/6/11, no. 11: John Knight to Fynn (report of Umswarele), 18 November 1878.

28 *BPP* (C. 2260), sub-enc. 19 in enc. 2 in no. 6: reply of Cetywayo to message from Lieutenant-Governor of 8 October 1878 (translated by J. W. Shepstone), 29 October 1878.

29 For an example of the many reports to this effect, see SNA 1/4/2, no. 63 (confidential): Wheelwright to SNA, 30 October 1878.

30 *BPP* (C. 2260), sub-enc. 23 in enc. 2 in no. 6: message to Cetywayo from the Lieutenant-Governor of Natal (signed by J. W. Shepstone), 30 October 1878.

31 SNA 1/6/11, no. 8: John Dunn to ASNA, 28 October 1878; Vijn, *Cetshwayo's Dutchman*, p. 8.

32 See, among the many reports to this effect, CSO 1925, no. C171/1878: Fannin to Colonial Secretary, 19 November 1878.

33 *BPP* (C. 2308), enc. 2 in no. 7: statement of Umlunge and Umlamula (taken by C. B. H. Mitchell), 6 December 1878.

34 GH 1399, pp. 237–41: Fynney to ASNA, 30 September 1878; Vijn, *Cetshwayo's Dutchman*, pp. 16–17; M. M. Fuze (H. C. Lugg (tr.) and A. T. Cope (ed.)), *The Black People and Whence They Came: A Zulu View*, Pietermaritzburg and Durban, 1979, p. 111.

35 For Mnyamana, Zibhebhu and Hamu, see Laband, 'Zulu polity', pp. 5–6.

36 For Hamu's strained relations with the king, see ibid., p. 6.

37 AU 25: Hamu to Landdrost of Utrecht (letter signed 'Home'), recd. 6 November 1878.

38 SNA 1/4/2, no. 31: message from Cetywayo to Fynney, conveyed by Ruqu, Umlamula and Unyumbana, 7 November 1878.

39 SNA 1/4/2, no. 79 (confidential): message from the chiefs of Zululand to Fynney, conveyed by Mavwanga and Ugodi, 13 November 1878.

40 AU 25: Gwegwana, Hamu's messenger, to Rudolph, 6 November 1878.

41 *Natal Witness*, 30 November 1878: Biggarsberg correspondent, 20 November 1878.

42 *BPP* (C. 2308), enc. 1 in no. 7: message from Bulwer to Cetywayo, 16 November 1878; ibid.: 25 November 1878.

43 Ibid., enc. 2 in no. 7: statement of Umlunge and Umlamula to Colonial Secretary, 6 December 1878.

44 CSO 1925, no. 4624/1878: Robson to Colonial Secretary, 5 December 1878.

45 *BPP* (C. 2308), enc. 2 in no. 7: report by J. W. Shepstone, 19 December 1878; Fynney, *Zulu Army*.

46 There was a rumour that Mnyamana had originally been part of the deputation, but that he had decided against joining it and had given as excuse that a wife of his was ill (*Natal Witness*, 17 December 1878).

47 See O. F. Raum, 'Aspects of Zulu diplomacy in the 19th century', *Afrika und Ubersee*, LXVI, 1983, pp. 34–5, 41.

48 There was nothing extraordinary about such feats of memory. Communications between the British and the Zulu king had almost invariably been conducted through verbal messages relayed with great accuracy. See J. Y. Gibson, *The Story of the Zulus*, London, 1911, p. 164.

49 See H. F. Norbury, *The Naval Brigade in South Africa during the Years 1877–78–79*, London, 1880, pp. 205–14. Norbury witnessed the proceedings.

50 *BPP* (C. 2222), enc. 1 in no. 59: Dunn to SNA, 18 December 1878; D. C. F. Moodie, *John Dunn, Cetywayo and Three Generals*, Pietermaritzburg, 1886, pp. 91–2.

51 CSO 1925, no. 250/1879: Fannin to Colonial Secretary, 12 January 1879; Webb and Wright, *Zulu King Speaks*, p. 28.

52 TS 35: Chelmsford to T. Shepstone, 13 December 1878.

53 CSO 1925, no. 4956/1878: Fannin to Colonial Secretary, 25 December 1878; Webb and Wright, *Zulu King Speaks*, p. 28.

54 SNA 1/1/31, no. 66: Fynney to ASNA, 23 December 1878; CSO 1925, no. 4994/1878: Robson to Colonial Secretary, 25 December 1878.

55 SNA 1/1/31, no. 69: message from Cetywayo to Fynney, 26 December 1879.

56 CSO 1925, no. C6/1879: Fannin to Colonial Secretary, 8 January 1879; Moodie, *John Dunn*, pp. 71–2, 74.

57 For a full description of the ceremonies, see *JSA* IV, pp. 115–17: testimony of Mtshayankomo.

58 Ibid. II, p. 317: testimony of Lunguza; ibid. IV, p. 118: testimony of Mtshayankomo; *Natal Colonist*, 24 October 1878: Lower Tugela correspondent, 21 October 1878.

59 *BPP* (C. 2242), enc. 4 in no. 4: Fannin to Officer Commanding Greytown Column, 22 December 1878.

60 Ibid., enc. 3 in no. 4: Capt. E. Woodgate to Col. R. Glyn, 19 December 1878. The new moon was on 23 December.

61 CSO 1925, no. 9/1879: Fannin to Colonial Secretary, 30 December 1878.

62 SNA 1/1/33, no. 26: Fynn to SNA, 8 January 1879; CSO 1925, no. 212/79: Fannin to Durnford, 10 January 1879; Webb and Wright, *Zulu King Speaks*, p. 56.

63 Moodie, *John Dunn*, pp. 71–3, 93–5; C. Ballard, *John Dunn: The White Chief of Zululand*, Craighall, 1985, pp. 114, 129–30, 133–4, 138.

64 WC II/2/2: Chelmsford to Wood, 11, and 23 December 1878.

65 CP 9, enc. in no. 5: Capt. N. MacLeod to Wood, 28 December 1878. Connections between Hamu and the Swazi were, in any case, close. Two of Hamu's favourite wives were Swazi, and most of his adherents, especially those in the north, were likewise married to Swazi.

66 The Zulu had the idea that under white rule the men would be sent to England to work, the girls married off to white soldiers and their cattle become the property of the government (Vijn, *Cetshwayo's Dutchman*, p. 15).

67 *JSA* IV, p. 209: testimony of Ndhlovu kaTimuni; ibid., p. 335: testimony of Ndukwana.

68 CSO 1925, no. 250/1879: Fannin to Colonial Secretary, 12 January 1879. The testimony of those interviewed for the supplement to the *Natal Mercury*, 22 January 1929, all confirms that they went to the king's to muster in their units for war and hear his instructions.

69 Filter and Bourquin, *Paulina Dlamini*, p. 69.

70 H. Ngubane, *Body and Mind in Zulu Medicine: An Ethnography of Health and Disease in Nyuswa-Zulu Thought and Practice*, London, 1977, pp. 77–8, 81, 86, 131, 133.

71 For full descriptions of doctoring at time of war, see *JSA* I, p. 124: testimony of Dunjwa kaMabedhla; ibid. IV, pp. 296–300, 306: testimony of Mpatshana; and Rev. Canon Calloway, *The Religious System of the Amazulu*, Leipzig, 1870, reprinted 1884, pp. 437–440. For the significance of the ceremonies, see Ngubane, *Body and Mind*, pp. 109–10, 119, 126, 129–30, 152.

72 *JSA* III, pp. 296–7, 313: testimony of Mpatshana; *Natal Mercury*, 30

January 1879: Wounded induna captured after the battle of Nyezane. There was also and earlier report of a war-doctor in October 1878 promising to make warriors in western Zululand invulnerable.

73 *JSA* III, pp. 306–7: testimony of Mpatshana. See also ibid. IV, p. 89: testimony of Mtshapi kaNoradu; and ibid., p. 371: testimony of Ndukwana. See too Moodie, *John Dunn*, p. 73.

74 *JSA* IV, p. 77: testimony of Mtshapi; ibid., p. 146: testimony of Mtshayankomo; ibid., p. 291: testimony of Ndukwana.

75 Bishop J. W. Colenso and H. E. Colenso, *Digest of Zulu Affairs*, Bishopstowe, 1878–88, series 1, part 2, p. 540.

76 CSO 1925, no. 221/1879: Fynney to ASNA, 11 January 1879.

77 SNA 1/4/1: message from Bulwer to Cetywayo, 12 January 1879.

3

Opposing armies

The two armies which faced each other in January 1879 across the Zululand border were very different in terms of their organization, dress, weapons, habitual tactics and intended strategies.

For the British, the conduct of colonial campaigns against warriors inferior in armaments, organization and discipline to regular troops trained in the European fashion was an art in itself. For unlike campaigns in Europe, where the foe could be expected to fight in a predictable fashion, those against less sophisticated enemies with varied military styles required considerable adaptability in both strategy and tactics.[1] Much also depended on the calibre of troops available. All these considerations are pertinent when assessing Lord Chelmsford's preparations for the Zulu campaign, which required the invasion of unfamiliar foreign soil against an untried but reputedly formidable foe.

For this operation, Chelmsford succeeded in putting together an army of 17 929 men, divided initially into five columns, later reduced effectively to three. Of these men, 5 476 were British regulars drawn from regiments in Natal, the Cape and the Transvaal; 1 193 were irregular colonial horse; and 9 350 were black auxiliaries, raised in Natal. The remaining 1 910 men were colonial conductors, drivers and voorloopers necessary to manage transport and supplies. Moreover, on Chelmsford's urgent request, an additional 2 188 regulars left Britain on 2 December 1878 to reinforce him, though their arrival at the front was not to be expected until late January 1879.[2]

The main striking-force of this army was the British regulars. Their numbers were limited, for the professional Victorian army was small, and its manpower and capabilities were constantly overstretched by a multiplicity of commitments, both routine and emergency, in defence of the British Empire across the globe. Paradoxically, recognition of its vital imperial role was accompanied by continuing public disparagement of soldiers as such.[3] For, without the familiarizing effect of conscription, the general public regarded the army as an alien institution, officered by a privileged and reactionary class and manned by the least respectable elements of the working class. Nor were such prejudices without foundation.

The forces of conservatism were deeply entrenched in an authoritarian and self-contained institution like the British army. No tropical uniform was issued to the British soldier, with the exception of those stationed in India, and war was still a matter of the scarlet tunic. The only concession to the African sun was the foreign service helmet, first issued in 1877. Nevertheless, the demands of imperial defence encouraged some reforms,[4] such as those carried through under Edward Cardwell, Secretary of State for War (1868–74). For the sake of economy and efficiency, Cardwell reduced Britain's military presence overseas by completing the withdrawal of troops from white settlement colonies, scaling down garrisons elsewhere (except in India), and thus establishing a better balance between home and imperial defence. The introduction of short service in 1870, whereby recruits spent six years in the regular army and six in the reserve, was intended to provide a large reservoir of trained reservists, reduce unhealthy service abroad, and save money. In 1872 Cardwell created brigade districts with two linked battalions to be attached to each depot. The battalions would alternate in recruiting at home and serving abroad, so (it was planned) ensuring that the empire was guarded only by seasoned troops. In 1871 the purchase of commissions was abolished to encourage the development of a professional officer corps.[5]

This system, although admirably suited on paper to an empire with scattered and diverse military requirements, did not work in practice. The reserve was only to be called out in the event of a national emergency, which meant that minor colonial campaigns could only be provided for by calling upon regular and reserve units for volunteers, and by reducing standing garrisons – thus breaching the principle of regimental *esprit de corps*. Moreover, as colonial commitments increased, a growing number of home-based and imperfectly trained battalions found themselves serving abroad. Thus in 1879 eighty-two battalions were abroad, and only fifty-nine at home depots. In order to maintain establishments and meet the larger turnover of men caused by short-term enlistment, the army had to lower physical standards.[6] Furthermore, as experienced soldiers now left the ranks earlier, the proportion of young men rose to such an extent that the efficiency of regiments for active service was undermined. Nor had the abolition of purchase substantially improved the calibre of the officer corps. Officers still came from the upper classes, and though some had received specialist training, most were still conservative and stereotyped in their approach.[7]

Consequently, many of the regular troops and officers available to Chelmsford – who was himself a typical product of the conservative military establishment – suffered from handicaps of youth and inexperience or inflated professional esteem, as well as a reluctance to adapt to local conditions.

Since the British regulars at Chelmsford's disposal were too valuable to be dispersed on garrison and convoy duty, they had to be augmented by black levies raised in the Natal Native Reserves and put under white officers. The Natal Native Contingent, as this force was known, was poorly armed and trained, and was consequently of doubtful morale. A far better fighting force, but underestimated by the British regulars, was the colonial irregular horse, whom the initial lack of regular cavalry made essential for patrol work.[8] Indeed, cavalry retained an importance in colonial war long after it had been lost in European. Vital in pursuit of a broken enemy, it was just as important for reconnaissance and raiding purposes, and the absence of sufficient horsemen was one of the greatest defects in Chelmsford's army.[9]

It is necessary for a commander to study in advance the military methods of the enemy so as to understand how best to overcome him. Chelmsford certainly turned his attention to preparing detailed information on the Zulu military system for his army, and to instructions on how the campaign should be conducted and fought. Nevertheless, officers and soldiers alike entered on the war wholly underrating the Zulus' fighting ability. Indeed, it was their genuine concern that the Zulu would not be prepared to stand and fight, let alone actually initiate an attack.[10] There is no doubt that this overconfidence derived from Chelmsford's recent campaign in the eastern Cape. His experience there misled him and all his men into presuming that the Zulu would be an only slightly superior adversary to the easily disposed of Gcaleka Xhosa, and that they too were no more than 'kafirs, who had only to be hunted'.[11] This discounting of Zulu military ability, allied to complete confidence in the superiority of British weapons, goes far to explain the strategy Chelmsford adopted for the invasion of Zululand.

To achieve the political objectives of the war, it was necessary to overthrow Zulu military might in the field, and naturally preferable to do this on Zulu rather than British soil. An offensive into Zululand would, however, leave the borders of Natal and the Transvaal vulnerable to a Zulu counter-thrust, while Colonel Rowland's unsuccessful campaign of 1878 against Sekhukhune meant that a British presence would have to be retained in the north-eastern Transvaal.[12] White settlers generally were in dread of a Zulu raid, and anticipated that the colonial blacks might well rise up in aid of the mobile and merciless Zulu.[13] Such potential raids were a far greater threat in the broken terrain of the Natal frontier than in the open country of the Transvaal, where they could be more easily detected and countered. However, Chelmsford noted with alarm that the Natal authorities' contingency plans in the event of a Zulu raid consisted in nothing more than advice that the settlers take refuge in the various government laagers, which were mainly situated in the small and widely scattered towns.

Accordingly, on 10 September 1878 he persuaded the Natal government to take more appropriate measures, and on 26 November the Colony was divided into Colonial Defensive Districts. However, since the garrisons of imperial troops along the army's line of communications into Zululand would be very small, and because the numbers of available colonial volunteers would be minimal, there would be enough armed men to hold only the fortified posts. To dissuade the Zulu from raiding the countryside in between, it was necessary to raise a large field-force of black levies in the border Defensive Districts, and this the Natal government authorized on 20 December 1878. Unlike the Natal Native Contingent, which had been recruited as imperial troops and were intended for service in Zululand, the border levies were Natal's responsibility. They were to be activated only in the event of a Zulu raid. Besides these part-time levies, the Natal government also provided for small standing reserves of Border Guards at strategic points, as well as Border Police along the river frontiers. On 11 January, when poised to invade Zululand, Chelmsford placed the entire crucial border region under military control.[14]

There was no doubt, though, that despite these arrangements border defences remained weak, and this consideration helped determine the timing of Chelmsford's offensive. As Bulwer wrote, 'our best friend is the river'.[15] The rivers along Natal's frontiers with Zululand were usually unfordable from January to March, except at a limited number of drifts which could be effectively guarded. By the time the rivers subsided, Chelmsford confidently expected the campaign to be over. Until then, the rivers would form an effective line of defence against Zulu raids. Indeed, as with many another campaign, the seasons helped determine its timing. Thus Chelmsford's planning was affected by the condition of the countryside after the late spring rains of 1878 and the consequently delayed harvest. So while the Zulu would still be short of food in January 1879, which would adversely affect their capacity to wage a campaign, the grazing, upon which the British draught animals subsisted, was plentiful. Soon, though, the grass would be higher and so afford the Zulu even better cover; while later still, in the winter months, grazing would give out and be dry enough to be burned by the Zulu. January 1879, then, was the optimum time to launch the invasion of Zululand.[16]

Success in a vigorous, offensive campaign such as Chelmsford intended to conduct depended upon firm logistics. These involved not only the prior accumulation of necessary supplies and ammunition, but also the organization of sufficient transport. In this sense, the Anglo–Zulu War exemplified one of the basic features of colonial warfare: it was a campaign against distance and natural obstacles as much as against hostile man, and one in which problems of supply were at the root of most of the difficulties encountered and, indeed, governed its whole course.

Since supplies could not be obtained from the theatre of war, they had to be carried. Chelmsford succeeded only with great difficulty and expense in assembling the 10 023 oxen, 398 mules, 977 wagons and 56 carts required to supply his invading army.[17] Yet wagons, even when drawn over favourable terrain by animals in peak condition, could hardly travel further than 19 km a day. Their pace would be even slower across the enormous distances and broken countryside of the Zulu theatre of war. Moreover, they required all-round protection on the march, and the larger the convoy the slower it moved.[18] Colonists, especially the Boers, advised Chelmsford to form defensive wagon-laagers when he halted in Zulu territory. But until the dreadful lesson of Isandlwana had been administered, the General was reluctant to laager because it was such a time-consuming procedure and his progress was already so slow.[19]

Indeed, the reliance of the British on their crawling supply-trains ruled out from the beginning any possibility of a war of manoeuvre.

In planning his strategy, therefore, Chelmsford was faced with certain constraints. When he advanced into Zululand he would leave his own frontiers inadequately protected; while his dependence on slow-moving and vulnerable supply-trains would limit both his flexibility and the size of the columns they were to support.

Chelmsford's solution to these problems was to send in a number of relatively small columns to converge on an appropriate point – oNdini. Such a division of forces is normally considered bad strategy, but Chelmsford hoped to move with greater speed with smaller columns, and to have more forage at the disposal of each. Moreover, the presence of a number of supporting columns would engross more of the enemy's territory, reduce the chance of their being outflanked, and presumably discourage Zulu counter-thrusts against the British frontiers. With the matter of Zulu raids particularly in mind, Chelmsford selected invasion routes in sectors considered vulnerable to Zulu attack. The advance across the lower Thukela would protect the coastal plain; that across Rorke's Drift, central Natal; and that across the Ncome River, the Transvaal. Moreover, by invading at several points, he hoped to force Cetshwayo to keep his *amabutho* fully mobilized in order to face the diverse threat, and so to present him with supply problems as great as his own.[20]

After Isandlwana, Chelmsford's strategy came under considerable criticism, not all of it well founded. It is true that, because of hopelessly unreliable maps and inadequate reconnaissance on account of lack of cavalry, he had no accurate conception of the terrain over which his columns were to advance.[21] In such circumstances, it was unlikely that several forces converging on a distant point such as oNdini would arrive simultaneously, or even be in a position to provide much mutual support. Why oNdini should have been the objective was also questioned. After all, there was no capital of Zululand in the European sense, and the king occupied many different royal homesteads as the wish took him. In sophisticated European states the capture of the capital, being the administrative and economic focus of the state, might often end a war. It was otherwise with differently structured societies, where the taking of the ruler's favourite residence would serve only to diminish his prestige. Nevertheless, oNdini did represent a legitimate target, for the Mahlabathini plain where it and many other *amakhanda* were concentrated was undoubtedly the heart of the Zulu kingdom. The *amakhanda* there, as well as those positioned elsewhere about the kingdom, were not only centres of the king's authority and rallying-points for the *amabutho*, but were also depots for supplies. That is why the systematic destruction of every *ikhanda*, culminating in that of oNdini, would ensure the reduction of the king's capacity to resist and fatally impair his ability to exercise authority.[22]

Unfortunately for the Zulu, Chelmsford well understood that almost the most effectual way of defeating a people such as the Zulu was 'through the stomach'.[23] This entailed the systematic destruction of less 'legitimate' military targets than *amakhanda*, such as ordinary *imizi* and their grain stores, as well as the capture of livestock. Mounted troops were essential for this raiding activity, which Chelmsford intended to maximize by dispersing his columns over a wide area. Of course, the British officially had no quarrel with the Zulu nation, only with its king,[24] which should have ruled out large-scale devastation at the expense of the civilian population. But after Isandlwana it was conveniently felt that it was no longer possible to observe any distinction between the king and his 'savage' subjects. Consequently, no restrictions were to be placed on military operations except the laws of civilized warfare[25] – which apparently sanctioned the complete destruction of the enemy's means of subsistence along the British line of march.

Protracted and desultory irregular warfare was to be avoided if at all possible, for it favoured the more mobile enemy fighting on home ground. It was therefore imperative to maintain the initiative at all times, which is why, despite the far-flung dispositions of his columns, Chelmsford preferred to conclude the campaign swiftly with a decisive battle.[26]

All the advantages in a pitched battle lay with properly trained troops, and a severe general engagement was calculated to bring home to the enemy the superiority of even heavily outnumbered regulars. This was especially important when, as in the case of Zululand, the war was undertaken to overthrow a militarily powerful state, whose army was its most potent manifestation. Naturally, when fighting a people with strong military traditions, there was a much greater chance of their being willing to risk all in battle, and the British confidently expected the Zulu to meet them in the open field. Chelmsford's operational gambit of dividing the army into several columns must consequently also be seen as a means of enticing the Zulu into attacking one or more of them. For it was only when they were committed to battle that the Zulu would discover that the numerical inferiority of the apparently weak columns would be more than compensated for by superior firepower and tactics.

A disciplined British force, once it was properly positioned and handled so as to give maximum effect to the destructive capabilities of modern breech-loading, rapid-firing rifles, Gatling guns and artillery, was normally invulnerable against the poorly armed mass attacks of warriors such as the Zulu.[27] The casualties it could inflict were, however, perhaps not as heavy as might be anticipated, as they depended upon both the range and the concentration of fire. For example, at close range (90–230 m), two minutes' Martini-Henry rifle fire at six shots per minute would only be 10 per cent effective. This would decrease to 2 per cent effectiveness at long range (630–1 260 m).[28] The fast-firing Gatling guns would be more lethal, but they were not dependable and tended to jam. Shrapnel bursts from the light seven-pounder mountain guns, which were the only artillery Chelmsford had at first, were not particularly damaging.[29] Therefore, it was necessary to deploy troops in close order so as to develop a weight of concentrated fire capable of halting a Zulu attack. The most effective way of doing this was to place troops in prepared all-round defensive positions, such as fieldworks (whether of earth or stone), or wagon-laagers.[30] It was to be repeatedly proved that the Zulu were helpless against even elementarily fortified posts or hastily arranged march-laagers. Consequently, in the wake of Isandlwana – which demonstrated conclusively that a massed charge could break through a loose skirmishing line no matter how superior the line's armament – it became the dominant British concern to entice the Zulu into destroying themselves against the invader's prepared positions.

A weak link in all this careful planning was lack of adequate intelligence work,[31] and in the days following their invasion of Zulu soil the British were in considerable doubt as to Zulu military dispositions and intentions. What they anticipated as the most likely Zulu move, once their slow-moving columns were fully committed to the difficult Zulu terrain, was a thrust into Natal at the poorly defended middle border below Kranskop by a considerable Zulu force, repeatedly reported to be concealed in the Nkhandla forest.[32]

King Cetshwayo, by contrast, was apparently well informed as to the strengths of the various invading columns, and their intended lines of advance. He gained such information from the effective deployment of spies. Spies were no novelty in Zulu society, for the king used them as a means of control, and normally had an 'eyes of the king' at the larger homesteads to keep him informed of what was occurring throughout his kingdom.[33] In time of war, spies were activated on a large scale to gain intelligence of the enemy, and the advancing British were always aware that they were under observation. The king expected his subjects in every district to keep lookouts and report the enemy's movements to him. In addition, the people along the borders were ordered in January 1879 to send spies into Natal and the Transvaal, as well as to Delagoa Bay, to collect what information they could.[34] Numbers, posing as deserters or refugees, managed to infiltrate British military positions, and sometimes were even employed as camp servants. It took some time before the military realized that these apparently harmless individuals were relaying information to the enemy and began to take precautionary measures.

In January there were reports that Zulu spies were moving along the Drakensberg towards Basutoland and Pondoland, and Bulwer ordered that any Zulu found in Natal without a refugee pass should be arrested.[35] He had some reason to be suspicious, for there is no doubt that, as the crisis intensified and war loomed, Cetshwayo was in search of allies against the British. Yet overtures to other chiefdoms were not primarily aggressive in intent, as was supposed by the British, but part of Cetshwayo's policy of taking defensive precautions. For on contemplating the possibility of going to war, any belligerent naturally assesses how intervention by outside parties might affect the course of the conflict. Such predictions, especially if optimistic, can play an important part in military planning. The irony of the situation was that in the past Cetshwayo had looked to Britain, as the strongest power in the sub-continent, for aid against his enemies, particularly the Transvaal. Now he had no choice but to turn to neighbouring chiefdoms for help.[36]

Cetshwayo's routine diplomatic relations with his black neighbours were consistently misrepresented by British officials and settlers as evidence that he was orchestrating a black conspiracy against white rule in southern Africa. The reality was that, during the process of the closing of the frontiers, African chiefs rarely succeeded in forming large-scale alliances, and though they might have maintained contacts, sectional advantage was ever placed before wider interests.[37] So it proved in 1879.

There was never any chance, despite some pre-war negotiation, of any help from Swaziland, which for far too long had been a victim of Zulu expansionism, and hoped rather for an end to Zulu military power.[38] Nor, despite the reported presence of Zulu emissaries in the region of Delagoa Bay, was there any possibility of cooperation with the Mabhudu-Tsonga, the dominant chiefdom across the trade route to Zululand. Although the Mabhudu-Tsonga paid tribute to the Zulu, and Muhena had been regent since 1876 with Zulu support, relations had been poor since the 1860s as both attempted to control the lucrative trade and smaller chiefdoms of the region. The Mabhudu-Tsonga therefore welcomed any diminution of Zulu power. To the south and west of the Mabhudu-Tsonga, and north of the Hluhluwe and Mkuzi rivers, lived various chiefdoms which had a strong cultural and tributary relationship with the Zulu state. Being so thoroughly within the Zulu orbit, men of the more southerly of these chiefdoms were expected to assist the Zulu in war, even though they were not part of the *ibutho* system.[39]

Further afield Cetshwayo had no chance at all of raising the black chiefdoms already under British suzerainty against their overlords. Though it is certain that he maintained diplomatic contact with certain BaSutho chiefs (who, since 1871, fell under the authority of the Cape Colony), his emissaries had no success in persuading them to rise up in 1878, if that was indeed their objective. Nor did Zulu emissaries fare any better in the eastern Cape, where, despite some diplomatic contacts, the Mpondo remained quite unaffected by the war brewing against Zululand.[40]

It might have been different with Sekhukhune, the Pedi chief, whom Shepstone accused of acting 'as a kind of lieutenant' to Cetshwayo,[41] and who maintained regular diplomatic contact with the Zulu king. Moreover, the failure by October 1878 of the British campaign against Sekhukhune might be expected to have encouraged an anti-British front, and there is evidence that Cetshwayo began seriously to pursue the possibility.[42] Even so, no active alliance was ever formed between the Zulu and the Pedi. The latter found it sufficient to pursue their own interests in their relations with the Transvaal administration, and avoided becoming involved in the Zulus' dispute with the British.[43] Consequently, Cetshwayo found that when it came to war he had to face the British alone.

The defensive was the essence of the Zulu king's military strategy in 1879. It conformed with his political programme of presenting himself as the pacific victim of an unwarranted attack, prepared only to fight in self-defence within the borders of his own country.[44] The weight of evidence (despite some testimony to the contrary, and the disbelief of British officials) indicates that it was his policy to resist the invader in as restrained a fashion as possible. He instructed his people not to attack the British until they had first fired on them, begun to build fortifications inside Zululand, or otherwise demonstrated their hostile intent.[45] Only when he learned that the British Right Column was across the lower Thukela, and that the Centre Column had defeated Sihayo's adherents on 12 January at Sokhexe, did the incensed Cetshwayo order his *amabutho* impatiently assembled at oNdini to drive the invader back.[46]

Nevertheless, he insisted that his armies, if successful, were not to follow up their victory with an invasion of Natal. He knew well from his white advisers, such as John Dunn, that the British had the resources overseas to reinforce their army in southern Africa until it was ultimately successful. Consequently, the longer the war lasted and the more extensive its scope the less chance the Zulu would have of winning it. If they violated British territory, they would provoke the British into persevering until Zululand had been crushed as a dire warning to all the other chiefdoms in the sub-continent. The campaign had therefore to be swift and limited, and the hope was that, if the Zulu armies were able through success in the field to menace the borders of Natal, the British would be pressured into concluding a peace favourable to the Zulu before reinforcements could arrive.[47]

The alternative of a protracted, guerrilla-style defensive strategy was not practicable. It could be argued that by withdrawing to traditional strongholds and avoiding conventional engagements the Zulu might have prolonged the campaign beyond Britain's endurance. Yet that consideration worked equally well in reverse. For how long could the men occupying Zululand's rocky fastnesses have been provisioned? Besides, the nature of the *ibutho* system and the Zulu economy made it imperative that the men be freed at vital times of the year to go about their domestic duties and serve the king; while the prevention of women and boys from planting and harvesting crops, and tending their precious livestock, would swiftly mean starvation and ruin for the entire community. Moreover, the prospect of permitting the British systematically to ravage Zululand was quite unacceptable to a warlike people who were more accustomed to raiding their enemies' territory. Thus, for reasons both material and psychological, only the conventional clash of armies in the open field was possible for the Zulu in 1879.[48] It could not be helped that this strategy played directly into the hands of the British, who also wished to avoid a drawn-out campaign, and sought a swift solution through direct and decisive military encounters.

It is difficult to estimate with any certainty the number of warriors the king had at his disposal. Fynney, in his booklet on the Zulu army which he compiled in 1879 on Chelmsford's orders, estimated the size of the Zulu army at 41 900 men. Naturally, the full complement of the Zulu army would never have been available for active service at a specific moment. Some of the senior *amabutho* were of too advanced an age to fight, while not every member of an *ibutho* could be expected to muster when summoned. The king and his councillors had consequently to devise a strategy that employed a considerably lower number of men than were nominally at their command. Fannin reported on the eve of the battles of Isandlwana and Nyezane that he had gathered from his intelligence sources that Zulu armies totalling 29 000 men had been deployed against the invader, a figure that was to prove substantially correct.[49]

Yet 29 000 effectives were barely sufficient for the king's strategic requirements. Three British columns were invading his territory from widely separated points. Besides, the Transvaal Boers could be expected to support the Left Column advancing from Conference Hill. Moreover, Cetshwayo feared that the British might attempt a seaborne invasion from St Lucia Bay or Delagoa Bay and, conceivably aided by the Tsonga, advance on the kingdom from the north-east; while the Swazi in the north could be expected to seize the opportunity to attack over the Phongolo.[50] Thus the king faced the risk of attack from every quarter, and had to place his limited forces as effectively as he could. In the event, he gave priority to his strategy of defeating the British in the field, and threatening the colony of Natal in order to force a peace. This decision required that he concentrate his efforts against the British columns operating from Natal.

There are indications that his council did not altogether approve of this plan, but the king was fully supported by his military commanders.[51] Since Chelmsford was accompanying the Centre

Column, and spies reported it to be stronger than the other columns, Cetshwayo naturally singled it out as the main British force. It had, moreover, already scored a victory at Sihayo's homestead on 12 January, and so was most deserving of a salutary lesson. The king consequently directed the crack *amabutho* of his main army against it. A much smaller force moved off from oNdini at the same time towards the coast to cooperate with local elements of the *amabutho* in impeding the advance of the British Right Column. It seems he also sent some reinforcements from oNdini to support the Qulusi *ibutho* and local irregulars who were preparing to face the Left Column and its Boer allies when they entered Zululand. Local irregulars (and not the large army feared by British intelligence) also collected in the Nkhandla forest area in order to repel any advance across the middle Thukela.

Having committed his available forces to the southern and western borders of his kingdom, the king had left the interior of Zululand apparently vulnerable to attack from the north and north-east. Certainly, he retained a reserve at oNdini to counter such a threat, and to intercept any possible dash by a British mounted force into the heart of the country – not that the British had sufficient cavalry for effective reconnaissance, let alone a venture of that sort. Yet this reserve consisted of what had been King Dingane's favourite *ibutho*, the iNdabakawombe, married men of about fifty-eight years of age, who could not have numbered more than 1 000. Elements of the uDlambedlu (izinGwegwe) *ibutho*, only two years their junior, also remained at oNdini, as probably did some other older warriors in their sixties.[52] The inadequacy of this reserve for countering any real threat indicates that, on balance, Cetshwayo and his military advisers had decided to discount a serious incursion from the sea or across the Phongolo. At one time the possibility had seemed real, for in October 1878 the British had investigated using Lourenço Marques as a port for a British invasion of Zulu territory, and the Portuguese had been willing to allow the passage of British troops. There is no doubt that had the British landed a force it would have prevented the king from denuding the north of defenders and concentrating on the Natal border.[53] But by January 1879 it was clear to the Zulu that the British were not going to exercise that particular strategic option.

The British had also seriously considered a landing further down the Zulu coast. Their activity close to land at St Lucia Bay, where boats from the frigate *Active* explored the shore, had seriously alarmed the Zulu. In September the king had even sent an armed force to the area to keep watch and to oppose a possible landing.[54] John Dunn fanned apprehensions of an amphibious landing on the coast of his chiefdom in the south-east of Zululand, and these were given substance by the unsuccessful attempt on 20–2 August 1878 of the steam tug *Adonis* to find a landing place at the Thukela mouth, or along the coast within 56 km to the north.[55] Nevertheless, it was apparent that no British landing was being contemplated in January 1879.

Nor was there any prospect of the Tsonga initiating hostilities against their Zulu overlords – in fact, the contrary was the case. As war approached, Tsonga, who supplied labour to Natal, and were allowed safe passage through Zululand in return for a 'head fee' to the king, began streaming out of the colony. Some made their way home, but others, as was to become apparent, remained in south-eastern Zululand to fight for King Cetshwayo, with whom their ultimate allegiance lay.

If the king was correct in calculating that he faced no likelihood of attack from the sea or the north-east, he was less confident in leaving his border with Swaziland exposed. Since the late 1860s Zulu homesteads had been expanding across the Phongolo to shore up Zulu influence in the area, and this process had proceeded at an accelerated pace once Cetshwayo became king. Yet Cetshwayo had always stopped short of an actual attack on the Swazi kingdom. He was prevented by the complex interaction between internal Zulu politics (powerful chiefs in northern Zululand had independent interests in Swaziland and feared the repercussions of war) and pressure from Natal and the Transvaal. This pressure increased once Britain had annexed the Transvaal and, in the latter part of 1878, induced Cetshwayo to make friendly overtures to the Swazi. The Swazi were not mollified, however. They had every reason to fear and hate their expansionist neighbour, and would have welcomed his overthrow. However, nothing would induce them to risk entering a war as allies of the British until they were absolutely certain that they were on the winning side.[56]

That was the crux of the matter. Throughout November and December 1878 Norman MacLeod, the Swazi Border Commissioner, made repeated overtures to King Mbandzeni. He offered inducements for Swazi intervention in the north of Zululand to protect the left flank of the advancing British, to expel the Zulu living north of the Phongolo, and to cut off a possible Zulu retreat to the north. But Mbandzeni wavered. While the Swazi along the Zulu border fell into a state of apprehension and began removing their cattle to places of safety,[57] he assured the British with one breath that he was ready to advance to their aid, while with the next he found that he could not. This was apparently because part of his army had already gone to the Lebombo mountains, where Zibhebhu was fortifying his caves, and he declared that in any case he had still to consult his council on the matter.[58] This sort of prevarication intensely frustrated the British, but it allowed Cetshwayo to neglect the Phongolo border and to concentrate on defeating the British advancing from the south.

King Cetshwayo sent his armies off to war in 1879 in the firm conviction that if they could only force the British to give battle in the open field they would overwhelm the enemy with their numerically superior forces deployed for the traditional mass frontal attack. After all, they had beaten the Boers in 1838 when the intruders had left the protection of their wagon-laagers. At the same time, Zulu tacticians were very aware after the disaster of Blood River during the same campaign of the dangers involved in trying to storm prepared positions such as laagers or forts. The king thus categorically forbade attacks on entrenchments.[59] Instead, he ordered his generals to bypass British positions and, by threatening their defenders' lines of supply and British territory to their rear, force them into the open in their defence. Otherwise, they were to surround the entrenched British at a distance (as was later to occur at Fort Eshowe) and attempt to starve them into submission or a disadvantageous sortie.[60]

Yet, sound as this strategy might have been in theory, it did not recognize sufficiently the difficulties involved in supplying a Zulu army in the field, nor the lack of patience and restraint likely to be exhibited by headstrong younger *amabutho* eager for glory. These factors made compliance with the king's sensible instructions by his generals unlikely, and Zulu success in the field dependent on catching the British in the open. That the British should ever have allowed this to happen was a consequence of the way in which Chelmsford and his staff, fresh from their easy successes in the eastern Cape, insisted (until taught otherwise) on underrating the Zulu.

There is contradictory evidence regarding what the Zulu wore on the campaign that was about to open.[61] The ceremonial attire of the *amabutho* that distinguished them one from another was lavish and intricate, and contained many rare and fragile items which were supplied through the king's favour.[62] It seems that only an abbreviated form of this precious and constricting costume was worn to war, and that it was a matter of some personal taste as to which items were retained. Men of status apparently wore more regalia than ordinary warriors as a distinguishing mark. Also, men who had killed in battle would wear their amulet necklaces (or *iziqu*) of willow wood to ward off the evil effects of the deed. Armies that had less distance to march generally kept more of their costume than those which had to strike further afield, while the more conservative men of the older *amabutho* preferred to wear more than the younger men, who laid most decorative pieces aside.

In 1879 Zulu fighting-men carried, in varied combinations, both traditional and modern weapons. The basic traditional weapon was the spear, of which there were some ten varieties.[63] The most deadly was the short-handled stabbing-spear (*iklwa*), reputedly introduced by King Shaka. It was used only at close quarters, when an underarm stab – normally aimed at the abdomen – was followed before withdrawing by a rip. This methodical operation required considerable skill and practice. The warrior carried in addition two or three throwing-spears with long shafts (*izijula*). Used also for hunting, they were well balanced in flight, and could find their target at up to thirty metres. Some warriors might also carry a wooden knobkerrie for close fighting (*iwisa*), or perhaps a few might have a battle-axe with a crescent blade (*isizenze*), of Swazi or Pedi origin. The making of spears was a skilled craft, the speciality of blacksmiths in the regions of the Nkhandla forest and Black Mfolozi. The spears were handed over to the king, who distributed them to his *amabutho*. The war-shield of cattle hide (*isihlangu*), which took great care and patience to manufacture, was also supplied by the king (whose property it remained) and was kept in a special hut in the *ikhanda* on account of its ritual properties. By 1879 the shield had generally shrunk to two-thirds of the man-height size stipulated by Shaka, though there are indications that full-size ones were still carried by chiefs, and perhaps some veterans of the older *amabutho*.[64] The uniformity of shield colours and patterns, which had distinguished the different *amabutho* in Shaka's time, was no longer observed, although younger *amabutho* carried predominantly black or reddish shields and married *amabutho* white ones. There is evidence that many *amabutho* carried shields of no particular hue.[65]

Many Zulu went into battle in 1879 armed besides their traditional weapons with firearms. These had entered Zululand in significant quantities from the late 1860s, when Cetshwayo's fears that his position as Mpande's heir might be usurped by one or other of his brothers, combined with threats of Boer encroachment, had compelled him to encourage their importation. The precise number and quality are uncertain. British consular officials reckoned that up to 10 000 guns a year were entering Zululand during the second half of the 1870s.[66] A correspondent of the *Natal Witness* in August 1878 estimated that there were 20 000 stands of European firearms in Zululand. From his observations he computed that these consisted of 500 superior British breech-loading rifles, a further 2 500 good rifles like the percussion Enfield, and 5 000 second-hand ones. The balance were inferior weapons, mainly muskets. For with the adoption by European armies in the 1860s and 1870s of breech-loading rifles with metallic cartridges, obsolete firearms were cheaply disposed of and dumped for a solid profit by unscrupulous dealers on the African market.[67] The general quality of these antiquated weapons can be assessed from those captured at the battle of Nyezane in January 1879. Most were ancient British Tower muskets (some dating from 1835), and the remainder were condemned Continental army ones, mainly of German manufacture, besides a few from the United States.[68]

Guns reached Zululand from Natal or through the Portuguese possession of Delagoa Bay, though not through the Diamond Fields, as few Zulu had yet become migratory labourers. In June 1875 the Natal government, fearing the threat guns posed to the security of the Colony, prohibited their direct sale in Zululand. Illicit gun-running persisted across the Thukela, nevertheless, with whites dealing mainly in the better-quality arms. Traders along the Zulu border carried on a brisk and open business in cartridges, percussion caps and lead. Yet it was the circumvention of Natal's ban by several merchants which provided the main source of firearms in Zululand. Quite legally, they transshipped arms from Durban or Cape Town to Delagoa Bay, where the agents of John Dunn, who was King Cetshwayo's most favoured and trusted trader, arranged for their transportation by porter to Zululand.[69]

By 1878, with the possibility of war with the Zulu looming, the

British decided that the wholesale import of arms through Delagoa Bay must be halted. By an agreement of February 1878 with Portugal, the sale of guns and ammunition to Africans was prohibited. The small Portuguese force at the Bay found it difficult to stop arms finding their way into Zululand, however, and it was not until August 1878 that the contraband traffic through northern Mozambique ports was effectively stopped. The Zulu were unable to bring about a relaxation of the arms ban, either through negotiation or the threat of hostilities, and consequently had no choice but to fight the war of 1879 with what arms and ammunition they already possessed, or with what they could manufacture themselves or seize from the enemy.[70]

It was the trader John Dunn who had convinced King Cetshwayo that a royal monopoly of firearms in the kingdom was essential for the maintenance of his power against external enemies and internal rivals. A complete monopoly was not possible, however, and it was no coincidence that the king's most dangerous and capable rival, Zibhebhu, whose chiefdom lay across the route to Delagoa Bay, was heavily engaged in trading for firearms, as was the discontented Prince Hamu in the north-west.[71] Nevertheless, the king, through his trader John Dunn, remained the main source of firearms in the kingdom. When, for example, the uVe mustered at oNdini on the eve of the war and possessed no firearms to speak of, it was the king who ordered that each must exchange a cow for one.[72]

The king also possessed the largest stores of ammunition in Zululand. In time of war he supplied it to his men, though there were quantities of gunpowder, percussion caps, lead and bullet-moulds over much of the country. Moreover, there were Zulu who had learned from white traders how to make gunpowder, and the king ensured that this skill was disseminated.[73] He stored his ammunition in the vicinity of his emLambongwenya and kwaMbonambi homesteads, a few kilometres north-east of oNdini. There he built both a hut for the Sotho gunsmiths he specially employed, and a magazine, which was a square, thatched house.[74] His close friend Somopho kaZikhala, chief of a section of the emaNgweni, was his chief armourer and supervised the manufacture of powder. This was stored in a deep cave in the side of a cliff near by. When the British blew it up in August 1879, the cache consisted of about 1 100 lb of powder packed in 178 barrels.

The power and prestige conferred by firearms were acknowledged by Cetshwayo when he armed some of the women of his *isigodlo* with carbines, and kept them by him as a bodyguard.[75] For there is no doubt that possession of the same weapons as the whites gave the Zulu confidence in confronting them on equal terms. Yet they seldom made full use of their firearms, or developed new tactics which would have exploited their potential more effectively. In contrast, people such as the Pedi – who were accustomed to take the defensive against raids by their neighbours – more readily adapted their methods of fighting to the new weapons. The Zulu, like the Ndebele,[76] preferred to rely on the traditional weapons upon which their successful aggressive tactics had been based. They consequently tended to employ their guns only as secondary weapons in place of throwing-spears, to be discharged at a distance and then caste aside in favour of the stabbing-spear as they charged home.

Perhaps the perceived limitations of the majority of their firearms, besides their inadequate mastery of them, account for this practice. After all, many of the older muskets were already condemned, while the barrels of many of the muzzle-loaders were covered in deep-seated rust, as the Zulu tended not to keep their guns clean and in working order.[77] Such weapons could be positively dangerous to their users, let alone inaccurate, a problem which was exacerbated by the use of eccentric bullets. Besides stones, it seems that favourite missiles for the muzzle-loaders were the broken pieces of legs from the three-legged cast-iron pots traders sold in Zululand.[78] The poor range or penetration of obsolete muskets was not improved by the often poor quality of gunpowder, nor by the Zulu custom of carrying a single bullock's horn, transformed into a powder-flask, which limited the powder available for a proper charge.[79] Loading muskets was a laborious procedure, limiting the rate of fire, and Gumpega Gwabe remembered that at Isandlwana after firing one shot there was no time to reload.[80] Wet weather could put an end to any firing at all.

Nevertheless, poor marksmanship had more to it than inadequate weapons, bullets and powder. Part of the problem may have lain with the 'extraordinary contrivances' employed by some as sights; with unfamiliarity with their correct use by others; or with the belief that putting the sights up to their highest point increased the power of the gun.[81] Nor must it be forgotten that many of the warriors issued with guns had little experience in using them, and it was reported in November 1878 that the king was putting his men through exercises to see how they would cope with them in battle.[82] In the first battles of the war they did poorly, blazing away even when out of range, and almost invariably firing high. The marksmanship of the majority never improved, but at Hlobane the rapidity and precision of some Zulu fire was first noticed, and again at Khambula. It would seem that the Zulu army probably contained a few hundred men who were familiar with modern firearms and were proficient in musketry, a skill probably learned while involved in the gun trade or hunting. Such men came into their own as snipers, and were most effective against small British scouting or foraging parties.[83] And though the Martini-Henry rifles captured during the course of the war were made good use of by these specialists, they were wasted in the hands of most of those who used them. The seven-pounder guns and rocket-troughs that fell into Zulu hands were never exploited, either, for, despite some efforts to load and fire them, they were eventually abandoned near emLambongwenya.

Yet if there were technological reasons why the Zulu failed to make the most effective use of their firearms, equally compelling was the force of military conservatism, which continued to favour the traditional tactics practised since the time of Shaka. As was well known to all their neighbours, these consisted essentially of surrounding the enemy and finishing him off in hand-to-hand combat. The British may have been under the mistaken impression that the Zulu favoured night attacks and ambushes, but in reality they preferred attack by day, in the open (unless heavily outnumbered), and according to an ordered and predictable formula.

Once the *amabutho* had been ritually cleansed of and protected against evil influences, the king decided which *ibutho* would have the honour of leading the army against the enemy, or of 'drinking the dew'.[84] The others followed according to their status. Until it reached enemy territory, the army marched in one great column. Only boys of over fourteen would be taken as *udibi*, or carriers, moving with the army some kilometres off on its flanks. Girls would accompany the army with food, but after a day or two they and the *udibi* boys would no longer be able to keep up with the army's advance. Thereafter, the men would carry their own belongings, and forage as they went. They tried to spare their own civilian population, and only began to plunder ruthlessly as they advanced through hostile territory. Once it neared the enemy, the column split normally into two divisions. Scouts, specially selected for their courage, preceded each division in extended order by about 18 km. These bodies of scouts were intentionally substantial (each about 500 strong), for they were supposed to trick the enemy into thinking they were the main body, and so if attacked to draw him on to the rest of the army – with which they were in close contact by runner and which would have been given time to prepare for action. But besides these advance-guards, which moved provocatively in the open as decoys, sometimes driving cattle to tempt the enemy, the Zulu also sent out spies in twos and threes to locate the enemy so that the army might have a chance of surprising him.

The intention of the advancing army was to engage the enemy in a pitched battle in the open. Not for the Zulu the harassing and oblique tactics employed by other black warriors against whom the British had fought in southern Africa, and which many commentators have thought might have been more effective. When the enemy had been located and the Zulu commander had taken the decision to engage, the army was drawn up in a circle (*mkumbi*). *Izinyanga*, who had accompanied the army, stirred up the medicines they had carried with them in a basket, and sprinkled them over the circle of warriors. The commander gave his instructions, and took up position with his staff on suitable high ground at some distance from the coming engagement. From this eminence he was able to direct operations by runner, to despatch a high-ranking officer to rally his men at a crucial moment, or even to retire unscathed should the battle go against the Zulu.[85]

The habitual tactical intention was to outflank and enclose the enemy in a flexible manoeuvre that could be readily adapted either to a formal battle or to a surprise attack. The army was divided into four divisions in a formation likened to an ox. The 'chest' or centre (*isifuba*), which consisted of the veteran *amabutho*, advanced slowly, while the flanking 'horns' or wings (*izimpondo*) of younger, more agile *amabutho* were rapidly sent out. One horn made a feint, while the other, concealed as much as possible by the terrain, moved with greater speed to effect a junction with the less advanced horn. The chest then charged the surrounded enemy and destroyed him in close combat, where the stabbing-spear came into its own. The 'loins' or reserve (*umuva*), traditionally kept seated with their backs to the enemy so as not to become unmanageably excited, had the task of supporting an engaged unit in difficulty, or pursuing the defeated enemy.[86] Similarly, a reserve of youths was sometimes held back from joining in an attack, but was later sent in for support, in pursuit, or to round up captured cattle. A very young *ibutho* might be confined to this role.

Contrary to the now generally accepted impression, the Zulu did not attack shoulder-to-shoulder in a solid body. What always impressed the British at the time was their skill and rapidity in utilizing ground, and the way in which they advanced in open skirmishing order in the best approved European fashion. They came on in short rushes, dropping to the ground every 50 m or so, and coming on again when the enemy's fire had slackened. They only concentrated when about to engage in hand-to-hand fighting, and this they prefaced with a shower of throwing-spears to distract the enemy as they rushed in at close quarters.

Imbued with their military ethic, dating back to the time of Shaka, each man vied to be first among the enemy, and rival *amabutho*, spurred on by the ritual challenges concerning their respective military prowess which they had exchanged before the king, contended to gain the honours. No quarter was ever given in battle, and not even women were generally allowed to escape, on the grounds that they bore fighting-men.[87]

This was the formidable and disciplined army the British were about to face. What made their persistent and negligent over-confidence regarding its quality all the more culpable was the expectation that the extent of Zulu perseverance in the coming war would depend on the outcome of the first encounter.[88] Only if they won it could the British hope for the short and easy campaign they were anticipating.

Notes

1 Col. C. E. Callwell, *Small Wars: Their Principles and Practice*, London, 1906, pp. 21–3, 25–9. Callwell's work summarized many years of discussion concerning the professional implications of Britain's characteristic mode of warfare in the second half of the nineteenth century.

2 War Office, *Narrative*, pp. 145–6; J. Mathews, 'Lord Chelmsford: British general in southern Africa, 1878–1879', unpublished D.Litt. et Phil. thesis, University of South Africa, 1986, pp. 89–90.

3 P. Burroughs, 'Imperial defence and the Victorian army', *Journal of Imperial and Commonwealth History*, XV, 1, October 1986, pp. 58, 66, 72.

4 See H. Strachan, 'The early Victorian army and the nineteenth-century revolution in government', *English Historical Review*, XCV, October 1980, pp. 782–809, passim.

5 For a recent synthesis of the considerable literature on the Cardwell reforms, see Mathews, 'Chelmsford', pp. 19–27.

6 For example, the standard height of a soldier, which had been fixed in 1870 at 5 ft 8 in, had fallen by 1881 to 5 ft 4 in.

7 H. Bailes, 'Technology and imperialism: a case study of the Victorian army in Africa', *Victorian Studies*, XXIV, 1, autumn 1980, p. 103; Burroughs, 'Imperial defence', pp. 70–1.

8 Laband and Thompson, *Field Guide*, pp. 9, 13–14.

9 Maj. W. Ashe and Capt. the Hon. Wyatt Edgell, *The Story of the Zulu Campaign*, London, 1880, pp. 188–9; H. Strachan, *European Armies and the Conduct of War*, London, 1983, pp. 84–5.

10 For example, see AC, p. 23: Clery to Alison, 18 March 1879.

11 AC, p. 27: Clery to Alison, 13 April 1879. See also A. Harness, 'The Zulu campaign from a military point of view', *Fraser's Magazine*, CI, April 1880, pp. 477–8.

12 Mathews, 'Chelmsford', pp. 90–2.

13 See J. P. C. Laband and P. S. Thompson, *War Comes to Umvoti: The Natal–Zululand Border, 1878–9*, Durban, 1880, pp. 15–17; and *The Buffalo Border 1879: The Anglo–Zulu War in Northern Natal*, Durban, 1983, pp. 19–20.

14 Laband and Thompson, *Field Guide*, pp. 13–14, 17; J. P. C. Laband, 'Bulwer, Chelmsford and the border levies: the dispute over the defence of Natal, 1879' in Laband and Thompson, *Kingdom and Colony*, pp. 150–3. See also Mathews, 'Chelmsford', pp. 64–70, 112.

15 Bulwer Letters: Bulwer to Edward Bulwer, 19 January 1879.

16 TS 95 (Uys Papers, vol. VI): O. C. Oftebro to G.C. Cato, 28 November 1878; Hallam Parr, *Kafir and Zulu Wars*, pp. 170–1.

17 War Office, *Narrative*, p. 146. By the end of the campaign, the British would have used 27 152 oxen and 4 633 mules for transport services (Intelligence Division of the War Office, *Precis of Information Concerning Zululand*, London, 1895, p. 58).

18 For a description of a column in Zululand on the march, see Commeline Letters: Commeline to Father, 6–9 June 1879.

19 Mathews, 'Chelmsford', pp. 105–6.

20 CP 24: Memorandum 'F', Chelmsford's review of the strategic conduct of the campaign, n.d.; Wood Papers, file 7, KCM 51074: Thesiger to Wood, 13 November 1878.

21 Mathews, 'Chelmsford', pp. 85–6.

22 Ashe and Wyatt Edgell, *Zulu Campaign*, pp. 306–6; *Illustrated London News*, 24 October 1879, p. 314: Sir E. Wood on the Zulu Campaign.

23 A574 (NAD): Lord Chelmsford (the General's father), to Biggs Andrews, QC, 15 May 1878, discussing his son's Pondoland campaign.

24 See GH 601, no. 12A/79: notification by His Excellency the High Commissioner, 4 January 1879.

25 See GH 602, no. G392a/79: Frere to Bulwer, 19 April 1879.

26 TS 35: Chelmsford to T. Shepstone, 28 November 1879.

27 Sir B. Blood, *Four Score Years and Ten: Bindon Blood's*

Reminiscences, London, 1933, p. 183.

28 H. Whitehouse, *Battle in Africa, 1879–1914*, Mansfield, 1987, p. 35.

29 For detailed discussion on the characteristics of these various weapons, see Maj. D. Hall, 'Artillery in the Zulu War – 1879', *Military History Journal*, IV, 4, January 1879, pp. 152–61; C. Wilkinson-Latham, *Uniforms and Weapons of the Zulu War*, London, 1978, pp. 53–7; D. Featherstone, *Weapons and Equipment of the Victorian Soldier*, Norwich, 1978, pp. 24–7, 36, 52, 58–62, 74, 83–5, 95–6, 106–9.

30 For a description of the various types of fortification and prepared defence employed by the British during the war, and their specific function, see Maj. W. C. F. Molyneux, *Notes on Hasty Defences as Practised in South Africa*, private circulation, passim; J. Plé, *Les Laagers dans la Guerre des Zoulous*, Paris, 1882, passim; Laband and Thompson, *Field Guide*, pp. 25–7; J. P. C. Laband, 'British fieldworks of the Zulu campaign of 1879, with special reference to Fort Eshowe', in Laband and Thompson, *Kingdom and Colony*, pp. 68–79, passim.

31 See J. Laband, 'Introduction' to *Companion to Narrative of the Field Operations Connected with the Zulu War of 1879*, Constantia, 1989, especially pp. 9–10.

32 Representative of the numerous reports to this effect is CSO 1925, no. 250/1879: Fannin to Colonial Secretary, 12 January 1879.

33 W. C. F. Molyneux, *Campaigning in South Africa and Egypt*, London, 1896, pp. 196–7.

34 'Zulu spies are sent into all parts of the white man's country' (CP 16, no. 13: statement by Zulu prisoner Mungundela, taken by Bengough's men on 13 May 1879).

35 GH 1421: minute, Bulwer to Colonial Secretary, 29 January 1879.

36 M. A. Monteith, 'Cetshwayo and Sekhukhune 1875–1879', unpublished M.A. thesis, University of the Witwatersrand, 1978, pp. 119, 133, 175–6.

37 Saunders, 'Political processes', p. 162.

38 See P. Bonner, *Kings, Commoners and Concessionaires: The Evolution and Dissolution of the Nineteenth-Century Swazi State*, Johannesburg, 1983, pp. 147–52.

39 See P. Harries, 'Labour migration from Mozambique to South Africa; with special reference to the Delagoa Bay hinterland, *c.* 1862 to 1897', unpublished Ph.D. thesis, University of London, 1983, pp. 147, 167, 179–81; 'History, ethnicity and the Ingwavuma land deal: the Zulu northern frontier in the nineteenth century', *Journal of Natal and Zulu History*, VI, 1983, pp. 12–13, 17, 21–2.

40 Colenso and Colenso, *Digest*, series 1, part 2, p. 639; Benyon, *Proconsul*, p. 120.

41 Martineau, *Frere*, vol. II, p. 235: T. Shepstone to Frere, 30 April 1878.

42 J. W. Shepstone Papers I: R. Du Bois to J. Shepstone, 23 September 1878. Du Bois talked to Cetshwayo's messenger to Sekhukhune, who had been instructed to say that 'next year they might combine and have a better chance' against the British.

43 Monteith, 'Cetshwayo and Sekhukhune', pp. 173–6; Delius, *Pedi Polity*, pp. 236, 238.

44 Webb and Wright, *Zulu King Speaks*, pp. 29–31; Vijn, *Cetshwayo's Dutchman*, pp. 31, 96–7; Haggard, *Cetywayo*, p. 34.

45 CP 9, no. 4, enc. f in Wood to Military Secretary, 30 December 1879: Lloyd to Wood, 28 December 1878; Webb and Wright, *Zulu King Speaks*, pp. 55–6.

46 CSO 1925, no. 444/1879: Fannin to Colonial Secretary, 20 January 1879; Webb and Wright, *Zulu King Speaks*, pp. 29–30, 56.

47 Ibid., pp. 30–1.

48 J. Guy, 'A note on firearms in the Zulu kingdom with special reference to the Anglo–Zulu War, 1879', *Journal of African History*, XII, 4, 1971, p. 565.

49 CSO 1925, no. 488/1879: Fannin to Colonial Secretary, 21 January 1879.

50 Webb and Wright, *Zulu King Speaks*, p. 55.

51 TS 38: Rudolph to Henrique Shepstone, 16 February 1879: statement of the refugee Ncagyama.

52 CSO 1925, no. 488/1879: Fannin to Colonial Secretary, 21 January 1878; Webb and Wright, *Zulu King Speaks*, pp. 30, 32.

53 CO 179, vol. 131, pp. 464–5: R. E. D. Morier to Lord Salisbury, 15 February 1879.

54 SS 306 (1878), no. R3466/78: Rudolph to Secretary of State, Transvaal, 27 September 1878.

55 CO 879/14: *African Confidential Print* 162, enc. in no. 248: Capt. E. Baynton to Commodore F. Sullivan, 23 August 1878.

56 Bonner, *Swazi State*, pp. 131, 133, 147–8, 151, 216–17. For details of connections by marriage with Swaziland of senior Zulu chiefs, see the *Times of Natal*, 18 July 1879: Utrecht correspondent, 10 July 1879.

57 CP 9, no. 5: enc. in memorandum from Wood, 7 January 1879: MacLeod to Wood, 28 December 1878; *Times of Natal*, 10 January 1879.

58 TS 36: MacLeod to T. Shepstone, 28 January 1879.

59 CP 8, no. 49: report by Bishop Schreuder on conversation with the *induna* Ulankana, son of Undikile, 10 February 1879.

60 Vijn, *Cetshwayo's Dutchman*, p. 39.

61 The most comprehensive recent discussion on Zulu war-dress is in I. J. Knight, 'The uniforms and weapons of the Zulu army, 1879', *Soldiers of the Queen*, XVI, February 1979, pp. 38–41. See also I. J. Knight, *The Zulus*, London, 1989, pp. 6–7.

62 See the descriptions of ceremonial dress in Fynney, *Zulu Army*, and Angus McBride's excellent set of illustrations in Knight, *The Zulus*, between pp. 32–45.

63 H. C. Lugg Papers, File I, MS 1405 b: List of weapons, 9 March 1942. See also J. L. Smail, *From the Land of the Zulu Kings*, Durban, 1979, p. 23.

64 Anstruther Papers: Col. P. R. Anstruther's Letter-Book, 12 August 1879.

65 *JSA* II, p. 243: testimony of Maxibana; ibid. III, pp. 318–19: testi-

mony of Mpatshana.

66 See Harries, 'Ingwavuma', p. l6, note 71.

67 *Natal Witness*, 22 August 1878: letter from 'Rufus'. The Zulu had specific names for the various types of guns. See *JSA* I, p. 63: testimony of Bikwayo.

68 *Times of Natal*, 14 February 1879: Lower Tugela correspondent.

69 The merchants were the firms of Lipperts and Deutzelman, A. Bennet, Beningfield and Sons, Randles Bros and Hudson and A. Fass. See also Ballard, *John Dunn*, pp. 115–17, 121.

70 During the Anglo–Zulu War some unscrupulous traders from Britain tried to ship gunpowder in through Zanzibar, but with little success.

71 See Ballard, *John Dunn*, p. 86.

72 *JSA* III, p. 305: testimony of Mpatshana.

73 SNA 1/6/11, no. 11: J. L. Knight to Fynn, 18 November 1878; Vijn, *Cetshwayo's Dutchman*, pp. 10–11.

74 In August 1879 the British found a quantity of pigs of lead, sporting cartridges and a large barrel of sulphur stored at the magazine.

75 *JSA* III, p. 328: testimony of Mpatshana.

76 R. Summers and C. W. Pagden, *The Warriors*, Cape Town, 1970, p. 41.

77 *Natal Colonist*, 21 January 1879: correspondent from Zulu side of the Tugela Drift, 14 February 1879.

78 *Times of Natal*, 7 March 1879: notes by 'a gentleman well acquainted with the Zulus'.

79 D. Blair Brown, 'Surgical notes on the Zulu War', Lancet, II, 5, July 1879, p. 6.

80 *Natal Mercury*, supplement, 22 January 1929: testimony of Gumpega Gwabe.

81 *Times of Natal*, 14 February 1878: Lower Tugela correspondent; Capt. W. E. Montague, *Campaigning in South Africa: Reminiscences of an Officer in 1879*, Edinburgh and London, 1880, p. 102.

82 SNA 1/6/11, no. 11: Knight to Fynn, 18 November 1878.

83 Guy, 'Note on firearms', pp. 562–3.

84 *JSA* IV, p. 92: testimony of Mtshapi. For the Zulu army on campaign, see Laband and Thomspon, *Field Guide*, pp. 5–7.

85 B. Mitford, *Through the Zulu Country: its Battlefields and its People*, London, 1883, pp. 91, 312–3.

86 Fynney, *Zulu Army*, pp. 6–7; Carl Faye Papers 8: diagram illustrating formation of attacking Zulu *impi*.

87 *JSA* I, p. 166: testimony of Mvayisa kaTshingili.

88 TS 69: T. Shepstone to Lord Chelmsford, 6 December 1878.

4

The battle of Isandlwana

At daybreak on 11 January 1879 the mounted men of the 4 700-strong British Centre Column began crossing into Zululand at Rorke's Drift. The following day a detachment stormed Sihayo's Sokhexe homestead in the Batshe River valley and, with little difficulty, put it to the torch. Gamdana kaXongo (a brother of Sihayo), who, since late December, had been in contact with the British and wished to avoid a similar fate, gave himself up to Chelmsford on 17 January. As it was British policy to encourage chiefs and their adherents to abandon the cause of Zulu national resistance, Gamdana, accompanied by a number of elderly headmen, women and children, was welcomed and relocated for the duration in Weenen County in Natal.[1] However, the remainder of Gamdana's adherents, including all the young men, refused to follow him into Natal and, driving their cattle for safety into the deep Mangeni gorge, prepared to resist the invaders.

After the deceptively easy success at Sokhexe, the Centre Column began slowly to advance into Zululand, and on 20 January encamped at Isandlwana, which Lord Chelmsford had selected as the next halting place on the road to oNdini. The name of the mountain indicates that the Zulu perceived it as looking 'something like a small house'.[2] To the British, the mountain resembled a sphinx, which, by some curious chance, was portrayed on the badge of the 24th (2nd Warwickshire) Regiment, who constituted the column's main striking-force. In the days following, Isandlwana was to take on the most sinister of implications for the British, and the Zulu victory there was to change the whole complexion of the war.

Oral evidence recorded today is of limited value when trying to reconstruct the complex details of a battle such as Isandlwana. The last of the Zulu participants would have been dead by the 1950s, and their descendants' knowledge of the battle can be no more than generalized. Fortunately, there are numbers of accounts recorded from Zulu participants which, when taken in conjunction with the evidence of British survivors, permit a reasonably full reconstruction of the battle from the Zulu perspective.

There has been considerable controversy over the composition, numbers and command structure of the Zulu army which marched on Isandlwana. The command structure is perhaps the least problematical. Chief Ntshingwayo kaMahole Khoza and Chief Mavumengwana kaNdlela Ntuli were the joint commanders, with Ntshingwayo apparently taking precedence. That was only natural, for the nearly seventy-year-old *isikhulu* Ntshingwayo was second only to Mnyamana on the king's council and his great friend. He was, moreover, *induna* of the kwaGqikazi *ikhanda*, and renowned for his abilities in war. Mavumengwana was also a man of great influence in the kingdom. He was the brother of the *isikhulu* Godide, the Ntuli chief and commander of the Zulu army facing the British Right Column. Their father, Ndlela, had been King Dingane's chief *induna*. Mavumengwana was senior *induna* of the uThulwana and a close friend of the king (they were both in their mid-forties and of the same *ibutho*). Though he had been one of the leading men in the appeasement party before the war, this did not affect the trust the king placed in him.

There is also the suggestion that Sihayo, in whose district the army was operating, had some powers of command. Ntuzwa kaNhlaka, the brother of Chief Sekethwayo of the Mdlalose and one of Cetshwayo's *izinduna*, accompanied the army to act as the king's 'eyes', and so to report both on the performance of its commanders and on its success in battle. Various other men of importance were with the army, though not always in a specified capacity. Prince Nugwende kaMpande, Cetshwayo's youngest brother, claimed to have been present, and Mehlokazulu kaSihayo, who was a junior *induna* of the iNgobamakhosi, certainly was there. Muwundula kaMamba, brother of the eMgazini chief and *induna* of kwaNodwengu, was with the army, as were Vumandaba kaNtati, one of the king's *izinduna* and an *induna* of the uMcijo, Chief Zibhebhu kaMapitha Mandlakazi, *induna* of the uDloko, and Sigcwelegcwele kaMhlekehleke, also an *induna* of the king, and commander of the iNgobamakhosi.

The size and composition of the Zulu army are related problems. The very names of *amabutho* present difficulties, and though modern authorities have attempted to synthesize available information, certain obscurities remain unresolved. Consequently, it is not always possible to be absolutely certain which *amabutho* were present at a battle and in what numbers, though there is enough corroborative evidence as regards Isandlwana to be reasonably sure. Certainly present in significant numbers were the uDududu, iSangqu, iMbube, uNokhenke, uMcijo, uMbonambi, iNgobamakhosi, uVe and elements of the uMxhapho. Those *amabutho* which remained in reserve and went on to attack Rorke's Drift were the uThulwana, iNdluyengwe, iNdlondlo and uDloko.

Some idea of the strengths of these *amabutho* may be gained from Fynney's lists, though it must be noted that the figures he gave were only approximations. Furthermore, he was referring to complete peacetime units, whose numbers can bear only a partial relation to a unit's active strength, especially when it is remembered that no single *ibutho* was ever complete in a battle. Members of an *ibutho* forming part of the main army who lived in a district threatened by another British force were kept back to defend their own locality. Thus significant elements of any *ibutho* mentioned as taking part in the Isandlwana campaign would have been detached to serve against the British Right and Left Columns. The British never fully grasped this fact, so that their estimates of Zulu strength, based on reports of Zulu units present correlated with Fynney's figures, were unreliable. However, Zulu computations of their own numbers were hardly better. They reckoned the strength of an army in *amaviyo*, or companies, no standard number of which made up an *ibutho*. The *amaviyo* themselves could vary between fifty and 200 men, depending on the favour in which the king held a particular *ibutho*. Consequently, even if the Zulu were to have agreed on the number of *amaviyo* present at a battle (which they did not), this would still not have provided an accurate indication of Zulu strength, for the local irregulars who were generally present would not have been taken into account. Consequently, the Zulu were themselves reduced to making broad estimates of numbers as unreliable as those hazarded by the British, and any conclusions reached by modern historians can be little more than the result of informed speculation. On balance, though, it would seem that a number approaching 20 000 Zulu were engaged at Isandlwana, while the remaining 3 000 to 4 000 men who made up the army went on to attack Rorke's Drift.[3]

The army left kwaNodwengu late in the afternoon of 17 January.

With the uNokhenke in the van, it marched 10 km in a great single column to its bivouac across the White Mfolozi in the emaKhosini valley. It was full of confidence, for the king had assured his warriors that it would take but 'a single day' to finish off the whites.[4] The next day it marched 14 km to the isiPhezi *ikhanda*, presumably near the Mpembeni River, and five months later its track was still plain, the long grass all trodden down in one direction as if a huge roller had passed over it. On 19 January the *impi* split into two columns which advanced parallel to and in sight of each other. Ntshingwayo commanded the left column, which consisted of the uNokhenke, uMcijo, uDududu, iSangqu and iMbube *amabutho*, while Mavumengwana led the remaining *amabutho* on its right. A few mounted men of Chief Sihayo scouted ahead. The columns traversed much the same distance as on the previous day, and slept on the tableland east of Babanango Mountain. On 20 January the columns proceeded across open country and bivouacked on the northern slopes of Siphezi Mountain, where it rained heavily. During the evening of 21 January the army moved in small detached bodies to the steep and rocky Ngwebeni valley, which abruptly opens up under the Mabaso heights. The valley, whose floor is sufficiently wide to shelter 25 000 men, is further concealed by the Nyoni heights from Isandlwana hill 10 km to the south-west, where Zulu scouts reported the British to be encamped. Stragglers continued to come up to the bivouac throughout the morning of 22 January.[5]

With better vigilance, or more experience of Zulu ability to conceal themselves in the folds of the undulating countryside, British patrols should have detected this protracted Zulu movement across open country. But one patrol which actually came in sight of a portion of the Zulu army failed to grasp the significance of what it had seen, while Zibhebhu (who superintended the Zulu scouts) drove off another before it came in view of the army.[6]

Once in their bivouac at the Ngwebeni, the Zulu lit their camp fires as usual. However, they soon put them out for fear of giving away their position, and remained quiet and under cover, waiting for the morning. The order of the encampment was as follows: on the extreme right were the men of Ntshingwayo's column; the iNgobamakhosi and uMbonambi formed the centre; and the uDloko, uThulwana, iNdluyengwe and iNdlondlo were on the left. The army was in good condition, for on the king's explicit instructions it had advanced slowly so as not to tire itself, and had collected enough grain and driven in sufficient livestock from the *imizi* on the line of march to keep the men well fed.[7]

There is doubt as to the intentions of the Zulu commanders that night. It seems clear that Cetshwayo had instructed them to continue negotiations with the British if possible, and to be prepared to give up Sihayo's sons and the cattle for the fine in earnest of the king's pacific desires. Only if the British remained hostile were they to fight.[8] According to the king, the commanders of the various *amabutho* came together at the bivouac at the Ngwebeni to decide which chiefs should go and confer with the British, and were again discussing the matter the following morning when the outbreak of fighting with a British patrol put an end to the conference.[9] Of course, the assembled commanders could just as well have been coordinating their plans for an attack on the British camp. For if the original intention had been to parley with the British encamped at Isandlwana, it seems quite clear that by 21 January the Zulu commanders had realized that they were presented with a military opportunity which would have been folly to forgo. For Chelmsford, despite his experience, had committed the elementary error of dividing and widely separating his force, so practically delivering himself into Zulu hands.

The intriguing question is whether the British had inadvertently presented the Zulu with an irresistible temptation, or whether the Zulu had successfully manoeuvred the British into their vulnerable position. On balance, it seems the latter was the case, and that the dispersal of the British forces was of the Zulu making.

Here the figure of Matshana kaMondisa becomes a central one. He was chief of the Sithole, and King Mpande had settled him and his adherents around Qudeni when, in 1858, Matshana had fled over the Thukela from Natal on account of his implication in witchcraft accusations. These circumstances had made him particularly beholden to the royal house. Report had it that he and Bheje (an *induna* of the Ngcolosi in Natal along the middle Thukela, who had defected to Zululand with his adherents in November 1878) were originally to have been the principal commanders of the Zulu army because (so the argument went), as refugees from Natal, their fate depended on the success of the Zulu in battle.[10] In reality, the other commanders were jealous of a 'Natal Kafir' being entrusted with high command, and mistrusted his loyalty. Perhaps they knew that in late December Matshana, like Gamdana, who had recently defected,

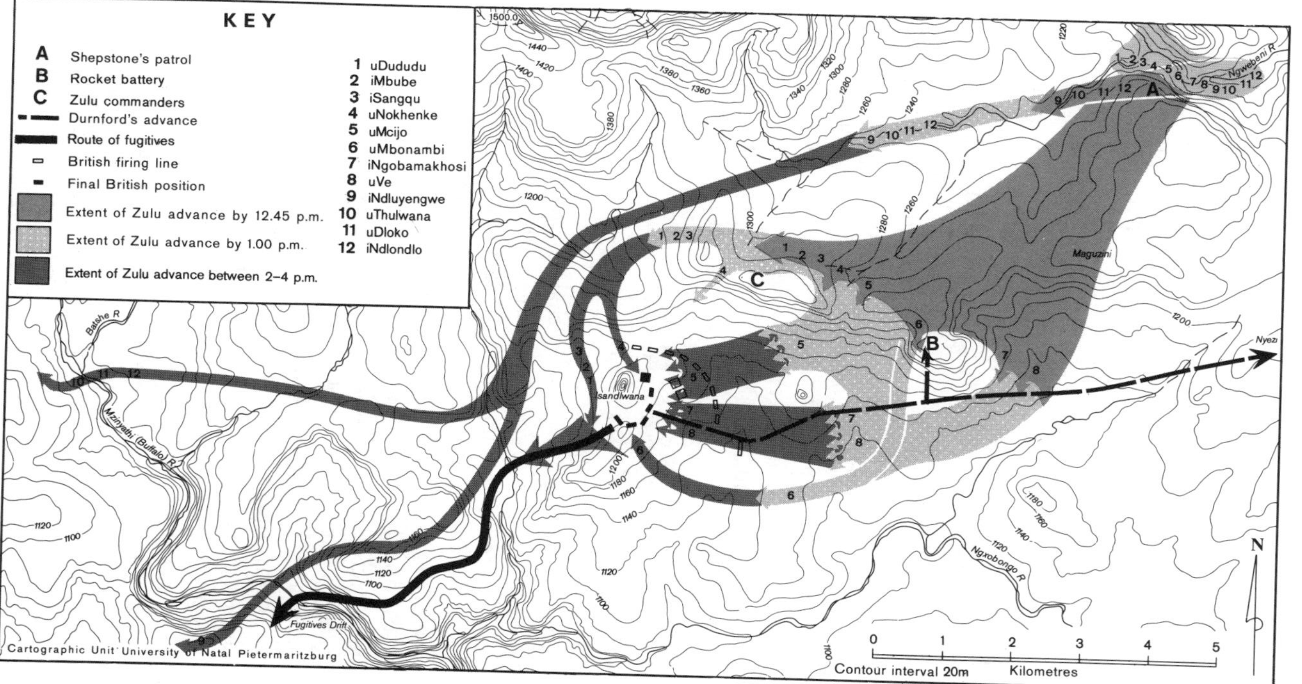

2 Isandlwana, 22 January 1879: a pitched battle in the open field, such as the Zulu preferred to fight

had expressed a desire to Fynn, the Resident Magistrate of Umsinga, to side with the British in the event of war.[11] In any event, the other commanders had apparently persuaded him to go forward late on 20 January with six *amaviyo* to the broken country south-east of Isandlwana, and while he was away led the army north-west to its bivouac at the Ngwebeni.[12]

What strategic objective, then, lay behind Matshana's move towards the hills surrounding the Mangeni stream, which were within the vicinity of his chiefdom? A plan initially considered by the Zulu commanders had been to advance down the Mangeni valley to the Mzinyathi, and then to fall on the British from behind when they pushed into Zululand, cutting them off from their base. But the movement of the main Zulu army to the Ngwebeni valley showed that option to have been abandoned.[13] So another construction should be placed on Matshana's mission. The British were subsequently to have few doubts that it was a deliberate ploy, devised by the Zulu high command, to split the British forces. If so, it was conducted with perfection. For reports of Zulu movements in the Mangeni region, where the General was scouting in order to find a site for his next camp, induced him to send out a reconnaissance-in-force on the morning of 21 January to investigate.

That day Matshana's men led Major Dartnell's force of generally inexperienced colonial troops a merry chase. Some 800 Zulu – local elements must have joined the small force Matshana had detached from the main army – kept gradually retiring before the British, at a safe distance of about 3 km. By evening about 2 000 of them were massed on the Magogo heights. When some mounted troops in the valley below attempted to approach them, the Zulu deployed with admirable precision into two horns, and came on in skirmishing order at the double in an attempt to envelop the British. Alarmed at this proficiency, the British withdrew. Dartnell encamped for the night in a hollow square on the Hlazakazi heights, across the valley from the Zulu, in a position he hoped would forestall a Zulu advance in the direction of Isandlwana. The Zulu lit fires all along their position and kept them going throughout the night. But these were a blind to mislead Dartnell, and when morning came there was not a Zulu to be seen. The fires had succeeded nevertheless in convincing Dartnell's men that a large force was facing them, and during the course of the night they were swept by a couple of demoralizing but false alarms.[14] The panic among his men convinced Dartnell that he urgently required reinforcements, and on receipt of his urgent message Chelmsford made the fatal decision to lead out a large force to his relief. At 4.30 a.m. on the morning of 22 January he marched out of his unentrenched camp, leaving Colonel H. B. Pulleine in command of its depleted garrison.[15]

Chelmsford arrived at Dartnell's bivouac at about 6 a.m. Spotting some Zulu on the Phindo heights to the north-east, Chelmsford sent Dartnell's men to engage them, while Glyn's force of regulars was sent to secure Silutshana Hill near by. The Zulu in the latter region conducted an orderly withdrawal north-east in the direction of Siphezi Mountain, drawing Glyn after them, further and further from Isandlwana. Dartnell's men, meanwhile, became involved in a heavy skirmish among the rocks and caves of the Phindo heights, where Matshana had his stronghold, and killed some sixty of the Zulu.[16] Matshana himself had a close shave. While his men were successfully engaged in luring the British along, he set off for the conference called by the other Zulu commanders at their bivouac at the Ngwebeni. He was surprised by mounted Natal Volunteers, and escaped only after a long chase.[17] But he had achieved his mission. The British had split their forces and, while more than half of them marched and counter-marched over the broken terrain of the Mangeni valley region, the remainder were left to hold the camp with numbers hardly sufficient to withstand a determined assault – should it come.

Yet at this crucial moment, with the British forces divided and the main Zulu army poised to descend on the unsuspecting garrison left at Isandlwana, a difficulty presents itself. For if it had been deliberate Zulu strategy to decoy part of the British force away from the camp; and if there was no serious commitment on the part of the Zulu commanders to follow the king's instructions and open negotiations with the British rather than fight them – then how is it that the Zulu were later unanimously to declare that they had had no intention of fighting that day, but were waiting for the morrow? The 22 January 1879 was the day of the new moon. She was to begin her new life at 1.52 p.m., and it was not customary for the Zulu to fight on her 'dark day', nor undertake any business of importance. It was a time of *umnyama*, when evil influences would overtake an *impi* to its enemy's advantage.[18] Consequently, when at midday Captain Shepstone and his detachment of Natal Native Horse stumbled upon the Zulu army, the Zulu had not yet been prepared for battle through the customary rituals. The warriors had not been drawn up in a circle and sprinkled with medicines to ward off *umnyama*, nor been addressed by their commanders.[19]

Nevertheless, these considerations do not prove that the Zulu were not preparing to fight later that day. Their refrain, reiterated after the event to their captors or conquerors, that the battle was triggered off a day early by the British patrol, must be seen as a way of attempting to lessen their responsibility for an encounter which had so shocked white public opinion.[20] After all, its being the day of the new moon had not hampered Matshana's remarkably successful diversionary operations, which were clearly part of a concerted strategy. The Zulu commanders, moreover, were in council that day, considering their next move, and they knew their enemy to be at a fatal disadvantage, which could not be expected to persist indefinitely. Nor, as events proved, was it likely that so large a force as theirs could maintain the advantage of surprise by keeping its presence hidden for a further twenty-four hours until the dawning of a more auspicious day. In any case, the Zulu army was clearly lying 'right under the British noses to put temptation in their way', and must have been prepared to engage if the British started fighting.[21] It can only be concluded, therefore, that the Zulu commanders were making ready for a Zulu assault on the camp later that day, and that Shepstone's patrol precipitated an action already decided upon.

Since early on the morning of 22 January parties of Zulu foragers had been astir, replenishing exhausted supplies from the deserted mealie-fields and abandoned livestock. It was such a group of foragers, driving a small herd of cattle, whom Shepstone and his patrol encountered and pursued north-east from Isandlwana, along the Nyoni heights. The foragers fled towards the safety of their bivouac, and together with their pursuers came over the edge of the Mabaso heights into sight of the right of the Zulu army, just where the uMcijo were concentrated. The Zulu bivouacked along the Ngwebeni were already keyed up, for they had been disturbed earlier in the morning by the firing coming from Chelmsford's encounter with Matshana. The uNokhenke had armed and run forward until ordered back to their place, as had the uMcijo, though the iNgobamakhosi had kept their discipline. When Shepstone's appalled men caught sight of the uMcijo, they dismounted, fired a volley and retired. This provocation was too much for the already jittery *ibutho*, who sprang up and broke away from the control of their commanders, followed by the other younger *amabutho*. As they pressed on, others moved up to support them.[22] Thus the uNokheke, uDududu, iSangqu and iMbube advanced on the right of the uMcijo, and the uMbonambi, iNgobamakhosi and uVe on their left. Ntshingwayo and Mavumengwana did all they could to restrain their men. They succeeded only with the uThulwana, iNdluyengwe, iNdlondlo and uDloko, who had been bivouacked furthest downstream of the Ngwebeni on the Zulu left. The two commanders formed them into the customary circle, where they kept them seated until they had received their instructions. Even so, some of their officers, like the fiery Qethuka kaManqondo, son of the Magwaza chief and an *induna* of the uThulwana, broke away to join the uMcijo.[23] After quite an interval the two commanders managed to deploy the circle into battle order. With several of the king's brothers in their company, they moved off considerably in the rear of the rest of the army, marching to the north of Isandlwana down the declivity that runs along the Nyoni heights, out of sight of the British. In this way, the Zulu left, as it had been in the bivouac, became the extreme right, while the right became the centre, and the centre the left.[24]

The main part of the Zulu army, which advanced at a very fast walking pace directly on the camp, made their usual dispositions for an attack, and were already in crescent formation as they traversed the Nyoni heights, driving Shepstone's men and their NNC supports before them. Confident in their strength, the advancing Zulu army had at first expected the British to flee without fighting when they saw the overwhelming numbers confronting them.[25] And indeed the Zulu were a marvellous sight as they spilled into the plain below, all the more terrifying for the perfect order and precision of their deployment. For as they became exposed to British fire from the camp, they extended their concentrated formation into light lines of skirmishers, one behind the other, which came on by rushes in the most approved European military manner, making good use of cover. Supports followed close in their rear. The right extremity of the Zulu line was thin, but broadened towards the centre and left to between 200 m and 300 m in depth, its constituent ranks of skirmishers varying in number between five and twenty, with ten or twelve perhaps being the mean. With no untoward hurry or excitement, they deployed methodically along the British front, so that their centre – or chest – went forward steadily against the left centre of the camp, while the left horn engaged and attempted to outflank the right of the British defences. A line of Zulu ultimately appeared right across the plain in front of the camp. Meanwhile, the right horn moved rapidly round to envelop the British from the rear. Only when the British were outflanked and surrounded did the Zulu finally charge home with the stabbing-spear. The reserve, which had followed in the army's wake, was then in position to take up the pursuit.

Those Zulu who had firearms kept up a continuous but wild fire at the British as they came on, either firing when still out of range, or aiming too high, as was typical of their defective marksmanship. Yet if Zulu fire did the British little harm, British firepower all but stopped the Zulu, numerous and determined though they were. They were seen to 'writhe, sway and shrink' before the steady volleys of the extended firing line of the seasoned 24th, who were 'cutting roads through them'.[26] Yet the Zulu did not seem dismayed, but filled up their gaps in perfect silence, and pressed on with the utmost bravery. Not that they were absurd in their courage. As they rushed forward they threw themselves upon the ground whenever the fire became too hot, and either edged forward on their hands and knees through the long grass, or waited for support before jumping up again. It was easier for them to avoid the shells from the seven-pounders than the rifle volleys. When they saw the gunners stand clear, they either fell down or parted ranks, allowing the shot to pass as harmlessly as wind, and leaving the British unsure as to whether their fire had taken effect or not. They took this evasive action with no hurry or confusion, but as if they had been drilled to it.[27]

As the Zulu attack unfolded, fortunes varied between the two wings and the centre. At about 11.30 Colonel A. W. Durnford, whom Chelmsford had ordered up with a detachment of his No. 2 Column to reinforce the camp in his absence, rode out to intercept some Zulu in the distance who he presumed were moving to reinforce Matshana. Durnford was 'as plucky as a lion but as imprudent as a child',[28] and anxious to prove his ability in the field. Unfortunately for the British, his ill-considered action forced Pulleine to detach units in his support, and so prevented him from concentrating at an early stage on the camp. It was some 8 km out of camp that Durnford encountered the rapidly deploying iNgobamakhosi and uVe of the Zulu left horn, who opened fire at about 800 m. Durnford retired steadily in skirmishing order, picking up on the way the survivors of his Rocket Battery, which had wheeled left up the Nyoni heights to support Shepstone's men. Just below Itusi peak they had encountered the advance-guard of the uMbonambi, and had only had time to fire an ineffectual rocket before being overwhelmed by a volley from the Zulu, followed up by hand-to-hand fighting. Durnford conducted his fighting withdrawal as far as a donga to the east of the camp, where he was reinforced by further colonial mounted units. Here the dismounted force of nearly 200 men held up the Zulu left horn as it attempted to sweep round to encircle the camp.[29]

Although the Zulu left moved in particularly open order, with even two men rarely close together,[30] it began to take heavy punishment. The young and inexperienced uVe, whose fleetness set them in the van, were repulsed, and retired until reinforced by the slower veterans of the iNgobamakhosi. These in turn were pinned down by the rifle fire from the donga, and by the two seven-pounder guns in the centre of the extended British firing line which Pulleine had deployed to the north of the donga. The guns first shelled them and then the uMbonambi on their right, who suffered the more severely. The Zulu responded to the shelling by opening their ranks still further, and a lateral movement to their left by the uMbonambi saved the left horn from stalling in front of the donga. They pushed forward behind and beyond the iNgobamakhosi to complete the intended turning movement around the British right flank, forcing the British to reinforce their right at the expense of their centre.[31]

The Zulu centre – which consisted of the uMcijo, elements of the uMxhapho, and those members of the reserve which had broken away from their generals' command – suffered the heaviest Zulu casualties. Shepstone's mounted men had retired steadily before them, fighting all the way, and with the support of some advanced companies of the 24th had managed to fall back to join the British firing line, which was deployed in skirmishing order along a low, rocky ridge. Thus, once in the hollow between the Nyoni heights and the rocky ridge, the Zulu chest was fully exposed to the musketry and artillery fire from the centre of the British position, where it was at its most concentrated. The chest's attack therefore stalled as the warriors took cover from the devastating fire directed at them.[32]

Meanwhile, the uNokhenke had come down from the Nyoni heights on the uMcijo's right and in line with the British left flank. They massed under cover of a homestead when confronted by the British fire, and scattered when shelled. Quickly recovering, however, they veered back on to the high ground, and ran out in the shape of a horn north of the camp, keeping under the cover of the long grass and the declivities in the terrain. The uDududu, iMbube and iSangqu, who had not attempted to come down into the plain, were already ahead of them, and all raced along in a wide, flanking movement, intending to effect a junction with the Zulu left horn behind the camp. The reserve proceeded in the wake of the right horn.[33]

By about 1 p.m. it was evident that the attack by the Zulu centre had stalled, but the situation was saved by the uMbonambi of the left horn. Driving a herd of maddened cattle before them to distract the enemy, they, and fleet-footed members of the uVe who had joined them, outflanked Durnford's position and began to pour into the camp.[34] At much the same time, the right horn completed its turning movement. The uNokhenke began to descend on the camp from the north-west, entering it from the rear, while the other *amabutho* of the right horn passed behind Isandlwana itself, seeking to join hands with the uMbonambi. Durnford's men, seeing they were outflanked, began to fall back on the camp, and so exposed the flank of the infantry on their left to the iNgobamakhosi. Realizing that his line had collapsed, and that he was in danger of being surrounded and attacked from the rear, Pulleine ordered a cease-fire and tried to pull his troops back to concentrate on the endangered camp.[35]

The Zulu commanders were, by this stage, stationed on an eminence directly north of the uMcijo.[36] It was customary for high-ranking Zulu officers and their staffs to remain at some remove from the field of battle, and to despatch subordinate officers to convey their orders and to spur on their men when they saw the need arising. When the British line suddenly began to fall back on their camp, they grasped that the moment had at last come to encourage the demoralized Zulu centre to advance and support the horns' encirclement of the British. The chiefs consequently sent Ndlaka, one of the *izinduna* of the uMcijo, running down the hill to rally his *ibutho*, calling out, 'You did not say you were going to lie down!' and that they would get the whole army beaten if they did not come on. For, he exhorted them, 'the little branch of leaves that beats out the fire [Cetshwayo] did not order this'. The *induna* fell dead, shot through the head, but he had succeeded in rousing the uMcijo to charge the retiring British.[37] To their left, Sikizane kaNomageje, an *induna* of the iNgobamakhosi, could then remind his *ibutho* of its ritual challenge in the presence of the king to the rival uMcijo: 'Why are you lying down? What was it you said to the Kandempemvu [uMcijo]? There are the Kandempemvu going into the tents.'[38] He then shouted: 'Stop firing. Go in hand to hand!' So the iNgobamakhosi took their firearms in their left hands and also fell upon the British.[39] The uVe were similarly roused by one of their *izinduna* to emulate the uMbonambi, who got among the British tents before them.

The Zulu advance up to that moment had been made with little noise of war-cries, but with a low musical murmuring, like a gigantic swarm of bees.[40] But when they saw the British fall back they began to call to one another as they made their almost simultaneous forward movement. The Zulu centre at first did not resume the attack at the run, but with steady determination at little more than a walking pace. At a distance of about 120 m, however, they raised the national cry, 'uSuthu!', and charged home at the double, pouring in a shower of throwing-spears.[41] The British guns fired case-shot to no effect, for the Zulu in the front ranks who might have flinched were pushed on by the force of the numbers concentrating behind. To one of the horrified British survivors the Zulu seemed to come up like a swarm of bees to get between the retreating British and their camp.[42] As it was, they became intermingled with the British soldiers as they drove them back, and the *amabutho* themselves lost formation and became mixed up as they carried the camp. It was later a matter of dispute among the Zulu as to which *ibutho* the honour should fall to of being the first in the camp, but it was eventually decided that it was the uMbonambi of the left horn, followed by the iNgobamakhosi and uMcijo.[43]

The uNokhenke had come round the shoulder of Isandlwana and seized its base, which commanded the camp, before the British realized what had happened.[44] The uDududu, iMbube and iSangqu poured into the valley behind Isandlwana, and drawing themselves into long lines between the camp and the river, cut the road to Rorke's Drift. Their intention was to join the iNgobamakhosi and uVe on the nek, and so entirely block off the British retreat.[45] But many of the uVe and iNgobamakhosi were diverted in pursuit of the mounted units and NNC already in flight towards the river, so that a narrow gap was left open for the attempted escape of those British still in the camp. The uThulwana, iNdluyengwe, uDloko and iNdlondlo of the reserve now made their appearance at the rear of the camp, but, seeing it to be in the process of being overrun, decided to continue on their way to Rorke's Drift.[46]

The fighting in the camp was hand-to-hand, the British being rushed before they had time to fire many shots. They were buried by clouds of warriors, so many of them that some of the Zulu were unable to get into the thick of the fight until the very end. Both Zulu and British were blinded by the smoke and dust and, pressed together in the mêlée, struck out wildly on every side. The horror was increased by the partial eclipse of the sun, which was at its greatest extent at 2.29 p.m. It made the dull, cloudy day darker still, and was taken by the Zulu as an omen of *umnyama* and considerable loss of life.[47] Each time a Zulu stabbed one of the British to death, he cried 'uSuthu!', or 'This is father's cow!'[48] Some of the young men had never before seen a white, so in the confusion they stabbed the mealie bags too as they had been told to kill everyone wearing clothes.

Seeing the road to Rorke's Drift blocked by the Zulu right horn, many of the British made a desperate rush for where the narrow gap in the Zulu encirclement remained open. Not many got through, however, and the Zulu were soon able to block the retreat of the infantry from where they had rallied at the nek. The Zulu suffered so many casualties in doing so, however, that they later wondered if it would not have been better to have allowed the infantry out and attacked them as they marched back to Rorke's Drift. There is no doubt that by this stage many of the British were overcome by a general panic as order collapsed and death or flight seemed the only alternatives.[49] However, many of those British who had not managed to break through the Zulu encirclement stood shoulder to shoulder and resolved to sell their lives dear. Contrary to their usual tactics, the Zulu preferred to break these formations by throwing their spears, thus keeping away from the deadly bayonet thrusts. The places where the British dead were later found corroborated the recollections of the participants as to where the British suffered their casualties: they were nearly all in and about the camp (especially near the nek) or down the fugitives' path. Very few were found where the firing line had been, showing that, until their flanks had been turned and they were forced to fall back in disorder on the camp, the Zulu had been able to inflict very little injury on the British.[50]

The uDududu, iMbube and iSangqu of the right horn had arrived on the scene too late to be much involved in killing the British in the camp. So, lest they be accused of returning without having fought, they joined the iNgobamakhosi and uVe of the left horn in pursuing the fugitives.[51] The ground down to the river was so bad that the Zulu went as fast as the mounted men and, mixed up in the mob of flying men and horses, stabbed them as they ran. Other Zulu following closely on the flanks of the fugitives subjected them to a galling fire. More than half of those who fled from the camp were killed before they reached the Mzinyathi, where many more were drowned in attempting to cross the swollen stream. Nor were they yet safe. Gamdana's adherents who had not submitted to the British fell upon the fugitives struggling across the river.[52] Those fugitives reaching the Natal bank were then treated to volley after volley fired after them, while a few of the more determined Zulu also took to the water and pursued them for a couple more kilometres, killing the exhausted stragglers. It was fortunate for the fugitives that most of those Zulu who decided to cross into Natal ran further upstream, where the drifts were safer.

It had been a singular aspect of the carnage in the camp and the pursuit that many of the Zulu had tended to spare the blacks in British service, especially those not carrying arms. Some of the British attributed this to the Zulus' supposed lifelong desire to get hold of a red jacket, which caused them to ignore those not wearing one.[53] But a far likelier reason lay with Cetshwayo's instructions to his army. He had insisted that his war was with the invading British, not the blacks of Natal, and that the latter should be spared, since it was the British who had caused them to fight.[54]

Of the sixty-seven British officers and 1 707 men involved in the battle, of whom 800 were white (including 581 regulars) and 907 black, fifty-two officers, 727 white troops and 471 black died. The Zulu, as was their custom, took no prisoners and spared no lives, despite pleas for mercy.[55] In the heat of battle they stabbed everything living they came across, even at first the highly prized livestock. All the wounded were killed. Zulu were later adamant that none of the British was tortured, as was suspected by their white interviewers. They also denied witnessing the mutilation of the bodies of the slain in order that medicine-men might use the pieces to 'doctor' the Zulu army, though they could not absolutely discount the possibility.[56] The British, nevertheless, were filled with horror at what they considered the Zulu atrocities committed against the dead. Some of the corpses, for example, had been scalped or decapitated.[57] Particularly shocking to Victorian sensibilities was the cruel fate of the little drummer boys, who were hung up and butchered.[58]

Yet what appalled the British most was to find all the corpses of their comrades disembowelled. They could understand (but not condone) that this practice was in obedience to a 'superstition' of the Zulu that if they did not slit open their slain enemies' stomachs *umnyama* would follow and they would swell up like the dead. In fact, disembowelment was only part of the Zulu rites for the removal of the contagious ritual pollution that followed homicide and the dangerous identification with death and the other world.[59] Equally part of the rites was the stripping of the dead man's clothes by the slayer so that he could put on all or part of them in place of his own – which had been polluted by the harmful influences of his victim's blood – in order that he might *zila*, or observe the customary abstentions after a death. He wore the apparel (a piece of which would come from each man he had stabbed) until he had been ritually cleansed on his return home.[60] The British, it seems, were not conscious of the meaning of this particular ritual. They were merely disgusted that their dead had been stripped, even though the Zulu had generally been content with taking the dead men's shirts and coats (which they could comfortably wear), and had decently left them with their trousers. The British were also shocked to find corpses 'stuck all over the body' with an unnecessary number of spear wounds.[61] Yet here again, the British failed to appreciate the meaning of a Zulu ritual, and one that did great honour to their dead. To *hlomula*, or to stab an adversary who had already been stabbed, was a practice connected with overcoming a formidable opponent in a hunt, such as a lion, buffalo or bush-pig. By observing this custom at Isandlwana the Zulu were recognizing that killing a foe such as the British was of the same high grade as lion-hunting.[62]

The Zulu left the British dead where they had fallen. Those *amabutho* who had been involved in taking the camp, rather than pursuing the fugitives or making for Rorke's Drift, went on (as was natural in a victorious army) to loot it.[63] The considerable numbers of surviving oxen, as well as the two field guns, were eventually taken to the king, as were four of the wagons – though Matshana also took two and Sihayo four. The tents were cut into convenient lengths and the 'bell' portion of each brought to Cetshwayo. What was not wanted of the canvas was burned. The Zulu carried off to their homes everything else which they personally valued: firearms, cartridges, blankets, waterproof sheets, axes, shovels and the like. Most of the horses were killed, as they were considered 'the feet of the white men' and because the king had not required them; but numbers were nevertheless taken to chiefs, like Hamu, who prized them. They also took watches, money and similar valuables from the slain. The most prized booty of all, naturally, were the rifles and ammunition. The king later insisted that he be shown the captured weapons, which included about 800 Martini-Henry rifles, but he was wise enough to allow those who had captured them to retain them as personal trophies.[64] The Zulu broke open the ammunition boxes with stones in their eagerness for the some 40 000 cartridges they contained. Those who had not managed to seize hold of a rifle tore open piles of cartridges with their teeth to extract powder and ball for their muzzle-loaders. They also found many bottles in the camp, and began indiscriminately drinking the contents, not having the means of knowing which were the alcoholic spirits they craved and which were more harmful, like paraffin or chemicals off the veterinarian's wagon. In consequence, while many became very drunk, others fell sick and even died of the effects of the poisons they had drunk. Perhaps alarmed by these unforeseen effects, the Zulu were suspicious of the more unfamiliar contents of the commissariat stores. So while they carried off the biscuit and maize, they stabbed most of the tinned articles and smashed boxes of other stores and scattered the contents over the veld. What they did not want they left tumbled about the camp: portmanteaux, camp-beds, boots, brushes, forges, bellows, sponges, books, photographs, gaiters, cricket-pads, papers of every description.

Those Zulu involved in the pursuit of the British did not return to the plundered camp, but proceeded straight to the king or dispersed to their homes.[65] The remainder, when towards evening they saw Chelmsford returning in battle order to his stricken camp with the forces Matshana had so successfully lured away that day, took up as much of the plunder as they could carry and, driving the captured livestock before them, retired in long lines on their bivouac of the previous night, passing in their thousands over the Nyoni heights. There is a suggestion that the Zulu withdrawal was rather precipitate, and was set prematurely in motion by Chelmsford's resolute advance on Isandlwana. Certainly, the Zulu were in no condition to risk further fighting, and the fact that they retired leaving their wounded whom they could not carry to die on the field would emphasize the haste of their departure.[66] The British could not be certain of their intentions, however, and spent an apprehensive night eyeing Zulu watch-fires lit between them and Rorke's Drift, and preparing for a Zulu attack at dawn.

After the battle, those of the Zulu army who did not immediately disperse stayed encamped close to the battlefield for three days, mainly on account of the large number of the wounded whom they could not move, many being in a critical condition.[67] There were also the dead to be considered. Although there is some evidence that the Zulu slain were left where they had fallen, with each corpse simply covered with a shield, whenever a friend or relative (who had that obligation) had been able to locate it, it seems clear that most were decently buried or hidden away in dongas, antbear holes and mealie-pits.[68]

But how many Zulu dead were there? The British, who had been driven from the field, could only estimate. Naturally, they initially multiplied Zulu casualties to unrealistic levels to compensate for their own defeat. Later, they would admit that not nearly so many Zulu had been killed as they had imagined – or hoped. Nevertheless, the Zulu considered Isandlwana their worst battle as regards casualties.[69]

That they remained masters of the battlefield would indeed have enabled the Zulu to gain a realistic appreciation of their losses, but calculations as to their number were essentially no less impressionistic than those of the British. For one thing, there is no indication that the Zulu ever conducted a body-count, as was the British practice if circumstances allowed. Nor had they muster rolls, and since much of the Zulu army dispersed home directly, no tally could in any case have been taken. Then, the Zulu way of calculating casualties in an *ibutho* was to reckon how many men of importance had been killed. In those unhelpful terms, the iNgobamakhosi were considered to have suffered the most.[70] (The only casualties of note whose names have been recorded are Mkhosana kaMvundlana, the Biyela chief and *induna* of the uMcijo, and Sigodi kaMasiphula, the eMgazini chief, whose father had been King Mpande's chief *induna*. Sigodi's brother, Maphoko, was severely wounded but recovered, though it seems that the two badly wounded sons of Ntshingwayo, the senior of the Zulu commanders, later succumbed. The *induna* Mzi kaManyosi of the Mbatha was also reported killed.)[71] And the final reason why no accurate figure for Zulu losses can be reached is that there were a great number of wounded who, although they were not so badly hurt that they had to be left by the retiring army to die on the battlefield, nevertheless perished later of their injuries.

Indeed, by most accounts it would seem that few of the wounded, who had struggled to their homes with the aid of their relatives (who alone had the obligation to help them), long survived the agonizing journey. Chief Sigodi was one of those who died at home of his wounds. That so many of the even relatively lightly wounded subsequently died caused the Zulu to imagine that the British bullets were poisoned.[72] However, considering the elementary nature of Zulu medicine, wounds inflicted by unanointed British bullets were quite sufficiently deadly in themselves. Spear wounds (and sword-bayonet thrusts too, no doubt), as Dr Brown discovered when treating British soldiers stabbed during the war, could be healed with the simplest of treatment, such as the Zulu possessed. Bullet wounds, on the other hand, which smashed bones and caused considerable internal injury, required much more sophisticated care.[73] Yet for treating fresh wounds the Zulu had nothing better than a poultice made from the leaves of the ubuHlungwana herb (*Wedelia natalensis*), or the powdered bulb of the uGodide (*Jatropha hirsuta*), which prevented inflammation. Open wounds would be tied up with grass. Fractures were set with splints, and certain herbs – particularly the powdered root of the uMathunga (*Cyrtanthus obliquus*) – were rubbed into incisions made at the point of breakage.[74] There is evidence that some Zulu had the limbs smashed by bullets amputated – and lived, and that some medicine-men were able to open broken skulls and remove harmful blood clots. Others survived multiple bullet wounds and smashed bones, but required very long periods for recuperation and were left with ugly scars.[75] Nevertheless, there is no doubt that hundreds, whom British-style medical attention could have saved, died of their wounds. Travelling through Zululand in 1882, Bertram Mitford was struck by how few of the surviving veterans of the war were men who had been wounded.[76]

Heavy fatalities among the wounded, often at some time after the battle, must add considerably to any casualty figures based on an impression gained from a sight of the battlefield alone. Consequently, the historian can do little better than the *Narrative of Field Operations*, and offer a figure of 'not less' than 1 000 Zulu dead as reasonable.[77]

The day's fighting did not end with the Zulu victory at Isandlwana. Part of the army went on unsuccessfully to attack the British depot at Rorke's Drift.

Notes

1 On 4 January Chelmsford had ordered that those Zulu living in the border region who surrendered must be relocated in British territory. Bulwer had already set out regulations for their reception and disposal. They were to be disarmed and issued with passes, and given rations only if necessary, for their cattle and other property were to be reserved for their own use. The able-bodied were to be secured for employment on public works or as servants. Gamdana and a few of his people were later allowed to return temporarily across the Mzinyathi to tend their crops.

2 Linguistically, the name Isandlwana is based on the rare Zulu formative *–sa–* (something like) and *–ndlwana*, the diminutive of *indlu* (house). See A. Koopman, 'Zulu place-names in the Drakensberg' in A. J. L. Sinclair (ed.), *G. S. Nienaber – 'n Huldeblyk*, University of the Western Cape, 1983, p. 302. This interpretation is to be preferred over the linguistically unsound alternative suggestion that the Zulu had named Isandlwana after the second, or honeycomb, stomach of a cow because its shape reminded them of that organ.

3 This discussion is drawn from Laband, 'Zulu army', pp. 35–8. The complicated calculations of J. Whybra, 'Contemporary sources and the composition of the main Zulu impi, January 1879', *Soldiers of the Queen*, LIII, June 1988, pp. 13–16, therefore have an air of unreality about them, though as it turns out his recondite reckoning concerning the size of the Zulu army ultimately corresponds to contemporary estimates.

4 *JSA* IV, p. 87: testimony of Mtshapi kaNoradu of the uMcijo.

5 C. L. Norris-Newman, *In Zululand with the British throughout the War of 1879*, London, 1880, p. 254: Cetshwayo's testimony whilst prisoner on board SS *Natal*; *BPP* (C. 2260), enc. 2 in no. 13: statement by Umtegolalo (captured on 23 January 1879).

6 Gibson, *Story of the Zulus*, p. 175: testimony of Ndabuko kaMpande (Cetshwayo's brother) and Zibhebhu; Webb and Wright, *Zulu King Speaks*, p. 57.

7 For a Zulu eye-witness account of foragers from the army, see G. H. Swinny, *A Zulu Boy's Recollections of the Zulu War and of Cetshwayo's Return*, London, 1884, edited and reprinted by C. de B. Webb in *Natalia*, VIII, December 1978, p. 10. It is likely that the *impi* would also have driven in wild game for consumption, and the Isandlwana area was renowned for the number of buck it supported.

8 WO 32/7717: Fannin to Colonial Secretary, 1 March 1879; Vijn, *Cetshwayo's Dutchman*, p. 116: Colenso's notes.

9 Webb and Wright, *Zulu King Speaks*, p. 57.

10 CSO 1926, no. 681/1879: Fannin to Colonial Secretary, 31 January 1879.

11 SNA 1/4/2, no. 4 (confidential): Fynn to SNA, 31 December 1878.

12 F. E. Colenso, assisted by Lt.-Col. E. Durnford, *History of the Zulu War and its Origin*, London, 1880, p. 411: statement of Uguku; A. N. Montgomery, 'Isandlwana: a visit six months after the disaster', *Leisure Hours Magazine*, 1892, p. 539.

13 H. F. Fynn, Jnr. Papers, file no. 26031: 'My recollections of a famous campaign and a great disaster', pp. 8, 13.

14 D. Child (ed.), *Zulu War Journal of Col. Harry Harford, C.B.*, Pietermaritzburg, 1978, pp. 26–8; L. T. Jones (ed.), *Reminiscences of the Zulu War by John Maxwell*, Cape Town, 1979, p. 1.

15 Mathews, 'Chelmsford', pp. 146–8.

16 WO 32/7731: report by Lt.-Col. J. C. Russell, 1 April 1879.

17 Colenso and Colenso, *Digest*, series 1, part 2, p. 549.

18 *JSA* III, p. 301, 323–6: testimony of Mpatshana; Vijn, *Cetshwayo's Dutchman*, pp. 119–20: Colenso's notes; Gibson, *Story of the Zulus*, p. 175.

19 *BPP* (C. 2260), enc. 2 in no. 13: Umtegolalo's statement, 23 January 1879.

20 Note Cetshwayo's later insistence that he had never ordered his army to attack the British at Isandlwana (WO 32/7717: Fannin to Colonial Secretary, 1 March 1879: Cetshwayo's message).

21 *Natal Mercury*, supplement, 22 January 1929: Nzuzi's account.

22 *BPP* (C. 2318), enc. 2 in no. 9: Fannin to Colonial Secretary, 2 March 1879: Cetshwayo's message.

23 *JSA* IV, p. 83: testimony of Mtshapi.

24 Colenso, *Zulu War*, p. 409: testimony of 'Zulu Deserter'; Gibson, *Story of the Zulus*, p. 177.

25 Conductor in the Transport Division's Diary of the Zulu War: 20 April, p. 55: testimony of Makwendu, Cetshwayo's half-brother; *Natal Mercury*, 7 April 1879: Kambula correspondent, 26 March 1879: testimony of Hamu's warriors who had fought at Isandlwana.

26 Col. G. Hamilton-Browne, *A Lost Legionary in South Africa*, London, 19[?], p. 131; F. Emery, *Marching over Africa: Letters from Victorian Soldiers*, London, 1986, pp. 69–70: Driver Elias Tucker to his parents.

27 Mitford, *Zulu Country*, p. 160: accounts by two warriors from the 'Undi corps' and one from the iNgobamakhosi.

28 TS 37: T. Shepstone to Offy Shepstone, 6 February 1879.

29 WO 33/34, enc. 1 in no. 80: Cochrane to J. North Crealock, 8 February 1879; ibid., enc. 3 in no. 101: Capt. C. Nourse to Cmdt. A. N. Montgomery, 17 February 1879; Norris-Newman, *In Zululand*, p. 80: Mehlokazulu's account; Mitford, *Zulu Country*, pp. 90–1: account of warrior of the uMbonambi.

30 A. F. Hattersley, *Later Annals of Natal*, London, 1938, p. 153: J. A. Brickhill's account.

31 *BPP* (C. 2260), enc. 2 in no. 13: statement by Umtegolalo, 23 January 1879; Norris-Newman, *In Zululand*, pp. 80–2: Mehlokazulu's account; Colenso, *Zulu War*, p. 409: account by Zulu Deserter.

32 Mitford, *Zulu Country*, p. 220: testimony of Vumandaba, *induna* of the uMcijo; Colenso, *Zulu War*, p. 407: Nugwende's account; ibid., p. 409: Zulu Deserter's account; ibid., p. 412: Uguku's account.

33 WO 33/34, enc. 2 in no. 91: statement by Nyanda, 25 January 1879; *BPP* (C. 2260), enc. 2 in no. 13: statement by Umtegolalo, 23 January 1879;

Colenso, *Zulu War*, pp. 412–13: Uguku's account; Mitford, *Zulu Country*, p. 94: testimony of warrior of uNokhenke; Hattersley, *Later Annals of Natal*, p. 153: Brickhill's account.

34 *JSA* III, p. 307: testimony of Mpatshana.

35 WO 33/34: enc. in no. 70: Captain Essex's evidence, 24 January 1879; ibid., enc. 2 in no. 90: statement of Nyanda, 25 January 1879; Richard Vause: Zulu War Diary, p. 6; Wood Papers 7, KCM 51103: Cmdt. G. Mansel to Col. E. Durnford, 1 November 18[?]: Colenso, *Zulu War*, p. 407: Nugwende's account; Norris-Newman, *In Zululand*, pp. 80, 82: Mehlokazulu's statement.

36 Mitford, *Zulu Country*, p. 91: account by warrior of the uMbonambi.

37 Ibid.; Fuze, *Black People*, p. 113; ibid., p. 176, note 6 to chap. 51; H. C. Lugg, *Historic Natal and Zululand*, Pietermaritzburg, 1949, p. 106.

38 *JSA* III, p. 307: testimony of Mpatshana.

39 *Natal Colonist*, 11 February 1879: account of four black wagon-drivers, told on 26 January 1879.

40 Gen. Sir H. Smith-Dorrien, *Memories of Forty-eight Years' Service*, London, 1925, p. 13.

41 Vause's Diary, p. 6; Cato Papers 1, MS 1602a: Cato to Richards, 2 February 1879.

42 F. Emery, *The Red Soldier: Letters from the Zulu War, 1879*, London, 1977, p. 101: Sgt. W. Morley to his family, 1 February 1879.

43 Colenso, *Zulu War*, p. 413: Uguku's account; *JSA* III, p. 307: testimony of Mpatshana.

44 Wood Papers 7, KCM 51103: Mansel to E. Durnford, 1 November 1879; Mitford, *Zulu Country*, p. 94: account by warrior of uNokhenke.

45 *Illustrated London News*, 8 March 1879: narrative of the Revd Mr Witt.

46 *BPP*(C. 2260), enc. 2 in no. 13: statement of Umtegolalo, 23 January 1879.

47 H. F. Fynn, Jnr. Papers, file no. 26031: 'My recollections', p. 12.

48 The implications of the latter exclamation relate to the ritual sacrifice of cattle and the favour of the ancestral spirits.

49 Among the many accounts to this effect, see *Natal Mercury*, 22 August 1879: Fort Evelyn correspondent in conversation with Zulu veterans of Isandlwana, 14 August 1879.

50 Norris-Newman, *In Zululand*, p. 123.

51 See *BPP* (C. 2318), no. 3: epitome of statements made by four Zulus of Hamu's tribe to Col. E. Wood, 17 March 1879.

52 *Natal Colonist*, 11 February 1879: account of four black wagon-drivers, 26 January 1879.

53 Cato Papers 1: MS 1602a: Cato to Richards, 2 February 1879; AC, p. 129, Russell no. 3: F. S. Russell to Alison, 31 July 1879.

54 *Times of Natal*, 26 February 1879.

55 *BPP* (C. 2454), enc. 1 in no. 32: statement of Sibalo, 1 June 1879.

56 Colenso, *Zulu War*, p. 410: Zulu Deserter's account.

57 Norris-Newman, *In Zululand*, p. 84: Mehlokazulu's account;

Emery, *Red Soldier*, p. 114: Archibald Forbes's description.

58 See Mason Papers, KCM 55067: Mason to Cary, Mary and Charley, 8 February 1879: '. . . the black buggers got the boys and tied them up by the hands to the waggons and butchered them cut there privates of and stick them in there mouth' [*sic*].

59 Ngubane, *Body and Mind*, p. 94.

60 *JSA* III, pp. 302–3, 318: Mpatshana's testimony.

61 Emery, *Red Soldier*, p. 94: Sgt. W. E. Warren to his father.

62 *JSA* III, p. 304: Mpatshana's testimony.

63 Among the many accounts of the looting of the camp, see *BPP* (C. 2260), no. 10: statement of Ucadjana, 3 February 1879; SNA 1/1/34, no. 143: Fynn to SNA, 19 July 1879; Norris-Newman, *In Zululand*, p. 122: Archibald Forbes's account of 14 March 1879; *Natal Mercury*, supplement, 22 January 1929: Gumpega's, Nzuzi's and Mbongozo's accounts.

64 War Office, *Narrative*, p. 48; *JSA* III, p. 318: Mpatshana's testimony.

65 *Natal Witness*, 2 October 1879: Mehlokazulu's account.

66 See representative comment in CSO 1926, no. 1185/1879: Fannin to Colonial Secretary, 23 February 1879: statement of two Christians from Ntumeni.

67 SNA 1/1/34, no. 73: statement of Sibalo, 1 June 1879; Webb and Wright, *Zulu King Speaks*, p. 31.

68 CSO 1926, no. 1667/1879: Fannin to Colonial Secretary, 22 March 1879: statement of Klaas, alias Barnabas; *JSA* III, p. 318: Mpatshana's testimony.

69 *Natal Colonist*, 14 June 1879: statement of Zulu messengers; Webb and Wright, *Zulu King Speaks*, p. 36.

70 *JSA* III, p. 303: Mpatshana's testimony.

71 FC 2/5: Fannin to his wife, 5 March 1879; Webb and Wright, *Zulu King Speaks*, pp. 31, 37; Fynney, *Zulu Headmen*; *JSA* IV, p. 300: testimony of Ndukwana.

72 See, for example, CP 7, no. 32: Fynney to Col. Law, 8 March 1879: statement of Magumbi.

73 Blair Brown, 'Surgical notes on the Zulu War', pp. 6–7.

74 A. T. Bryant, *Zulu Medicine and Medicine-Men*, Cape Town, 1966, pp. 77–8.

75 Molyneux, *Campaigning*, pp. 195, 198; *JSA* IV, p. 342: testimony of Ndukwana.

76 Mitford, *Zulu Country*, p. 241.

77 War Office, *Narrative*, p. 49.

5

The battle of Rorke's Drift

The British regarded their defence of Rorke's Drift as an epic action which secured Natal from the horrors of a Zulu invasion.[1] It also provided them with much-needed propaganda to counter the Zulu success at Isandlwana. In reality, however, the battle merely diverted a large Zulu raiding party from going about its short-term business of ravaging the Mzinyathi valley in the vicinity, and not from marching on Pietermaritzburg. Yet it did have the important consequence of serving the Zulu notice that their traditional tactics were ineffective against prepared positions. This lesson, which the Zulu were to prove reluctant to absorb, was to be crucial to the future conduct of the war.

When the British Centre Column advanced across the Mzinyathi into Zululand on 11 January, it left behind a small garrison, consisting of a company of the 2/24th Regiment, a company of the 2/3rd NNC and various detached personnel, to secure its depot at Rorke's Drift. Not anticipating a Zulu attack, the British had neglected to fortify the Swedish mission church and house at the place, which had been converted respectively into a commissariat store and hospital. Shortly after 3 p.m. on 22 January some fugitive horsemen from Isandlwana arrived at the drift below the post with the alarming intelligence that the Zulu army had overrun the British camp, and that a large Zulu force was making for Rorke's Drift.

Lieutenant J. R. M. Chard, RE, the senior officer present, resolved that the garrison must stand and defend itself until it could be relieved. The post was hastily fortified by erecting a breast-high barricade of large 200 lb mealie bags, which, incorporated with two wagons, connected the barricaded and loopholed store with the similarly prepared hospital, and then ran back along the top of a rocky terrace to a stone-walled cattle kraal next to the store. Since the Zulu had no artillery, and were inadequately equipped with firearms, it was hoped that these improvised fortifications would be sufficient, especially since the Zulu would have to face the concentrated Martini-Henry rifle fire of the garrison. Moreover, their usual tactics of enveloping the enemy's flanks would lose their effectiveness against an all-round defensive position. While this work was in progress, about 100 men of the Natal Native Horse, who had formed part of Durnford's ill-fated No. 2 Column, arrived at the drift from Isandlwana. Chard positioned them at the river to give warning of and to retard the Zulu advance.[2]

The approaching Zulu force consisted of the uThulwana, iNdlondlo, iNdluyengwe and uDloko *amabutho*.[3] They were the reserve that had not been engaged with the rest of the army at Isandlwana but had passed north of the British camp to form up on the high ground above it. Their combined strength, inevitably, is difficult to compute, but it is reasonable to suggest that it was somewhere between 3 000 and 4 000. They did not advance in one unit from Isandlwana towards the vicinity of Rorke's Drift, but in three separate contingents. The younger men of the iNdluyengwe moved in open order in advance of the others around the rear of Isandlwana, following the path of the British fugitives and searching out and killing those making for Sothondose's (or Fugitives') Drift across the flooded Mzinyathi. The other two contingents first went through various disciplinary exercises – dividing, wheeling and reforming – before also moving off at some distance from each other in open order, sweeping the country in the direction of the drifts upstream of Sothondose's.[4]

Their leader was Prince Dabulamanzi kaMpande, the king's over-confident and aggressive half-brother. He was not actually one of the generals of the army appointed by the king, but his royal status and domineering personality gave him natural precedence over the other officers of the reserve. His undoubted intelligence, as well as his notorious unscrupulousness, showed in his handsome face, which was adorned with a well-cared-for moustache and pointed beard. Indeed, he was a sophisticated man. At ease socially with whites, he liked to wear European clothes, had developed a distinct taste for gin, and was a magnificent shot with the rifle. A vigorous forty years of age, he was finely muscled, though he was fat about the legs, which was typical of all King Mpande's sons. He was not, however, a general of proven ability.

The iNdluyengwe forded the Mzinyathi just up from Sothondose's

Drift where the water was calmer, and sat down to rest and take snuff on a small hill on the Natal side. The uThulwana, iNdlondlo and uDloko crossed further upstream where the Batshe runs into the Mzinyathi. They spent a long time in the river, cooling down and forming long human chains to assist each other through the water, which only reached up to their waists. When they gained the opposite bank, having brushed aside the foolhardy attempt of some of the Natal Native Horse posted along the river to oppose their crossing, they too sat down on reaching the higher ground and took snuff. (It is known that before battle the Zulu often took narcotics, such as *Cannabis sativa*, so perhaps the snuff-taking should be understood in this light.)[5]

Chief Zibhebhu, *induna* of the uDloko and unquestionably the most imaginative Zulu commander in the field, turned back when the reserve reached the Mzinyathi. It seems he had sustained a slight wound, but there is the distinct likelihood that he used it as an excuse to avoid crossing the river into Natal and so extending the scope of the conflict. He would have been fully aware that it was the king's explicit policy, as the victim of unprovoked British aggression, to fight only in defence of Zulu soil. Nor was Zibhebhu alone among the Zulu commanders in his scruples about invading Natal. The dignified and influential Vumandaba kaNtati (who was second-in-command of the uMcijo, a personal friend of the king, one of his most trusted *izinduna* and consequently privy to his intentions) reportedly shouted to the iNgobamakhosi, who were beginning to cross the river in pursuit of the fugitives at Sothondose's Drift, to come back, as the king had not given them permission to invade Natal. The exhausted iNgobamakhosi were probably relieved to obey him.[6] The uMbonambi were also disinclined to prolong their day's fighting, and so declined to obey the aggressive exhortations of Prince Ndabuko kaMpande, the king's younger full brother, who urged them to join the reserve in invading Natal. Not unreasonably, they insisted that they should rather tend the wounded that they had left behind on the battlefield.[7] So they turned back to Isandlwana, setting up the great battle-song of King Dingane.

It is perhaps typical of the arrogance and pretensions of some of the king's brothers that both Ndabuko and Dabulamanzi should have acted in such blatant disregard his orders. More significant, perhaps, was the contrasting response of their men to their commands. It underlined what had already been made disquietingly apparent in the opening moments of the battle of Isandlwana: Zulu warriors were only prepared to obey their commanders if their inclinations coincided. Dabulamanzi, as he was later freely to admit, was chagrined at having missed the fighting at Isandlwana, and 'wanted to wash the spears of his boys'.[8] His 'boys' felt similarly, and feared that should they return without having fought, they would be the laughing-stock of all Zululand. So they followed him on to British territory.

Yet it seems certain that, tired and hungry as they were after their already long march, they had no plans for a serious incursion into Natal. Their intention was simply to scour the countryside as far as the foot of the Helpmekaar heights, burn the farms and *imizi* they encountered, lift what cattle they could find, and then retire to Zululand with honour salvaged. In other words, what they had in mind was something akin to the limited but destructive raid across the middle Thukela River to the foot of Kranskop which about 1 000 Zulu were later to make on 25 June 1879. Dabulamanzi's men, however, were diverted from the normal course of a punitive raid into enemy territory when they came up to the little post at Rorke's Drift, or KwaJim, as they knew it, garrisoned by a handful of British soldiers. It seemed a tempting and prestigious prize, to be snatched up lightly on the way. Never did they suppose that its determined defence would compel them to commit all their strength to attempt its capture, and force them to curtail their intended ravaging of the plain.[9]

It would appear, then, that the more sophisticated strategic motives ascribed to the Zulu by the British – namely, either to prevent any help reaching Isandlwana from Rorke's Drift or, conversely, to cut off Chelmsford's retreat to Rorke's Drift – were unfounded. To people in Zululand, Dabulamanzi's attack on Rorke's Drift seemed afterwards to have been both unpremeditated and absurd. As they said, 'You marched off. You went to dig little bits with your assegais [stabbing-spears] out of the house of Jim, that had never done you any harm!'[10]

While the two contingents of older *amabutho* were taking their snuff near the confluence of the Mzinyathi and Batshe, an advance-guard of about ten men of the iNdluyengwe scouted up the valley between Rorke's Drift and the Macembe and kwaSingindi hills to its rear. The main body of iNdluyengwe duly followed them at an easy pace. Meanwhile, some detached sections went about their primary objective of ravaging the plain in the direction of Helpmekaar, and set fire to the farmhouse and *imizi* of a white farm neighbouring Rorke's Drift. The first of the two contingents of older men, having rested for about half an hour, set off in their turn. They bore to their left behind Shiyane Mountain, apparently to support the iNdluyengwe in their advance. The remaining contingent sent out a number of scouts, who ran hard up the river bank towards the main drift below the post. It then proceeded in their wake, led by two stout chiefs on horseback, one of whom must have been Dabulamanzi, who was a practised horseman. The advancing Zulu forces started rietbuck and duiker, driving them along before them. But none of the Zulu took any notice of the game, for a far greater prize had come in sight.[11]

At about 4.20 p.m. the British garrison heard the sound of firing coming from behind Shiyane Mountain, which overlooked Rorke's Drift from the south-east. It seems that the Natal Native Horse, who were deployed along the river, were skirmishing with the Zulu as they advanced. An officer of the NNH reported the proximity of the Zulu force, and then galloped off with his men to the safety of the heights at Helpmekaar, where there was a strong British post. The company of NNC followed their craven example, so depriving the post of about 200 of its defenders. The perimeter of the fortified position was now too long for the remaining garrison of eight officers and 131 men (thirty-five of whom were sick) to hold. Chard ordered it to be halved by building a 1.2 m high barricade of heavy, wooden biscuit boxes across the position from a corner of the storehouse to the mealie bags along the stony ledge. But as it was still incomplete when the Zulu attacked, and since not all the sick had yet been evacuated from the hospital, which would have been left outside the reduced defensive position, the depleted garrison was forced to try and hold the original perimeter.[12]

Nevertheless, the Zulu had lost the advantage of surprise, and the British were waiting for them behind prepared defences. It did not matter that these were incomplete and rather inadequate, for they were sufficient to prevent the Zulu from employing their usual tactics. All-round defence meant that, extend as they might, the Zulu could not turn the British flank. Nor did it help them to envelop the position, for the garrison's concentrated and effective cordon of rifle fire meant that Zulu could not charge through it in the open to engage in their preferred hand-to-hand fighting. They had therefore to seek out suitable cover, and could mount attacks only where it was available.

At about 4.30 p.m. the Zulu came in sight of Rorke's Drift around the southern side of Shiyane.[13] Considering the direction of their advance, they must have been of the iNdluyengwe. Only about twenty appeared at first, formed in a line in skirmishing order, just as the British had been trained to do in similar circumstances. They were rapidly reinforced until they were between 500 and 600 in number, so that their fighting line, formed silently in the classic crescent shape,[14] extended from Shiyane towards kwaSingindi to its south-east. Keeping up a heavy if ineffective fire, the Zulu in this formation then wheeled to their right and advanced at a steady trot against the south wall. Stooping with their faces near the ground, they took the fullest advantage of the cover afforded by the many anthills, dongas and steeply banked streams on their line of approach. The British opened fire at between 500 m and 600 m, dropping many of them. Undeterred, some of the Zulu rushed on to within 50 m of the south wall. There they were caught in such heavy cross-fire from the hospital and storehouse that they could proceed no further in that direction. Without stopping, the majority then swerved to their left in search of a less well defended sector. Those pinned down before the south wall occupied the cookhouse ovens and took advantage of the cover provided by numerous banks and ditches on that side of the post.

Those Zulu continuing to manoeuvre surged around the western end and back of the hospital, and made a rush at the building and the north-western line of mealie-bags. This was a much better sector to attack than the southern perimeter, for there was less chance of being caught in cross-fire, and plenty of cover was available because the defenders had not had time to cut down the bush or trees. The Zulu consequently succeeded in advancing right up to the walls in what was to be one of the three most determined onslaughts of the day. There were a few moments of desperate hand-to-hand fighting before they were repulsed and took cover among the bushes and behind the stone wall below the terrace, and in the garden of mealies and peach trees. A feature of that brief struggle, which was to have important implications for the further course of the battle, was the Zulu disregard of bullets but reluctance to face cold steel. It was an inexplicable though oft repeated feature of Britain's colonial wars that the warrior people they encountered, although trained from childhood in the use of spear or sword, nevertheless dreaded the infantryman's sword-bayonet.[15]

A frequent habit with the Zulu was to abandon an engagement after an initial repulse. In this case they persisted. Perhaps this was because their first attack had been unsupported, and reinforcements were at hand who could hardly march on and leave them to their fate. Indeed, the other two contingents of older *amabutho*, who had apparently joined up in the meantime to the east of Shiyane, now came up round the southern shoulder of the mountain. Their options were limited, for they found the iNdluyengwe fully committed to their attack on the post and the lineaments of the battle already formed. So while some lined the ledges of rocks and caves on the mountainside, and from this position, overlooking the British, kept up a constant harassing fire in support of those already firing from the ovens below, the majority moved on to the north-west of the post. They kept further to their left than the iNdluyengwe had done – and so more out of range of the British fire – and occupied the garden, sunken road and bush on that side.

This considerable reinforcement encouraged the iNdluyengwe already there. Because of the effective cover, they and the new arrivals were able to advance with relative impunity right up to the British defences. They then launched a series of desperate assaults on the hospital and along the wall of mealie bags as far as the bush reached, which was about up to where the cross-wall of biscuit boxes began. The Zulu seem not to have thrown their spears at all, but to have kept them for stabbing the defenders once they reached them.[16] Once the garrison had repulsed each charge in intense hand-to-hand fighting, the Zulu took cover in the bush, kept up their fire on the defenders while regrouping, and then tried again with great determination. If it had not been for the dead ground to the north-west of the post, the wall and thick bush, it is difficult to see how they could have maintained their position in dangerous proximity to the post for so many hours. From the dead left upon the ground, the British were able to establish that it was the uThulwana, with whom the iNdluyengwe were incorporated, who must have borne the brunt of this violent second stage of the fighting. Meanwhile, the snipers on Shiyane were taking the British completely in reverse, and though on account of their bad marksmanship the damage was not as great as it should have been, it was serious enough.

At length, at about 6 p.m., as the shadows gathered, the Zulu began to extend their attack further to their left beyond the bush along the more exposed parts of the north-western perimeter. In doing so, they were embarking on what was to be their only night battle of the war. The Zulu did not usually fight at night, but in this case they had unfinished business to complete, and perhaps they hoped that the gathering darkness would compensate for the lack of other cover. In any event, they began to develop their formidable and prolonged third assault. Chard, fearing that in their determination the Zulu would get over the wall behind the line of biscuit boxes and breach his position, and anxious at the mounting casualties from the snipers on Shiyane, decided to withdraw to the shorter position he had prepared behind the biscuit boxes. The Zulu immediately occupied the wall the defenders had abandoned and, in emulation of the British, used it as a breastwork to fire over.

At first, a heavy fire from the biscuit boxes prevented the Zulu from getting over the mealie bags and into the hospital, which its occupants were attempting to evacuate, but at length they succeeded in setting the thatched roof alight at its western end and burst into the building. The hospital garrison retired room by room, bringing out all the sick they could. As was to be anticipated, the Zulu ritually slit open the bellies of those whom they succeeded in killing.[17]

The capture of the hospital and the retreat of the British behind the line of biscuit boxes greatly increased the Zulus' confidence. While some looted the camp of the company of the 24th outside the defences, the majority pressed their attack with renewed vigour. Whenever repulsed, they retired for ten or fifteen minutes to have a war-dance and work themselves up for a renewed assault. While some attempted (without ultimate success) to fire the roof of the storehouse, others began an assault on the stone cattle kraal which formed the defenders' eastern perimeter. Faced with the real possibility that the storehouse might have to be abandoned and that the line of defences would be breached there and elsewhere, the British set about converting two great heaps of mealie bags into a sort of redoubt. This redoubt provided a second and elevated line of fire all round, and could serve as a final defence should it come to that, which for a time seemed quite likely.

Ironically, the glare from the burning hospital, whose flames only died out towards midnight, probably saved the British. When setting it alight, the Zulu had not reckoned on the advantage the light would give defenders with superior firearms whose attackers were thrown up into silhouette. Moreover, by illuminating the whole battlefield, the Zulu lost the advantage of night and the possibility of launching surprise attacks from unexpected quarters. Despite this inadvertent loss of advantage, the Zulu managed after several repulses to clear half the cattle kraal of its defenders and to take possession of the wall across its middle. However, the wall was too high for them to fire over effectively, and they were shot down by the British holding the inner wall as soon as they showed themselves.

The capture of half the kraal and subsequent stalemate there marked the turning of the tide. For as darkness finally fell, the Zulu seemed to pause, and some of the British swore they had just seen redcoats advancing in support down the road from Helpmekaar. Indeed, two companies of the 1/24th had marched towards Rorke's Drift, and by sunset their advance-guard was within 5 km of the post. But on being opposed by a body of Zulu, and seeing the hospital in flames, they incorrectly concluded that the post had already fallen, and retired to secure the depot at Helpmekaar from anticipated attack.[18]

Even so, the Zulu were unsettled by the knowledge that further British troops were moving unpredictably in the vicinity. This, coupled with the uncertainties of night and the awareness of their persistent failure to carry the post despite repeated efforts and heavy losses, made them increasingly reluctant to attempt a fourth full-scale assault. Consequently, although they maintained their positions along the walls the defenders had abandoned, and kept up a heavy fire from all sides until about midnight, they did not actually charge again in a body after about 9 p.m. or 10 p.m. They nevertheless maintained the garrison in a state of alarm by every now and again setting up a confused shout of 'uSuthu!' from one side and then another, leaving the defenders in doubt as to where they intended to attack. They kept this up into the early hours, as well as a desultory fire from Shiyane and the garden and bush on the opposite side. But as the Zulu later admitted, it was no longer fighting, merely an exchange of salutations.[19] Even this ceased at about 4 a.m. The British remained on the alert, however, for they feared that the Zulu would renew their assault at dawn. If only the Zulu had known, the garrison were down to one and a half boxes of ammunition, and could not have defended themselves for much longer against a determined attack.[20]

Yet when day broke the Zulu were out of sight, having retired in the direction they had come, around the southern shoulder of Shiyane. The majority moved back across the Mzinyathi towards Isandlwana, only to encounter Chelmsford's column.

The surviving portion of the Centre Column had spent a dreadful night encamped among the dead at Isandlwana. At first light it had begun to move off towards its threatened base at Rorke's Drift. Once across the Manzimnyama stream, and into the more open country that gave way to the Batshe valley, the column came in sight of the Zulu returning from their unsuccessful assault on Rorke's Drift. The Zulu were south-west of the British, advancing in the direction of the very drift over the Manzimnyama which Chelmsford's men had just traversed. Yet no encounter took place. Although large numbers of the Zulu advance-guard appeared on the right of the road within a few hundred metres of the British rear-guard, they remained squatting, gazing at the British like sightseers at a review, and exchanging a few shouted words. The main mass of the Zulu was moving up the Mzinyathi valley on the British left, but this also avoided a confrontation, so that the two columns moved off harmlessly at angles from each other.

This extraordinary episode can be explained, however. Chelmsford refused to offer battle as reserve ammunition was short, the Batshe valley had still to be traversed and the situation at Rorke's Drift and along the Natal border was unknown. Furthermore, there is no doubt that his forces were in a vulnerable position, strung out on a line of march nearly a kilometre in length, with Zulu both to left and to right. Indeed, the British feared that they had fallen into a Zulu ambush, and there was great relief when the Zulu passed on.[21] For their part, the Zulu were just as grateful that the British had not attacked, and felt the spirits had been protecting them. For they were sure that they would have been able to put up only a feeble resistance, as they were exhausted from lack of food and sleep and from crossing the swollen Mzinyathi, and were demoralized after their repulse at Rorke's Drift.[22] There is no need, therefore, to explain their reluctance to fight as the consequence of superstitious apprehensions that the British were the dead redcoats of Isandlwana come back to life. They would have known that part of the Centre Column had not been engaged at Isandlwana, and their main concern (as was that of the British) was to withdraw in order to recover.

Meanwhile, the garrison at Rorke's Drift, who had no means of knowing that the main Zulu force had retired across the river, and who had no idea when they were to be relieved, feverishly strengthened their defences against further attack. And duly, at about 7 p.m., a large body of Zulu, who had remained in the vicinity of Rorke's Drift, appeared in growing numbers on kwaSingindi hill to the south-west of the post. The garrison presumed that they were intending to renew the attack,[23] but Chard later came to believe they had gone up to the high ground to observe Chelmsford's advance. Certainly, as Chelmsford's column came in sight of Rorke's Drift at about 8 a.m. the Zulu finally melted away.

Chard had been fairly certain that the Zulu were in no condition to attack again on the morning of 23 January because of the unacceptably heavy casualties they had sustained. What gives force to this conclusion is the fact that the majority of Zulu began their withdrawal from Rorke's Drift while Chelmsford was still encamped at Isandlwana, and posed them no immediate threat. Independent of considerations concerning being caught by the arrival of a relieving British force, or being terribly short of food and sleep, must have been the stark awareness among the surviving Zulu that their companions had vainly died, literally in heaps, before the British defences. Certainly, after their experience before Rorke's Drift, the Zulu flinched at even the suggestion of ever pressing on to Pietermaritzburg. It was sufficient to say, 'There are strongholds there.'[24]

Zulu casualties had indeed been insupportable at Rorke's Drift, perhaps around 15 per cent of those engaged. In future battles of the war, considerably less severe losses sustained in attack were to prove quite sufficient cause for the Zulu to retire. In those situations, moreover, British mounted pursuit was to be responsible for a large proportion of the total Zulu losses. At the battle of Ulundi, for example, where the Zulu casualty rate was about 10 per cent, nearly half the losses occurred during the rout. At Rorke's Drift the Zulu were able to withdraw without hindrance or loss, which underscores the atypical extent of their casualties, and draws attention to their extraordinary bravery and persistence.

When the British inspected the abandoned field that morning, they found the Zulu dead piled in heaps, sometimes three deep. They lay especially thick in front of the verandah outside the hospital, and round the walls on the north-western and north-eastern sides of the post, their heaped bodies sloping off from the top of the barricades. Most were grotesquely disfigured, mutilated by Martini-Henry bullets (often fired at point-blank range) and frozen by death in extraordinary attitudes. About 100 guns and rifles and some 400 spears were also found upon the field, where the Zulu had abandoned them.[25]

If only for hygienic reasons, the British immediately set about burying the rapidly putrefying Zulu dead. The men of the 3rd NNC and 24th Regiment of Chelmsford's relieving column provided the fatigue parties. Since the NNC had a great repugnance to touching the dead for fear of the effects of *umnyama*, it was arranged that they should dig the necessary pits, to which the 24th dragged the bodies with the aid of leather *rieme*, or thongs, there being few carts or draught animals available for the gruesome task. The corpses were then burnt with wood cut from thorn-trees before being finally covered over with earth. The operation took two days.[26]

Chard reported that they buried 351 Zulu,[27] though in reality the number of Zulu dead must greatly have exceeded any figures based on body-counts. What makes any accurate computation especially difficult is the fact that the Zulu were not forced to retire in haste. This meant that relatives were enabled to dispose of unknown numbers of their dead in dongas and the river, and were allowed to carry off many of their wounded with them. Some of these drowned while trying to cross the Mzinyathi,[28] and a large (but unknowable) percentage of the remainder would inevitably have died of their wounds on their way home, or soon afterwards. Many other wounded were too seriously injured even to attempt to withdraw into Zululand. For months afterwards the garrison at Rorke's Drift was coming across bodies where the wounded had crept away to die in the long grass, in caves and among the rocks a great distance away. But the British no longer bothered to keep an accurate tally of the dead.

There is an even darker side to the fate of the Zulu wounded, one which the British would rather have suppressed, and certainly attempted to rationalize.[29] On the very morning after the battle, a further 200 Zulu dead were reported to have been found a way off from those killed and buried near the post.[30] Unfortunately, there can be but little doubt that a great many of these 'dead' had actually been wounded or exhausted Zulu lying hidden in the orchard and mealie garden and on Shiyane. They had been systematically finished off with bayonet, rifle butt and spear by British patrols who were trying to conserve their ammunition.[31] Of course, it must not be forgotten that the British troops had been worked up to an implacable fury by the sight of their disembowelled dead, both at Isandlwana and at Rorke's Drift; and it should be accepted that it was the custom of the NNC (as it was of the Zulu too) to kill any wounded they encountered. Consequently, as they expected no quarter, the Zulu wounded instinctively fought back when located by the British, their 'treachery' usefully justifying their inevitable despatch.[32] In the end, only three wounded Zulu were taken alive, and these were ostentatiously cared for by the surgeons with the British. This publicized concern could not disguise, however, how merciless and thorough the British mopping-up operation had been.

How many Zulu did die, then, in the battle of Rorke's Drift? It is impossible to know exactly, but when to the bodies counted by the British are added the numbers of wounded they killed and those who subsequently died of their wounds, the estimate of 600 (which Henrique Shepstone had from Marulumba kaThinta of the Mdlalose) is a reasonable figure.[33]

In comparison, the British casualties of fifteen men killed and one officer and nine men wounded (two mortally) were relatively light.[34] Because they had fought behind walls and barricades their wounds were all in the upper parts of the body, and those who died had been hit in the head. If Zulu fire had been more effective, there is no doubt that the British casualty rate would have been much higher. But even in subsequent battles, when they had the Martini-Henry rifles captured at Isandlwana, the Zulu failed to make proper use of them. They persisted in mass frontal attacks with the objective of engaging in hand-to-hand fighting. In doing so, they disregarded the lesson of Rorke's Drift, which proved that as long as the British could hold an all-round defensive perimeter with a reasonable field of concentrated fire, they were secure from a conventional Zulu assault.

The battle of Rorke's Drift thus provided the model for all successful British engagements throughout the remainder of the war, and vividly demonstrated the inadequacy of traditional Zulu tactics against fortified positions. Ordinary Zulu, however, did not necessarily see the implications of the failure to take Rorke's Drift, and jeered at the 'shocking cowards' whom they considered to have been so ignominiously repulsed: 'You! You're no men! You're just women, seeing that you ran away for no reason at all, like the wind!'[35] How unfortunate for Dabulamanzi's men that they should have marched into Natal to avoid becoming laughing-stocks for missing the battle of Isandlwana, only to become objects of derision for failing to take so apparently weak a position as Rorke's Drift.

After a victory, it was customary for a Zulu army to return in triumph to the king in order to report and to share out the spoils. If beaten, an army would scatter, each man making for his home.[36] The fact that after Isandlwana and Rorke's Drift only the *izinduna* and a relatively small part of the army appeared before the king seemed to indicate that the army did not consider itself victorious.[37] The senior women about the king were inclined to blame Cetshwayo for the only partial success of the campaign. Once fleet-footed messengers had brought him word that battle had been joined, he had taken his seat on the *inkatha*, thereby ensuring that his influence would reach out to his warriors, inspiring them not to waver. But against the women's advice he had left the *inkatha* now and then, and the consequences were as they had warned.[38]

The king, however, could not immediately confront his warriors. They had first to be purified of the evil and contagious influences of homicide and to ornament themselves correctly before reporting to the king, rejoining their companions or resuming normal domestic life. The majority of those warriors who returned to the Mahlabathini plain did so on the fifth day after the battle. For four days, those who had killed, or who had ritually stabbed the dead, were separated from their companions who were barracked in the *amakhanda*, placed in special homesteads and fed with cattle captured at Isandlwana. Daily, they washed ritually in the White Mfolozi, and then returned to *ncinda*, or suck medicine from the fingertips and ritually squirt it in the direction of their foes. In this way they hoped to obtain occult ascendancy over the spirits of their vengeful victims, the blood from whose fatal wounds formed a dangerous bridge between the living and the dead, and to ward off *umnyama*. Because many of the warriors had carried the medicines necessary to *ncinda* with them, an *inyanga* was not required, except to sprinkle medicines on the final day.[39]

Once they were ritually clean, those who had killed in battle presented themselves with their weapons in the cattle enclosure before Cetshwayo. There, with the king seated in their midst, the *amabutho* exchanged accounts of the fighting and renewed the challenges they had made before setting off to war. But already the king had held the customary extensive discussions to discover who had distinguished themselves in the campaign, or had been revealed as cowards. So Cetshwayo acknowledged the uMbonambi, led by their *induna*, Ntuzwa kaNhlaka, brother of the Mdlalose chief, as deserving of the great honour of having been the first to stab the enemy, and rewarded them with cattle. The cowards were publicly humiliated at the same time.[40]

Nevertheless, despite the public ceremonies and reports of victory, Cetshwayo had little cause for satisfaction. Sitshitshili kaMnqandi, one of the king's *izinduna* who had accompanied the army to report on its performance, complained that the commanders had lost control and allowed the army to attack without being properly doctored. Thus no credit was given either to Ntshingwayo or Mavumengwana, for the battle had been fought in breach of their commands.[41] The unsuccessful attack on Rorke's Drift doubly angered the king, for he had forbidden any forays into Natal. Moreover, he was displeased that his commanders had been unable to prevent his army from largely dispersing, carrying off home the bulk of the plunder won at Isandlwana before it could be brought to him for distribution, as was customary. He was particularly incensed that the two seven-pounder guns had been abandoned on the field, necessitating their retrieval by the people living in the vicinity. Besides which, he was most put out that no British officers had been taken prisoner, for they could have been most useful to him.[42]

Above all, he was deeply shocked at the casualties his army had sustained at the hands of such small British forces, and there were unconfirmed reports that he had ordered the execution of several leading *izinduna* for their poor generalship.[43] What was particularly alarming was how the greatly outnumbered British forces at Isandlwana had almost managed to stem the Zulu attack, and had actually done so at Rorke's Drift. This boded very ill for Zulu chances of success in the future, so that instead of being elated by their victory at Isandlwana the Zulu were generally discouraged by the implications. It is true that at first, when the word was shouted from hill to hill that the army had killed the whites at Isandlwana, there was a moment of euphoria in Zululand, and people believed that the whites had been driven out and would be afraid to return.[44] But as news of the ignominious repulse at kwaJim's filtered through, and as the wounded straggled home with word of so many comrades whom they had left dead behind them, weeping and mourning began to fill the land, and continued for many weeks.[45] Moreover, the ordinary Zulu could not but be cowed by the realization that further sacrifices would be required of them.

At oNdini the king told those warriors gathered there to disperse to their homes, both to complete their ritual purification and to recuperate. For he warned them that the British were still coming, and that they must reassemble in a month's time to resist them. So while those veteran warriors who had not gone on campaign remained behind to guard the king, the remainder made *iziqu* (amulets) of willow wood or horn to wear round their necks as token that they had killed in battle, threw away their defiled garments, and fixed new hafts to their spears in preparation for the next battle.[46]

Isandlwana had been an unsatisfactory victory, and its implications were confirmed by the defeat at Rorke's Drift. Mnyamana was prompted to go straight to the king to advise him to make peace while he still had the upper hand. And in this sense Isandlwana had given Cetshwayo hopes of saving his kingdom, for he anticipated that now the British would be prepared to negotiate.[47] In fact, the very degree of Zulu success at Isandlwana (only partially negated by the subsequent fighting at Rorke's Drift) had ensured that the British must proceed until the Zulu army was crushed, and the king had acceded entirely to their demands.

Notes

1 For a detailed account of the battle, see J. P. C. Laband, ' "O! Let's go and have a fight at Jim's!" The Zulu at the battle of Rorke's Drift', in Laband and Thompson, *Kingdom and Colony*, pp. 111–30.

2 WO 32/7737: Lt. Chard's report on the defence of Rorke's Drift, 25 January 1879 (henceforth Chard's report); Col. G. Paton, Col. F. Glennie and W. Penn Symons (eds.), *Historical Records of the 24th Regiment from its Formation in 1689*, London, 1892, p. 247: Revd G. Smith's account, 3 February 1879 (henceforth Smith's account); N. Holme (comp.), *The Silver Wreath: Being the 24th Regiment at Isandhlwana and Rorke's Drift*, London, 1979, p. 63: Pte. A. H. Hook's account (henceforth Hook's account); Lt.-Col. I. H. W. Bennet, *Eyewitness in Zululand: The Campaign Reminiscences of Colonel W. A. Dunne, C.B.: South Africa, 1877–1881*, London, 1989, pp. 95–6; Laband and Thompson, *Buffalo Border*, p. 107; *Field Guide*, pp. 25, 59.

3 The men of the uThulwana were forty-five years old in 1879, those of the iNdlondlo forty-two, and of the uDloko forty-one. The men of the iNdluyengwe, who were incorporated with the uThulwana, were only thirty-three years old. (E. Krige, *The Social System of the Zulus*, Pietermaritzburg, 1974, p. 406.)

4 Holme, *Silver Wreath*, p. 50: Maj. J. R. M. Chard's account of the battle of Rorke's Drift, January 1880 (henceforth Chard's account of 1880);

Natal Mercury, 7 April 1879: the defence of Rorke's Drift by an eye-witness (henceforth Eye-witness's account); SNA 1/1/34, no. 73: statement of Sibalo, 1 June 1879; SNA 1/1/34, no. 85: statement of Sihlahla, 3 June 1879.

5 Eye-witness's account; *Illustrated London News*, 8 March 1879, p. 218: narrative of the Revd Mr Witt; Cato Papers I, MS 1602a: Cato to Richards, 2 February 1879.

6 *Natal Colonist*, 11 February 1879; Vijn, *Cetshwayo's Dutchman*, p. 97: Colenso's notes.

7 Gibson, *Story of the Zulus*, p. 182: testimony of Ndabuko.

8 Capt. W. R. Ludlow, *Zululand and Cetewayo*, London and Birmingham, 1882, p. 61.

9 TS 37: H. C. Shepstone to T. Shepstone, 9 September 1879; John Shepstone Papers 10: 'Reminiscences', pp. 109–10; Mitford, *Zulu Country*, p. 161: warrior of the Undi's account.

10 Webb, 'Zulu boy's recollections', pp. 12–13.

11 Eye-witness's account; *Illustrated London News*, 8 March 1879, p. 218: narrative of the Revd Mr Witt.

12 Chard's report; Chard's account of 1880, p. 50; P. S. Thompson, 'The Natal Native Contingent at Rorke's Drift, January 22, 1879', in Laband and Thompson, *Kingdom and Colony*, pp. 131–2.

13 The basis of the following account of the battle is drawn from Chard's report; Chard's account of 1880, pp. 50–3; and Smith's account, pp. 251–4.

14 Holme, *Silver Wreath*, p. 61: Cpl. J. Lyons's account, 13 June 1879; ibid., Pte. F. Hitch's account, p. 62 (henceforth Hitch's account).

15 Callwell, *Small Wars*, p. 399; Hitch's account, p. 62.

16 Eye-witness's account.

17 Holme, *Silver Wreath*, p. 61: Sgt. G. Smith's account, 24 January 1879.

18 War Office, *Narrative*, p. 47; Chard's account of 1880, p. 52.

19 Webb, 'Zulu boy's recollections', p. 12: comment of Munyu, who fought at Rorke's Drift.

20 WC II/1/6: A. F. Pickard to Wood, 14 October 1879.

21 H. F. Fynn, Jnr, Papers, file no. 26031: 'Recollections', p. 16; Child, *Henry Harford*, p. 35; Jones, *John Maxwell*, pp. 6–7; Norris-Newman, *In Zululand*, p. 64; Hattersley, *Later Annals of Natal*, p. 148–9: Trooper F. Symons's account; H. P. Holt, *The Mounted Police of Natal*, London, 1913, p. 67.

22 John Shepstone Papers 10: 'Reminiscences', p. 110; Colenso, *Zulu War*, p. 406: Dabulamanzi's testimony.

23 Hallam Parr, *Kafir and Zulu Wars*, p. 245; Hitch's account, p. 65.

24 Webb, 'Zulu boy's recollections', p. 13.

25 H. F. Fynn, Jnr, Papers, file no. 26031: 'Recollections', p. 17; *Natal Mercury*, 7 April 1879: the defence of Rorke's Drift by an eye-witness.

26 Laband and Thompson, *Buffalo Border*, p. 44.

27 Chard's account of 1880, p. 53.

28 H. C. Lugg, 'Short account of the battle of Rorke's Drift', 1 September 1944, typescript in Natal Archives.

29 See the arguments in Hallam Parr, *Kafir and Zulu Wars*, pp. 263–7.

30 FC 2/4: Fannin to his wife, 23 January 1879.

31 Hamilton-Browne, *Lost Legionary*, p. 152; Hattersley, *Later Annals of Natal*, p. 150; Symons's account.

32 KCMS 31185: W. J. Clarke, 'My career in South Africa', part I, p. 27; Hook's account, p. 65.

33 TS 37: H. Shepstone to T. Shepstone, 9 February 1879.

34 War Office, *Narrative*, p. 158.

35 Webb, 'Zulu boy's recollections', p. 12.

36 *JSA* I, p. 125: testimony of Dunjwa kaMabedhla.

37 CSO 1926, no. 1393/1879: Fannin to Colonial Secretary, 6 March 1879; *BPP* (C. 2260), no. 10: statement of Ucadjana, 3 February 1879; Webb and Wright, *Zulu King Speaks*, pp. 31–2; Colenso, *Zulu War*, p. 410: Zulu Deserter's account.

38 Filter and Bourquin, *Paulina Dlamini*, pp. 69–70.

39 Webb and Wright, *Zulu King Speaks*, p. 31; *JSA* III, pp. 302–4: testimony of Mpatshana; Ngubane, *Body and Mind*, p. 121.

40 *JSA* III, pp. 141, 305, 307: testimony of Mjobo kaDumela and Mpatshana; ibid. IV, pp. 147–8: testimony of Mtshayankomo; Zulu Tribal History Competition, file 25, KCM 64795: Vivian Maphanga, 'The life of a male from birth to marriage', p. 2. For the punishment of cowards, see *JSA* IV, pp. 88–9: testimony of Mtshapi.

41 *JSA* IV, p. 147: testimony of Mtshayankomo; Gibson, *Story of the Zulus*, p. 188.

42 Webb and Wright, *Zulu King Speaks*, p. 32; Vijn, *Cetshwayo's Dutchman*, pp. 30–1; *Natal Witness*, 2 October 1879: Mehlokazulu's account.

43 Webb and Wright, *Zulu King Speaks*, p. 32; FC 2/4: Fannin to wife, 23 January 1879; 19 February 1879.

44 TS 38: Rudolph to H. Shepstone, 16 February 1879.

45 *BPP* (C. 2260), no. 10: statement of Ucadjana, 3 February 1879; Vijn, *Cetshwayo's Dutchman*, pp. 28–9.

46 CP 8, no. 49: letter from Bishop Schreuder, 10 February 1879; *JSA* III, p. 317: testimony of Mpatshana; ibid. IV, p. 148: testimony of Mtshayankomo.

47 *Natal Colonist*, 25 September 1879: Cetshwayo's comments from the *Cape Times*.

6

Defeat on the coast and disarray in the west

The Zulu in the south-east of the kingdom did not oppose the advance on 13–14 January of Colonel C. K. Pearson's No. 1 Column of 4 750 officers and men, 384 wagons and twenty-four carts across the lower Thukela drift below Fort Pearson.[1] False rumours circulated among the British of a large Zulu force near by, but the only Zulu in the vicinity were those few plundering John Dunn's abandoned homesteads, or the scouts Cetshwayo had directed to observe Pearson's movements and signal his approach with beacon fires. Otherwise, the whole district was deserted. The warriors had mustered at oNdini, and their families had driven their cattle into the interior.[2]

On Saturday 18 January Pearson divided his column into two mutually supporting sections, and began his march from the newly completed Fort Tenedos to the abandoned Norwegian mission station at Eshowe, where he intended to establish a supply depot. The incessant rain of the previous weeks had reduced the tracks to mud and swollen the rivers, so that his progress was considerably slowed. By 21 January the column was only crossing the amaTigulu River. While this was in progress, a patrol advanced to the deserted and undefended kwaGingindlovu *ikhanda* just south of the Nyezane stream, and put it to the torch. Cetshwayo had built kwaGingindlovu after his victory over his brother Mbuyazi in 1856, and the Zulu considered this destruction of the locus of royal authority in the district an extremely provocative act, and one that required retaliation.[3] Thus far the Zulu scouts had been able to do no more than keep watch on British movements from the hills to their front. But now a Zulu army was approaching, intent on confronting the invader.

When the main Zulu army moved off from kwaNodwengu on the afternoon of Friday 17 January to oppose Chelmsford, it was initially accompanied by the smaller and qualitatively inferior force detailed by the king to confront the lesser threat of Pearson's column. Its crack element was the major portion of the uMxhapho *ibutho*, whose members were in their prime of life. The smaller contingents of warriors from the accompanying uDlambedlu and izinGulube *amabutho* were in their mid-fifties, however, and could hardly be expected to be equally effective on campaign. Nor were the reinforcements they were to pick up as they moved through the coastal region to be of much better quality. These consisted of small local elements of the iNsukamngeni, iQwa, uDududu, iNdabakawombe and other *amabutho* still mustered at the coastal *amakhanda*, as well as numbers of local irregulars. The latter made up about a fifth of the combined Zulu force, which probably numbered between 4 000 and 6 000.[4] In command was the seventy-year-old Godide kaNdlela, hereditary chief of the Ntuli, whom Shaka had settled along the middle Thukela, an *isikhulu*, and *induna* of the uDlambedlu *ibutho*. His younger brother, Mavumengwana, was joint commander of the army marching to Isandlwana. Godide's lieutenants would seem to have included Chief Matshiya kaMshandu of the Nzuzu near Eshowe, the aged Mbilwane kaMhlanganiso, *induna* of the kwaGingindlovu *ikhanda*, Masegwane kaSopigwasi, an *inceku* of the king, and Phalane kaMdinwa, a royal *induna*.

On 18 January Godide's force separated from the main Zulu army, and marched south-east, bivouacking the night on the high, open ground at kwaMagwaza. There the men were overcome by cold and hunger, and many began to suffer from dysentery, conceivably brought on by the full meat diet at oNdini after the many months of dearth. Consequently, the army was forced to remain at kwaMagwaza until the morning of Monday 20 January, when it was sufficiently recovered to resume the advance. On the night of 20 January it slept at the original oNdini *ikhanda*, which King Mpande had built for Cetshwayo in the 1850s between the lower Mhlatuze River and Ngoye Mountain.

At this stage, Godide was not certain how far Pearson had advanced, and was still intent on marching straight towards the lower Thukela drift to confront him, bivouacking on the way at the kwaGingindlovu *ikhanda*.[5] However, when kwaGingindlovu was reached after dark on 21 January, it was discovered to be no more than a smouldering ruin, with the British encamped for the night near by. The Zulu then stealthily surrounded the British as they slept, but eventually retired without initiating an attack. They were alarmed by the shouted passwords of the British vedettes, which persuaded them that the British were prepared to defend themselves; while they were in any case not confident of their ability to mount a successful attack at night.[6] Besides which, they had already chosen the place where they preferred to give battle.

It was not Cetshwayo's practice to issue his commanders with precise instructions, and he had left it to Godide to drive Pearson back in the manner he thought best – so long as he did so without fail.[7] However, it seems that in this case the king's familiarity with the terrain (in 1856 he had campaigned in the vicinity against his brother Mbuyazi) had led him to suggest the ideal battlefield. Just north of the Nyezane stream the open plain gives way to a range of hills. The ascent is along a low ridge running up a valley (then thickly overgrown with bush and reeds), between two grass-covered hills which rise steeply either side.[8] Here – a fortunate precedent – the Zulu had won victories in the past, and hoped to do so again.

A British column on the march was vulnerable to attack, especially on its flanks, which made it imperative that patrols move parallel to it or reconnoitre the broken ground ahead to give ample warning of the enemy. Because of the rapidity and suddenness of Zulu attack, it was also essential that a column keep well closed up. In this case, Pearson's reconnaissance had not been thorough, mainly because the enemy was underrated, and the column stretched out for 8 km.

At about 8 a.m. on the morning of 22 January, Pearson decided to halt for breakfast with the head of his column on the level ground between the Nyezane and the looming hills. He was as yet unaware that the Zulu lay concealed in their strong and well chosen position.[9] It was unfortunate for the Zulu that Pearson noticed some of their scouts on Wombane, the eastern of the two hills before him, and ordered a company of the NNC forward to disperse them. This movement had the effect of prematurely springing the carefully laid Zulu trap. The younger warriors could not be restrained from rushing into the attack, so revealing the Zulu position. However, the older men kept to the intended plan and hung back, so dislocating Zulu strategy, which evidently aimed at engaging the column in front while sweeping round both its flanks and enveloping it. With Zulu intentions made plain, Pearson was able to take action to forestall them.[10]

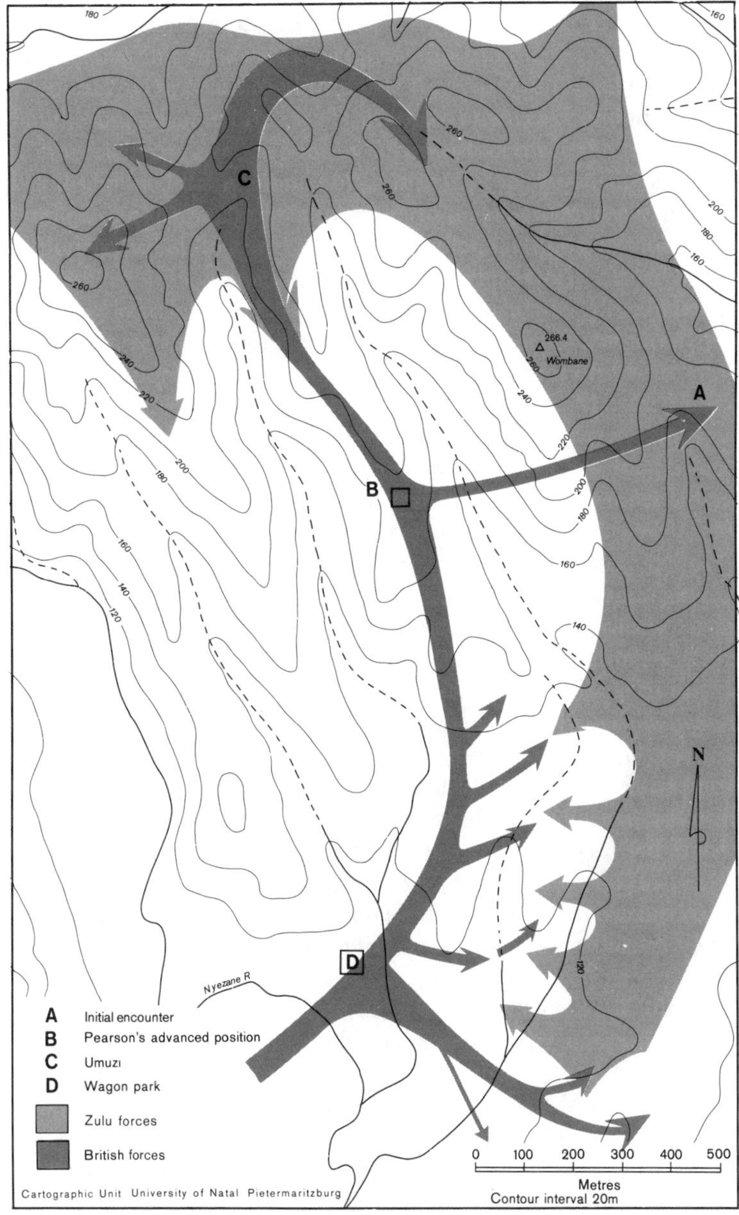

3 Nyezane, 22 January 1879: the unsuccessful Zulu ambush of a British column on the march

When they heard the faint buzzing of the Zulu lying concealed in the grass, the unhappy NNC being led up the slopes of Wombane knew they were walking into an ambush but could not make their white officers understand.[11] The Zulu then leap up with a great shout of 'uSuthu!', opened fire and routed the NNC. Within a few minutes their attack was fully developed. While the centre moved cautiously forward, five distinct streams of Zulu, who made up the left horn, ran straight at the British wagon train at right angles to its length, clearly trying to surround the first part of the column and to bisect the line of wagons. Rushing from bush to bush, they skirmished in extended order in the finest approved style to within 150 m of the wagons, firing with great rapidity and retiring under cover to reload, or to receive fresh muskets which had been loaded for them. Their form of attack surprised the British, who had expected to be confronted by great masses of warriors in the open, not men armed with guns and adept at skirmishing.

Zulu confidence had been greatly enhanced by the 'doctoring' they had received at oNdini, for they had been smeared with *muthi* which was supposed to ensure that British bullets would glide off harmlessly.[12] However, they were rapidly disabused. Pearson smartly sent forward the troops at the head of the column – two companies of the 2/3rd Regiment (the Buffs), and two companies of the Naval Brigade, accompanied by two seven-pounder guns, a rocket tube and a Gatling gun – to a knoll close by the road at the base of the pass from which the whole Zulu position could be seen and raked with fire.[13] Meanwhile, the convoy continued to close up and park, and when it was sufficiently concentrated Pearson directed a further two companies of the Buffs, who were guarding the wagons half-way down the column, to clear the Zulu left horn from the bush. Already astonished and unnerved at the concentration of British fire, the Zulu withdrew rapidly but in an orderly manner before the Buffs' determined skirmishing line, only to be fully subjected to the shells, rockets and musketry from the knoll when they were flushed on to the open hillside.

The dispersal of the Zulu left horn released the British troops who had remained near the Nyezane to guard the wagons, and the Mounted Infantry and Volunteers, as well as a company of Royal Engineers, moved forward on the Buffs' right to intercept those Zulu trying to retire across the Nyezane further downstream. They were supported by two half-companies of the Buffs and the 99th Regiment from the rear column, coming up under Lieutenant-Colonel W. Welman.

The Zulu, however, were not yet beaten, and exhibited courage, tenacity and a degree of ordered control which the over-confident British had not anticipated. From the bush they continued to direct a heavy fire on the knoll, and seemed to be aiming particularly at the British leaders. Both Pearson and Lieutenant-Colonel Parnell had their horses shot under them. Soon after the retreat of their left horn, the Zulu attempted rather belatedly to advance their right and outflank the British on the opposite flank, and occupied the high hill to the west of the road and an *umuzi* about 400 m from the knoll. A portion of the Naval Brigade, supported by some of the NNC, checked the Zulu movement. They forced the Zulu to evacuate the *umuzi* and set it alight, then gained possession of the high ground to the west of the Eshowe road, dispersing the Zulu right horn. Supported by a company of the Buffs, this force now proceeded – despite heavy fire from the considerable numbers of the Zulu centre still in possession – to clear the heights beyond the *umuzi* and to take the dominating crest of Wombane. On losing Wombane and the key to their position, the Zulu rapidly dispersed in comparatively good order down the far side, many too tired to do other than walk, even though under fire from the victorious British. Gun and rocket fire helped break up any groups that reformed near by. The last shots died away at about 9.30 a.m.

The old men and the women of the vicinity had climbed the hills to see what they could of the battle, for the Zulu had not anticipated that they would be defeated.[14] The warriors had consequently not previously selected ground for a possible withdrawal. Nevertheless, the majority managed to collect on a flat-topped hill 6.4 km away, scaling the sides along different routes in dense files. They remained there shouting, singing and dancing while the British halted to bury their dead and attend their wounded. Many were surprised that the British made no attempt to pursue them, but the invaders dared not do so over the broken, unscouted country, and were indeed apprehensive of falling into a further ambush.[15] Instead, the British column reformed, and at noon continued its march on Eshowe, camping for the night 8 km short of the place, which it reached the following morning. Abandoning the fiction that the war was against the king alone, and not his subjects, they burned all the *imizi* along their route to show their displeasure at being attacked.[16]

Of the ninety-five British officers and 2 687 men (1 660 of whom were black) who took part in the engagement, only two officers and six men of the NNC and three men of the Buffs were killed, and one officer and fourteen men wounded.[17] In comparison, the Zulu casualties were heavy. The British officially estimated these at about 300 killed, though any accurate figure is impossible to reach. The Zulu practice of disposing of their dead in the thick bush, in holes and between rocks meant that more would have been killed then were located by the British. In any case, most of those who had been wounded were reported subsequently to have died.[18] That the British found only two wounded Zulu gives no indication of their true number, since the Zulu always did their best to carry off the wounded, while those who could still move hid themselves in the bush.

What is certain, though, is that the Zulu were impressed with the steady bravery of the British and appalled at the effects of their firepower. This was, indeed, devastating, despite the better than usual marksmanship required on account of the good Zulu use of cover.[19] The Zulu dead were found lying about in heaps of seven or eight, while in one place ten corpses were found close together, and in another thirty-five. While it seems that these concentrations of corpses were mainly the consequence of the steady Martini-Henry volley-fire and the Gatling gun (employed in action for the first time by the British army in this battle), there is little doubt that the artillery – and especially the rockets – caused the greatest consternation. The rockets, even though they did little actual damage, were nevertheless perceived as lightning called down from heaven by the British, and spectacularly underlined their alarming superiority in armaments.[20] The inferior range of the Zulus' generally antiquated firearms meant that they had been subjected to a fire they could not effectively return. That their left horn had captured a few breech-loading rifles was hardly adequate compensation, especially since the Zulu had jettisoned many of their existing firearms in their retreat.[21]

It is hardly surprising, therefore, that the outmanoeuvred and outgunned Zulu of the battle of Nyezane were left demoralized. They were fully aware that only part of the British column had been sufficient to defeat them, and that British losses were insignificant compared to their own. All the advantages of a carefully picked position, surprise and enemy lack of preparation had come to naught. No wonder King Cetshwayo was angry with Godide, and considered that as a general he had mismanaged the battle.[22]

Nor were the Zulu wrong to have read so much into their failure. It is true that Nyezane was an unusual battle. There was little hand-to-hand fighting in what was essentially a running fire-fight, and both sides showed a degree of ineptitude. Yet the difference was that the British had the discipline to retrieve the situation, while the Zulu had not. Their failure to coordinate the attack of the horns, and the mettlesome uMxhapho's reluctance to hold back in the interests of a wider strategy, were to prove typical Zulu weaknesses in future battles. And while the British absorbed the lesson that tight defensive formations were absolutely necessary, the Zulu persisted in their traditional frontal attacks against modern weapons. Ultimately, this inability to draw the proper military lessons was of far greater import than the defeat itself.

After the battle of Nyezane, the Zulu did not at first disperse as was customary for ritual purification. Expecting Pearson to continue his march north-west towards oNdini, they concentrated in the thorny valley of the Mhlatuze River with the intention of again ambushing him. Instead, the British dug in at Eshowe and gave the Zulu some opportunity to recover before proceeding to blockade the British position.[23]

Pearson's instructions had been to form a depot at Eshowe by utilizing the buildings of the deserted Norwegian mission for stores, and to fortify it by throwing up earthworks.[24] Work was already in progress, and the British were confident of soon being ready to advance, when on 28 January word arrived from Lord Chelmsford informing Pearson of the disaster at Isandlwana, and leaving his future movements to his discretion. At a council of war the decision was narrowly taken to hold fast. It was felt that the continued presence of the column deep in Zululand would have a positive effect on morale in Natal, and tie up Zulu forces which might otherwise be free to attempt an invasion of the colony. Even so, limited supplies made it necessary to reduce the garrison, and nearly the whole of the two battalions of the NNC and the mounted men were sent back to Natal. The lack of sufficient mounted men was to be sorely felt. For without regular patrols it was impossible to learn of the Zulus' movements or to mount punitive raids, such as Wood was soon to be sending out from Khambula with such effect. The 1 339 white and 355 black soldiers and noncombatants remaining in Fort Eshowe consequently settled down with little positive to do except wait to be relieved. They filled their time by constantly improving the fort, making occasional minor forays outside the walls, nursing their dwindling supplies and tending the growing numbers of sick and dying.[25]

Meanwhile, in north-western Zululand, the British were also forced in the wake of Isandlwana to retire on fortified positions. However, in comparison with the coastal region, the initiative remained with them.

The north-west had long been a volatile region. Since the late 1860s the Zulu in their search for grazing had been staking out claims northwards across the Phongolo River, and in so doing had challenged the interests of the Swazi and certain lesser chiefdoms, though Cetshwayo had stopped short of full-scale hostilities. The land-hungry Transvaal Boers were also competing for the resources of the region, and from the Utrecht and Wakkerstroom Districts were spilling over the undefined borders of their republic and laying claim to great tracts of land which the Zulu claimed as theirs, and which were to become known as the Disputed Territory.

During the tense months of the latter part of 1878, while the Zulu waited for the British to show their hand, confrontation centred on the successful little German settlement of Luneburg, established in 1869 by the Hermannsburg Mission Society 3 km north of the Phongolo.[26] Cetshwayo was not prepared to accept the unchallenged presence of the Luneburgers in a region into which he was expanding. The Qulusi were his instrument. They were attached to the ebaQulusini *ikhanda* which King Shaka had established under the supervision of his aunt, Mnkabayi, near present-day Vryheid. The people of various clans attached to it occupied the valley of the Bivane River, and regarded themselves as linked to the royal house. Thousands strong, they were not drafted into conventional *amabutho* where they would be amalgamated with the other young males of their age from throughout the kingdom, but fought together as a royal section. They were in charge of *izinduna* appointed by the king to represent the royal house.[27] During 1877 and 1878 their unpredictable and hostile presence greatly disquieted the Luneburgers.

Even more alarming for the settlers were a series of raids during October 1878, led by Mbilini kaMswati.[28] The proverbially cruel and shrewd Mbilini was the eldest son of the late Swazi king's first wife. He lost the disputed succession after Mswati's death in 1865, and in late 1866 fled for support to Zululand. King Mpande accepted his allegiance, and allowed him to settle in the upper reaches of the Phongolo. There he gathered about him adherents, chiefly of Swazi extraction, who did not form part of the regular Zulu military system, but operated as a guerrilla force of auxiliaries. From his caves and rocky fastnesses Mbilini maintained a degree of turbulent independence, raiding his neighbours on all sides, but particularly the Boers of the Disputed Territory and the Swazi of the faction who had ousted him. In doing so, he aided covert Zulu action against Boer and Swazi alike. His relative autonomy made him particularly useful as a cat's-paw, for Cetshwayo could always disown him if it became necessary. Between 1870 and 1877 Mbilini's raids became increasingly provocative, and in February 1877 he was forced to flee to Cetshwayo for sanctuary from the Boers. Shortly before the raids of October 1878, Cetshwayo allowed Mbilini to establish a new homestead in the Qulusi country near ebaQulusini itself. It was on the south side and half-way up Hlobane Mountain and called iNdlabeyitubula – 'they [the Boers] gave my home a shove'.

Mbilini's October raids were the final straw for the white settlers of the Phongolo region. It was to dissuade them from abandoning the area to Zulu influence, and thus strategically separating the British from the Swazi, with whom they hoped to cooperate, that Colonel Evelyn Wood, commander of the British troops stationed at Utrecht, dispatched the garrison of two companies of infantry to Luneburg. The soldiers strengthened their position there and during November built Fort Clery. As feared, their presence provoked the Qulusi, who came to protest, as did Manyonyoba, a local *induna* who acted as Cetshwayo's representative.

Manyonyoba, who had been much longer established in the region than Mbilini, was equally self-serving and independently minded. His father, Maqondo (Magonondo), had been an independent chief who had accepted Shaka's overlordship. Manyonyoba was therefore considered to owe Cetshwayo his allegiance. His adherents were the debris of various chiefdoms conquered by Shaka and Dingane – Zulu, Swazi, Sotho – who had gone begging for land until allowed to settle north of the Phongolo, in the caves along both steep banks of the Ntombe River. From this fastness Manyonyoba was in the habit of raiding the surrounding countryside. The presence of troops, however, complicated his position. He had a record of past co-operation with the British, so it came as no surprise that for the time being he was prepared to hedge his bets and profess friendliness to the Luneburg garrison, which was strengthened during December with mounted men. However, he was left feeling exposed when, in response to the British ultimatum which demanded Mbilini's surrender, the king ordered Mbilini to move out of harm's way with 200 of his armed adherents to Hyentala Mountain, 65 km from Luneburg. It seems that Cetshwayo soon reassured Manyonyoba with promises of aid should the British attack him, and on Christmas day his men were 'doctored' for battle. Consequent uncertainty as to his intentions, as well as further small raids in the vicinity, persuaded all the local farmers and their farmworkers to seek refuge in the Luneburg laager by mid-January 1879.

Early in January the Left (No. 4) Column of 2 278 men assembled near Balte Spruit, and by 10 January was encamped at Bemba's Kop on the Ncome River awaiting the expiry of the ultimatum. Its commander was Colonel Evelyn Wood. The Zulu called him 'Lukuni', after the hard wood from which knobkerries were made, a sobriquet which was not only a play on his name but a tribute to his military ability.[29]

Chelmsford's plans for the initial advance of the Centre and Left Columns required that Wood move down the Ncome River and subdue the Zulu to his front and left in order to take pressure off the Centre Column as it crossed the Mzinyathi. The Left Column would also support the Centre Column by covering its left flank and the Transvaal border, and by forming the link between it and Colonel Rowlands's No. 5 Column to the north. The No. 5 Column, however, was not (as originally intended) to join the others in the advance on oNdini. As a consequence of Rowlands's unsuccessful operations during September–October 1878 against the Pedi, Chelmsford decided that his column should remain in garrison on the Phongolo frontier to keep Sekhukhune and predatory local chiefs like Mbilini in order, and to protect the Wakkerstroom District from Zulu inroads. Consequently, Rowlands's column did not advance beyond its posts at Derby and Luneburg except to take part in localized expeditions. The column consisted of 1 565 officers and men. When on 26 February the hostile attitude of the Transvaal Boers necessitated the return of Rowlands and his staff to Pretoria, No. 5 Column was attached to Wood's command.[30]

The mobility of the several hundred mounted volunteers and

infantry of Wood's column, imaginatively led in their scouting and skirmishing by Lieutenant-Colonel Redvers Buller, made them an extremely effective force. During the campaign of January and February, which saw many minor actions but no battles, Wood was able to establish his supremacy in north-western Zululand, ready, like a spider in the centre of its web, to pounce on any hostile force rash enough to penetrate his zone of control.[31]

It was Chelmsford's hope that the Zulu could be induced to surrender, rather than fight, and he had been encouraged by Hamu's overtures. Consequently, he had ordered Wood on 16 December 1878 to make every effort to induce the Zulu along his line of advance to come under his protection, and to relocate those who submitted in his rear.[32] In this spirit, Wood had an interview on 9 January 1879 with Bemba, an *induna* of the important Chief Sekethwayo kaNhlaka Mdlalose, an *isikhulu* in the north-western districts and the *induna* of the kwaNodwengu *ikhanda*. Wood agreed to protect and feed Bemba who came in the next day, along with eighty of his adherents and over 800 head of livestock. His people surrendered their arms, and were relocated in the Utrecht District.[33]

Bemba's submission was satisfactory, but it was Sekethwayo's that Wood sought. Because Sekethwayo was much embittered against the Transvaalers for their land claims in his territory, he was logically expected to be firmly against the British and of the war party. But instead, old and infirm, he was inclined to temporize, and Wood hoped to be able to reel him in.

On the eve of hostilities, most Zulu across the Ncome from Wood were still living in their *imizi* with their herds and flocks. Only the young men had gone in answer to their king's call to arms. Before he crossed into Zululand, Wood considerately warned the Zulu to his front that the war would begin the following day, and that they must decide whether to be friends or foes. Yet the speed of his mounted men's advance on 11 January to within 20 km of Rorke's Drift caught the Zulu by surprise, so that they had time only to make for the hills, leaving their livestock behind. These the British rounded up, taking about 2 000 cattle belonging to Sihayo, and another 2 000 to 3 000 from the adherents of Sondolosi, Sekethwayo's deceased brother. In addition they drove off some 2 000 sheep, besides goats and horses.

Sekethwayo, thoroughly alarmed, that very day sent word to

Wood of his desire to accept the British terms for surrender. But negotiations to this effect, which Wood eagerly entered into, terminated abruptly on 15 January. An *impi*, despatched from oNdini by the king, had entered Sekethwayo's territory and brought the errant chief smartly back into line. A handful of Sekethwayo's adherents had been able beforehand to give themselves up to the British, but among these women, children and old people looking for food and shelter there were no able-bodied men.[34]

Meanwhile, on 12 January, one of Wood's mounted patrols raided Mbusa's adherents, who lived on the lower Bivane, captured 538 head of cattle and dispersed the Zulu, killing seven. The Qulusi collected the survivors on 16 January, and returned with them to ebaQulusini. Wood sent a strong reconnaissance patrol in the direction of the Batshe on 15 January, and it became involved in a skirmish with about 500 Zulu. This skirmish was typical of the many running fights that marked the course of the war, including the battle of Nyezane. The Zulu tried to draw the British on to unfavourable ground, and sniped at them from the rear and flanks. The British, on the other hand, secured their flanks with mounted men and drove the Zulu back with a line of skirmishers. These were reinforced at the right moment, and broke through the Zulu force. The mounted men completed the Zulu rout, but did not pursue far for fear of an ambush.[35]

Wood, who had marched his force back to Bemba's Kop on 13 January, began an advance on the White Mfolozi on 18 January. During the march some of Wood's Irregulars (black troops raised in the Transvaal) had a successful skirmish across the White Mfolozi near Cerekoma Mountain with a party of Sekethwayo's adherents, and brought in 400 cattle.[36] At this stage, Wood had cause to be content with his progress. He had successfully cleared Chelmsford's left flank, and the discomfited Mdlalose had evacuated their *imizi* with their livestock. Wood spared their huts and standing crops from burning, for he still hoped to accept Zulu as refugees rather than to fight them. And indeed, on 20 January Thinta, Sekethwayo's uncle and chief *induna*, surrendered to Wood, and he and his adherents were relocated in Utrecht. They had been taking refuge in caves, for they expected to be attacked by the Qulusi.[37] This antagonism of the doggedly loyal Qulusi towards the Mdlalose introduced a new element into the situation: potential conflict between those wishing to accommodate the British, and those who were determined to stand by Cetshwayo.

As Wood was to discover, a far more determined foe now faced him in the Qulusi than in the equivocal Mdlalose. Cetshwayo had ordered the Qulusi to stand against Wood's column, and all had concentrated at the ebaQulusini *ikhanda* to do so, even those from as far away as the Phongolo valley.[38] Wood realized that he would have to defeat them, especially as they could disrupt his lines of supply. Consequently, he obtained Chelmsford's approval to strike north-east towards ebaQulusini, clearing the Ityenteka range of the Qulusi, before resuming his advance in support of the Centre Column.

On 20 January Buller led a mounted force consisting of eighty-two Frontier Light Horse and twenty-three Dutch Burghers under Piet Uys across the White Mfolozi to reconnoitre the top of eZungwini Mountain, where Mbilini had reinforced the Qulusi. They attacked Mabomba's *umuzi* on the south-eastern spur, killing twelve for the loss of a man wounded. However, the British were prevented from ascending the mountain by a force of about 1 000 Zulu on the summit. These came down the mountain in the traditional formation of three columns, the two horns (which moved in disciplined skirmishing order) quite outflanking the British. Buller had no option but to make a fighting retreat across the White Mfolozi, where he made a stand on the open ground, driving the Zulu back. This sharp reverse, and two more wounded, had a salutary effect on the British. The Qulusi had proved themselves far more serious fighting-men than the Mdlalose. Not only were the majority armed with guns, but they were under regular command and discipline and were sure of their skirmishing tactics, which were attuned to the broken terrain of their own territory.[39]

Wood could not allow the Qulusi to retain the advantage they had won, even if they did not seem able to make proper use of it by launching an offensive of their own.[40] In the early hours of 22 January he himself led out a strong patrol of infantry as well as mounted men to eZungwini.[41] A few hundred Zulu on the south-eastern summit retired precipitately at the sight of them, abandoning 250 head of cattle and about 400 sheep and goats to the British. From the top of eZungwini, however, Wood had a sobering sight. Under Hlobane Mountain he saw about 4 000 Zulu drilling with great ease and precision, forming squares, triangles and circles. These disciplined warriors would clearly have to be defeated if his column were to regain the initiative. Consequently, on 24 January

Wood led out a patrol between the Ityenteka range and eZungwini Nek, taking about 3 000 Zulu by surprise. Those who attempted a stand were dispersed by the two seven-pounder guns and were pursued and scattered by the mounted men, mainly retiring up Hlobane. About fifty Zulu lost their lives in the affray, including two sons of the prominent Qulusi *induna* Mcwayo kaMangeda, as well as three other *izinduna*.[42] It seems that Msebe kaMadaka, the senior Qulusi *induna* and cousin of Cetshwayo, had been in charge of the force, which had consisted – besides the Qulusi *ibutho* and local irregulars (including Mbilini's men) – of some members of other *amabutho* who lived in the area.[43]

The Qulusi were greatly disheartened by their ignominious setback,[44] but Wood's position had also suddenly deteriorated. During the skirmish he learned of the destruction of the British camp at Isandlwana and the consequent collapse of Chelmsford's strategy. Wood at once withdrew to his camp on the White Mfolozi. In order to cover Utrecht from Zulu attack and to maintain communication with No. 5 Column, and at the same time to be in a position to strike at the Qulusi, he moved north-west on 31 January to a strongly fortified camp at Khambula hill, where water and fuel were available. There he intended to stand fast, making his presence constantly felt in a 66 km radius through mounted patrols, until Chelmsford was ready to resume the march on oNdini.[45]

Meanwhile, all Manyonyoba's fighting men, who could not have numbered more than 1 000, were defeated on 26 January south of Luneburg by a patrol from the garrison. Manyonyoba took to his caves with his women, children and infirm, as well as his own cattle, while royal cattle in his care were driven towards oNdini. Commandant Schermbrucker intercepted these at the junction of the Ntombe and Phongolo, capturing 365 of them and some 200 goats besides. Half of Manyonyoba's discomforted warriors joined the Qulusi opposing Wood, while the remainder, operating in groups of 100 to 200, kept up raids from the Ntombe caves and made the Luneburg–Derby road unsafe for small parties of British. The garrison at Luneburg was too well fortified for them to attempt to attack it, however, while in turn the garrison was too small to risk assaulting the caves.[46]

In the west, therefore, as on the coast, there was apparent stalemate. This was not on account of Zulu success in these theatres, for the Zulu had generally been thoroughly worsted, but rather the consequence of the main Zulu army's victory at Isandlwana. It was this which had quite dislocated Chelmsford's offensive strategy and forced his various columns on to the defensive. Whether the Zulu could take advantage of the situation was, however, another matter.

Notes

1 A number of Zulu observing the crossing were surprised and captured by the mounted men.

2 Anti-Slavery Society Papers, G 12: statement of one of the Native Contingent with Col. Pearson's Column, made to the Bishop of Natal; *BPP* (C. 2252), no. 20: Pearson to Frere's Military Secretary, 17 January 1879; Norbury, *Naval Brigade*, p. 220–2.

3 WO 32/7717, enc. in Fannin to Colonial Secretary, 1 March 1879: message of two Ntumeni natives from Cetshwayo.

4 Inevitably, there is lack of clarity in the sources (which consist of information drawn from Zulu spies and prisoners as well as hearsay) on the precise composition and size of this Zulu army.

5 CSO 1925, no. 444/1879: minute, Fannin to Colonial Secretary, 20 January 1879; CP 8, no. 49: Bishop Schreuder's despatch, 10 February 1879; *Natal Mercury*, supplement, 22 January 1922: Chief Zimema's account.

6 Anti-Slavery Society Papers, G 12: statement of one of Natal Native Contingent to Bishop Colenso; Zulu War, File 1, KCM 42329: Col. Harry Sparks, 'Chelmsford's Ultimatum to Cetewayo'.

7 Webb and Wright, *Zulu King Speaks*, p. 30; *Times of Natal*, 5 February 1879: correspondent with Pearson's Column, 24 January 1879.

8 Today the hills are being covered by commercial timber plantations, though the lower ground is relatively unchanged.

9 B. M. Hart-Synnot (ed.), *Letters of Major-General Fitzroy Hart-Synnot C.B., C.M.G.*, London, 1912, p. 113.

10 See especially Turner Letters: Turner to his parents, 1 March 1879; Hart-Synnot, *Letters*, pp. 105, 113–14; W. R. C. Wynne, *Memoir of Capt. W. R. C. Wynne, R.E.*, Southampton, n.d., p. 27: 24 January 1879; Norbury, *Naval Brigade*, pp. 232–3; *BPP* (C. 2260), enc. 3 in no. 4: Pearson to Hallam Parr, 23 January 1879.

11 Cato Papers I, Ms 1602 a: Cato to Richards, 2 February 1879.

12 *Natal Mercury*, 30 January 1879.

13 The description of the engagement at Nyezane is primarily based upon the following sources: *BPP* (C. 2260), enc. 3 in no. 3: Pearson to Hallam Parr, 23 January 1879; WO 32/7708: report by Commander Campbell, 24 January 1879; WO 32/7708: Lt. T. W. Dowding to Capt. A. Campbell, 23 January 1879; AC, p. 153: Capt. MacGregor to Col. Home, 14 February 1879; War Office, *Narrative*, pp. 23–4; Norbury, *Naval Brigade*, pp. 229–32; Hart-Synnot, *Letters*, pp. 107–13, 148; Wynne, *Memoir*, p. 29.

14 *Natal Mercury*, supplement, 22 January 1929: Chief Zimema's

account.

15 Turner Papers: Turner to Ellis, 30 January 1879; Turner to his parents, 1 March 1879.

16 *Times of Natal*, 5 February 1879: correspondent, 24 January 1879; Norbury, *Naval Brigade*, p. 235.

17 War Office, *Narrative*, p. 155.

18 CP 7, no. 32: Fynney to Col. Law, 8 March 1879.

19 WO 32/7708: Commander Campbell's report, 24 January 1879.

20 See CSO 1926, no. C19/1879: statement of Unxakala and Udhlozi, 4 February 1879; SNA 1/1/34, no. 85: statement of Sihlahla, 3 June 1879; *Natal Mercury*, supplement, 22 January 1929: Chief Zimema's account.

21 *Natal Witness*, 26 June 1879: *Mercury* correspondent, Fort Napoleon, 24 June 1879.

22 CSO 1926, no. 1147/1879: Fannin to Colonial Secretary, 20 February 1879.

23 CP 8, no. 49: Bishop Schreuder's despatch, 10 February 1879; WO 32/7730: Pearson to Military Secretary, 9 April 1879; Webb and Wright, *Zulu King Speaks*, p. 31.

24 For details of the fortifications, which were daily improved, see Laband, 'British fieldworks', pp. 70–7, passim.

25 WO 32/7730: Pearson to Military Secretary, 9 April 1879; War Office, *Narrative*, pp. 54–7; Lt. W. N. Lloyd, 'The defence of Ekowe', *Natalia*, V, December 1975, p. 18.

26 P. Schwarz, 'Gemeinde Luneburg, Natal', in Pastor J. Schnackenberg (ed.), *Geschichte der Freien ev.–luth. Synode in Sudafrika 1892–1932*, Celle, 1933, pp. 24–5.

27 Vijn, *Cetshwayo's Dutchman*, p. 127: Colenso's notes; *JSA* IV, pp. 277–8: testimony of Ndukwana.

28 For Mbilini and Manyonyoba and the situation in the Phongolo region on the eve of war, see Laband, 'Mbilini' pp. 189–93.

29 Field Marshal Sir E. Wood, *From Midshipman to Field Marshal*, London, 1906, vol. II, p. 54 (note); Mitford, *Zulu Country*, p. 218 (note).

30 War Office, *Narrative*, pp. pp. 8–10, 20, 143–4.

31 F. Schermbrucker, 'Zhlobane and Kambula', *South African Catholic Magazine*, III, 1893, p. 337.

32 WC II/2/2: Chelmsford to Wood, 16 December 1878.

33 Woodgate's Military Diary: 10 January 1879. Turncoats such as Bemba were nevertheless not esteemed by the British. Local magistrates complained that refugees accepted for resettlement were always sneaking back to Zululand, while the relatively small number of able-bodied men among them (on average about a quarter) indicated that most were still fighting for Cetshwayo while they allowed the British to feed and care for their families.

34 Woodgate's Military Diary: 11, 14 and 15 January 1879.

35 *BPP* (C. 2252), no. 20: Wood to Military Secretary, 18 January 1879; Ashe and Wyatt Edgell, *Zulu Campaign*, pp. 33–5.

36 Woodgate's Military Diary: 1—January 1879.

37 WO 32/7712: Journal of Operations of No. 4 Column, 20 January

1879.

38 Webb and Wright, *Zulu King Speaks*, pp. 32–3.

39 *BPP* (C. 2260), enc. 2 in no. 13: report by Buller, 21 January 1879; Wood Papers 7, KCM 51124: Buller to Wood, 20 January 1879.

40 See Mbilini's complaint that the Qulusi did not take his advice to attack Wood's camp at night (*Natal Mercury*, 28 February 1879: correspondent, sources of the White Mfolosi and Pemvana, 17 February 1879).

41 Accounts of operations against the Qulusi can be found in WO/7712: Spalding to Quartermaster-General: Journal of Military Operations, 22, 24 January 1879; and Woodgate's Military Diary: 22, 24 January 1879.

42 CP 9, no. 12: Lloyd to Wood, 29 January 1879; *BPP* (C. 2260), no. 10: statement of Ucadjana, son of Matendeka, 3 February 1879.

43 *BPP* (C. 2374), enc. in no. 9: Wheelwright to Colonial Secretary, 18 February 1879: statement of Undobolonkwana.

44 *BPP* (C. 2260), no. 10; statement of Ucadjana, 3 February 1879.

45 *BPP* (C. 2260), enc. 3 in no. 4: Wood to Military Secretary, 25 January 1879.

46 Laband, 'Mbilini', pp. 194–5.

7

The lull

Once the battle of Isandlwana had brought the British invasion to a temporary halt, and thrown the aggressors on to the defensive, the conditions had apparently been created for Cetshwayo to exploit his ephemeral military advantage to force a negotiated settlement. In reality, however, the British were never prepared to entertain such a possibility. Chelmsford immediately set about gathering reinforcements in order to defend Natal, renew the offensive and avenge Isandlwana. Yet the resumption of full-scale hostilities was as unpalatable for Cetshwayo as peace negotiations were considered desirable. There were signs of Zulu demoralization as a consequence of the heavy casualties they had suffered, and discontent among some of the leadership with the progress of the war.[1] The king could consequently not be sure how his subjects would react should he call on them again to take the war to the British. On the other hand, once the British had built up their forces sufficiently to resume their advance on oNdini, there was the possibility that the kingdom might begin to unravel under the strain of a fresh round of battles. Cetshwayo was consequently left with no obvious way of taking advantage of the lull that followed the blunting of the first British invasion.

The British, staggering under their defeat, naturally expected Cetshwayo to take the offensive. Intelligence constantly reaching them in the weeks following Isandlwana indicated that the king planned to send a large army to storm Fort Eshowe, before sweeping on to invade Natal.[2] Such, however, was not Cetshwayo's intention. Even had he wished to exploit the military situation, only limited strategic options would have been open to him.

Superficially, it might have made sense to march on Natal while 'the white people were still tired',[3] but the king was in no position to do so. For one thing, the sudden rise of the Thukela and its unpredictability during the summer months made incursions into Natal too hazardous until the winter, and he ordered the border people to make no raids on their own account until he was ready to move. Those opposite Defensive District VI of Natal consequently confined themselves to occasional threats and shots exchanged across the lower Thukela;[4] while further upstream, opposite Defensive District VII, the Ntuli under Chiefs Godide and Mavumengwana, the Magwaza under Chief Manqondo (whose eldest son, Qethuka, was an *isikhulu* and close friend of the king), and the Cube under Chief Sigananda (who exercised authority in place of his blind father Sokufa), were as inactive.[5] The Zulu across the Mzinyathi from Defensive District I were relatively more aggressive, however, and did not heed the king's order not to raid. Even so, no major incursions were attempted. Only small raiding parties (in which those adherents of Gamdana who had not surrendered with him to the British in January were especially prominent) troubled the plain between the river and the Helpmekaar heights. The British responded with limited counter-raids, and the district continued to witness low-grade military activity until March, when the local warriors began to respond to Cetshwayo's call for his army to reassemble.[6]

Another reason why Cetshwayo could not have contemplated an invasion of Natal was that his council objected to further operations until the mealie crop was ripe and more food was available.[7] Furthermore, there were threats from other fronts to consider. Exaggerated and unfounded fears persisted that the British were still planning an amphibious landing at St Lucia, while the intentions of the Swazi remained somewhat uncertain. The British certainly desired Swazi participation, but after Isandlwana the Swazi were chary of any commitment until they were certain that the British were indeed the winning side, and clearly preferred (despite prevarications to the contrary) to stand on the defensive behind their own borders.[8] Chelmsford soon had no alternative but to regard them as 'out of the game'.[9] Cetshwayo was obviously heartened by Swazi reluctance to intervene, and by their readiness to take care of some 5 000 Zulu cattle driven over the border for safety. Towards the end of February he even went so far as to open negotiations with King Mbandzeni regarding sanctuary should the 'wild animals' who had come against him eventually prevail.[10]

Yet if the Swazi could be safely disregarded (at least until the

British emerged the clear winners), there still remained the untested British No. 5 Column in the Phongolo region. And, most dangerous of all, Wood continued to raid aggressively from Khambula and threaten the whole of north-western Zululand. The greatest obstacle, nevertheless, to any strategic planning – especially of an offensive nature – was the uncertain morale of the Zulu army.

It was normal for the Zulu to disperse after battle for ritual purification. The king expected them, though, to have reassembled at oNdini within a month of the first round of battles.[11] But after their heavy casualties, discouragingly inflicted by such a numerically inferior foe, his *amabutho* were most reluctant to try conclusions again, and could not be made to muster during February. Until the regular *amabutho* were prepared come together, the king had to make do with what operational forces he still had in the field. One such force was the Qulusi in north-western Zululand, whom the king ordered to watch Wood's very active column, and to attack it if the opportunity arose.[12]

The Qulusi, however, were finding themselves no match for Wood, who was determined to maintain the initiative. The first strike from his strategically placed camp at Khambula was on 1 February against the ebaQulusini *ikhanda* itself, 50 km to the east. To destroy it would establish British dominance in north-western Zululand. The Boers regarded ebaQulusini as impregnable, for it was situated in a basin surrounded by precipitous hills. But in a raid that exemplified the value of rapidly moving mounted troops, Buller's 140 Frontier Light Horse and Dutch Burghers took the place by surprise, scattering the 100 or so inhabitants and killing six of them. They then burned the *ikhanda* – which formed a great circle 300 m wide, and consisted of 250 huts – before retiring with 270 cattle.[13] It was indicative of drooping Qulusi morale that parties of between 100 and 300 were seen hovering in the area, but made no attempt to obstruct Buller. For the Qulusi had decided after their series of reverses to abandon the open country, and to take up a strictly defensive position on their mountain fastnesses, such as Hlobane.

Wood had planned to attack Hlobane next, but after the destruction of the Qulusis' rallying-point at ebaQulusini and the consequently damaging blow to their military prestige, he no longer considered it necessary. He contented himself with neutralizing the Hlobane stronghold, and on 10 February Buller carried off another

490 head of cattle from its environs.[14] Hlobane, though, persisted as a potential threat. It continued to harbour large numbers of Zulu and their herds, even if by the end of March the grazing was giving out. Cetshwayo, meanwhile, seeing the plight of the Qulusi huddled on the mountains out of reach of Wood's patrols, ordered their women to fall back east with their cattle to the Nongoma region. To Wood's rear, by contrast, the majority of Sekethwayo's hungry adherents were returning home from the mountain tops. The war had swept over them, and they were content to submit so long as they were left in peace.[15] But for the Qulusi it was not so easy. Since they had been involved in actual fighting, they feared that if they gave themselves up they would be killed. Yet they were utterly disheartened by their defeats and wearied by Wood's unremitting raiding. It was imperative for their survival that Wood's column be neutralized. But since the Qulusi themselves had no answer to Wood's raids, and were in no position to attack his fortified camp at Khambula, they had no option but to petition the king to send them strong reinforcements of regular *amabutho* for the task.[16]

The situation was less one-sided in the Phongolo region.[17] Although Manyonyoba had seemed increasingly prepared after his January setbacks to open negotiations with the British, he was overborne by his chief *induna*, Sityuwabunto/Situwabemba, who wished to intensify the raiding. Accordingly, on the night of 10–11 February, Manyonyoba led as strong a force as he could muster to join a war party, led by Mbilini and the Qulusi *induna* Tola kaDilikana, which had advanced from Hlobane. The objective of the combined Zulu force of about 1 500 men was the Christianized blacks (*amakholwa*) and farmworkers of the Ntombe valley. In the course of their audacious raid in the early hours of 11 February, they burned the *amakholwas*' and farmworkers' houses in the valley, killed a total of forty-one of its inhabitants, and drove off hundreds of cattle and thousands of sheep and goats to Manyonyoba's caves. Significantly, certain Wakkerstroom Boers who owned farms in the region had entered into a pact with the Zulu, for in return for their cooperation as guides the raiders spared their property.

The British retaliated on 15 February, when Buller led a force of fifty-four mounted men and 517 black auxiliaries from Khambula and Luneburg against Manyonyoba's caves. Buller succeeded in burning five *imizi*, killing thirty-four Zulu (including two of Manyonyoba's sons) and driving off 375 cattle, 254 goats and eight sheep for the loss of only two black auxiliaries. But though he had evened the score somewhat, he had failed to dislodge Manyonyoba. As equivocal a success as Buller's raid was the one launched on the same day by Colonel Rowlands. The constant raiding from Khambula had caused many of the Zulu between Luneburg and Derby to abandon the open country for the relative security of the Ngongama Mountains and the broken terrain at the confluence of the Phongolo and Bivane rivers. One such stronghold was Talaku Mountain, some 32 km north-east of Luneburg in the Swazi zone, where some of the Qulusi had taken refuge with their cattle. Rowlands, despite inflicting casualties in a running skirmish and capturing livestock and noncombatants, had nevertheless to leave the Qulusi in possession of the mountain. The story was repeated on 20 February when a patrol from Luneburg attacked Makateeskop, 16 km to the south-east, where Zulu cattle were being driven for safety; and again on 25 February when Rowlands failed in another attempt to dislodge Manyonyoba.

The British were beginning to accept that they could achieve no decisive result in the Phongolo region. As indication of their lack of success the Zulu continued to command the road between Derby and Luneburg. And as Mbilini was to demonstrate, not even large parties were secure. Supplies for the Luneburg garrison were forwarded from Derby, and on 7 March a company of the 80th Regiment under Captain D. Moriarty moved out of Luneburg to meet a convoy of eighteen wagons carrying ammunition and supplies, and to escort it in. By 9 March the convoy and escort had reached the north bank of the Ntombe, but the rain-swollen river prevented all but two wagons crossing the drift. While waiting for the river to subside, Moriarty and seventy-one men pitched camp on the north bank and formed a V-shaped laager. A detachment of thirty-five men under Lieutenant H. H. Harward encamped on the south bank.[18] Moriarty's defensive arrangements were inadequate, as gaps were left between the wagons, and the flanks of the laager were not secured on the river.

This soft target was evidently a sore temptation for Manyonyoba, who called on Mbilini to help him attack it. His appeal came at the right moment, for Mbilini was in any case preparing for a fresh offensive, and had been collecting men from all parts of the surrounding countryside.

On the evening of 11 March Mbilini himself is said to have come into the unsuspecting laager and, while eating mealies, to have spied out the British dispositions. Before dawn on 12 March, and under cover of a thick river mist, Mbilini and a force of at least 800 (though estimations go as high as 9 000) advanced the 5 km from his fastness, a huge, flat-topped mountain north-east of the sleeping camp. His men approached unchallenged to within 65 m of the laager, when they fired a volley and rushed upon the panicking British with their spears. A detachment crossed the Ntombe to attack Harward's men and to cut off the British retreat from the north bank. Colour-Sergeant Booth managed to rally a few of the fugitives and to conduct a fighting withdrawal, which caused the Zulu to give up the pursuit after about 5 km. In the camp they had overrun, the Zulu – as at Isandlwana – ritually disembowelled the dead, killed the dogs, broke open and looted the boxes of ammunition, scattered mealies and flour about, shredded the tents and drove off 250 cattle.

On being alerted, Major L. Tucker, who was in command of the Luneburg garrison, marched on the Ntombe with 150 men. However, lacking mounted men, he was unable to prevent Mbilini's force from withdrawing at the trot and in a dense mass on Mbilini's stronghold. It was able to carry off most of its wounded, and the British later found only thirty Zulu bodies on the banks of the river. The British themselves had lost 1 officer and sixty men, a civil surgeon, two white wagon conductors and fifteen black drivers: casualties which were to prove the third highest after Isandlwana and Hlobane suffered in an engagement during the course of the Anglo–Zulu War.

Mbilini returned to his homestead on Hlobane with his captured rifles and ammunition, doubtless well satisfied with his resounding success. In Luneburg the stunned garrison stood in expectation of imminent attack. On 25 March, in retaliation and to keep spirits up, a mounted patrol from Khambula once more ravaged the *imizi* and mealie fields in the Ntombe valley belonging to Manyonyoba's adherents, and this time encountered no resistance.

The general success of the British No. 4 and No. 5 Columns (leaving aside the Ntombe disaster) in dominating their theatre of operations in north-western Zululand was a consequence of the number of experienced mounted men at Wood's disposal, and his ability to strike rapidly at great distances from base. This made him a greater immediate danger than the immobile Pearson at Eshowe. Cetshwayo and his council were therefore persuaded to send their army – once it had eventually reassembled and they had taken the decision to resume the offensive – against him rather than the Natal border or the Eshowe garrison. In the interim, while the Swazi could be ignored and the Natal border was looking after itself, Pearson remained a thorn in the Zulu side (albeit less sharp than Wood), and had to be dealt with.

Cetshwayo might be exceedingly indignant that Pearson had settled himself down in the middle of Zululand, as if he had already conquered it,[19] but he knew it was more than he could do to turn him out. The Zulu could despise the British for burrowing into the ground 'like wild pigs' and not fighting in the open like men,[20] but the king dared not ignore the lesson of Rorke's Drift. The strategy adopted, therefore, was one of blockade rather than assault. The Zulu investing the fort were charged with cutting the garrison off from all supplies and communication with Natal, and with preventing attempts to relieve it. The intention was to force the starving garrison into evacuating the fort, and then to attack it in the open.[21] This operation was assigned to men of all the *amabutho* living in the coast country, augmented by local irregulars. About 500 of them were constantly employed in keeping watch on Fort Eshowe in parties of between forty and fifty, while the remainder (perhaps as many as 5 000), were distributed in small groups at different local *imizi* and *amakhanda*. They were to form an army to prevent Pearson's relief, or to attack him if he made a sortie.[22] Dabulamanzi and Mavumengwana, who lived close by each other in the vicinity of eNtumeni, seem to have been in command.

Because the British in the fort had little information regarding Zulu movements, and were fully employed working on the entrenchments, standing guard or foraging in the nearest mealie and pumpkin gardens (inevitably to the sorrow of the women who had raised the crops), they remained almost entirely on the defensive.[23] For their part, the Zulu generally kept a prudent distance, though they watched the fort day and night and subjected it to long-range fire. Scouts would creep up undetected to within a few metres of the earthworks, or the unsuspecting outlying vedettes. Indeed, the vedettes, unpractised in commando-type operations, were easy prey for the practised Zulu, and on a number of occasions were surprised and suffered casualties.[24] Nevertheless, the garrison's chief anxiety was finding adequate pasturage for their remaining several hundred head of oxen. The grass close to the fort was soon eaten down, or was deliberately burned by the Zulu, so the British were forced to graze their cattle under strong escort many kilometres from the fort. What puzzled them was that, apart from a faint-hearted attack on 22 February, the Zulu made no attempt to capture the livestock. This failure was as much a relief to the British as was the relative lack of Zulu activity at night. They never quite understood that the Zulu were merely keeping watch until the garrison moved out into the open, and that the boastful exchanges between the black cattle guards Zulu were simple banter.[25] For the Zulu had absolutely no intention of storming the fort or suffering unnecessary casualties.

To break the dreadful monotony of their situation, and to strike a blow at the base of the parties of Zulu harassing the cattle guard, Pearson decided to attack eSiqwakeni, the *ikhanda* near eNtumeni of which Dabulamanzi was *induna*. Accordingly, Pearson marched out at 2 a.m. on 1 March with 450 men and a seven-pounder gun.[26] Despite all precautions, the Zulu detected their approach and streamed out of eSiqwakeni to safety before the British arrived at dawn. The disappointed British shelled the fugitives and burned the *ikhanda*, which consisted of fifty huts. Dabulamanzi's own *umuzi* was close by, but Pearson feared he would suffer too many casualties attempting to burn it. He therefore withdrew, destroying three small *imizi* on the way home. Dabulamanzi, who was recognized mounted on a black horse,[27] directed some 500 Zulu in close pursuit of the withdrawing British, and harassed the column all the way back to Eshowe. The British had to admire the expert way in which the Zulu on their flanks skirmished. If their shooting had not been so inferior, they would have inflicted considerable casualties. As it was, the Zulu were not completely wrong in their opinion that they had administered a decided reverse to the British expedition.

By early March the garrison was in growing expectation of being reinforced or relieved, and on 7 March set about improving and shortening the road to Nyezane by which their rescuers would come. The Zulu collected every day from the neighbouring *imizi* to fire on the work parties, but from long range and with little effect. Then, on 11 and 12 March, strong parties of Zulu, many thousands strong, were seen moving towards the Thukela, obviously with the intention of opposing the reinforcements the garrison was expecting daily. However, on 13 March the garrison learned that relief was postponed until 1 April, and so good was Zulu intelligence that on 15 March the Zulu were observed marching back from the direction of the Nyezane to resume position about the fort.[28]

In the first week of March the sole Zulu force assembled was still the one watching Eshowe. There was clearly continuing unwillingness to obey the king's orders to muster, and most men remained at their homes. However, with Chelmsford's palpable preparations for a major military strike, and Wood's train of successes in the north-west, the attitude of the warriors inevitably changed, and by the second week of March they were willingly complying with the urgent order going out for the whole army to assemble by the new moon (or 22 March).[29] By 20 March the absence of men was made apparent by women coming down to tend their gardens along the middle Thukela armed with gun and shield, and it was soon reported by one of John Dunn's agents that the great bulk of the Zulu army was indeed assembled at oNdini and being ritually prepared for war.[30] The king was using the opportunity to review his *amabutho* to ascertain their casualties, and to gather the notables of the kingdom around him for consultation on the best means of prosecuting the war. Dabulamanzi and Mavumengwana, who had been directing the blockade of Eshowe, were among them.

There was another reason besides consultation on military matters why Cetshwayo had summoned his *izikhulu* and all the *abantwana*: Hamu had finally defected to the British in early March, and it was necessary to be assured of the loyalty of the rest of the Zulu leadership. Indeed, Hamu's defection had been a real blow to morale. It was a matter to be mentioned only in whispers, for it was perceived among the Zulu as portending the break-up of the kingdom.[31]

When all Zulu defections up to the end of January are taken into account, they must be seen to be of limited significance. Dunn's flight had been the most serious, though Sekethwayo's, had it not been foiled at the last moment, would have been nearly its equal. As it was, those who had surrendered (Dunn excepted) were merely *izinduna* with limited followings, and only noncombatants had given themselves up with them. Nevertheless, the British continued to pin much hope on Hamu's promised defection. Yet he was not a free agent. At the outbreak of war he was at oNdini, held there by the king as a hostage for his adherents' cooperation in the struggle. Even so, Hamu contrived to pursue his negotiations with the British. Through his chief *izinduna*, Ngwegwana and Nymubana, who were still in his district, he exchanged secret messages with Wood, plaintively reaffirming his loyalty to the British and asking for advice on how to escape from oNdini. Simultaneously, he continued to treat with the

Swazi king regarding sanctuary should he flee Zululand. The British at last decided to aid him openly by convincing the Swazi that if any of Hamu's cattle should be driven across their border for safety they should be looked after, as Hamu was not to be considered a hostile belligerent.

Throughout early February Cetshwayo and Hamu were reported to be regularly quarrelling over responsibility for the war. Then at last, reportedly at Mnyamana's urging, Hamu managed to slip away from oNdini. Cetshwayo sent after him with a gift of cattle in a vain attempt to appease him. On 17 February two messengers from Hamu arrived at Khambula, urgently desiring Wood's aid in bringing Hamu and his wives to safety. For on hearing that Hamu was making for the British lines, Cetshwayo had despatched an *impi* in pursuit (made up of Mandlakazi and ukuBaza), which had captured some of his cattle and wagons and was also apparently committing atrocities against Hamu's adherents. It seems Mbilini also made an attempt to intercept Hamu, but was too late. Eventually, the harried Hamu took refuge across the Phongolo in Swaziland, whence he was escorted by a British patrol to Khambula, arriving there on 10 March 'in a most awful state of funk'.[32] Over the next few days his adherents continued to trickle into camp, until they finally numbered about 1 300. The fighting-men were drafted into an existing unit known as Wood's Irregulars, while the noncombatants, including Hamu and his many wives, were located near Utrecht.[33] Some of his adherents, trying to join him there, were massacred by the king's *impi*; and as late as May Ngwegwana, his chief *induna*, reported that forces placed by the king at the drifts across the Phongolo had prevented repeated attempts by some of Hamu's leading *izinduna* and other adherents to escape. Furthermore, to punish these would-be defectors, the king sent men during March and April to help themselves to their mealies and grain stores, while Mnyamana seized the greater part of Hamu's cattle south of the Phongolo on behalf of the king (though he retained them for his own use). Cetshwayo and his chief *induna* succeeded between them in stripping the district bare, so contributing to bitter animosities that were to manifest themselves in civil war in the 1880s.

North-western Zululand, where Wood's raiding continued so effectively to demoralize the inhabitants, and which had witnessed Hamu's defection, seemed the region most likely to be detached from its loyalty to Cetshwayo.[34] Sekethwayo's allegiance had only been secured by threat of force, and to the king's concern the Mdlalose chief was steadfastly refusing to attend him at oNdini. Significantly, Msebe kaMadaka, a second cousin of Cetshwayo's and an *induna* of the Qulusi, disheartened by his people's plight, began to consider defection. On 22 February, while Hamu was attempting to make his escape, he let the prince know that he too wished to join the British but, being a cautious man, and in fear of retaliation by those Qulusi who remained loyal, wanted to wait until Hamu had successfully led the way. However, Mahubulwana kaDumisela, a senior *induna* of the Qulusi, foiled Msebe's plans. Mahubulwana informed the king that Msebe, as well as Mcwayo kaMangeda, another Qulusi *induna*, were in contact with Hamu and in league with the British. Furious, Cetshwayo ordered their deaths, but spared them on the intercession of Mhlahlo kaKhondlo, a Qulusi *induna*, and instead placed them under surveillance. However, the consequences of their intended treason were grave for their adherents. The hostility of loyalist Qulusi forced them to quit their *imizi*, and to take refuge in caves until their eventual surrender to the British in August.

With such developments in mind, Major H. Spalding of Chelmsford's headquarters staff optimistically pronounced in early March that Zululand appeared 'to be breaking into fragments'.[35] However, he was reading too much into the implications of the defections and incipient civil war of north-western Zululand. Mnyamana's loyalty might be reported suspect, but there was clearly never any probability of his following Hamu's example,[36] and his adherents had been active in attempting to foil the latter's flight. Nor was it likely that Zibhebhu would defect at that stage, despite suggestions by Hamu's adherents that he was contemplating such action.[37] Even so, defections (especially Hamu's) and incipient disloyalty were undoubtedly causing consternation among the Zulu leadership gathered at oNdini.

It was not automatic that the king and his councillors would sanction a major new offensive, even though the army was being mustered in response to Chelmsford's accelerating military preparations. However, the apparently desirable diplomatic alternative was exploited with neither haste nor great vigour, possibly because it never really seemed feasible. Only on 1 March did two of the king's messengers cross the Thukela and deliver the king's message to his old friend, Bishop Hans Schreuder, at his mission station, kwaNtunjambili, near Kranskop. In substance, the king begged the

British to withdraw their forces from Zululand and to resume talks on a peaceful settlement.[38]

In making this new overture, Cetshwayo probably did not comprehend that *au fond* the British were not prepared to negotiate.[39] On 17 January Chelmsford had laid down that any further Zulu emissaries must communicate with him only, and that no overtures would be considered which were not 'preceded by . . . the unconditional acceptance of all demands [set out in the ultimatum] as before notified'.[40] Consequently, the British response to the king's latest feeler was harsh. Chelmsford straightforwardly dismissed Cetshwayo's protestations, and Frere was unprepared to accept anything less than Cetshwayo's unconditional surrender and the general disarmament of the Zulu people. Nor was the High Commissioner ready to consider any message that did not come in a form to 'bind' the king.[41] Yet the British were always quite prepared to seize any advantage created by the Zulu willingness to treat, and accordingly coolly spun out negotiations in order to gain time to complete their plans for a renewed offensive.

Cetshwayo's messengers had returned from kwaNtunjambili with 'long faces' to report,[42] but the king and his assembled advisers decided to persevere in their negotiations. On 22 March two emissaries delivered the king's message at Middle Drift, but were coldly received and sent back with a reminder of the terms of the ultimatum. To British officials, aware that the king and his council were at that very moment planning the coming campaign, Zulu messengers could not be other than spies. Thus when on 23 March two additional messengers from the king approached Fort Eshowe, instead of being accorded the traditional sanctity they expected to enjoy as emissaries, they were clapped into irons as spies.[43]

The king and his council, apparently undeterred by these rebuffs, and at the very moment when they were reaching the decision to renew the offensive, chose to despatch fresh messengers to the middle Thukela border. Perhaps, after the consistently uncompromising British responses to his earlier feelers, the king was simply pursuing his diplomatic initiative without any real hope of the outcome. But, whatever his purpose, the simultaneous despatch of fresh emissaries and his armies on campaign inevitably reinforced the existing British conviction that all Zulu messengers must be spies. Consequently, when on 28 March (the very day the battle of Hlobane was fought) three messengers appeared at Middle Drift they were instantly sent under strict guard to Fort Cherry. One of these messengers was Johannes, a Christian convert from Schreuder's eNtumeni mission; the other two, Mfunzi and Nkisimana, were elderly and respected messengers of the king, who over the preceding six years had been sent on many important missions to the Natal government. Although ignominiously treated as spies, and detained in Fort Buckingham pending the successful relief of Eshowe, their message was dignified: Cetshwayo saw no reason for the war against him and asked the Natal government to appoint a place at which a peace conference could be held. But the launching of the Eshowe Relief Column and the Zulu offensive against Wood had already ruled out such a possibility.

Besides once wishing to exploit British disarray after Isandlwana to reopen peace negotiations, Cetshwayo had naturally hoped that his victory would have impressed the neighbouring black chiefdoms. Perhaps, should negotiations have failed and the war regained its momentum, they would have been encouraged to come to his aid. Certainly, the British distinctly feared that Isandlwana had provided the signal for an uprising of all the black chiefdoms around, and would spark off a rebellion among the discontented Transvaal Boers.[44] But, if Cetshwayo had entertained any hopes in this regard, he was disappointed here as well. His diplomatic feelers succeeded only in alarming the British and, despite reports of contacts with Griqualand West and Kuruman, the Pondo, Sotho, Pedi and even the Ndebele of Lobengula, nothing at all came of them.[45] Even British precautions against communication between Cetshwayo and the Natal border population proved unnecessary, for there was never any likelihood of his being able to incite them to rebellion. By the time the king had assembled his council in March, it was clear that the Zulu would have to undertake any further fighting against the British quite alone.

The major upshot of the great assembly of March was the decision to resume the war with the utmost vigour. In response to the pleas of the hard-pressed Qulusi, the main Zulu army mustered at oNdini was to be sent against Wood at Khambula while the warriors already in the vicinity of Eshowe were to be reinforced against Chelmsford's relieving column. There was indeed no alternative remaining other than capitulation. Any of the hopes entertained during the post-Isandlwana lull of a negotiated end to the war had had to be abandoned. And in its readiness to fight on alone to maintain its independence the Zulu nation was demonstrating its essential cohesiveness and continuing loyalty to the king – despite the defections and incidences of disloyalty, and some initial reluctance among the *amabutho* to muster again after the gruelling first round of battles.

Notes

1 See CSO 691, no. 1344/1879: Fannin to Colonial Secretary, 7 February 1879.

2 For a summary, see WO 32/7717: Chelmsford to Secretary of State for War, 2 March 1879.

3 *BPP* (C. 2374), enc. in no. 9: Wheelwright to Colonial Secretary, 30 January 1879.

4 P. S. Thompson, 'Captain Lucas and the border guard: the war on the lower Tugela, 1879', in Laband and Thompson, *Kingdom and Colony*, p. 172.

5 Laband and Thompson, *Umvoti*, pp. 23–4, 35–41.

6 Laband and Thompson, *Buffalo Border*, pp. 58–61.

7 CSO 1926, no. C18/1879: Fynn to Colonial Secretary, 3 February 1879.

8 Bonner, *Swazi State*, pp. 152–3.

9 WC II/2/2: Chelmsford to Wood, 3 February 1879.

10 CP 9, no. 30: memorandum, MacLeod to Wood, 24 February 1879.

11 TS 38: Rudolph to H. C. Shepstone, 16 February 1879: statement of Ncagyama.

12 *BPP* (C. 2260), no. 10: statement of Ucadjana, 3 February 1879.

13 See CP 9, no. 19: Buller to Military Secretary, 1 February 1879; Woodgate's Military Diary: 1 February 1879.

14 All this captured livestock had to be disposed of in a regular fashion to prevent freebooting. Consequently, it was either sold to the commissariat or auctioned off in Natal and the Transvaal.

15 TS 38: Rudolph to H. C. Shepstone, 16 February 1879.

16 CP 8, no. 49: Bishop Schreuder's report, 10 February 1879.

17 See Laband, 'Mbilini', pp. 194–8, for the Phongolo region during February and early March 1879.

18 For the Ntombe engagement, see ibid., pp. 198–9.

19 CSO 1926, no. 1185/1879: Fannin to Colonial Secretary, 23 February 1879; AC, p. 79: J. N. Crealock to H. H. Crealock, 2 March 1879.

20 Vijn, *Cetshswayo's Dutchman*, pp. 40–1.

21 CSO 1926, no. C19/1879: statement by Unxakala and Udhlozi, 4 February 1879; *BPP* (C. 2374), enc. in no. 9: statement by Fokazi and Umpothlo, 7 February 1879.

22 CP 7, no. 32: Fynney to Law, 8 March 1879; Webb and Wright, *Zulu King Speaks*, p. 33

23 WO 32/7730: Pearson to Military Secretary, 9 April 1879.

24 Reminiscent of the aftermath of Isandlwana, on one occasion the Zulu carried away the beard of the soldier they had killed (Colenso and

Colenso, *Digest*, series 1, part 2, p. 615).

25 'If you come and eat our pumpkins, we'll come into Eshowe and drink your coffee' (Norbury, *Naval Brigade*, p. 246).

26 WO 32/7730: Pearson to Military Secretary, 9 April 1879.

27 Colenso and Colenso, *Digest*, series 1, part 2, p. 616: Native account of the doings of the Coast Column.

28 Norris-Newman, *In Zululand*, pp. 150–1; Norbury, *Naval Brigade*, pp. 257–8, 260–1; Wynn, *Memoir*, pp. 53–4; Lloyd, 'Defence of Ekowe', p. 24.

29 See CP 14, no. 8: L. H. Lloyd, Political Assistant: report of three spies, 24 March. Submitted by Wood to Military Secretary, 27 March 1879.

30 AC, p. 81, Crealock no. 15: J. N. Crealock to Alison, 15 March 1879.

31 CSO 1926, no. 1346/1879: Fannin to Colonial Secretary, 3 March 1879. For the following account of the defection of Hamu, see Laband, 'Zulu polity', p. 10.

32 TS 39: H. C. Shepstone to T. Shepstone, 23 March 1879.

33 Some 947 of Hamu's cattle, which the Boers across the Phongolo and the Swazi had taken, were returned to him in batches between March and June 1879.

34 See Laband, 'Zulu polity', pp. 10–11, for Qulusi defections.

35 WO 32/7715: Diary of Operations, 10 March 1879.

36 CSO 1927, no. 2702/1879: Fannin to Colonial Secretary, 30 May 1879.

37 CP 9, enc. in no. 37: MacLeod to Wood, 1 March 1879.

38 CSO 1926, n.n.: Fannin to Colonial Secretary, 1 March 1879.

39 For Anglo–Zulu negotiations during March 1879, see J. P. C. Laband, 'Humbugging the general? King Cetshwayo's peace overtures during the Anglo–Zulu War' in Laband and Thompson, *Kingdom and Colony*, pp. 49–52.

40 *BPP* (C. 2252), no. 20: Lord Chelmsford's Order of 17 January 1879.

41 *BPP* (C. 2318), enc. 2 in no. 9: Frere to Chelmsford, 3 March 1879.

42 FC 2/5: Fannin to his wife, 10 March 1879.

43 Still in irons, they were brought into Natal after the relief of Eshowe, and only released in early April after interrogation by Lord Chelmsford.

44 Littleton Papers, no. 91: Littleton to Ciss, 14 February 1879.

45 See Monteith, 'Sekhukune', pp. 149–51, who has noted and discussed all these contacts.

8

The turning-point

'We are the Boys from Isandhlwana!' shouted the Zulu forces as they advanced against Khambula camp, known to them as inqaba kaHawana (or Hawana's stronghold).[1] They were then still buoyed up with their spectacular victory earlier in the war, but their rout on 29 March at Wood's hands was the turning-point of the Anglo–Zulu War. The Zulu defeat had the effect of raising British spirits by demonstrating that the Zulu warriors were not, after all, invincible; while the high morale of the Zulu army was irreparably affected in the four hours of desperate fighting. Word of its flight and heavy casualties 'shook the country',[2] and King Cetshwayo instantly grasped that from that moment there could be no doubt as to the inevitable outcome of the war.

After the Isandlwana disaster, a mood of extreme caution had prevailed among the British. The Ntombe debacle of 12 March had only reinforced their determination never again to be caught unprepared by the Zulu. Chelmsford had consequently resisted marching to the relief of Eshowe until sufficient reinforcements had arrived, and enough transport had been assembled, to allow him to do so with confidence. He did not expect to relieve Eshowe unopposed, however, and believed the bulk of the Zulu army to be concentrated near kwaGingindlovu. He thus considered it necessary to create some diversions in order to draw off elements of the force facing him and to secure his flanks.

The forces guarding the Natal bank of the Thukela were accordingly put to positive use, and ordered to mount a number of raids and demonstrations.[3] Major A. C. Twentyman, the commander of the Greytown garrison, began his demonstration on 24 March, and raided across the middle Thukela on 2 and 3 April.[4] Because of the swollen state of the river only small forces could be ferried across. Little damage was done except to burn a few *imizi*, including that of

Mabedla kaManqondo, the Magwaza *induna* opposite Middle Drift whose men had been involved in the border incident of September 1878 which had provided one of Frere's *causi belli*. Just how much of a diversion they created in favour of Chelmsford's advance is debatable. The Zulu moved themselves and their cattle out of range, but were sufficiently provoked to threaten retaliatory raids once the opportunity offered. As prophesied by Sir Henry Bulwer, who had always feared the consequences of militarily activating that stretch of border, a cycle of raid and counter-raid had been created. Downstream, in Defensive District VI, Captain G. A. Lucas demonstrated at the drifts from 27 March, but could attempt no serious crossing because the river was too high.[5] His show of force consequently did no more than frighten the Zulu along the opposite bank into temporarily abandoning their *imizi* and fleeing with their livestock into the hills. Whether this succeeded in distracting or confusing the Zulu to the front of the Eshowe Relief Column is open to doubt. At Rorke's Drift Major W. Black led an extended patrol 16 km into Zululand without encountering any Zulu, and obviously without creating any sort of diversion worth the name.[6]

Meanwhile, Wood (whom Chelmsford had given *carte blanche* to take any diversionary action he considered suitable) decided to raid Hlobane, the Qulusi stronghold and cattle depot. He intended thereby to tie down the local irregulars and prevent them from reinforcing the army Cetshwayo was expected to despatch against Chelmsford. Conversely, he also hoped to draw off a portion of the force blockading Eshowe. In doing so, he discounted the intelligence (which was to prove only too accurate) that the Zulu intended to move with their fullest strength against Khambula, and to place only secondary forces to face Chelmsford.

During March Cetshwayo had summoned his army to reassemble at oNdini. Men of all *amabutho* were called up, except those living in the coastal strip, who were to oppose Chelmsford. By the third week of March the full army was present at oNdini, though it was not expected to move off for another week on account of the need for some units still to be ritually prepared for war.[7] A spy reported to the British that the army was made up as follows: thirty *amaviyo* of the uMcijo *ibutho*; forty of the iNgobamakhosi; twenty of the uMbonambi; forty of the uNdi corps[8] (uThulwana, iNdlondlo and iNdluyengwe *amabutho*); twenty of the uNokhenke; 30 of the uDloko; and thirty of the uNodwengu corps (uDududu, iMbube and iSangqu *amabutho*). That is, a total of 210 *amaviyo* or about 17 000 warriors, if the average number in an *iviyo* is taken at eighty. On the march they were to be reinforced by local units, especially the Qulusi *ibutho* and irregulars. The Qulusi strength was estimated by the spy to stand at between thirty-five and forty *amaviyo*, thus making a combined force of probably about 20 000.[9] This total was reasonably corroborated by the testimony of Zulu prisoners interrogated after the battle.

As for the actual Zulu units involved, a degree of uncertainty also persists, despite the spy's apparent precision in this regard. This is attributable to the fact that while most *amabutho* were present in almost their full strength for the Khambula campaign, varying elements were absent operating against Chelmsford. What is certain is that this army was at least as large as the one sent against Isandlwana, and that all the crack *amabutho* were present.

More than any other engagement of the Anglo–Zulu War, Khambula was King Cetshwayo's own. He himself gave the most minute instructions to his commanders on how to attack, on what ground to occupy, and on what dispositions they were to make. After planning the battle so carefully, he never dreamed, as he was subsequently to admit, that it could result in defeat.[10]

Fully conscious of the folly of storming prepared positions, Cetshwayo ordered that no entrenchments were to be attacked, but that his army should 'seize the camp cattle and so draw the white men away from their wagons and tents'.[11] If the Zulu army nevertheless failed to lure Wood's force into the open, it was to pass on into Transvaal territory and, by threatening white farms, Utrecht and Wood's line of supply, was to force the British out in their defence. This strategic objective was the consequence of the 'inflating conviction' the Zulu evolved after Isandlwana that any numerically overwhelming Zulu force must crush the British in the open field.[12]

Yet, considering Cetshwayo's apparently clearly expressed orders, it is a matter of some puzzlement why Wood's spy reported on the eve of the battle that he had been informed by the warriors of the advancing army that the king's instructions had been to attack and sack Wood's camp, as they had done at Isandlwana.[13] Perhaps this intelligence reflected the potentially disastrous gap between Cetshwayo's and his generals' perception of British preparedness on the one hand, and on the other the unrealistic expectations of the ordinary warriors, which were to lead them on the day of the battle to their fatal disregard of their commanders' orders.

The Zulu army set off from oNdini on 24 March. It advanced north-west by forced marches, covering the ground somewhat faster than in the Isandlwana campaign. From the fact that the corpses of several of the Zulu who had managed to penetrate Wood's laager during the course of the battle were found with their hands and mouths full of food taken from the British cooking pots, it has been assumed that the Zulu marched without provisions in the expectation that they would eat when the British camp fell into their hands.[14] It was normal, however, for a Zulu army to live off the land after the first day or so as it advanced. Moreover, in the case of the Khambula campaign, the supply of food had become more plentiful with the advance of the season than it had been at the time of Isandlwana, and the warriors were probably better fed and in better condition than on the earlier campaign. This apparent contradiction regarding provisioning is resolved when it is noted that on the day of the battle itself the Zulu army, which had been on the move since early morning, had not stopped again to eat, intending to do so once it had taken the camp.[15]

On the afternoon of 27 March Wood's Irregulars, scouting beyond Hlobane, saw smoke and fires to the east, which they correctly assumed to be the camp fires of a Zulu army. They refrained, however, from commenting on them to the white mounted troops with them (to whom the camp fires were equally visible), as they had long since learned that their words were never heeded.[16]

Unaware, therefore, of the near presence of the Zulu army, Wood proceeded with his plans to raid Hlobane, where shortly before nearly 2 000 cattle had been seen grazing under the mountain. At 3.30 a.m. on the misty morning of 28 March, Buller and 675 men started to scale the eastern slopes of Hlobane, while the 640 men of Lieutenant-Colonel John Russell's force moved from the west on to the adjoining Ntendeka Mountain. The plan was that Russell's column would create a diversion, and draw the defenders away from the eastern side of Hlobane, where they were concentrated, as well as creating the impression that the attackers were more numerous than they actually were.[17]

The steep slopes of Hlobane culminate in a belt of sheer cliffs, at the foot of which is a jumble of huge slabs of rock, the gaps and crevices between them forming a kind of cave system. This terrain provided the perfect opportunity for the Qulusi and Mbilini's men on the mountain – who were variously estimated at up to nearly 3 000 strong, though the number may have been as small as 500 – to ambush the British struggling up the difficult path. Despite the Zulus' cleverly laid trap,[18] Buller led his men in skirmishing order through a heavy cross-fire with relatively few casualties (five dead) and gained the summit. Although dismayed at the extent of the grassy plateau and the task before him, Buller extended his force and advanced west across the mountain top. Brushing aside the sniping Zulu, his men rounded up all the cattle that they could find on the southern side of the plateau (about 2 000 of them), and only halted when they reached the precipitous Devil's Pass at the western extremity. From there they exchanged hot fire with the Zulu, who had built their huts under the krantzes on the north-western side of Hlobane.[19]

The British were pleased with their progress, but the Zulu on Hlobane, who knew an army was approaching from oNdini – indeed, they had been expecting it since dawn and were dismayed that it had not yet arrived as arranged[20] – were drawing Buller into a trap. For when at 9 a.m. Buller began to call in his scattered detachments preparatory to descending with his booty, resistance began steadily to stiffen in order to hamper his withdrawal until the Zulu army had appeared in support. Increasing numbers of Zulu mustered on the higher ground of the northern side of the plateau, and harassed the British as they began to fall back across the summit. It was then, between 10 and 11 a.m., that Buller beheld an awesome sight. A great Zulu army was rapidly advancing on Hlobane from the south-east like the shadow of a dense cloud across the grassy plain, its horns thrown out either side of the chest in traditional order of battle. The British would naturally never have gone up Hlobane if they had credited the main Zulu army to have been so close.[21] Now, their first priority was to get down the mountain again as quickly as possible, not only to save themselves, but for fear that the Zulu army might move directly on Khambula and its depleted garrison.

The Zulu commanders had planned initially to advance on Khambula past the southern flank of Hlobane, but cognizance of the situation on its summit caused them to change direction in support of the Qulusi and Mbilini's people.[22] In the event, it was not necessary for the army to move up the mountain. It proved sufficient to detach an *ibutho* (either the uMcijo or the iNgobamakhosi)[23] to cut off in the plain many of Buller's force whom the defenders harried down the mountain in their precipitate retreat. Indeed, panic overcame Buller's men as the Zulu on the summit determinedly closed off their flight eastwards and forced them down the almost sheer Devil's Pass to the west.[24] Those horsemen already in the plain, as well as those who managed to get down the eastern side of Hlobane, were engulfed by the Zulu army. Russell's force on Ntendeka withdrew as rapidly as it could, in its haste giving little support either to Buller's horsemen or to the black auxiliaries who were doing their best to bring in the captured cattle. These auxiliaries succeeded in saving about 300 head from recapture, but were most indignant at the way in which the white troops had abandoned them.[25]

The British fell back in disorder on Khambula, leaving fifteen officers and seventy-nine men dead behind them, as well as over 100 of their black levies. The Zulu took no prisoners, and killed even the officers, despite Cetshwayo's orders to bring a few back to oNdini for interrogation.[26] The heavy British casualties can be attributed, besides other factors such as the difficult terrain, panic and Zulu ruthlessness, to far more rapid and accurate Zulu marksmanship than in the past. In accounting for this, the British were probably right in supposing that the Zulu had more rifles than in previous encounters, some possibly being the spoils of Isandlwana and Ntombe. Yet the skill of the Zulu irregulars of north-western Zululand should not be discounted, for Hlobane was their preferred type of running battle, waged on their terms.

Buller acknowledged the British debacle on Hlobane as 'a bad day', such as he hoped never to see again.[27] Others vehemently agreed. Indeed, there is little doubt that had it not been for the great British victory at Khambula the following day, which drew a veil over the Hlobane disaster, both Wood's and Buller's reputations would have been seriously damaged. As it was, the only redeeming feature for the British about the Hlobane affair – which had been an undoubted Zulu victory – was that by diverting the main Zulu army it may have delayed its assault on Khambula for a day, thus giving the garrison time to concentrate and prepare. For, rather than continuing far on its march, the Zulu army decided to encamp for the night on the banks of the White Mfolozi, near Nseka Mountain (Tinta's Kop).

Consequently, despite their defeat on Hlobane, the British remained in a strong position. It was axiomatic that in the 'small wars' of the colonial period the advantage always lay with the

European armies of regulars. This was especially so if they were able to maximize their superior armaments and discipline by selecting and fortifying their own ground, and inducing their opponents to forgo their one advantage of superior mobility by mounting a frontal attack on their prepared position.[28] In this particular case, the outcome of the campaign hinged on whether the Zulu were successful in drawing the British into the open, as the king had intended; or whether, by a combination of circumstances, they decided to take the unfavourable gamble of directly assaulting the camp. The latter alternative was indeed foolhardy, for Khambula camp was strong and well prepared, manned by a force armed with breech-loading rifles, supported by artillery, and with an almost unlimited supply of ammunition.

According to the official account, Wood had under his command 2 086 officers and men. The infantry consisted of eight companies of the 90th Light Infantry (711 men), and seven companies of the 1/13th Light Infantry (527 men). The mounted force, under the command of Lieutenant-Colonel Buller, was made up of one squadron of Mounted Infantry (99 men), four troops of the Frontier Light Horse (165 men), two troops of Raaff's Transvaal Rangers (135 men), and troopers of Baker's Horse (ninety-nine men), the Kaffrarian Rifles (forty men), the Border Horse (sixteen men), the Mounted Basutos (seventy-four men), and a local commando of Dutch Burghers (forty-one men). There were also fifty-eight of Wood's Irregulars remaining, the rest, as with many of the Boers, having decamped after Hlobane. In addition there were eleven Royal Engineers and the 110 men of No. 11 Battery, 7th Brigade, Royal Artillery, with their six seven-pounder guns.[29]

This garrison had few preparations still to make, for every man had long been allotted his duties and place behind the defences. The key to the position was an elongated earthwork redoubt on a narrow ridge of tableland. In it were placed two of the guns. The redoubt was connected to the main wagon-laager 20 m below and 280 m behind it by the four remaining guns. The wheels of the wagons of the laager were chained together, each wagon-pole was lashed to the wagon in front, and sods were thrown up under the wagons to form a rampart. Bags of provisions were placed along the outside buckrails of the wagons, with regular interstices for firing through. Below the redoubt and to its right was a smaller wagon-laager, connected by a palisade, into which the force's 2 000 cattle were crammed. Its right outer edge, and that of the main laager, stood on the edge of a rocky ravine, affording any assailant a considerable amount of cover. To the left of the position the ground sloped gently away, giving a much better field of fire. The main force was stationed in the laager, with small garrisons in the redoubt and the cattle-laager. All points around the camp had been carefully measured and range markers set up to aid the accuracy of the defenders' fire.[30]

Such preparations minimized the ability of the Zulu ever to come close enough to the British defences to employ their traditional method of hand-to-hand fighting. Sheer courage and weight of numbers might prevail, but at the cost of fearful casualties. Yet once they had determined to attack a fortified position, the Zulu seem not to have contemplated any form of attack other than variations of the mass charge. This is not to say that other methods were impossible, especially as a large portion of the Zulu coming against Khambula were equipped with firearms of some sort. Most of these, as is confirmed by an analysis of the firearms captured by the British during the battle, were of very inferior quality. Muzzle-loaders predominated (as at Isandlwana and Nyezane), and were mainly Tower muskets and Enfield rifles. Of the 325 firearms taken, only fifteen were breech-loaders. One of these was a Snider carbine marked as belonging to the Royal Artillery, and the other fourteen had belonged either to the 24th or to the 80th Regiments, showing that they had been captured either at Isandlwana or Ntombe.[31] The likely reason why more of these prized breech-loaders were not recaptured at Khambula is that whenever the possessor of one was disabled, it was immediately taken over by one of his comrades.

It was most fortunate for the British that on the whole the possession of these firearms did not substantially change Zulu tactics. The likely reason was that the Zulu had little reason to set particular store by them, as their wild and ill-aimed fire had little apparent effect. Thus while at Khambula they subjected the British to heavy fire, their poor marksmanship (as usual, they generally aimed too high) meant that their own men on the far side of the laager – rather than the British within – were often the victims.[32] The few British casualties suffered mainly high scalp wounds, all except two being from Martini-Henry fire. It is possible to speculate what the cumulative effect might have been had the Zulu been content to harass the camp with long-range fire. As it was, firearms were (as at Isandlwana) only allowed to play a subordinate harassing role to the mass charge.

When the morning of the 29 March dawned, it was clear that much would depend on the ability of the Zulu commanders to conform to the strategy laid down by their king, and to resist pressure from their warriors to adopt the traditional tactic of the mass frontal assault.

Chief Mnyamana, the commander of the army, had the direction of the campaign as a whole. However, it was as a statesman, rather than as a general, that he had made his considerable mark. His presence at the head of the army was thus an indication of the king's personal concern with the conduct of the campaign. Rather than Mnyamana, it would be Chief Ntshingwayo who would lead the army into actual battle. He was a general of considerable personal renown, and had been the senior commander at Isandlwana. Nevertheless, it was Mnyamana who, as commander-in-chief, formed his men into the traditional circle at their bivouac on the White Mfolozi in order to harangue them.[33] According to the testimony of Mpatshana kaSodondo, who was a member of the iNgobamakhosi *ibutho*, Mnyamana's eloquence had an unsettling effect. Doubtless only too conscious of the consequences to the kingdom of the outcome of the campaign, he allowed it to become apparent that he was 'unduly apprehensive and fearful of the results'. So, while stirring up the *impi* to 'burn like a fire', he also left it in a state of alarm.[34] It is no longer known what he actually said, though it must be presumed that, although ordering an advance on the British camp, it was to carry out the king's strategy, and not to mount a direct assault.

The British were forewarned of the Zulu advance. Information came from one of Hamu's men who had been fighting with Wood's column since his chief's defection in early March. To save himself at the battle of Hlobane, he had divested himself of his British insignia and had attached himself to his old *ibutho*. He had marched with them as far as the White Mfolozi, when in the early morning he gave his unsuspecting comrades the slip. He fell in with a patrol of Raaff's Transvaal Rangers, who sent him back with his intelligence to the camp. He told Wood that the *impi* was already on the march, and accurately conjectured that it would attack the camp at 'dinner time'.[35]

Commandant Raaff's reconnaissance brought him to the edge of the eZungwini plateau, and when the morning mist lifted at about 10 a.m. he saw the Zulu army cooking its meal on the banks of the White Mfolozi and a tributary stream (where Vryheid now stands), only a few kilometres north of their overnight bivouac near Nseka Mountain. At 11 a.m. Raaff reported that the Zulu army was advancing north-west against the British camp some 19 km away. Wood immediately called in all outlying units and prepared to meet an assault. The Zulu army made its approach in five principal columns at considerable intervals. As their line of advance tended to the west, Wood feared that his intelligence had indeed been faulty, and that the Zulu (in accordance with Cetshwayo's strategy) actually intended to march on Utrecht, whose citizens had begged him in vain to garrison their town against such an eventuality. But when the Zulu army reached the hills some 6 km south-east of the camp, it halted. There it stayed in its dense masses for over an hour, in full sight of the anxious British garrison, who could only wait for the Zulu council-of-war to decide on its next move. The British became aware that a decision to attack the camp had finally been reached when the Zulu army began to deploy, moving slowly and deliberately so as to conserve the warriors' energy for the struggle ahead.[36]

The Zulu centre stayed where it was, while the left horn resumed the march in column in the direction of Utrecht, until at about 1 p.m. it wheeled to the right and began a rapid advance on the camp, halting about 5 km away. The right horn, meanwhile, which had further to go, spread out to the north of the camp, where it halted about 2.5 km away, just out of range of the guns.[37] A portion of the army was detached to secure about 200 of the camp cattle which had not been rounded up in time and had strayed. Wood estimated that when fully deployed the Zulu front stretched for over 16 km,[38] and a nervous young officer confided to his mother that 'the whole country round was black with the enemy and it seemed as if these legions would swamp us completely'.[39] The Zulu warriors, poised to charge, had discarded their ceremonial and distinctive regalia for the battle, and wore nothing besides their loin-covers and necklaces of charms and medicine wood.

Why had the Zulu commanders decided to launch an attack on the camp, despite the king's instructions to the contrary? Mpatshana later claimed that when it came to the point Mnyamana lost control of his army and that it took up position by itself.[40] There are indications that the commanders were overruled by the young men when they came in sight of the camp. For as the king himself complained, the success of the previous day at Hlobane had greatly elated the warriors, and the prospect of the small and apparently vulnerable British position convinced them that they had another easy victory in their grasp.[41] Moreover, they were greatly encouraged when at 12.45 p.m., dinner being over, Wood ordered that the tents be struck and the men take up their battle-posts. The Zulu took this sudden striking of the tents as a sign that the British were preparing for immediate flight, and abandoned whatever remaining hesitations they had about attacking the camp.

Expecting to be attacked by the Zulu left, which had been the most active in its deployment, the British were surprised when the Zulu right horn suddenly broke from its stationary line into column, and began to advance at a tremendous pace. This movement persuaded some of the British onlookers that it must be the Zulu strategy to refuse their left, and by feinting with their right to draw some of the British defenders into the broken and difficult ground of that salient, so weakening the camp for a subsequent blow from the Zulu left. A far more likely reason, however, for this premature movement by the right horn, which was in closer striking distance of the camp than was the left, lay in the intense rivalry between the crack *amabutho* of the two wings. Hamu's adherents explained to the British that there was a dispute as to whom belonged the honour at Isandlwana of being second among the British tents after the uMbonambi: the iNgobamakhosi or the uMcijo. It had thus apparently been agreed that when the army came upon Khambula the other *amabutho* would look on while the iNgobamakhosi of the right horn, and the uMcijo of the left, settled the issue by vying to be first into the camp.[42]

Possibly, though, this was a rationalization by the Zulu of what actually occurred. Mehlokazulu made the suggestion that the iNgobamakhosi only advanced as they erroneously thought that the rest of the army was in position to attack.[43] But whatever the cause, the advance of the Zulu right horn was a godsend for the British. It was a standard manoeuvre in 'small wars' against troops whose discipline was not so tight as that of the British to attempt to draw part of the opposing force into a premature and uncoordinated attack, thus weakening the remainder and throwing it off balance. This was best achieved through a feint attack or simulated retreat.[44] When Wood saw the forward movement of the Zulu right horn at 1.30 p.m., he immediately sent out Buller and two squadrons of his mounted men to egg it on into a fully committed but unsupported attack on the camp.

Buller's force rode out of the main laager when the Zulu were just over a kilometre away.[45] Clouds of Zulu skirmishers, fed by supports and reserves, preceded the main body of the right horn. Buller led his force to within good rifle range, and ordered it to dismount and open fire. The sight of this puny body of some hundred men was too much for the mettle of the over 2 000 iNgobamakhosi, who swept forward determined to overrun it, their skirmishers falling back, to reveal the more solid line of the dense column. Buller's men remounted, fell back, dismounted and fired again, repeating the operation with great precision and coolness, drawing the iNgobamakhosi on with complete success. That the Zulu did not comprehend the purpose of Buller's manoeuvre is borne out by the comments they later made, denigrating the 'mounted redcoats' who were 'very much afraid, and quickly cried and ran away'.[46] As it was, they taunted Buller's men, calling out, 'Don't run away Johnnie; we want to speak to you!'[47]

Buller's action rapidly drew the iNgobamakhosi to within the distances previously marked for artillery practice, and the guns opened fire at 1.45 p.m. The artillery did not do the damage it was anticipated it would because the Zulu were able to take advantage of the cover afforded by some broken terrain between the flats and the camp.[48] But when the right horn came to within nearly 300 m of the camp, it was checked by the accurate rifle fire of the 90th Light Infantry and the enfilading fire from the redoubt. Finding this fire quite untenable on the open ground, the iNgobamakhosi were eventually forced to fall back to the cover of some rocky outcrops to the north-east of the camp.

The luring on and subsequent repulse of the Zulu right horn, all within the space of three-quarters of an hour, was a brilliant success for the British. It helped disrupt Zulu strategy, for the intention of the right horn must surely have been to complete a flanking movement along the left of the British position, eventually to join up with the less advanced Zulu left horn, and so completely surround the camp. Such at least were classic Zulu battle tactics. But Buller's sortie deflected the right horn from its purpose, while its repulse and the devastating blow to its morale ensured that it made no further effort to outflank the camp. Instead, it was content to keep up fire on the British from the rocky ledges to which it had retired. The result was that for the remainder of the engagement the left and rear of the British position remained unsurrounded and unthreatened, freeing the garrison to face the unsupported Zulu onslaught from the opposite quarter.[49]

As the attack from the Zulu right dwindled away, the heavy masses of the left and centre began at about 2.15 p.m. to develop their own belated assault. The centre moved against the south-eastern side of the redoubt, while the left, taking advantage of the cover provided by the steep ridge on the south side of the laager, assembled in the dead ground to attack the position from that direction. Mnyamana, as was the usual custom with high-ranking Zulu officers, did not come under fire, but watched the battle (which was presumably occurring despite his instructions or intentions) from a hill about 5 km away. The actual direction of the day's operations devolved upon Ntshingwayo, who was seen to take up position at about 2.30 p.m. about 650 m from the camp, and to remain there under cover of a low hill until his men retreated.[50] This unusual action by a senior commander – which could only have encouraged his troops – was an indication of the vital importance the Zulu put on this battle.

The British who witnessed the waves of the assault could not but admire the Zulus' striking courage under fire, their 'dash, elan and fearlessness'.[51] Despite the effects of the artillery in particular, which drove great roads through their ranks, they closed up and came on, keeping to a steady trot. This is not to say that the Zulu were utterly foolhardy, and did not make use of whatever cover was offered. But they had to cross the numerous small streams which form the headwaters of the White Mfolozi, and to traverse at least 700 m of open ground commanded by the defenders' fire. The left horn could make for the ravine on the right flank of the camp and take cover there, though when they charged out of it they faced the concentrated fire from the laager at a distance of less than 100 m.[52] The chest and right horn had to take what little cover they could in the open ground, though the centre could utilize the partially obliterated remains of Wood's previous camp, which he had been forced to abandon on sanitary grounds. Sihlahla, a member of the uMxhapho *ibutho*, admitted that he took cover behind a large white marker stone placed by the British,[53] and others were reported to have carried large stones on their heads, which they threw down to shelter behind.

Yet there was inevitably a limit to what even the brave Zulu could stand. The destructive effect of artillery shells on whole groups was particularly disheartening, especially as they could not be easily dodged, despite every effort. There were certainly moments when heavy and accurate fire paralysed Zulu movements and sowed panic. As has been seen, the iNgobamakhosi were demoralized by such fire and had eventually to fall back to the shelter of the rocky outcrops. The other horn and the chest who came on after them were 'literally mowed down'[54] until they too had to retire. This is not to denigrate the extraordinarily courageous endeavour of the Zulu army. As Trooper Mossop put it, assaulting a prepared position defended by modern artillery and rifles with spears and inadequate firearms amounted to attacking it with bare hands.[55] And the marvel is that there was even a moment when it looked as if the left horn might carry the laager. Yet the nightmare quality of this desperate effort was expressed in the shocked comment of some Zulu after the battle who, doubtless having seen the pets kept by the British garrison, swore that among the defenders were dogs and apes 'clothed and carrying firearms on their shoulders'.[56]

The sustained attack of the Zulu centre and left, although ultimately unsuccessful, was extremely determined. It went through several phases. To the British onlookers, the as yet unengaged units of the Zulu army seemed to be resting and taking food while the right wing was being repulsed. Then, with a great rattle of shields and spears, they poured down the slopes opposite the centre and right of the camp in a series of great waves and, keeping as much as they could to the shelter of the bed of the little stream in the dead ground along the right flank of the camp, finally charged up in successive lines to assault the British position. The main body remained concentrated in the dead ground, evidently waiting to make a decisive rush once the first waves had gained a foothold on the defences. The uNdi corps, and notably the uNokhenke *ibutho*, succeeded in getting into the cattle kraal, and eventually drove out the garrison of one company of the 1/13th. From the vantage of captured wagons they opened fire on the main laager. Encouraged by this success, a column of about 1 000 to 1 500 Zulu (evidently the uMbonambi) formed up west of the cattle kraal for an assault on the main laager. Wood saw some thirty *izinduna* exhorting their men, while their commander waved them on with a red flag.[57] To meet this crisis, Wood ordered two companies of the 90th under Major Hackett to counter-attack with the bayonet. This force marched out as if on parade, and took the Zulu greatly by surprise. Their unexpected and determined advance down the slope between the two laagers broke up the Zulu concentration, forced the warriors to abandon the advantage they had previously gained, and to retire sullenly to the cover of the stream bed and to sheltered positions to the right and left of Hackett's force. Once sufficiently down the slope, Hackett's men opened fire, supported by case-shot from the artillery. Fire from the redoubt and the guns also swept the cattle laager, making it untenable for the Zulu.

The two companies of the 90th were then in their own turn forced to retire on the main laager, for the Zulu caught them in a most telling cross-fire, kept up by marksmen armed with Martini-Henry rifles positioned in the vacated huts of Wood's Irregulars, and behind the camp's refuse dump 330 m away. At much the same time, Wood was obliged temporarily to withdraw a company of the 1/13th posted at the right rear of the main laager because of the Zulu enfilading fire. The fact that this fire inflicted almost all the most serious casualties of the day on the British shows what the Zulu might have achieved with proper use of their weapons, and with tactics other than the frontal assault. In the end, the British cleared the huts of the Zulu posted there with artillery fire, while they flattened the rubbish-dumps with volleys of rifle fire. Sixty-two dead Zulu were found behind them the next day. Almost simultaneously with Hackett's sortie at about 3 p.m., a company of the 1/13th was also constrained to advance out of the south-west corner of the main laager to drive off a dense mass of the Zulu left horn with the bayonet. This was the uMcijo *ibutho* whose impetuous rush came near enough for them to grasp the rifles of the defenders.[58] Altogether, it was a most critical moment for the main laager, for a wagon had to be removed for the sortie, and when the company retired, fresh Zulu who had been in support rushed forward to try and seize the gap.

The temporarily successful Zulu attack on the cattle-laager, followed by the two effective British sorties, marked both the limit of Zulu success and the turning-point of the battle. Henceforth, the advantage lay with the defenders.

There followed, nevertheless, some two further hours of fierce Zulu attacks at different points of the camp. At one time the Zulu came almost within grasp of the Artillery horses, which were kept outside the redoubt in the open between it and the laager; while at another they came right up to the very trenches along the right flank of the redoubt. At 4.30 p.m. the Zulu switched the focus of their attack away from the south of the British position, and made a second attempt at the north and north-east faces. Simultaneously, the iNgobamakhosi from the position among the rocks where they had retired earlier, and elements of the uNdi corps from the shelter of the remains of Wood's previous camp, charged the British position. But they came again under a heavy cross-fire at about 300 m from the laager and redoubt and, enfiladed by the guns, had to retire.[59]

By about 5 p.m. it was obvious to the British that the Zulu attack was at last beginning to slacken. Within half an hour, as the sun began to go behind the ridge to the west of Khambula camp, it became evident that the Zulu had finally accepted that they could not take the position, and that they were preparing to retire. Noting this, Wood at 5.30 p.m. ordered a company of the 1/13th to clear the cattle-kraal, where some Zulu still crept among the oxen they had been unable to remove. He advanced a company of the 90th on its right to the edge of the krantz in front of the cattle-laager, where it first pushed the Zulu back with the bayonet, and then poured a heavy fire into the Zulu in the stream-bed below. Everywhere the Zulu were now falling back, at this stage 'in the most orderly and leisurely style', while a great cheer from the defenders rang in their ears.[60]

The Zulu, however, were not to be allowed to retire with impunity in their own time. As the garrison poured its fire into the retreating masses, and the guns discharged canister-shot, the bugles sounded to horse, and every mounted man in the laager started in hot pursuit. One of the chief functions of cavalry is to complete a victory by turning an orderly retreat into a rout leading to the dispersal of the enemy.[61] This the mounted men at Khambula achieved with complete success. Three columns under Buller's command dashed upon the demoralized Zulu. With nearly 16 km of open country before them, with a couple of hours before darkness remaining, with fresh horses and with a quarry already on the point of exhaustion, the slaughter was awful. The carnage lasted for more than two hours. It was after 9 p.m. before the last of the mounted men returned to camp, having followed the Zulu up to the foot of eZungwini Mountain, when night saved the fugitives.[62]

Once their flight began in earnest the Zulu seemed to lose their capacity to resist, and in their own words the British horsemen 'turned them about as if they were cattle'.[63] It seems Mnyamana made some attempt to rally his men and to persuade them to take advantage of the fact that the British were at last in the open. But Chief Zibhebhu, one of his senior commanders and a man of great military reputation, dissuaded him, pointing out that the rout, once begun, was irreversible.[64] Indeed, the exhausted Zulu were soon unable to move faster than at a walk, and were too dazed even to fire in their own defence. That the Zulu were 'completely done up'[65] was only to be expected, considering the prodigious physical and emotional effort they had been called on to make since early morning. It is not to be wondered at, therefore, that in their flight they were 'falling down in every direction',[66] that some tried to simulate death or to creep into hiding places such as antbear holes, reeds or long grass. But the British infantry and their black auxiliaries scoured the immediate neighbourhood of the camp and killed as many of those hidden away as they could find. There are reports of some of the fugitives begging on their knees for their lives, but most met their death with silence and valiant stoicism, some turning to expose their chests to their pursuers, others just standing waiting to be shot. It was reported that some, sooner than die at British hands, stabbed themselves.[67]

It is well that most of the flying Zulu expected no quarter (they usually gave none themselves), for they received none. Their pursuers were out to avenge Isandlwana and Hlobane only the day before, and as Major D'Arcy of the Frontier Light Horse exhorted his men, 'No quarter, boys, and remember yesterday!' He reported that they heeded his words, 'butchering the brutes all over the place'.[68] They shot them down at only 10 m to 15 m range, and lamented the lack of sabres for more efficient killing, as shooting Zulu when they became exhausted took too much time. Many therefore made do with captured spears, using them as if 'giving point' with the sabre, and thereby also economized on ammunition. Schermbrucker saw Buller 'like a tiger drunk with blood',[69] a condition he doubtless shared with many of his men.

Harried mercilessly, it was inevitable that the Zulu army should fall into great disorder and begin to break apart in various directions. The general line of flight was eastwards towards eZungwini Mountain, and the main body continued on in the direction of Hlobane, though smaller groups broke off to the north and west. Strong elements remained on Hlobane for the next few days, not fully evacuating it until 3 April, but the main force withdrew towards the south-east. Most did not return to oNdini to report to the king as was customary, but, considering themselves thoroughly beaten, mainly dispersed to their own homes, despite the efforts of the *izinduna* to keep them together. To Mnyamana's entreaties they replied quite simply that they had had enough. The unhappy Mnyamana had to be content to go on with only the fraction of his defeated army which consented to stay by him to inform Cetshwayo of the disaster which had befallen the forces under his command.[70]

The extent of the losses which the Zulu army had suffered is a matter of some debate. Certainly, the British did not take over-many prisoners. They were not inclined to spare many in the heat of the pursuit, while their black auxiliaries were in the habit of killing all the wounded they found as a matter of course. The survival of any of the wounded at all was the consequence of Wood promising the auxiliaries the reward of a 'stick' of tobacco for each prisoner they brought into the camp. Those prisoners whom Wood himself interrogated he released in the direction of eZungwini Mountain. The badly wounded received medical attention and were put in the care of the auxiliaries, who were rewarded with an ox to slaughter at the end of the week.[71]

These prisoners were the lucky few. The alternative of death or flight was the option for the great majority. Yet how many Zulu did die in the battle or as a consequence of the wounds they had received? Their losses were undoubtedly out of proportion to those suffered by the British. For, considering the length and intensity of the engagement, these were light: eighteen NCOs and men killed, eight officers and fifty-seven NCOs and men wounded. It is true that three officers and seven men subsequently died of their wounds, and that a considerable number of unrecorded casualties occurred among the black non-combatants in the camp. Compared with these low figures, the official British estimation put the Zulu losses at 'nearly 2,000'.[72] Captain Woodgate reported 785 dead Zulu (some horribly mutilated by shell-fire) collected in the two days following the battle,[73] though the work continued for some days more, and further bodies were brought in. The Zulu corpses were buried 750 m outside the British lines in large pits, described as being 60 m long, 6 m broad, and 3 m deep. Wagon load after wagon load of bodies were deposited in them.[74] Yet the Zulu dead were collected only within a 2 km radius around the camp, and because the Zulu had done their best to keep under cover when assaulting the camp, fewer dead were found in its proximity than the British had anticipated. The ground in the direction of their rout, on the other hand, was thickly strewn with bodies. On the line of pursuit which he had followed, Captain D'Arcy the next day counted 157 bodies. It was also his significant reflection that there were 'hundreds and hundreds of them some miles off, that are being eaten by dogs and vultures'.[75] Indeed, for months afterwards patrols were coming across Zulu corpses at great distances from the battlefield.

This surely is the crucial point when estimating the number of Zulu casualties. The battle had taken place in one of the more sparsely inhabited parts of the Zulu kingdom, so the wounded had to press on to find succour, and had no means of travelling the often great distances to their homes except by foot. British scouts near Hlobane reported that in the retreating *impi* nearly every two men carried a wounded comrade between them,[76] but there was a limit to how long they were prepared to do so, or how long the wounded man could survive. A month after the battle patrols along the line of the *impi's* retreat found various bodies buried head-first in antbear holes, each covered with a shield. In the end, it seems that only the walking wounded ever reached their homes. Of these, it is unrecorded how many subsequently died.

It is therefore impossible to arrive at an accurate casualty figure based on the number of bodies found near the British camp. That is why the British had to estimate, and why the Zulu had to do so as well. What is clear, though, is that the Zulu felt the casualties they had sustained at Khambula were at least comparable, if not greater, than those suffered at Isandlwana. However, as King Cetshwayo himself pointed out, there is the difficulty that at Isandlwana the Zulu were left masters of the battlefield and could realize the extent of their losses, which they were unable to do at Khambula. He consequently did not consider a comparison really valid.[77]

No one could quibble, though, over the devastating impact of the Zulu losses on the kingdom as a whole. Natal Border Police were awed to hear the terrible sounds of lamentation coming from the Zulu homesteads near the confluence of the Mzinyathi and Thukela rivers, a region where almost the whole male population had been called up for the Khambula campaign, and in which they had suffered badly. Two of the most important chiefs of the region, Godide of the Ntuli and Manqondo of the Magwaza, were both reported to have lost a number of sons.[78] What made it worse was that it was the flower of the army which had died, the young men of the crack *amabutho*. Those burying them in the pits near Khambula noted their fine physiques and the fact that few wore the head-ring of the married man.[79] It seems those *amabutho* which suffered the greatest casualties in the attack on the camp were, in order of their loss, the uMbonambi, uNokhenke and iNgobamakhosi.[80] The Qulusi, who were less disciplined, lost most heavily in the rout. Among the dead were a great many *izinduna*, more than in any other battle of the war. For, as the king commented, they 'exposed themselves a great deal, attempting to lead on their men'[81] – a fact Wood had noted. Men of the highest status among the dead included the king's own cousin, Madlangampisi kaThondolozi, two sons of Mnyamana, and the sons of various other important chiefs and royal councillors,[82] such as Godide and Manqondo, mentioned above.

King Cetshwayo was understandably furious with his army for its defeat and dispersal. He attached particular blame to its commander, Mnyamana, for not following his instructions and allowing a frontal attack on Wood's prepared position.[83] The extent of the king's displeasure was not sufficient, though, to decide Mnyamana to take refuge with the British; nor for the king to carry out his original intention of executing the commander of the iNgobamakhosi for permitting the crucial unsupported attack of his men.[84] As for the warriors themselves, although they had finally learned the basic lesson that it was hopeless to attack laagers or otherwise fortified posts, they were still prepared to fight the British if they could be brought into the open, and were apparently still determined to continue the war in the hope that they would be able to do so. The king laboured under no such hopes or illusions. Although his warriors would not confess themselves beaten, the battle of Khambula had taught him that he could no longer win the war in the field, and that his only salvation still lay in negotiations with the British – if they would consider entering into them after their decisive victory.[85]

Notes

1 D. C. F. Moodie (ed.), *The History of the Battles and Adventures of the British, the Boers and the Zulus in Southern Africa*, Sidney, Melbourne and Adelaide, 1879, p. 290. For a detailed account of the Khambula campaign, see J. P. C. Laband, 'The battle of Khambula, 29 March 1879: a re-examination from the Zulu perspective', in Laband and Thompson, *Kingdom and Colony*, pp. 80–110.

2 SNA 1/1/34, no. 73: statement of Sibalo, 1 June 1879.

3 See Laband, 'Border levies', pp. 154–8.
4 See Laband and Thompson, *Umvoti*, pp. 47–51.
5 See Thompson, 'Border guard', pp. 172–4.
6 See Laband and Thompson, *Buffalo Border*, p. 63.
7 CP 14, no. 9: report by Lloyd, submitted by Wood to Military Secretary, 27 March 1879; Webb and Wright, *Zulu King Speaks*, p. 33.
8 This was a British term for a number of *amabutho* all attached to the same *ikhanda* and known collectively by its name.
9 TS 39: H. Shepstone to T. Shepstone, 30 March 1879.
10 *Natal Colonist*, 20 September 1879: report by *Natal Mercury* correspondent on the march with the king to the coast.
11 SNA 1/1/34, no. 85: statement of Sihlahla, 3 June 1879.
12 CP 8, no. 49: Schreuder to Chelmsford, 10 February 1879.
13 Woodgate's Military Diary: 29 March 1879.
14 See E. D. McToy, *A Brief History of the 13th Regiment (P.A.L.I.) in South Africa*, Devonport, 1880, p. 53.
15 Zulu War File no. 3, KCM 53791: Trooper C. Hewitt (Frontier Light Horse) to his sister Annie, 3 January 1920.
16 TS 39: H. Shepstone to T. Shepstone, 30 March 1879.
17 Schermbrucker, 'Zhlobane and Kambula', p. 342.
18 'Umbilini did a very crafty thing on top of that mountain' (Magema's statement in Vijn, *Cetshwayo's Dutchman*, p. 127: Colenso's notes).
19 Buller Papers, WO 132/1: Buller to AG, 30 March 1879; Moodie, *British, Boers and Zulus*, pp. 271–2, 279, 283.
20 Woodgate's Private Diary: 21 April 1879. Apparently Mbilini was later to blame Mnyamana for not arriving at daybreak to surround Hlobane as arranged.
21 TS 38: Piet Uys Jnr's statement, 29 March 1879.
22 Apparently the clear voices of the defenders of Hlobane carried to the army below, acquainting them with the situation.
23 It is quite possible that elements of both *amabutho* were involved.
24 G. Mossop, *Running the Gauntlet*, London, 1937, p. 61; Moodie, *British, Boers and Zulus*, pp. 280, 284–5.
25 Schermbrucker, 'Zhlobane and Kambula', pp. 346–7.
26 Wood, *Midshipman*, vol. II, p. 55 (note).
27 Buller Papers, WO 132/1: Buller to AG, 30 March 1879.
28 Callwell, *Small Wars*, pp. 90–1, 279–81.
29 War Office, *Narrative*, p. 161.
30 Wood, *Midshipman*, vol. II, p. 59; War Office, *Narrative*, p. 79; Schermbrucker, 'Zhlobane and Kambula', p. 376; Norris-Newman, *In Zululand*, p. 163.
31 Woodgate's Military Diary: 30, 31 March 1879.
32 E. Clairmonte, *The Afrikander: A Plain Tale of Colonial Life*, London, 1896, p. 106.
33 Woodgate's Military Diary: 29 March 1879.
34 *JSA* III, p. 314: testimony of Mpatshana.
35 The informant has been identified as Mbangulana, an *induna* of Hamu (Gibson, *Story of the Zulus*, p. 197).

36 *Natal Colonist*, 10 April 1879: Kambula correspondent, 31 March 1879.

37 The maximum range of the seven-pounder was 2 790 m.

38 Emery, *Red Soldier*, p. 176: Wood to Sir A. Horsford, 6 April 1879.

39 Slade Papers: Slade to his mother, 29 March 1879.

40 *JSA* III, p. 314: testimony of Mpatshana.

41 Webb and Wright, *Zulu King Speaks*, p. 33.

42 TS 39: H. Shepstone to T. Shepstone, 30 March 1879; Mitford, *Zulu Country*, p. 278: testimony of Warrior of the Tulwana.

43 Vijn, *Cetshwayo's Dutchman*, p. 114: Mehlokazulu's testimony.

44 Callwell, *Small Wars*, pp. 228–30.

45 Not all the mounted men were stationed in the main laager during the battle. Wood had permitted the Mounted Basutos under Maj. Cochrane to fight in their own fashion outside the camp, hovering on the extremes of the Zulu horns, harassing them whenever possible.

46 Vijn, *Cetshwayo's Dutchman*, p. 38.

47 Montague, *Campaigning in South Africa*, p. 263. The Zulu had picked up this term for the British from the Sotho.

48 Shrapnel fired by seven-pounders had in any case little effect because of the low muzzle velocity of the guns and the small bursting charge of the common shell.

49 Buller Papers, WO 132/1: Buller to AG, 30 March 1879.

50 CP 14, no. 21: Wood to DAG, 3 April 1879.

51 Schermbrucker, 'Zhlobane and Kambula', p. 378.

52 The edge of the ravine was just 200 m from the wagons, and because of the rapidly falling ground there were only 100 m of clear fire.

53 SNA 1/1/34, no. 85: statement of Sihlahla, 3 June 1879.

54 McToy, *13th Regiment*, p. 51.

55 Mossop, *Running the Gauntlet*, p. 75.

56 Vijn, *Cetshwayo's Dutchman*, p. 38.

57 Wood, *Midshipman*, vol. II, p. 61.

58 Moodie, *British, Boers and Zulus*, p. 286: correspondent to *Cape Argus*; Schermbrucker, 'Zhlobane and Kambula', p. 379.

59 Ashe and Wyatt Edgell, *Zulu Campaign*, p. 142.

60 Norris-Newman, *In Zululand*, p. 164.

61 Callwell, *Small Wars*, pp. 172, 211.

62 Buller Papers, WO 132/1: Buller to AG, 30 March 1879.

63 SNA 1/1/34, no. 73: statement of Sibalo, 1 June 1879.

64 Vijn, *Cetshwayo's Dutchman*, p. 37.

65 Moodie, *British, Boers and Zulus*, p. 275: correspondent to a Natal newspaper.

66 *Natal Colonist*, 10 April 1879: Kambula correspondent, 31 March 1879.

67 McToy, *13th Regiment*, p. 52.

68 Moodie, *British, Boers and Zulus*, p. 279: Capt. C. D'Arcy to his parents.

69 Emery, *Marching over Africa*, p. 65: letter by Schermbrucker, 1 May 1879.

70 SNA 1/1/34, no. 73: statement of Sibalo, 1 June 1879; SNA 1/1/34, no. 85: statement of Sihlahla, 3 June 1879; Vijn, *Cetshwayo's Dutchman*, pp. 36–7.

71 Wood, *Midshipman*, vol. II, pp. 67–8.

72 War Office, *Narrative*, p. 81.

73 Woodgate's Military Diary: 30, 31 March 1879.

74 Schermbrucker, 'Zhlobane and Kambula', p. 380.

75 Moodie, *British, Boers and Zulus*, p. 278: Capt. D'Arcy to his parents.

76 *Natal Colonist*, 24 April 1879: Kambula correspondent, 2 April 1879.

77 Webb and Wright, *Zulu King Speaks*, pp. 36–7.

78 CSO 1926, no. 1939/1879: Fannin to Colonial Secretary, 9 April 1879.

79 *Natal Colonist*, 10 April 1879: Kambula correspondent, 31 March 1879.

80 SNA 1/1/34, no. 73: statement of Sibalo, 1 June 1879; SNA 1/1/34, no. 85: statement of Sihlahla, 3 June 1879.

81 Webb and Wright, *Zulu King Speaks*, p. 37.

82 Woodgate's Military Diary: 30, 31 March 1879; CP 14, no. 21: Wood to DAG, 3 April 1879.

83 SNA 1/1/34, no. 85: statement of Sihlahla, 3 June 1879.

84 Vijn, *Cetshwayo's Dutchman*, p. 115: Mehlokazulu's testimony.

85 *Natal Colonist*, 25 September 1879: Cetshwayo's comments taken from the *Cape Times*.

9

The battle of Gingindlovu

When Cetshwayo and his council resolved to send the main Zulu army against Wood at Khambula, they also decided to reinforce the forces already in the vicinity of Eshowe with more men raised locally, or with the coastal elements of *amabutho* sent back from oNdini. On 2 April this army attempted valiantly but unsuccessfully at Gingindlovu to halt Chelmsford and the Eshowe Relief Column. In one sense, its effort was a vain one, for the battle of Khambula had already been fought, and the war effectively lost. Nevertheless, had it succeeded in defeating Chelmsford, it is probable that the course of the war would have changed once again, and a negotiated peace might have become a real possibility.

The garrison at Eshowe saw daily evidence during the last week of March of a growing Zulu concentration. Large bodies of Zulu filed down the distant hills towards the Nyezane, and their cooking fires multiplied in its valley. It appears that the Thembu lineage head, Somopho kaZikhale, senior *induna* of the emaNgweni *ikhanda*, chief gunpowder manufacturer and armourer to the king, and his close personal friend, commanded the forces bivouacked along the Nyezane. These were reported to have been made up of 3 000 irregulars mainly from up the coast in the region of St Lucia Bay, and of 1 500 local members of *amabutho* connected with the burnt kwaGingindlovu *ikhanda*.[1] Dabulamanzi continued to direct the 1 000 local warriors centred on eNtumeni who were keeping an eye on the fort. North of Eshowe, 3 000 warriors made up of elements of the iNgobamakhosi, uMcijo, uNokhenke and uMbonambi *amabutho* were barracked at the Hlalangubo *ikhanda* (the old oNdini), and 1 500 of the iNdluyengwe were at the isinPuseleni *ikhanda* near by. They would seem to have been jointly commanded by the tall and broad-shouldered Sigcwelegcwele kaMhlekehleke, a royal *induna* and favourite, proud commander of the iNgobamakhosi and Ngadini lineage head; and by the large and handsome Phalane kaMdinwa of the Hlangezwa with his ornaments of beaten brass about neck and ankles, and his 50 mm-long nails (white as ivory), who was *induna* of the royal Hlangezwa section. Once Chelmsford marched, this force of 10 000 would concentrate and fall upon his column.

On 28 March the Eshowe Relief Column advanced across the Thukela into Zululand.[2] John Dunn rode with the column to organize effective forward reconnaissance and advise on laagering procedures, for the General was determined to rectify the deficiencies that had led to the Isandlwana disaster. Dunn, who knew the country well, also suggested a route closer to the coast which, by going for most of the way through open terrain, would reduce the danger of ambush. On 29 March the British formed an entrenched laager at the Nyoni River. Thus far, nothing had been seen of the Zulu except signal fires burning on the hills, but reports of Zulu movements on 30 March suggested they were concentrating to oppose the invaders. Chelmsford therefore decided to devote all of 1 April to crossing the swollen amaTigulu River with every precaution and to laager just beyond. His care was apparently justified, for the Zulu were reported to be in force and to have crossed the river upstream of the British, threatening their left rear. But the Zulu in the vicinity had been directed to 'sit still' for the moment, and are said to have contented themselves with smoking dagga *(Cannabis sativa)* while the British crossed.[3] Meanwhile, Major Barrow and some of the mounted men pushed on some 19 km towards the Ngoye Forest, close to the Mlalazi River. They saw only small bodies of Zulu, but on the way burned the *umuzi* of Makwendu kaMpande, the king's half-brother, and six other *imizi*. The following day the mounted men patrolled 10 or 13 km inland towards Eshowe, seeing a good many Zulu in the distance.[4] Their patrols were of importance, however. They effectively shrouded the movements of the column from the Zulu scouts, so that the Zulu were left unsure of its strength and movements.

On 1 April the column marched to within 2 km of the Nyezane stream, just south of the kwaGingindlovu *ikhanda*. The undulating and boggy country was covered with very high grass, broken by clumps of palm and undergrowth, which could provide excellent cover for the Zulu. On either side of the Nyezane there was a belt of bush and high reeds. John Dunn selected the best position available for the camp on the summit of a slight knoll. The wagon-laager was made 117 m square so as to give sufficient room inside for the 2 000 oxen, 300 horses and 2 280 black troops. The 3 390 white troops would advance during combat to the enclosing shelter-trench, which was 144 m square and about 13.5 m in front of the wagons. The corners, which were always the weakest sectors of a square, were reinforced by nine-pounder guns, Gatling guns and rocket tubes. Darkness fell before it was possible to cut down the tall grass and bush that came up to 100 m of the laager, which were to afford the Zulu welcome cover on the morrow. A heavy thunderstorm in the late afternoon and rain during the night made conditions in the crowded and sodden camp most uncomfortable and sleep impossible.

The British were anticipating an attack. Pearson had signalled soon after the column had encamped that a large force of Zulu was on the march towards the Nyezane.[5] Scouts had seen columns of smoke in the afternoon rising from the Zulu bivouacs across the Nyezane, and during the night pickets reported numerous camp fires on the hills to the north. Although that night there no longer appeared any immediate danger of attack, tension rose, and at midnight Chelmsford ordered the shelter-trench to be strengthened. It must have been with relief that the British stood to their arms at 4 a.m., the customary hour before dawn. At about 6.15 a.m. the sun rose, breaking through the heavy morning mists. Since earliest dawn an hour before, the mounted scouts and picquets had already been out, and at 5.45 a.m. reported that the Zulu were advancing to the attack.

It made sense that the Zulu should attack the Relief Column at some distance from the fort, for they must have been aware of the danger of being taken in the rear by the garrison.[6] The position of the British, camped out in the open plain, was an added inducement for the Zulu to attack them there, using their traditional enveloping tactics, which they felt the broken terrain at the battle of Nyezane had disrupted.[7] Some time had been required for the various Zulu forces bivouacked about Eshowe to concentrate, and there is evidence that not all arrived in time for the battle.[8] The more seasoned *amabutho*, who had been in the vicinity of the old oNdini, only reached the main Zulu camp in the hills some 8 km north of the Nyezane on the evening of 1 April.[9] It was too late then to probe the British position, and they were in any case tired and hungry. Some of the commanders wished nevertheless to mount an attack immediately, but Dabulamanzi reportedly persuaded them to delay until morning, by which time they would have eaten and rested.[10]

The Zulu commanders identified by British intelligence at the end of March as being in the vicinity of Eshowe all seem to have been present, including two of the commanders at the earlier battle of Nyezane – Masegwane and Mbilwane – as well as Sintwangu, a chief of a section of the Cele. Mavumengwana was clearly also there, and has sometimes been described as having been in command, as has Dabulamanzi. It seems plain, nevertheless, that the commander-in-chief was Somopho, and that all the others, including Sigcwelegcwele and Phalane, were his lieutenants.[11] There is lack of clarity regarding the composition and size of the Zulu army at Gingindlovu, though here again the intelligence reports of the Zulu concentration around Eshowe provide the best guide. Since only coastal elements of the *amabutho* are known to have fought at Gingindlovu, while the main elements marched against Khambula, it is probable that almost all *amabutho* were represented, though some by stronger contingents than others.[12] What does seem certain is that local irregulars, especially the Tsonga and neighbouring peoples of north-eastern Zululand, made up a substantial part of the army.[13] From prisoners' statements Chelmsford estimated the Zulu numbers, including the reserves who never came into action, to have consisted of no more than 11 000 men.[14]

At almost exactly 6 a.m. on Wednesday 2 April the Zulu on the far side of the Nyezane, and on top of Misi Hill to the west of the laager, came in sight of the British. The clouds of skirmishers which masked their advance drove in the British pickets and mounted scouts. The British, however, were quite ready for the rapidly developing attack. The ammunition boxes were open, the shelter-trench was manned two-deep, and the tops of the wagons had their load of riflemen. In contrast to Isandlwana, the British were in the ideal formation for repelling a traditional Zulu onslaught. And it was soon apparent that the Zulu were intent on repeating their usual tactics, which were first to surround the enemy before pressing home their attack.[15] A strong Zulu column divided and crossed the Nyezane, the left division (or left horn) advancing at the north-east corner of the laager, and the right (or chest) at its northern face. Meanwhile, a somewhat weaker column (or right horn) emerged from the bush to the north of Misi Hill and deployed, so that one part confronted the western face of the

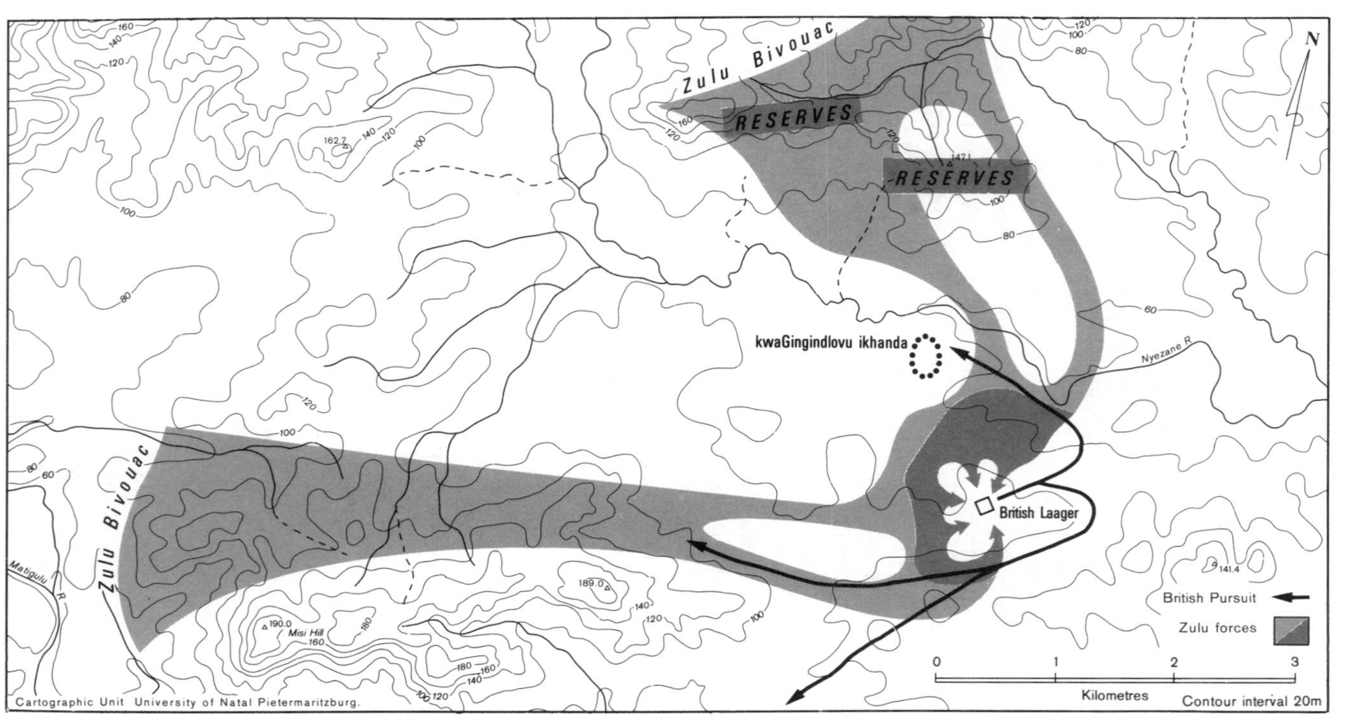

4 Gingindlovu, 2 April 1879: a typical Zulu attempt to storm a prepared British position

laager, and the other the southern. All the columns deployed in open order at the double, so that within ten minutes of their first being sighted they were formed in the classic crescent shape around three sides of the British position. Reserves waited on the hills beyond the Nyezane, while the large body of women and boys carrying food for the army stayed safely away near Eshowe.[16]

Contrary to British expectations, the Zulu did not wear ceremonial dress, but were generally stripped for action to their loin-covers, as they had been at Khambula.[17] What impressed the British enormously was the rapidity and courage of the Zulu attack – and its professionalism. For once the enveloping Zulu crescent was in position, most of the Zulu broke into three distinct lines, and advanced skirmishing towards the laager in knots and groups of between five to ten men, creeping up under cover of the anthills, bushes and long grass in splendid, disciplined style, keeping up a brisk but inaccurate fire the while, the puffs of smoke alone revealing their positions. The British noted with relief the characteristically poor Zulu marksmanship.[18] This could be partially attributed to the inefficient muzzle-loaders carried by most, which fired bullets, old pieces of iron and stones high over the heads of the British. The few casualties they inflicted (two officers and eleven men killed, four officers and forty-four men wounded – of whom one was killed and four wounded in the subsequent mounted pursuit)[19] were mainly caused by the sprinkling of modern rifles in their possession.[20]

The attack of the Zulu left horn and centre on the north-eastern and northern perimeter of the laager developed a little before the more hesitant one of the right horn on its western and southern flanks, where the terrain afforded less cover. The engagement was begun by the Gatling guns at 1 000 m range, and when the Zulu closed to within 400 m or 300 m the firing on both sides became incessant. With cries of 'They are encircled!' and 'uSuthu!' the Zulu tried to close in,[21] but despite several desperate charges never succeeded in approaching nearer than within 20 m of the north-east corner of the laager. For even with their extraordinary courage – 'brave to madness'[22] – they were unable to break through the wall of fire set up by the massed rifles, Gatling guns, artillery and rockets. Inevitably too, as they converged on the entrenched laager, their concentrations became denser, and thus more vulnerable. In their grim determination they ceased to shout, and doggedly held their ground, taking cover behind their fallen comrades. But now they were in range of the marksmen on top of the wagons, and subjected to a double tier of fire. No troops in the world could long have stood such punishment. As Sub-Lieutenant Smith-Dorrien put it, 'The poor Zulus hadn't a ghost of a chance.'[23]

This is not to say that the British fire was as effective as it should have been. Many of the soldiers, especially the younger recruits who lacked training and steadiness, had never before been under fire, and were nervous and excited.[24] Their behaviour contrasted adversely with the disciplined Naval Brigade. Yet even among the more experienced soldiers there was a dearth of good marksmen, which meant that independent firing was wasteful of ammunition and only controlled volley-fire had an effect. Even so, volley-fire was not properly suited to stop an enemy rapidly advancing in skirmishing order, and it is clear that the rifles were on occasion incorrectly sighted and were firing high.[25] If the shooting of the soldiers was frankly disappointing, that of the rockets and guns seems to have been little better. Only the Gatlings, serviced by the Naval Brigade, were handled really successfully. During the battle 1 200 rounds were fired from the Gatlings, and about forty rounds of case and shrapnel from the nine-pounders. The average shot fired per regular soldier was 6.2 (compared to the 6.4 to 7 at Ulundi); while the average for the whole force including irregulars was 10. This figure was the normal average for pitched encounters in 'small wars',[26] and shows why, for all its relative ineffectiveness, the British zone of fire was too hot for the Zulu to penetrate.

At 6.40 a.m., when the Zulu chest attacking the northern face of the laager could stand the concentrated fire no longer, and began to retire into the long grass, Chelmsford ordered out the 120 Mounted Infantry and Natal Volunteers under Major Barrow to keep them on the run. But the Zulu quickly recovered from their momentary loss of nerve, and closed round to cut Barrow off, forcing him to fight his way back into the laager.[27] The chest then executed a change of front, and with perfect discipline circled to their right to reinforce the left division of the Zulu right horn attacking the laager's western face. Meanwhile, at 7 a.m., the right division of the right horn was just beginning its assault on the rear, or southern, face of the laager. This was to prove the most determined and furious of the whole day. The Zulu were erroneously encouraged by the presence of the NNC inside the rear of the laager to believe that there were not enough British soldiers to man the entire position, and that the southern face must consequently be less strongly held than the others. Dabulamanzi on horseback directed this final effort, and he suffered a flesh wound above the left knee as he urged his men on from the thick of the fight.[28]

However, this attack stalled like the others before the impenetrable British fire, and the demoralized Zulu began to retire to the low ground below the rear of the laager. Chelmsford then directed Barrow and his mounted men, including the Mounted Natives (about 280 men in all), to move out of the laager's unengaged eastern face and open fire on the Zulu right horn's eastern flank. Barrow's sortie was enough for the wavering Zulu to give up their last hopes of taking the laager. After standing for a few moments and firing at the mounted men, they gave up the effort and commenced their retreat. Seeing them turn, the NNC advanced out of the laager at 7.15 a.m. in pursuit, though the regular troops were ordered to remain in position lest the Zulu flight be a feint designed to break their formation. Part of Barrow's force charged the Zulu flank with drawn sword, quite breaking its morale and turning its withdrawal into a rout. In their efforts to escape, the Zulu abandoned weapons and accoutrements. Though some Zulu turned pluckily at bay, most who could not get away threw themselves down without any attempt to resist, to be speared by the NNC who followed up the charge. Barrow's men pursued the Zulu for about 2 km towards Misi Hill, and some kilometres southwards towards the amaTigulu River. The other part of Barrow's force wheeled north to pursue the Zulu who were retiring from the front of the laager, and followed them up towards the kwaGingindlovu *ikhanda*, driving them through the flooded Nyezane.[29]

The two large bodies of Zulu reserves on the hills beyond the Nyezane retreated when they saw the army put to flight. Fire from the nine-pounder guns dispersed a considerable number of the right horn who, thinking they had gone far enough to be out of danger, had rallied on Misi Hill. After this bombardment, the Zulu made no further attempt at a stand, but dispersed north and west.[30] Long lines of dispirited warriors were seen from Fort Eshowe trekking away northwards along the coast country to the Mlalazi River, where they halted for a while before breaking up. Some elements seem later to have rallied further north in the Mhlatuze valley to oppose a possible British advance, but they were the exception. Those who lived further away returned to their homes, while the men of the Eshowe region took refuge with their families and cattle in the Nkhandla and Ngoye forests.[31]

Because the Zulu army at Gingindlovu was routed and rapidly dispersed, it had no means of assessing its casualties. The British, on the other hand, took what amounted to a sportsman's interest in their bag. Chelmsford reported that 471 Zulu had been buried within 900 m of the laager, and that another 200 dead had been found near the scene. These, and the great number of horribly mangled dead found lying in awful positions within a radius of 8 km, led him to estimate the Zulu loss at 1 000.[32] Pearson and other officers considered Chelmsford's tally an under-estimation. The War Office accepted their opinion, and put the figure at 'nearly 1 200',[33] or between a 10 per cent and 12 per cent Zulu casualty rate. Nor does this seem an exaggeration, especially when it is accepted that few of the wounded would have lived. Part of the reason for this lies with the nature of the Zulu rout. In their desperation to leave the field their comrades abandoned the wounded or were unable to carry them across the swollen Nyezane.[34] Those left in this way fell victim to the pitiless NNC who (as was their usual practice) never considered taking prisoners but stabbed every Zulu they came across, dead, dying or wounded. And even if the wounded did succeed in evading the NNC, and reaching their homes, most of them eventually died there of their injuries.[35] It seems only two Zulu officers of note died at Gingindlovu, but a great many sons of chiefs and well-to-do men were among the slain.[36]

The morning following the battle, Chelmsford left a garrison with the reduced laager while the remainder of the column marched up to relieve Fort Eshowe. Not a Zulu was seen, though they had partly destroyed the track in two places. Chelmsford had decided to abandon the fort altogether, not least because he considered the coastal route more suitable for subsequent operations. While Pearson supervised the evacuation of the fort on 4 April, Chelmsford accompanied a patrol of 225 men led by Major Barrow to destroy Dabulamanzi's eSulwini (eZuluwini) *umuzi* at eNtumeni, which had escaped burning during the raid of 1 March. A small force of forty Zulu led by Dabulamanzi, who had returned home after the battle and who was typically mounted on a black horse, kept up fire from a neighbouring hill, but were this time unable to prevent the British from completing their vindictive mission.[37]

On 5 April the relieving column and garrison set out from Fort

Eshowe for Natal, leaving behind six officers and thirty-five men lying in the little cemetery. The Zulu immediately set fire to the buildings at the abandoned fort, but did not in any way harm the British graves and crosses.[38]

As for Cetshwayo, he might have been rid of the detested British presence at Eshowe, but that was small compensation for the disastrous defeat suffered by his coastal forces. That, coming on top of the rout of the main army at Khambula, made it inevitable that the successful British would pursue the war to its conclusion. No wonder, then, that Cetshwayo found fault with the way the battle of Gingindlovu had been conducted, and furiously castigated his generals for their ineptitude.[39]

Chelmsford, meanwhile, buoyed up by the realization that after the overwhelming victories at Khambula and Gingindlovu his forces had entirely regained the initiative, was determined that the Zulu be given no chance to regain their balance. Consequently, on 7 April he sent orders from Fort Pearson for continued raids to be made across the Natal–Zululand border. The flooded state of the Thukela, however, prevented the border troops from doing more than hover menacingly at the unfordable drifts, and by the last week of April the Zulu along the river considered it safe to return to their *imizi*.[40] It was different at Rorke's Drift, where on 9 April Major Dartnell led 2 000 men on a raid up the Batshe valley and back over Fugitives' Drift. They burned three of Sihayo's *imizi* and nine others that had hitherto escaped the attentions of the mounted patrols launched from Rorke's Drift, as well as the crops standing in their gardens. The Zulu had deserted the whole region, and had had sufficient warning of the raid to be able to drive their cattle and horses eastwards out of range. The British therefore encountered no resistance, but for weeks afterwards were anxious lest the Zulu attempt a retaliatory raid.[41]

Wood's force remained undisturbed at Khambula after their victory, and his operations were confined to sending out mounted patrols which engaged in several light skirmishes with the few Zulu still in the neighbourhood.[42] By 3 April all the Qulusi and Mbilini's adherents had gone from Hlobane. They moved north to raid the Phongolo region once more, accompanied by Mbilini, who reportedly travelled in a cart because of a superficial wound to the forehead, sustained either at the battle of Hlobane or at Khambula. Once in the north, they broke into several small parties, one of 150 men even raiding as far away as the Mkhondo River valley. On the night of 4 April several parties, making up a force perhaps 1 200 strong, raided the Phongolo valley opposite Luneburg. They retired rapidly in the direction of Makateeskop with their booty of cattle. On the way they encountered two companies of the 2/4th Regiment on their way to relieve the Luneburg garrison. The British at once formed laager, and the Zulu, who had learned their lesson well at Khambula, left them unmolested and broke into several small parties which proceeded to ravage the countryside as they went. It was while following up one of these small parties that a patrol from Luneburg under Captain Prior became engaged in a skirmish near the Ntombe. It killed Tshekwane, a younger son of Sihayo who had often accompanied Mbilini on his marauding expeditions,[43] and wounded another Zulu horseman. He turned out to be Mbilini himself, and had been shot in the back through the right shoulder, the bullet coming out below his waist. He managed nevertheless to make his escape, but died within a few days of his dreadful wound, and before he could regain his *umuzi* at Hlobane.

The death of the veritable hyena of the Phongolo left his adherents leaderless. They ceased to be a factor in the region, and by May were reported to have been ordered by Cetshwayo to leave Hlobane and to move to Ngwegwe Hill, over the Phongolo. As for Manyonyoba, constant patrols during May by the Luneburg garrison and by Commandant J. A. Rudolph, whose Burghers operated from their laager on the Bivane River close by Fort Lawrence (which had been built by a company of the 2/4th), kept him bottled up in his caves.

The British consequently considered that the Zulu of the north-west could safely be contained by the existing garrisons in the area. This was vital, for Chelmsford was preparing for his second invasion of Zululand, and Wood's forces – which were required for the renewed advance – could hardly have been employed if moving them were to have meant leaving the Transvaal frontier open to Zulu raids. Confident, then, that little risk to the frontier communities would be incurred, on 5 May Wood moved south from Khambula to join Chelmsford's force. The men of the Utrecht garrison caught up with him on 28 May, and on 17 June Wood effected his rendezvous with Chelmsford.[44] This time, their march on oNdini would be inexorable.

Notes

1 Despite the conflicting and unreliable information coming out of Zululand, the British were able to form a detailed picture of the Zulu concentration around Eshowe at the end of March. Zulu dispositions and numbers are based on CP 7, no. 38: Drummond to Chelmsford, 27 March 1879: report of spy Magumbi.

2 For the British advance to Gingindlovu, see WO 32/7727: Chelmsford to Secretary of State for War, 10 April 1879; and Mathews, 'Chelmsford', pp. 248–54.

3 Anti-Slavery Society Papers, G 12: statement of one of the Native Contingent with Col. Pearson's Column, made to the Bishop of Natal.

4 Stainbank Diary: 31 March, 1 April 1879.

5 *Illustrated London News*, 26 April 1879, p. 398.

6 Lloyd, 'Ekowe', p. 26.

7 Anti-Slavery Society Papers, G 12: statement of one of the Native Contingent to Colenso: testimony of prisoners.

8 Webb and Wright, *Zulu King Speaks*, p. 33; Norris-Newman, *In Zululand*, p. 142.

9 For a description of the Zulu camp three days after the battle, see Norbury, *Naval Brigade*, pp. 278–9. The commanders seem to have occupied a large sort of hut, made from covering the drooping branches of a tree with grass.

10 Norris-Newman, *In Zululand*, p. 142.

11 Webb and Wright, *Zulu King Speaks*, p. 37.

12 Lt.-Gen. Sir E. Hutton, 'Some recollections of the Zulu War', *Army Quarterly*, XVI, April 1921, p. 70.

13 JSA I, p. 63: testimony of Bikwayo kaNoziwawa; *Illustrated London News*, 26 April 1879, p. 398; Vijn, *Cetshwayo's Dutchman*, p. 40.

14 WO 32/7727: Chelmsford to Secretary of State for War, 10 April 1879. Other estimations varied only slightly.

15 Sir F. T. Hamilton Papers, HTN/103: Journal, 2 April 1879.

16 See especially War Office, *Narrative*, p. 64; Norris-Newman, *In Zululand*, pp. 137–8; Norbury, *Naval Brigade*, p. 271; Molyneux, *Campaigning*, p. 131; H. L. Hall, 'With assegai and rifle: reminiscences of a transport conductor in the Zulu War', *Military History Journal*, IV, 5, June 1979, Appendix VIII, p. 200.

17 Hutton. 'Recollections', p. 70.

18 'They cannot hit a laager, not even a thundering big one' (FC 2/5: Barton to Fannin, 16 April 1879).

19 War Office, *Narrative*, p. 163; CP 7, no. 50: Major Barrow's report.

20 The wagon-and-a-half full of guns abandoned by the Zulu in the rout and collected by the British reflected the preponderance of obsolete weapons: five Martini-Henry rifles; four shotguns; one revolver and 425 guns and rifles, mostly muskets.

21 Anti-Slavery Society Papers, G 12: statement of one of the Native Contingent to Colenso.

22 Conductor in the Transport Division's Diary, p. 24: 2 April 1879.

23 Smith-Dorrien Papers, SMD/1: Scrap-book, unnumbered pages.

24 A. C. B. Mynors, *Letters and Diary of the Late Arthur C. B. Mynors, Lieut. 3rd Batt., 60th Rifles*, Margate, 1879, p. 30: 2 April 1879.

25 Moodie, *John Dunn*, pp. 102–3.

26 Ashe and Wyatt Edgell, *Zulu Campaign*, p. 170; J. Laband, *The Battle of Ulundi*, Pietermaritzburg, 1988, p. 32.

27 For the closing stage of the battle, see CP 7, no. 50: report by Major Barrow; and WO 32/7727: Chelmsford to Secretary of State for War, 10 April 1879. Additional information on the Zulu rout can be found in Stainbank Diary: 2 April 1879; AC, p. 147, Barrow no. 2: Barrow to Alison, 14 June 1879; Hamilton-Browne, *Lost Legionary*, pp. 209–13; Dawnay, *Private Journal*, pp. 14–15; and Norris-Newman, *In Zululand*, pp. 139–40.

28 *Natal Witness*, 19 July 1879: correspondent with Crealock's Column, 13 July 1879.

29 Vijn, *Cetshwayo's Dutchman*, p. 40.

30 WO 32/7750: Diary of 2nd Brigade, 1st Division, 21 April 1879.

31 SNA 1/1/34, no. 10: Fynney to ASNA, 8 April 1879; CSO 1926, no. 2051/1879: Fannin to Colonial Secretary, 17 April 1879.

32 WO 32/7727: Chelmsford to Secretary of State for War, 10 April 1879.

33 War Office, *Narrative*, p. 65.

34 Mynors, *Letters and Diary*, Diary p. 34: 6 April 1879; Hutton, 'Recollections', p. 73.

35 Conductor in the Transport Division's Diary, p. 54: 20 April 1879: Makwendu kaMpande's report.

36 Webb and Wright, *Zulu King Speaks*, p. 37.

37 WO 32/7727: Chelmsford to Secretary of State for War, 10 April 1879; Ashe and Wyatt Edgell, *Zulu Campaign*, pp. 179–82; Molyneux, *Campaigning*, pp. 141–3.

38 Norbury, *Naval Brigade*, pp. 299–300.

39 CSO 1926, no. 2051/1879: Fannin to Colonial Secretary, 17 April 1879; SNA 1/1/34, no. 85: statement of Sihlahla, 3 June 1879.

40 Laband and Thompson, *Umvoti*, pp. 50–1; Thompson, 'Border guard', pp. 172–4.

41 Laband and Thompson, *Buffalo Border*, pp. 63–5.

42 For operations in the Phongolo region during April and May, see Laband, 'Mbilini', pp. 201–2.

43 For doubts expressed concerning the dead man's identity, see Vijn, *Cetshwayo's Dutchman*, p. 124: Colenso's notes.

44 War Office, *Narrative*, pp. 100–3.

10

Warding off the falling tree

While Chelmsford had been relieving Eshowe, his forces still in Natal had been considerably augmented by the arrival in Durban of the main body of reinforcements which he had requested from England. Consequently, on his return to Natal on 7 April, Chelmsford was able to launch his long-delayed major offensive. For this cautiously executed final thrust into Zululand, he decided that he would employ two columns instead of one in order to screen both the Transvaal and Natal from a Zulu counter-blow. He arranged that part of the assembled forces (7 500 men), now styled the First Division under the command of Major-General H. H. Crealock, would advance into Zululand from Fort Pearson. The remaining 5 000 men were to concentrate at Dundee as the Second Division under Major-General E. Newdigate. In their advance they would cooperate with the 3 200 men of Wood's command, to be known as the Flying Column. For a number of reasons Chelmsford chose Dundee as the Second Division's chief depot in preference to Helpmekaar: the roads were better by way of Ladysmith than by Greytown and less exposed to the Zulu border; and Dundee was nearer the Orange Free State, whence considerable supplies were being obtained. Yet one potent reason lay behind all these excellent considerations: no one wished to invade Zululand again by a road signposted by the dreadful field of Isandlwana and its unburied British dead. Instead, the Second Division would advance by an unfamiliar route that would require considerable reconnaissance.[1]

During the first week of May the Second Division began to mass at Landman's Drift on the Mzinyathi. From this fortified depot Chelmsford sent out various patrols. They were not only to reconnoitre the country ahead, but were to keep the Zulu off balance and prevent them from considering an attack on the Division or the Transvaal. Chelmsford considered the best way to achieve this was to deny the Zulu bases and supplies in the area of operations by burning the *imizi* and standing crops, and by driving off the livestock.[2]

Accordingly, on 13 May a combined force of mounted men and NNC circled south around Telezeni Hill, their destructive raid in which hundreds of huts were burned being marked by a perfect line of fires. This was followed up on 16 May with a large mounted raid on Telezeni Hill itself to clear the area of all Zulu who might interfere with reconnaissance patrols. However, the British found that there were no Zulu left in the vicinity. At Rorke's Drift on 15 May, a patrol investigating the Isandlwana battlefield was fired upon by small parties of Zulu. These local groups of warriors dared make no further resistance when on 21 May Major-General F. Marshall, commanding the Cavalry Brigade attached to the Second Division, made a reconnaissance in force to the battlefield. Burning every surviving *umuzi* in its path, his force commenced the burial of the British dead before returning to Landman's Drift.

As a results of these sorties, Chelmsford could be confident that the country to his front and on his immediate right was clear of any Zulu force large enough to threaten the Second Division or the Natal border. Meanwhile, in order to draw away the Zulu further east who might later fall upon his right flank or the colony, he ordered a new series of raids to be mounted across the Thukela.

At Middle Drift the river was at last sufficiently low and the drifts passable, and on 20 May Major A. C. Twentyman, the commander of Defensive District VII, led 1 700 men across in a three-pronged raid.[3] Resistance was minimal, as the Zulu were caught completely off guard by this unexpected offensive. They had time only to drive off their cattle, abandoning their food supplies and caches of ammunition. In all, the raiders burned an estimated nineteen *imizi* (including that of Godide, the Ntuli chief), destroyed great quantities of grain, and drove off a herd of 150 cattle.[4] The Zulu immediately responded to this provocation. That evening small parties raided the Natal blacks of the Thukela valley, throwing Umvoti County into its greatest panic since Isandlwana. But the Zulu were also demoralized. For fear of fresh raids they abandoned those *imizi* near the river which had escaped burning, and withdrew deeper into Zululand with their remaining cattle and food supplies; while in order to protect their families, the local fighting-men were reportedly determined to stay with them within easy distance of the refuge afforded by the Nkhandla and Qudeni forests, and to resist calls to muster at oNdini. The British border officials consequently came to the welcome opinion that the Zulu border population, though still hostile, was effectively cowed and neither of future military value to Cetshwayo, nor of danger to Chelmsford or Natal.

Further downstream, Captain G. A. Lucas of Defensive District VI sent in two diversionary raids on 28 May, in which two *imizi* were burned. That was the last raid across the lower Thukela, for, as in Defensive District VII, the objective of clearing the border had been achieved and there were apprehensions of Zulu retaliation. The decision was therefore taken to stand on the defensive until Chelmsford had gained his decisive victory.[5]

The mounted reconnaissances undertaken during May from Landman's Drift had established that the shortest route for the Second Division to follow to oNdini was to the north-east across the Ncome River below Koppie Alleen. A new depot was accordingly established there, and on 31 May the Second Division began to cross into Zululand to effect its junction with the Flying Column for their combined march on oNdini. Chelmsford could advance, confident in his belief that the Natal border on his right flank was secure, as was the Transvaal's to his rear. The border garrisons in their chain of forts were left behind to watch drowsily over the deserted Zulu banks of the Mzinyathi and Thukela rivers, where no one laboured in the forlorn mealie-gardens, where no smoke rose from the destroyed or abandoned *imizi*, and where a profound silence reigned over all.

However, in north-western Zululand the situation (with Mbilini dead and the Qulusi lurking in their mountain fastnesses) was not quite as stable as Wood had supposed when he marched from Khambula to join Chelmsford.[6] It was still necessary to patrol the Transvaal border, but the anti-British Boers of the Wakkerstroom District were unwilling to take the field, even when it was rumoured that Manyonyoba was intending to raid towards the Mkhondo River. (Indeed, there were strong indications that the Boers of the region were in league with the Zulu, and many wintered close to the Phongolo, actually among the Zulu *imizi*.) The lack of mounted men to defend the region meant that on 4 June a party of fifty Zulu was emboldened to attack the blacks living on a white farm on the banks of the Bivane River, while on 7 June a larger force (quite possibly made up of Qulusi and Mbilini's former adherents) swept the cattle off another farm near Luneburg, and near the Ntombe River cut off a patrol trying to intercept them. A young white volunteer and six black border policemen were killed. The depleted Luneburg garrison was too weak to take further action. The Zulu, for their part, did not risk attacking the fortified post, but retired over the Ntombe with their booty. The local blacks friendly to the settlers took to the mountains and caves, and left the Zulu masters of their mealie-gardens. From 7 until 21 June, when they finally passed back across the Phongolo, large forces of Zulu raiders swept with impunity between the Ntombe and Mkhondo, attacking *imizi* in the area and driving off thousands of cattle and sheep. Manyonyoba's men occupied the hills opposite Luneburg, and remained there throughout June with impunity. It was they who constituted the greatest danger to other blacks in the vicinity, for after the raids already mentioned no other serious Zulu activity occurred elsewhere in the upper Phongolo region.

The activities of the Zulu in the north-west, abetted by the Boers, though very uncomfortable for the settlers of Luneburg and their black dependants, were ultimately not sufficiently intensive or widespread to threaten Wood's rear or Chelmsford's left flank. Similarly, a sudden and successful Zulu raid on 25 June at Middle Drift, which at a blow reasserted Zulu ascendancy along the Natal border, was not enough to deflect the British from their joint march on oNdini to the defence of the colony.

At daybreak on 25 June, when fog still shrouded the river, a Zulu *impi* of 500 men crossed into Natal at Hot Springs, upstream of Middle Drift.[7] The Zulu rampaged up to the foot of Kranskop, killing the Ngcolosi people living between the river and the high land, setting fire to their *imizi* as they went, and driving off livestock. Below Kranskop the *impi* joined up with another force of about 500 which had crossed some 16 km downstream and had been similarly engaged against the Hosiyana and Bomvu. The joint force retired by way of Middle Drift, shrugging off the belated attempts at interception by the completely surprised border forces. Zulu strategy had mirrored that adopted much less successfully by the British in their major raid of 20 May. On this occasion, the Zulu burned seventy-three *imizi*, killed thirty of the border population, took captive another forty, drove off 678 cattle and 771 goats and – adding insult to injury – looted £170 sterling intended for the hut tax. Quite clearly, the Zulu had had much the better of the raiding exchange, and the Natal authorities and border population were only too aware of the fact. There was some speculation that Cetshwayo had sanctioned the raid to divert Chelmsford from his advance on oNdini, but it was most likely that the raid was a retaliatory blow of purely local initiative, in which the Magwaza of Chief Manqondo and the Ntuli of Chief Mavumengwana took the lead. In any event, the British border forces were thrown entirely on to the defensive, and remained there until Chelmsford's victory at Ulundi transformed the situation.

Chelmsford, when planning his advance into Zululand from Koppie Alleen,[8] naturally had to prepare against Zulu attack. He consequently instructed his troops to form wagon-laagers every evening. His extended columns of men and slowly moving wagons were more vulnerable when on the march, but he hoped that efficient scouting and screening by the cavalry would effectively prevent the Zulu from considering an attack. Accordingly, his advance was marked by the systematic burning of homesteads, destruction of crops and stored mealies, and capture of cattle, as his cavalry strove to create an extensive zone about the vulnerable columns free of Zulu forces and their sources of supply and shelter. In doing so, the cavalry were also indirectly waging war on the civilian Zulu population in an effort to diminish both their ability to sustain men in the field and their desire to resist.

Ironically, an incident at the very beginning of the advance from the Ncome involving a small mounted patrol engaged in such activities caused more consternation in Britain than the battle of Isandlwana itself. On 1 June the Prince Imperial of France, an observer on Chelmsford's staff, was killed when a Zulu scouting party of sixty men, drawn from local elements of the iNgobamakhosi, uMbonambi and uNokhenkhe *amabutho*, fell upon his group while they were off-saddled at the *umuzi* of the *induna* Sobhuza in the Tshotshosi valley. The Prince was abandoned by his panicked comrades, and the first to stab him was Xamanga of the uMbonambi, who was later killed at the battle of Ulundi. The Prince's sword was taken to Cetshwayo.[9] The tragic event, which extinguished a dynasty's hopes of restoration to the French throne, tarnished Chelmsford's reputation beyond redemption. Unhappily for King Cetshwayo, it also effectively obliterated any residual Zulu hopes of a negotiated end to the war, for Chelmsford was left with a greater need than ever to compensate for his disasters with a brilliant victory in the field.

On 3 June the Second Division resumed its advance and crossed the Tshotshosi River behind the Flying Column, which had moved beyond the Nondweni River. On 4 June Baker's Horse reported a large force of Zulu to their front, and sustained casualties when outflanked in a running skirmish.[10] Major-General Marshall and the Cavalry Brigade accordingly started at 4.30 a.m. on 5 June to reconnoitre as far as the valley of the uPhoko River. Here they joined a mounted party from the Flying Column under Buller, who had just routed some 300 Zulu on the eastern side of the uPhoko and chased them into the thorn bush on the lower slopes of eZungwini Hill. Colonel D. Drury-Lowe foolhardily advanced with three troops of the 17th Lancers and came under heavy fire from the Zulu who had taken cover among the long grass, bushes, dongas and anthills. The Zulu, if they had known how to use their firearms effectively, might have done considerable harm. As it was, Lieutenant Frith, the adjutant of the 17th Lancers, was shot dead, and a squadron of the King's Dragoon Guards had to be moved forward to cover the Lancers' withdrawal. The ineffectiveness of regular cavalry in broken terrain and irregular warfare was confirmed, as was Zulu skirmishing ability.[11] The following days were not only to reinforce these propositions, but were also to demonstrate how irregular horse, when led by an officer of Buller's ability, could regain the ascendancy.

The difficulty and slowness of his progress, which averaged just 3 km a day (it would take the British twenty-eight days to advance the 104 km from the Ncome to the Mthonjaneni heights overlooking oNdini), forced Chelmsford to halt to establish storage depots and entrenched posts along his line of communications. The Second Division built Fort Newdigate on 6 June, and on 7 June moved forward to the left bank of the uPhoko, where it remained until 17 June while supplies were brought up under heavy escort and the tracks improved. During this period reconnaissances were made by Buller in order to clear the area of the Zulu who had been so successful in the skirmish of 5 June. On 7 June near eZungwini Buller engaged a force of nearly 1 000, consisting of adherents of Sekethwayo, Sihayo and Msebe. Eleven of the Zulu were mounted, and Buller was impressed with their leader's generalship. The Zulu were nevertheless forced to retire, and Buller burnt a number of large *imizi* in the vicinity, which contained equipment evidently looted at

Isandlwana. The following day Buller outflanked and routed some 400 Zulu near by and burned more large *imizi*, while on 10 June his active patrols brought in another 300 cattle. On 15 June Buller's men crossed the Mfolozi to Thabankhulu Mountain, 40 km north of his camp, and not surprisingly caught the Zulu completely unawares. They captured 300 cattle and 100 sheep and also killed twelve Zulu, captured a number and burned twenty-four *imizi*.[12] These far-flung and successful patrols by Buller's Frontier Light Horse cleared the country between Conference Hill and Rorke's Drift of Zulu, as well as that in advance of the British as far as Babanango.

It was only on 18 June, though, after the Second Division had effected its rendezvous with the Flying Column and built Fort Marshall, that Chelmsford was free to order a general advance. The following day the combined force reached the Babanango heights, when forty-five of Baker's Horse skirmished with 500 Zulu in a thickly populated valley near by, probably the Mpembeni. The Zulu failed to tempt Baker's men into unfavourable terrain by driving past a herd of 3 000 cattle. Meanwhile, the women and children swarmed out of the *imizi*, making for the nearest mountain with their possessions on their heads.[13] Here as elsewhere, the British found the *imizi* which they routinely destroyed near the line of march deserted, though the large supplies of corn which they regularly contained suggested that they had been precipitately abandoned.[14]

The Flying Column built Fort Evelyn on 23–4 June, within sight of oNdini in the Mahlabathini plain below. Large bodies of armed Zulu were seen keeping watch on the British from the crests of the hills or from the valleys to the north of the Babanango ridge, but they were never strong enough to attack.[15] Buller, meanwhile, when reconnoitering on 24 June towards the Mthonjaneni heights where Chelmsford intended to camp before marching down into the plain for his final confrontation with the Zulu army, surprised and dispersed about seventy Zulu who were burning the drying winter grass along the line of the British advance. This attempt, as well as earlier ones elsewhere, could, if they had been successfully and persistently carried out, have further delayed the advance of the British, who were chronically short of forage. But because the British were well aware of the threat, their mounted patrols were constantly on the look-out for Zulu burning the grass, and were able to prevent it.[16]

Chelmsford had intended Major-General Crealock's First Division to play a vital part in his strategy for the second invasion of

Zululand. As he stipulated on 12 April 1879 in his instructions to Crealock, the First Division's task was to support the Second Division's and Flying Column's advance on oNdini by marching up the coast and forcing Cetshwayo to detach fighting men from the main Zulu army in defence of the south-east of his kingdom. That is why Crealock's initial objective was to be the destruction of the emaNgweni and old oNdini *amakhanda*, which were within 16 km of each other either side of the Mhlatuze River, for it was presumed that Cetshwayo would not allow them to be burned without making some attempt to protect them. For this ploy to be useful, however, it was essential that Crealock should move quickly and anticipate – or at least keep up with – Chelmsford's progress.[17]

Yet speed is what 'Crealock's Crawlers' were quite unable to achieve. Granted, Crealock had to grapple with extremely difficult supply and transport problems,[18] but these were compounded by his over-methodical approach, which required the construction of numbers of strong and well supplied advance posts. Disgruntled subordinates scoffed at the First Division's dilatory advance, and pointed out that it failed even in its primary objective of forcing Cetshwayo to divide his forces.[19]

There were indications that Cetshwayo had initially planned to 'eat up' the First Division before turning his attention to Chelmsford's joint force.[20] However, when the king realized that Crealock would never be able to arrive in time to join Chelmsford in his advance on oNdini, he decided to ignore the First Division's presence and concentrate on Chelmsford's more immediate threat. Consequently, when he called up his army, he left only a few irregulars living in the coast country with their families to protect the cattle and, if possible, to drive them out of reach of Crealock's patrols.[21]

It is not certain when Cetshwayo started summoning his *amabutho* against the likelihood of a final stand against the invader. Mobilization would have taken some time, for it was necessary to send out the order by runner or signal to the far corners of the kingdom. Besides, after the defeats of March and April there was a natural reluctance to face the British again,[22] though many warriors evinced a grim preparedness to do so if it was required of them. Perhaps a factor in their determination – as well as a manifestation of their irrational fears in the face of impending defeat – was the extraordinary rumour sweeping Zululand that if they were to yield, the whites would take their wives and castrate all the surviving Zulu males. This was corroborated in Zulu minds by the fictitious tale that Gamdana, who had defected in January, had already been mutilated and sent away to an island.[23] Practical considerations also played their part, and the king was persuaded to delay insisting upon a full muster at oNdini until the *amabutho* recuperating at their homes had reaped their crops and stored the grain.[24]

It was clear to Crealock's patrols at the coast that by the end of May the fighting-men from that part of the country were making for oNdini. By early June there was positive intelligence that the coastal elements of the *amabutho* had been called up, as well as those living along the Natal border and in the upper districts of Zululand. It was of considerable significance that the great majority of the *amabutho* still seemed prepared to fight on for their king, despite their undeniably lowered morale, and the continuing reluctance of some elements to respond to the king's reiterated command to reassemble.[25]

Thus even before the First Division's advance was fully under way by mid-June, the large parties of Zulu irregulars reported in May to have been in the region between the Mlalazi and Mhlatuze rivers, as well as a rumoured *impi* ordered to oppose the column at the Mlalazi, had either largely dispersed or gone to join the army at oNdini. The First Division consequently moved through a countryside clear of people, except for some concentrations beyond the Mlalazi and around Ngoye. Resistance was naturally minimal, even when the British were at their most vulnerable, crossing rivers. Besides occasionally cutting the First Division's telegraph wire,[26] the only aggressive action the Zulu took was to fire harmlessly every now and again from great range at British forward patrols on the south bank of the Mlalazi.[27]

In the demoralized post-Khambula period it was clear that Zulu allegiance to the king was at last beginning to waver.[28] On 21 April, near kwaGingindlovu, Prince Makwendu kaMpande, with 130 men, women and children, gave himself up to the advance-parties of the First Division. He told his captors that it had been the intention of all his adherents to surrender, as they saw the war could no longer be won. The king, however, learning of this intention, had sent an *impi* to intercept part of his following, killing some and taking his cattle.[29] Makwendu was a prince of little influence, with only a small following who, born of the same mother as Hamu, might have been expected to have followed the lead of his elder brother in joining the

British. All the same, the defection of another member of the royal house must have been as alarming for Cetshwayo as it was encouraging for the British, especially as there were persistent rumours that some of the major *izikhulu* of the southern coastal region were contemplating surrender. Dabulamanzi and Mavumengwana were both reported to be arguing the case for submission, and there were rumours that it was only by despatching loyal troops (as in the case of Makwendu) that the king had prevented their escaping into Natal with their followings.

Talk of their intended surrender persisted into May. Mfunzi and Nkisimana (Cetshwayo's emissaries) might have officially assured Fannin while held at Fort Buckingham that Dabulamanzi harboured no intention of deserting the Zulu cause, and that the Zulu nation would in any case stand by its king to the last. Privately, however, they had earlier confided that they themselves were anxious to submit and knew of thirty homesteads that would follow their lead, only because they lived in the heart of Zululand they were unable to defect with safety. A similar hedging approach was made to Wood at much the same time when a petty chief, Bangakama, let him know that he would submit once the Flying Column had advanced sufficiently for him to do so with impunity. There were reports that some chiefs were declaring that with their *imizi* full of wounded they were not prepared to fight any more, and that the women were beseeching the king to yield.[30]

Faced with such waverings, and uncertain how best to prosecute the increasingly disastrous war, in mid-May Cetshwayo summoned the principal men of his kingdom to give of their advice. It was reported that they opposed the continuation of the war and strongly urged peace.[31] Apparently unnerved by the disaffection of his *izikhulu* (not least Zibhebhu's), and himself despairing of fighting off the British – despite brave fighting words to the *amabutho* beginning to muster at oNdini – Cetshwayo consented to begin a new peace initiative.[32]

The king's most recent emissaries, Mfunzi, Nkisimana and Johannes, had remained incarcerated at Fort Buckingham until 15 April. They were then informed that should they wish to make any peace proposals they should do so at Wood's camp in Zululand, whither Chelmsford was moving. This was the consequence of Chelmsford's renewed stipulation that all communications from the Zulu king must be sent to him direct. His insistence in this matter not only reflected his determination that Cetshwayo must accede in full to the British terms, but was also an aspect of his campaign to keep anything pertaining to the conduct of the war out of Bulwer's civilian hands. For Bulwer feared with reason that Chelmsford's instructions would cause unnecessary difficulties and delays, and hamper the cessation of hostilities which the Natal government desired. The vicissitudes to which Mfunzi and Nkisimana were subjected were amply to bear out the Lieutenant-Governor's disquiet.

On account of a degree of confusion over who had the authority to permit them to proceed (or perhaps it was a ploy deliberately to delay them), the two messengers remained at Fort Buckingham until an enquiry prompted by Bishop Colenso resulted in their leaving for Zululand on 9 May. On 12 June they appeared under flag of truce in Pietermaritzburg, sent on by Fynn, the Resident Magistrate at Rorke's Drift. It would seem from their conversation with General Clifford in the Natal capital that after leaving Fort Buckingham they had gone, not to Chelmsford, but to consult the king and his councillors. These had essentially confirmed their previous message calling for peace negotiations, and had sent Mfunzi and Nkisimana back with an injunction to hurry. But the messengers were old and the rains heavy, and Chelmsford's precise whereabouts were unknown to them. This is why they had fetched up at Rorke's Drift. Clifford sent the exhausted messengers back in the direction of Babanango, where he supposed Chelmsford to be.

Before Mfunzi and Nkisimana could locate Chelmsford, they and the message they bore were quite outstripped by events. In any case, they had let slip an observation to Clifford which pinpointed the fundamental limitation of all Zulu peace initiatives thus far: they admitted they had no authority to talk about the actual terms of peace, only the king's desire to negotiate. This was in accordance with Zulu custom. Messengers were sent out to make arrangements only for a meeting of chiefs, who alone had the power to discuss terms. Yet since March Frere had been insisting that he was not prepared to consider any message that did not bind the king to the terms of the ultimatum. Diplomatically the Zulu and British had reached an impasse.

Moreover, the British had become firmly wedded to the concept of victory in the field. On 4 April Frere had directed that 'no overtures of any kind must be allowed to delay military operations', at least until 'complete military command' of Zululand had been secured –

when the British could dictate any terms they desired. Complementary to this policy was Frere's authorization that overtures for peace would be acceptable from any other chief but the king.[33] For as the war turned decisively against Cetshwayo, so the opportunity increased to detach his chiefs from his cause.

Meanwhile, Major-General Crealock, laying the ground for his laborious advance up the coast, was soon complaining that he was 'in a state of chronic messengers from the king and his indunas'.[34] Not that he did any more than direct them to Chelmsford via Wood, as insisted upon by Frere.

On 15 May the first of this series of messengers, Chief Ndwandwe of the Langa in southern Zululand, came into Fort Chelmsford[35] with Cetshwayo's plaintive message: 'What have I done? I want peace – I ask for peace.'[36] Chelmsford responded to word of this message by evolving fresh terms for surrender over and above those contained in the ultimatum of December. All captured weapons and prisoners were to be surrendered, 10 000 stands of firearms handed over, as well as at least 10 000 cattle or 20 000 sheep: crushing and impossible terms surely designed to elicit resistance until Chelmsford had achieved his desired victory in the field. Frere capped these terms with his harsh directive that the king's messengers were to be informed that unless acts were substituted for 'idle words', and until the Zulu made genuine efforts to comply with the terms, their land would be devastated.[37]

Crealock learned on 27 May that the king was sending him further messengers, and that he had ordered that whites were not to be fired upon during the period of negotiations. There could no longer be any doubt that Cetshwayo was attempting to treat in earnest. But could he and his advisers possibly accept the inflexible British terms?

The messenger who arrived on 28 May was Sintwangu, an *inceku* (or high official in the king's household), and a well known emissary who had attended the ultimatum ceremony in December as the king's eyes and ears. In conversation with John Dunn on 31 May he reiterated Ndwandwe's message, and begged the renegade white chief to use his influence to achieve peace. Such pleas were to no avail, and Sintwangu was sent off like the other messengers to negotiate direct with Chelmsford – if he could find him. This was also the fate of Ndwandwe, who reappeared on 7 June with another relay of messengers, purveying what Crealock called his 'peaceful lies from the king'.[38]

Chelmsford, meanwhile, remained obdurate that there could be no permanent peace until the king were deposed, which rendered Cetshwayo's attempts to negotiate with the British advancing from the north-west as futile as his deflected efforts to treat with those slowly moving up the coast.

Three messengers, Mgcwelo, Mtshibela and Mpokitwayo, reached Wood's camp at the Nondweni River on 4 June. They had left Cetshwayo at his emLambongwenya homestead on 30 June, and had at first made for Khambula, which the Flying Column had already left. It would seem that they had set out at the same time as Sintwangu had been despatched to Crealock, and Mfunzi and Nkisimana to Rorke's Drift. The three messengers carried a message which Cetshwayo had personally given them before his chief councillors. Genuine emissaries though they might have been, they made a bad impression on the prejudiced British, who found them 'villainous-looking scoundrels'.[39] In turn, they were so strongly impressed with the spectacle of British armed might that they assured their interrogators in their preparatory interview that they would 'strongly recommend' on their return that the king come to terms. They also let it be known that Cetshwayo was finally of intention to send Mnyamana and other 'officers of state' to treat,[40] as Frere had always insisted they should.

However, in their formal interview on 5 June with Chelmsford, the General laid down conditions which were a refinement on the additional ones he had evolved in May, and which Bishop Colenso could only categorize as 'preposterous'.[41] Firstly, Chelmsford made it plain that on grounds of developments along the coast he no longer believed that the king was being obeyed, and that unless Cetshwayo could provide proof of his continuing authority and desire for peace, the General would rather continue negotiating with his chiefs. He therefore warned that he would continue his advance unless, in earnest of his power and genuine intentions, the king sent in the oxen at his royal homesteads and the two seven-pounder guns captured at Isandlwana, as well as promised that all the other firearms in Zululand would be collected and given up. In addition, an *ibutho*, to be named by Chelmsford, must come into the British lines and lay down its arms. Then, and only then, would Chelmsford even entertain peace discussions, which, naturally, would be based on the original terms of the ultimatum.

Their mission rendered futile by these preconditions, the disconsolate messengers left the British camp on 6 June, bearing with them Chelmsford's written statement of his impossible terms. This punctilious sop to correct diplomatic form (for who in the Zulu camp would be able to read his words?) did not disguise the General's transparent cynicism. Cetshwayo had already made it plain that, although desperate to negotiate, he could not accede to the demands of the ultimatum. How then could he even consider these outrageous preliminary conditions? How could Chelmsford have ever expected him to? Clearly he did not. His conditions were merely for the record, since his intentions were to fight and win his battle and so destroy the king whose warriors had ruined his reputation at Isandlwana. It made not a jot of difference that there were reports of the king calling on his people to send him cattle to help buy off the British and make peace; nor that he did not intend that the British should be attacked unless they continued to advance on oNdini. By way of contrast, Chelmsford's instructions of 16 June laid down that chiefs, on submitting to designated authorities, be required only to give up their arms and the royal cattle in their keeping. In return, their adherents were to be spared and protected. Only the king could expect no mercy.

Though being pushed into a situation where he must fight to the last, Cetshwayo attempted even more urgently than before to negotiate. Two new messengers, Ntanjana and Sibungu, arrived at Fort Pearson on the lower Thukela on 25 June (the very day of the Zulu raid at Middle Drift), begging that the British stay their advance until negotiations could take place. They explained that if the British continued to march on oNdini, Cetshwayo would have no choice but to resist, 'as there will be nothing left but to try and push aside a tree that is falling upon him'.[42] Unregarded as all those before them, the messengers left on 29 June. Sintwangu appeared on a new mission the following day, when he came into Crealock's camp at Fort Napoleon[43] on the Mlalazi River bearing an enormous elephant tusk – the symbol of peace and friendship – in earnest of the authenticity of his mission.[44] He made the unfortunate impression messengers seemed now automatically to create in the minds of the British, one of whom described him as manifesting 'a curious mixture of dogged determination, savage cunning and treachery'.[45] His interview with Crealock did not last twenty minutes, and when directed to address himself rather to Chelmsford, he took the rebuff as if he had expected it – as well he might have.

Chelmsford's written conditions, which the two messengers had taken off on 6 June, still required an answer. It had been the General's condition that this be returned within eight days. Yet even in this emergency Zulu dignity did not 'permit of hurry'.[46] And, as Cetshwayo could not read the message when it did arrive, it was necessary to bring Cornelius Vijn, the trader whom the war had overcome in Zululand, to the king to do so for him. Vijn was detained at a distance, so it was not until about 17 June that he had arrived at the kwaMbonambi *ikhanda* where the king was resident, translated the note and penned Cetshwayo's response. The king, doubtless affronted by Chelmsford's impossible demands, dictated a proud and dignified reply. Despite his perilous situation, he deprecated negotiations while the British were advancing and plundering as they went. This letter never reached Chelmsford. The four messengers to whom it was entrusted were denied entry when they arrived before Fort Marshall on 22 June and, fearing they would be shot, returned with the note undelivered.

Vijn wrote again. The three messengers, Mgcwelo, Mtshibela and Mpokitwayo (who had first carried Chelmsford's written terms to Cetshwayo), were sent with Vijn's letter in a cleft stick, carrying two great tusks of ivory and driving a herd of 150 of the cattle captured at Isandlwana. They were intercepted on 27 June by a British patrol and brought into Chelmsford's camp on the Mthonjaneni heights, which his combined force had reached that day. The tone of this second letter was much more placatory than that of the undelivered one, and probably reflected Cetshwayo's cooler second thoughts. However, it did not come to grips with the conditions Chelmsford had laid down. The General consequently declared that he would continue his advance, and so would not accept the symbolic tusks. Nevertheless, in order to give the king a last chance to comply, he undertook not to cross the White Mfolozi immediately, and condescended to keep the cattle as a sign that he was still willing to negotiate.[47]

With this the messengers had to be content, and left the next day, telling the interpreter as they went that they 'would have to fight now' as it was impossible for the king to comply with Chelmsford's terms.[48] For his part, the General remained prepared to 'stop hostilities' only if his conditions were complied with in full.[49] For though he credited Cetshwayo and his councillors with a genuine desire to end the war – their desperate situation demanded nothing less – he was convinced that it was still only on their terms, and not on his own.

The king's alarm and desire to negotiate had been greatly increased by political developments in the kingdom, especially in the path of the First Division's advance. Members of Chief Ndwandwe's peace delegation to Crealock at Fort Chelmsford on 15 May admitted that more chiefs would already have given themselves up but for fear and jealousy of the others. Spurred on by this intelligence, John Dunn immediately sent messages out to all the chiefs in the vicinity, inviting them to surrender, or to stay with their king and be destroyed.[50] Two of Dunn's scouts were Mfazi and Fanane. The latter was a half-brother of Sigcwelegcwele, the influential *induna* of the iNgobamakhosi, and the two were sent to him at Ngoye to persuade him to surrender. There they found the king's messengers, sent to summon him to oNdini. Sigcwelegcwele refused to go, sending a brother in his stead. At the same time, he publicly assured Dunn's messengers that he could not be the first to desert the king, thereby effectively hinting at the possibility. In addition, he conceded that he considered the war a great mistake on the king's part. Fanane, on the strength of a subsequent private interview with his half-brother, reported that the *induna* and his people were most relieved that the king was negotiating for peace, as they were very tired of the war.[51]

The impression of Zulu war-weariness which the British were gaining was confirmed for another region by the prisoner Sibhalo kaHibana, who came from south central Zululand. He told his interrogators that the people 'would gladly settle in their kraals again and live in peace', but added that the king, by detaining his chief men about him at oNdini, held the 'whole country in his hands' and so ensured that the people would continue to fight for him.[52] John Dunn disputed this conclusion, for, on the strength of a conversation on 31 May with the royal messenger Sintwangu, he was coming firmly to the opinion that Cetshwayo was beginning to find his influence 'passing away', and that in reality he was not being obeyed as he was said to be.[53]

An example of the king's weakening hold was the response of Muhena, regent of the Mabhudu people to the north-east of Zululand, who had been ruling for his nephew since 1876 only through Cetshwayo's support. In May Cetshwayo ordered him, and the other chiefs in the region who were in a tributary relationship to the Zulu, to join him with their forces as they had for the battle of Gingindlovu. At this stage H. E. O'Neill, the British Consul at Zanzibar, intervened, and persuaded Muhena not to comply with the king's demands. Instead, he ensured that Muhena would pledge his support to the British. Clearly, considerations in Muhena's decision were O'Neill's threats concerning future loss of independence should he aid Britain's enemies, coupled with promises of commercial advantages if he did not. As weighty, though, was the regent's belief that Cetshwayo must inevitably lose the war.[54] By the end of June his messengers were assuring the authorities in Natal that, far from still being Cetshwayo's ally, he was friendly towards the British and desired their protection against possible Zulu retaliation.[55]

Yet it was along the coast that a series of the most significant defections occurred, sufficient to deprive the king of his control of the south-east of his kingdom. In early June, just before the First Division was finally ready to commence its full advance, Prince Dabulamanzi began at last to treat with the British, so confirming the earlier rumours concerning his intention to do so. On 8 June his messengers arrived at Fort Pearson, where Crealock maintained his headquarters until 17 June, and stated that he was 'anxious to come in', but that he had been dissuaded to date by messengers from the king who wished him to negotiate peace on his behalf.[56] Towards the end of June, after the Second Division had advanced, two of the king's messengers, Ntanjana and Sibungu, communicated to Fynney (the Border Agent in Defensive District VI) a private message entrusted to them by Dabulamanzi and Chief Mavumengwana. Both wished to assure the British that it was not out of deceit that they had failed to give themselves up, but that ever since Prince Makwendu's defection on 21 April they had been closely watched (a fact the British had already ascertained), and that they were now awaiting a chance to slip away.

While Dabulamanzi and Mavumengwana gingerly negotiated, two other major figures along the coast took positive steps to come to terms. Phalane kaMdinwa, chief of the Hlangezwa and a commander at Gingindlovu,[57] and the even more prestigious Chief Somopho kaZikhala of the Mthembu, senior *induna* of the emaNgweni *ikhanda*, and commander-in-chief at Gingindlovu, sent to Crealock on 5 June admitting they were beaten and asking for terms. They took this step openly, for they also informed Cetshwayo that their men would not reassemble at oNdini, as he had ordered them to do. These overtures, coupled with a number of defections by minor chiefs along the coast, persuaded Chelmsford to formulate definitive terms for chiefs wishing to submit. He laid down that, on surrender, a chief, with a small personal following, would be relocated to British territory. They would hand over their arms and the royal cattle in their keeping, and the chief would instruct the *izinduna* left in charge of his adherents to submit once troops entered his district. In return, their people were to be spared and protected.[58]

During the third week of June the First Division began to reconnoitre the coast in the vicinity of the open landing-place at Port Durnford, through which it was to draw all its supplies after 9 July. The earlier naval identification of this landing-place had revitalized all the nascent Zulu fears of an amphibious landing. On 24 April, when detached boats from the gunboat HMS *Forester* were taking soundings off Port Durnford, they were fired on from the beach by a large party of Zulu. The gunboat returned fire, killing over thirty cattle which had apparently been driven to the water's edge to entice the British into landing. On 6 May there was a near repetition of the incident, but by the time two steamers arrived at Port Durnford on 30 June with supplies the Zulu had abandoned the vicinity.[59]

Once the First Division crossed the Mlalazi on 22 June, its patrols became much more aggressive. Successively on 23, 24, 26 and 30 June they scoured the countryside bounded by the Mlalazi, Port Durnford, the Mhlatuze and the foothills of the Ngoye range, driving the Zulu and their cattle into the sanctuary of the Ngoye forest. In the course of these punitive sorties, in which the Zulu made little attempt to resist, but fled leaving their stores of mealies intact and their potatoes sown, the British killed five Zulu and captured many others, besides lifting 378 cattle, twenty-seven sheep and twenty-nine goats. They also destroyed over fifty *imizi*, including the principal ones of Sigcwelegcwele and Phalane.[60] On 4 July a strong patrol under Major Barrow fulfilled one of the Division's official objectives by burning the emaNgweni *ikhanda* and twelve other *imizi* in the vicinity, as well as capturing 600 cattle. EmaNgweni consisted of 310 huts, and seems to have been unoccupied for some time. The principal hut, like Cetshwayo's audience building at oNdini, was built in European fashion. It consisted of three rooms and had glass windows, wooden doors, whitewashed walls and a thatched roof.[61] On 6 July Major Barrow and his men burned the 640 huts of the old oNdini *ikhanda*. Like emaNgweni, it was deserted and undefended.[62]

It seemed a questionable necessity to destroy the homes and livelihood of a coastal population which seemed already resigned to submission. Nor did the destruction of emaNgweni and the old oNdini divert a single warrior to their defence; indeed, there was almost no Zulu resistance at all in the coastal zone between the evacuation of the Eshowe garrison and the end of the war. Nevertheless, Crealock was undoubtedly partly right when he attributed the widespread and early submissions of the coastal population to their absolute lack of military success. The battles of Nyezane and Gingindlovu had been disasters, as had the blockade of Eshowe; while since April the Zulu had seen their country progressively occupied by laagers and forts, and their *imizi* burned at will by the enemy.[63] Yet what likely weighed most heavily in the coastal peoples' decision to surrender was their sense that their king had turned his back on them. For while he bent all his energies towards warding off the British advance from the west, his coastal subjects were left at the mercy of the First Division's ruthless patrols.

On the same day the emaNgweni *ikhanda* was burned, and before the news of the battle of Ulundi could have been known, a number of chiefs surrendered to Crealock with 300 fighting-men, 1 500 women and children and 1 327 cattle.[64] They included Mbilwane kaMhlanganiso, *induna* of the kwaGingindlovu *ikhanda*, and a commander at both Nyezane and Gingindlovu; Manyonyo kaZongolo, an *induna* of John Dunn's and an officer in the iNgobamakhosi; and Hobana kaMzwakeli, chief of the Dube and also an officer in the iNgobamakhosi. At the same time, Somopho, Phalane, and the very influential *isikhulu*, Chief Somkhele kaMalanda of the Mphukunyoni, a first cousin of the king's (and an officer of the uThulwana) who dominated the northern coastal plain,[65] as well as the *isikhulu* Chief Mlandlela kaMbiya of the Mthethwa, a cousin of the king's and strongly under the influence of John Dunn, besides several other lesser *izinduna*, all sent word that they were 'coming in', and that the people, as far north as St Lucia Bay, wished to submit. On 5 July the chiefs, all wearing a piece of coloured calico flowing loose over their bodies,[66] tendered their formal submissions at an impressive general parade of the First Division, when they were astonished at the playing of the bagpipes of the 91st Highlanders. After a harangue by Major-General Crealock, in which they were reminded that they were thoroughly beaten and must give up their allegiance to Cetshwayo, they were issued with passes and sent home.

Crealock's lenient terms, which Frere had given him permission to devise, and which were accompanied by threats that *imizi* would be burnt and cattle confiscated if they were not complied with, offered the Zulu their lives and property in return for surrendering their arms and royal cattle.[67] This meant that the local economic and power structures were left minimally disturbed, and persuaded the war-weary people that in submitting they were sacrificing nothing essential. Thus, even before the final battle of Ulundi had been fought, or its consequences could be thoroughly felt, and before much of the coastal plain had even been penetrated by the British, the entire region had abandoned the royal cause and come to terms with the invaders.

Yet the coast made up but part of the kingdom, and because the chiefs of the region were submitting it did not mean that the coastal elements of the *amabutho*, who had been mustering at oNdini since early June, would be unwilling to fight once more in defence of their king. During mid-June the white trader Vijn, who was being held in northern Zululand, saw nothing but great numbers of fighting-men going up continually to join the king.[68] Information from negotiating chiefs and from prisoners confirmed for the British that by the third week of June the bulk of the Zulu army was assembled at oNdini and neighbouring *amakhanda* awaiting the king's instruction. From Vijn it would seem that Cetshwayo was himself at oNdini by about 24 June,[69] and his presence confirmed that he was determined to fight the British should they continue their advance. No options remained save the military one if he intended to keep his throne and his people's independence.[70] With the closing of the frontiers the days had passed when, like Mzilikaze, he could abandon Zululand and establish a kingdom to the north. His fate, and that of his kingdom, would be decided in the Mahlabathini plain.

Notes

1 The most recent and comprehensive account of Chelmsford's preparations for the second invasion of Zululand is to be found in Mathews, 'Chelmsford', pp. 263–91.

2 For British patrols during May across the Mzinyathi, see Laband and Thompson, *Buffalo Border*, pp. 67–73.

3 For Twentyman's raid, see Laband and Thompson, *Umvoti*, pp. 56–67.

4 The lost cattle were the king's, and he was reportedly furious with Godide for not safeguarding them properly.

5 Thompson, 'Border guard', pp. 174–5.

6 For Zulu activity during late May and June in the Phongolo region, see Laband, 'Mbilini', pp. 202–4.

7 For a full account of the Zulu raid of 25 June, see Laband and Thompson, *Umvoti*, pp. 67–78.

8 For the advance of the Second Division and the Flying Column as far as Mthonjaneni, see Mathews, 'Chelmsford', pp. 293, 297–8, 301–2, 312–14.

9 For the Prince Imperial's death, see in particular WC II/1/2: statement of evidence elicited at Ityotyosi River, 26 May 1880: testimony of Umbooza, Umparlarz, Luabagazi and Dabayan; Vijn, *Cetshwayo's Dutchman*, pp. 145–6: Colenso's notes: testimony of Mnukwa; Mitford, *Zulu Country*, pp. 124–5: Sabuza's testimony.

10 *Natal Mercury*, 25 June 1879: Ishangwane correspondent, 11 June 1879.

11 For this skirmish, see *BPP* (C. 2454), enc. in no. 33: Maj.-Gen. Marshall to Maj.-Gen. Newdigate, 5 June 1879; *Times of Natal*, 20 June 1879: correspondent at Ezunganyan camp, 10 June 1879; W. H. Tomasson, *With the Irregulars in the Transvaal and Zululand*, London, 1881, pp. 103–10.

12 Milne Papers, MLN 202/2, Naval Diary: 7, 8, 15 June 1879; St Vincent Journal: 8, 10 June 1879; *BPP* (C. 2454), enc. 1 in no. 51: Buller to Marshall, 16 June 1879.

13 *Natal Witness*, 10 July 1879: Ibabanango correspondent, 19 June 1879; Tomasson, *With the Irregulars*, pp. 131–4.

14 For a description of the routine burning of *imizi* along the British line of advance, see Montague, *Campaigning in South Africa*, pp. 213–17.

15 T. St Lo. Malet, *Extracts from a Diary in Zululand*, Upper Norwood, 1880, pp. 21–2.

16 Ashe and Wyatt Edgell, *Zulu Campaign*, p. 328; Gen. Sir R. Harrison, *Recollections of a Life in the British Army*, London, 1908, p. 181.

17 WO 32/7728: memorandum for guidance of Major-General Crealock, C.B., by Chelmsford, 12 April 1879.

18 J. Mathews, 'Lord Chelmsford and the problems of transport and supply during the Anglo–Zulu War of 1879', unpublished M. A. thesis, University of Natal, 1879, pp. 111–16, 121, 136–7.

19 See AC, p. 43, Clery no. 18: Clery to Alison, 12 July 1879.

20 CP 13, no. 46: telegram, Maj.-Gen. Crealock to Chelmsford, recd. 10 June 1879.

21 Webb and Wright, *Zulu King Speaks*, p. 34; CP 35, no. 16: summary of information by Faenane, 28 May 1879.

22 Rumours reached Natal that Cetshwayo, finding his orders to reassemble being ignored, had despatched an *impi* to the western Nkhandla region to kill a few malingerers to encourage the others.

23 See CSO 1926, no. 1957/1879: Fynn to Colonial Secretary, 11 April 1879; CSO 1927, no. 2090/1879: Fannin to Colonial Secretary, 21 April 1879.

24 SNA 1/1/33, no. 11: Fynn to SNA, 10 May 1879: statement of Mabotyobana, wife of Voboza; CP 9, no. 52: Wood to Military Secretary: statement of scouts from the Zulu Country, 10 May 1879.

25 See particularly CP 13, no. 40: notes by Drummond on the report of Cetywayo's peace messengers, 5 June 1879; CP 16, no. 35: Maj.-Gen. Crealock to Chelmsford, 8 June 1879: statement of Zulu refugee Umsutu; CP 16, no. 40: Drummond to Assistant Military Secretary, 16 June 1879: statement of Umgaunzi.

26 WO 32/7754: 2nd Brigade, 1st Division, Diary ending 15 June: 12 June 1879.

27 WO 32/7750: Diary of 1st Division: 7, 18 May 1879; Stainbank Diary: 13 May 1879.

28 For coastal submissions during April and May, see Laband, 'Zulu polity', pp. 12–13.

29 As Makwendu had no cattle and was consequently destitute, the British gave him rations when he was located over the lower Thukela. He was allowed to return to Zululand in July 1879.

30 KCM 4275: Watson Letters, pp. 40–1: 16 April 1879.

31 CP 35, no. 3: telegram, Maj.-Gen. Crealock to Chelmsford, 15 May 1879.

32 CP 9, no. 52: Wood to Military Secretary, 16 May 1879: statement of scouts from Zulu country; Webb and Wright, *Zulu King Speaks*, p. 34. For the following account of Zulu peace initiatives during May and June, see Laband, 'Humbugging the general', pp. 52–8.

33 CP 13, no. 5: minute by Frere, 4 April 1879.

34 AC, p. 113: Maj.-Gen. Crealock to Alison, 31 May 1879.

35 Fort Chelmsford was built on the amaTigulu River on 23 April by an advance party of the First Division.

36 WO 32/7750: Diary of the First Division, 15 May 1879; WO 32/7740: telegram, Maj.-Gen. Crealock to Chelmsford, 16 May 1879.

37 *BPP* (C. 2374), enc. 10 in no. 32: telegram, Frere to Chelmsford, recd. 30 May 1879.

38 AC, p. 115: Maj.-Gen. Crealock to Alison, 7 June 1879.

39 Harness Letters: Harness to his sister Co, 4 June 1879.

40 CP 13, no. 40: notes by Drummond on the report of the king's peace messengers, 5 June 1879.

41 Colenso and Colenso, *Digest*, series 1, part 2, p. 571.

42 SNA 1/1/34, no. 117: translation of a message from Cetywayo by Fynney, 25 June 1879.

43 Fort Napoleon was begun by the First Division on 25 June and occupied the next day.

44 The tusk was 2.1 m in length and 0.45 m in circumference. It was subsequently forwarded to Queen Victoria.

45 Ashe and Wyatt Edgell, *Zulu Campaign*, p. 317.

46 Gibson, *Story of the Zulus*, p. 209.

47 In a curious incident, the king's further messengers of 30 June refused Chelmsford's request for them to take the cattle back. The British believed at the time that this was because the cattle had been doctored to ensure Chelmsford's defeat, and that the Zulu feared that if they accepted them back the magic would be turned on them instead (*The Graphic*, 30 August 1879, p. 198).

48 WO 32/7761: Gen. Newdigate's Diary for the week ending 29 June 1879: 28 June 1879.

49 WO 32/7751: telegram, Clifford to Secretary of State for War, 3 July 1879.

50 Chelmsford had invited Dunn to join the First Division as Chief of the Intelligence Department. Dunn later wrote that he accepted because he felt he could be of service by inducing the Zulu to give up fighting and by facilitating the submission of the local chiefs, with whom he was well acquainted (Moodie, *John Dunn*, pp. 105, 109–11).

51 For Zulu submissions from late May to June to the First Division, see Laband, 'Zulu polity', pp. 13–15.

52 SNA 1/1/34, no. 73: statement of Sibalo, 1 June 1879.

53 WO 32/7747: correspondence regarding peace: summary of conversation between John Dunn and the king's messenger, Usitwangu, 31 May 1879.

54 CO 179/131, no. Natal/12358: O'Neill to Lord Salisbury, 7 June 1879.

55 GH 1424, pp. 91–3: Bulwer to Wolseley, 1 July 1879.

56 CP 15, no. 4: telegram, Maj.-Gen. Crealock to Military Secretary, recd. 8 June 1879.

57 For Phalane's view in 1882 that Cetshwayo had been the cause of the fighting and that his people had become tired of the war, see Ludlow, *Zululand and Cetywayo*, p. 72.

58 *BPP* (C. 2454), enc. 7 in no. 51: message from the Lieutenant-General . . . to the Zulu chiefs, 16 June 1879.

59 AC, p. 105: Maj.-Gen. Crealock to Alison, 1 May 1879; WO 32/7750: proceedings, 'Forester', 6 May 1879; Norbury, *Naval Brigade*, pp. 294–5.

60 WO 32/7772: Maj.-Gen. Crealock to Wolseley, memorandum of operations of the First Division, 18 April to 7 July 1879; Stainbank Diary: 23, 24, 26, 30 June 1879.

61 *Natal Witness*, 22 July 1879: special correspondent at Port Durnford, 5 July 1879.

62 WO 32/7772: Maj. Barrow to Maj.-Gen. Crealock, 5, 8 July 1879.

63 WO 32/7772: Maj.-Gen. Crealock to Wolseley, memorandum of operations of the First Division, 18 April to 7 July 1879.

64 See Laband, 'Zulu polity', p. 15.

65 When Harford visited Somkhele in late July 1879, he found him living in great state in a huge homestead with a double row of huts and a centre space at least 200 m wide. He was surrounded by his own *izinduna* and at least a thousand warriors. He had become fat and unwieldy-looking, and sat with an old worsted shawl of many colours thrown over his shoulder

(Child, *Harford*, pp. 69–73).

66 *Times of Natal*, 9 July 1879: Port Durnford correspondent, 6 July 1879.

67 WO 32/7772: Maj.-Gen. Crealock to Wolseley, report of operations of First Division, 21 July 1879.

68 Vijn, *Cetshwayo's Dutchman*, pp. 43–4.

69 Ibid., p. 49.

70 *Natal Mercury*, 7 July 1879: correspondent with Newdigate, 16 June 1879: statement of Zulu prisoner.

11

The battle in the plain

The British called the last pitched engagement of the war the battle of Ulundi, their preferred form of oNdini.[1] By naming it after the strategic objective of their invading armies, they signified that to them it was the climax of the campaign. The Zulu, however, normally referred to it as the battle of kwaNodwengu, after the *ikhanda* nearer which it was fought, and also with reference to the old kwaNodwengu near by, which had been built by King Mpande and where he was buried. Curiously, it was once equally well known as oCwecweni, the battle of the corrugated-iron sheets. Doubtless, it was the flashing of the bayonets, swords and gun-barrels along the four sides of the compact British formation which gave rise to this impression. The king himself always maintained that the British had fought from behind iron shields,[2] a view genuinely held by many Zulu who had taken part in the battle. Indeed, some went so far as to insist that the British had hung red coats on the iron palings in front of them, off which the Zulu bullets had harmlessly bounced.[3]

All such tales were perhaps necessary for the Zulu to explain why they, having caught the British in the open, away at last from their forts and entrenched laagers, had yet been unable to overcome them.

There is a tendency among historians today to minimize both the intensity and the significance of the battle. Since the British were determined to restore the image of white invincibility among the black people of southern Africa, it is said that for propaganda purposes they elevated Ulundi to the status of a great and crushing victory, despite its being a half-hearted encounter in comparison with the earlier battles of the war. Moreover, it is contended that the Zulu defeat in the field did not end the war, as has been conventionally accepted. Rather, the rapid winding down of hostilities in the weeks following the battle is explained as the consequence of the desire on both sides to have a rapid end to the war, and of the lenient

British peace terms, which made submission acceptable to the Zulu.[4]

Though there is some truth to this argument, it under estimates the intense Zulu effort during the battle, as well as the widespread consequences that can result from a military encounter. There is more than enough evidence to show that this final overthrow of his army was fatal for the king's authority, as his men were no longer prepared to fight on to preserve the integrity of the Zulu state.

On 26 June, as Chelmsford's joint force approached Mthonjaneni from Babanango, they came in sight of the *amakhanda* in the emaKhosini valley on the right bank of the White Mfolozi. This was a particularly sacred spot for the Zulu, as Cetshwayo's royal ancestors were buried there. Wood moved down into the valley with a strong force with the intention of putting the *amakhanda* to the torch. A Zulu force of between 500 and 600 men of the uNokhenke and uMxhapho guarding them set three on fire themselves before hastily retiring. The British burned six more and the immense quantities of mealies stored in them. The burnt *amakhanda* whose sites are known today were esiKlebheni, kwaDukuza, kwaKhangela, ezinGwegweni, kwaNobamba and emaKheni. The whereabouts of the remaining three – oDlambedlwini, oQeketheni and ekuDabukeni – have still to be established.

Unbeknown to the British, Wood's patrol had committed an act of the greatest symbolic importance to the Zulu. The *inkatha yezwe yakwaZulu* had been kept at esiKlebheni. Handed down from King Shaka himself, it was the symbol of Zulu unity and very nationhood. When it perished in the flames, it was a dire forewarning of the imminent fall of the Zulu kingdom.

Chelmsford was by now probably aware that he had been subordinated in his military command – as had Frere and Bulwer in their civil powers – to General Sir Garnet Wolseley, whom the British government had sent out with chief authority in south-east Africa to end the embarrassing war in Zululand with speed and honour.[5] He certainly knew that Wolseley was eager to delay operations until he could arrive at the front to take personal command. If Chelmsford were to achieve the victory which might wipe out the shame of Isandlwana and the Prince Imperial's death, he must act immediately.

Before he could march down into the Mahlabathini plain, however, it was first necessary to prepare a strong wagon-laager at Mthonjaneni against possible Zulu attack, and to garrison it adequately. The work was completed by the morning of Monday 30 June, when at 8.45 a.m. Chelmsford led out some 5 500 men for the final blow against the Zulu kingdom. All were lightly equipped, marching without kits or tents, and with rations for only ten days. Supplies were carried in 200 ox-wagons, and there were mule-carts for the regimental reserve ammunition. Cavalry reconnoitring to their front soon spotted three armed bodies of Zulu, each about 5 000 strong, on the move towards the White Mfolozi. Their purpose was clearly to guard the drifts should the British attempt to cross. But the invaders did not proceed beyond the foot of Mthonjaneni, and after a difficult march of only 8 km through the thick thornveld halted at about 3.30 p.m.

At midday the by now extraordinarily well-travelled and footsore Mfunzi and Nkisimana finally caught up with Chelmsford.[6] They carried yet a third letter penned by Vijn, and in earnest of their mission presented the sword taken from the body of the Prince Imperial and promised the speedy arrival of the two captured seven-pounders and more cattle. Yet, unbeknown to them, Vijn had done the king an evil turn. The letter carried a postscript in which the trader informed Chelmsford that it was his opinion that the king and people, if not the princes and chiefs, still intended to fight to the end.

Nevertheless, Chelmsford's response to this latest embassy was an easing of his earlier terms. He now declared himself prepared to accept 1 000 rifles captured at Isandlwana in lieu of the surrender of an *ibutho*. Furthermore, he announced that Cetshwayo had until noon on 3 July to comply with his conditions, and that his troops would remain on his side of the White Mfolozi up to that moment. This apparent magnaminity had a purpose, however. The difficult terrain at the foot of Mthonjaneni made it almost impossible for cavalry to operate, and Chelmsford was naturally concerned that the Zulu might attempt to attack his force while it was strung out on the line of march. Continuing diplomatic exchanges would shield the British until they were more favourably placed.

As it turned out, Chelmsford's disingenuous reply never reached Cetshwayo, for the king's councillors denied Mfunzi and Nkisimana access to their royal master. It seems that the councillors were 'hopeless and desperate' and had no desire to prolong negotiations which they recognized as a sham.[7] Nor had Chelmsford's diplomatic duplicity even been necessary. The Zulu were in fact reluctant to attack the advancing column in the thornveld between the foot of

Mthonjaneni and the white Mfolozi because they anticipated that the British would immediately form a laager, and they still hoped to be able to attack them in the open.[8] Moreover, they were unwilling to launch an offensive until they were better informed as to the British position and intentions, and for the present the mounted British patrols were successfully deterring the Zulu scouts and keeping their commanders in the dark.

The British resumed their advance at 7.30 a.m. on 1 July with the seasoned Flying Column in the lead, and Buller and his mounted men reached the drift across the White Mfolozi at about 10.40 a.m. From the vantage-point of a small koppie they were able to watch the Zulu army manoeuvring in the plain beyond. These experienced men of the Flying Column realized that the Zulu were not forming up for an immediate attack, but were being drilled and ritually purified and strengthened in preparation for the fighting to come. Some *amabutho*, about 8 000 strong, came chanting and marching in companies from an *ikhanda* in the extreme north-west of the plain (almost certainly kwaKhandempemvu) and filed into the kwaNodwengu *ikhanda* in splendid order. Within half an hour four more *amabutho* were seen on the march from various points to the emLambongwenya *ikhanda* north-east of oNdini, where the king had gone that morning to address his *amabutho*. There they formed up, filling the space in a huge circle. At about 11.40 a.m. the *amabutho*, duly prepared, poured out in three long, broad columns, causing even Buller's veterans to fear for a moment that they intended to attack. In fact, the British need not have been alarmed, for Cetshwayo had instructed his *amabutho* to bar any British attempt to cross the river, but not to fire first upon them.[9]

Convinced that the Zulu were not planning an offensive that day, the Flying Column began calmly to construct its laager about 1 km from the drift. But before it was completed, and while the wagons of the Second Division were still on the road, a sudden Zulu movement at about 1.30 p.m. towards the river caused a panic among the British, especially the less experienced Second Division. The Zulu did not take advantage of the invaders' patent state of disarray, and by 5 p.m. the *amabutho* had all retired to their quarters, a possibly great opportunity missed.[10]

The following morning, 2 July, the Second Division moved forward to join the Flying Column and formed an entrenched double wagon-laager anchored on a small, stone-built fort. The whole position was designed so that a small garrison could effectively defend the position when the main force advanced across the river.

While the British were strengthening their position, Zibhebhu, who was possessed of a keen tactical eye, decided to ignore the king's injunction not to fire on the British until they had crossed the river. He posted marksmen in the rocks on a high bluff overlooking the river just below the drift. From there they opened fire on British details clearing the way down to the crossing-place, and on watering and bathing parties. British pickets were hurried up to return the Zulu fire, and soon pinned the Zulu down behind their rocks.

Feeling more secure as their fortified post progressed, the British ceased to be disturbed by the regular movements of large bodies of Zulu across the river. On both 2 and 3 July, the Zulu advanced on the river in the morning and then, having made their show of strength and hopefully deterred the British from attempting a crossing, returned at about 9 a.m. to the vicinity of kwaNodwengu, where they cooked a meal before marching off in the direction of oNdini.[11]

Cetshwayo made his last attempt to treat with the invader on 2 July. He ordered a herd of at least 100 of the royal white oxen to be driven towards the British camp as a peace offering. But the young men of the uMcijo turned them back, declaring that there should be no surrender while there were still warriors left to defend their king.[12] The king was not impressed. In a powerful speech to his *amabutho* gathered at oNdini, he made it clear that he considered the uMcijo's gesture foolhardy, for he was convinced that when fighting resumed the British must inevitably win, seeing that the Zulu armies in the past had been unable to halt their advance. Moreover, he voiced his very realistic fear that in defeat his army would disperse, leaving him no option but flight and ultimate capture. At this, his army protested and swore that they would defend him to the last. The king knew better, and sternly warned them that if they did fight, it was against his advice.[13] But seeing that his *amabutho* were determined to offer battle, he issued his instructions. They were not to attack when the British were stationary, for that would suggest they had entrenched, and bitter experience had shown the fatal consequences of an attack against a prepared position. If they did manage to catch them in the open and defeat them, the *amabutho* were not to pursue the British across the river for fear of the guns in the double laager.[14] So the final battle was not to be avoided, and that night the anxious British saw all around them the camp fires of the Zulu, eager to prove themselves against the invader.

Punctually at noon on 3 July, when the space Chelmsford had allowed for a reply to his conditions of 30 June had expired, the cattle, which Cetshwayo had sent in on 27 June as proof of his genuine desire to negotiate, were driven symbolically back across the river. Now that all pretence of negotiation was at an end, Chelmsford was free at about 1 p.m. to send a reconnaissance-in-force under Buller of approximately 500 mounted men of the Flying Column across the river.[15] While about 100 men under Commandant Baker crossed by the wagon drift and seized the bluff where Zibhebhu's snipers were positioned, Buller and the larger part of the force forded the river downstream and wheeled in pursuit of the surprised Zulu. His objective was to advance as far as possible along the road to oNdini, both to observe the ground and to decide where the best position would be for the British to take a stand if the Zulu attacked their advancing force. In fact, he was about to fall into a most cunningly devised ambush.

Buller's horsemen encountered some twenty Zulu scouts who had been deliberately placed to lure them on. With great skill and courage the scouts ran before the horsemen, leading them as far as kwaNodwengu, where other Zulu, driving a large flock of goats, were deployed to draw them towards oNdini. Galloping Zulu horsemen, of whom Zibhebhu was one, then took up the task and brought Buller's force to the valley of the Mbilane stream, where the ambush was prepared. About 4 000 Zulu, among whom the uMxhapho were prominent,[16] were concealed in two lines at right-angles to the British right. The long grass near the banks of the stream had been carefully plaited to trip or impede the horses. But the experienced Buller was beginning to sense a trap, and called a halt when a Zulu presence in the grass was noticed. Upon this, the concealed Zulu rose and fired a volley at the British at about 70 m range. The Zulu fire was as high and as inaccurate as ever, and the British instantly wheeled about. Two other Zulu forces, which had been hidden on both flanks of the British as they had passed unwittingly between them, now began to close together to cut off the route back to the laagers. Buller was saved by Commandant Raaff's horsemen, who covered his retreat from where he had positioned them near kwaNodwengu, and by Baker's men still near the bluff, supported by fire across the river. But Buller was lucky to reach the drift before the Zulu could cut him off, with the loss of no more than three killed and four wounded.

The experience had been something of a shock to the British. They could not but admit that the Zulu had shown themselves to be excellent strategists, and had to admire the professional Zulu skirmishing order and courage as they came on as far as the drift in pursuit of Buller's horsemen. For their part, the Zulu were naturally much elated with their near success. Some who later came down to the river's edge chaffed the British outposts, and with derisive laughs gloated over their victory that day, promising that none would escape should the British again leave the protection of their laager.[17]

Yet the British were well content. Buller had been able to fix on the ideal position for the coming battle. (Ironically, this very spot, just to the north-east of kwaNodwengu, had also been selected by Cetshwayo as the place where the British should be brought to battle.)[18] Moreover, his reconnaissance had revealed that the likely Zulu tactical intention in the battle, which Chelmsford intended to fight the following day, would be to surround the British and to cut them off from their base on the opposite bank.

It was a bitterly cold night of bright moonlight. The British were startled at about 11 p.m. by a sound which seemed at first like distant thunder, but was in fact the noise of the Zulu *amabutho* being prepared for their last great battle in defence of their kingdom. The roar of men's voices and the shrill cries of the women as they danced and sang was quite terrifying to the British. Some of the singing came from a large contingent who had arrived that very night from the coast and were greeting the king. Blacks with the British force made out some of the words of the songs, the refrains of which consisted of defiance of the British and laments over the men who had fallen that day.[19] There was in addition much movement as the Zulu marched from *ikhanda* to *ikhanda*. At one stage they approached the river, firing off occasional shots. But they did not go on to attack the British and, still singing, marched away at about midnight, apparently to take up their positions for the coming day.

At 3.45 a.m. on that fateful Friday, 4 July 1879, the British began their preparations in bright moonlight. The total strength of the force being marshalled was 4 166 white and 958 black soldiers, twelve pieces of artillery and two Gatling guns. At 5.15 a.m. the bugles sounded a bogus reveille at the normal hour in a feeble attempt to deceive the watching Zulu into supposing that nothing untoward was in progress. As day broke the British began to cross the river. They left behind them five companies of the 1/24th in the laager and one company of Royal Engineers in the fort, as well as other small detachments – 529 white and ninety-three black troops in all. Colonel W. Bellairs was in command, and it was his duty to hold the camp should the Zulu attempt to capture the British base once the main force was committed in the plain.[20]

Buller's mounted irregulars crossed by the lower drift at about 6 a.m. and took up position on the bluff which overlooked the drift over which the rest of the force had passed soon after 7 a.m. Despite British fears, the Zulu did not oppose the crossing. The Zulu plan was to allow the British into the plain and to force them to fight in the open, so they could be destroyed as at Isandlwana. They feared that, if they attacked them at the drift before they were properly across, the British would fall back on their impregnable fortified position.[21]

About 2.5 km from the drift, when at 7.30 a.m. the British had struggled through the rough and bushy ground into the open country, the Flying Column (which was in the lead) halted with the great circle of huts of what was probably the kwaBulawayo *ikhanda* to their left. While Buller's men continued to reconnoitre in the direction of kwaNodwengu, the Flying Column formed the front half of a hollow square, which was completed by the Second Division marching up behind them. The regular British infantry were ranged four deep, with the guns distributed at the faces and at the angles, where the formation was its most vulnerable. At this stage all the mounted men continued outside the square, but reserve companies (who might be required to plug a gap), the Royal Engineers, attached Native Pioneers, the NNC, ammunition wagons, water-carts, stretchers and medical personnel all took up position inside. Shortly before 8 a.m. the square set off towards the north-east, following a route between the supposed kwaBulawayo and kwaNodwengu *amakhanda*.[22]

Chelmsford's square was already an archaic formation in European warfare, devised originally as an infantry tactic for repelling cavalry. Yet this shoulder-to-shoulder formation was finding a new lease of life in colonial warfare, where it was particularly effective in all-round defence against an enemy who sought like cavalry to envelope flank and rear with great rapidity, and then to overwhelm the European invaders with shock tactics and superior numbers. Isandlwana had demonstrated that a widely spaced firing-line (even when equipped with the most sophisticated weapons), though necessary in European warfare against a similarly armed enemy, was ineffective against such an attack. On the other hand, the experience of Rorke's Drift, Khambula and Gingindlovu had shown that the Zulu had little chance against disciplined, concentrated fire by well drilled troops in an all-round position. An infantry square was naturally not as secure as an entrenched laager or fort, but it possessed their tactical advantages and its tight formation improved the confidence of the troops. Moreover, once an enemy's attack had broken before the square's disciplined ranks, he would be vulnerable to a devastating counter-attack by cavalry which had been kept in reserve within the safety of the square. The square's chief disadvantage – which was vulnerability to effective gunfire – did not apply in Zululand, where Zulu marksmanship had consistently proved to be poor.[23] There was also a moral advantage beyond the purely military to be gained by forming square. By advancing against the Zulu and beating them as thoroughly in the open plain as they had done hitherto from behind the security of a fortified laager, the British would demonstrate once and for all that further resistance was pointless.[24]

The square (which was a clumsy formation to manoeuvre) proceeded in rather loose formation across the plain, where the grass stood 0.6 m high. It was unharassed by the Zulu, for Buller's men were fanned out in advance and about 0.8 km away on the flanks to 'touch' the Zulu and keep their skirmishers away. The irregular horse of the Second Division, who made up part of the rear-guard, set light to kwaBulawayo as they passed. On approaching kwaNodwengu, Chelmsford ordered the square to 'half right turn', so that the *ikhanda* remained on his right flank and the front of the square now faced oNdini, and brought it to a halt at about 8.30 a.m. on the spot Buller had selected the previous day. The guns were got into position and the ammunition boxes opened. While the men standing in the rear of the four ranks filled the gaps between the men standing in the third, the front two ranks kneeled. All fixed their bayonets. Wood's men began to throw up a slight shelter trench outside their part of the battle formation.[25]

The position was ideal. The ground sloped gently down for several hundred metres on every side from the level top of the slight knoll, providing a perfect field of fire and scope for cavalry pursuit. It was uncommanded from any point, and there was little bush for cover, only the long grass. There Buller's men found and buried the naked corpses of their comrades who had been killed in the reconnaissance of the previous day, and whom the Zulu had ritually disembowelled.[26]

When at daybreak the Zulu saw the British crossing the White Mfolozi without the great number of wagons necessary to form a defensive laager, they thought the invaders must have taken leave of their senses so to deliver themselves into their hands.[27] The necessarily deliberate advance of the British square gave the Zulu time, moreover, to develop their strategy. Not a Zulu showed himself to the British until some allowed themselves to be spotted in a donga 0.8 km from the river, after which they drew Buller's men from each donga to the next. For it was the Zulu intention to repeat their ploy of the day before and, unnecessarily as it proved, lure the square to the battleground of their mutual choosing between kwaNodwengu and oNdini.[28] Perhaps the British were right to have believed that the Zulu would have been wiser to have attacked them while forming square, or moving through broken ground unsuitable for cavalry – but that was not the Zulu plan. In fact, it was only at about 8 a.m., as they were approaching kwaNodwengu, that the British first saw the Zulu gathering in any strength, and began to understand from their movements that it was the Zulu intention to envelop them, as their prior experience of Zulu strategy had always led them to suppose it would be.

To the west an estimated six *amaviyo* were collecting, and twelve *amaviyo* were forming 1 350 m to the north. These bodies continued to swell as they were joined by warriors streaming out of the *amakhanda*, so that the British were acutely conscious of the dark clusters of Zulu lining the crests of the hilltops to their left. The Zulu, moving at first in a straggling column parallel to the British square, began to form up in good order for the attack, while, to the east, in the stream beds of the thornveld around oNdini, great masses of warriors began to appear through the early morning mists and the smoke from their camp fires which had previously obscured them. The Zulu on the hills, and in the thornveld to the left, front and right of the British square first joined up to form the classic crescent battle formation, and then at about 8.20 a.m. the concentration to the front and right extended at the double to pass around kwaNodwengu to the rear of the square, and so to complete a great circle around the British, over 14 km in length.[29]

While the British were advancing on kwaNodwengu, two Zulu

forces, perhaps about 5 000 strong, were moving out of an *ikhanda* near the river to the right of them (whose name it has not been possible to establish) in the direction of the entrenched camp across the White Mfolozi. It is conceivable that their intention had been to dispute the British crossing and that they had been caught unawares by the early start; but it is most likely that their purpose was to capture the British base and cut off the square's retreat. At 8.10 a.m. the two *izimpi* came close enough to the drift for the garrison of the post to go on the alert, and some Zulu even crossed the river and came to within 450 m of the laager. However, they never seriously threatened the garrison, and the two *izimpi* soon melted away to join in the battle developing in the plain.[30]

There, the British watching the Zulu advance could only wonder at the skill and timing which, considering the difficult terrain and the varying distances they had to traverse, allowed the Zulu units to synchronize their envelopment. As the Zulu moved down the hills towards them they appeared at first to the British to be almost indistinguishable from the aloes that covered the slopes. It was soon apparent, though, that the Zulu were closing in, keeping the most 'splendid order' in loose undulating lines of companies about four deep, with intervals between the *amabutho*, followed by others in file to the rear. They were preceded by irregular waves of skirmishers (just as 'modern tactics' required, the admiring British realized), who opened a desultory fire at a great distance. In all, the Zulu advance was a revelation to the recent British reinforcements who, unlike the veterans of the Flying Column, had not before met the Zulu in pitched battle, and who had been led to expect a rush from dense, irregular masses rather than the 'splendid manoeuvring' in half-open order which they were witnessing.[31]

The size of the Zulu army converging on the British is a matter of some debate. Contemporaries could not agree on a figure. The official British estimation was 20 000,[32] though other figures varied between 30 000 and 10 000. King Cetshwayo himself declared that all his *amabutho* were represented at the battle, and that the army was about the same size as that which had fought at Isandlwana,[33] which has been estimated at nearly 20 000 strong. Frances Colenso, however, very sensibly pointed out that as the Zulu army had gathered from over such a wide area, and as some *amabutho* had suffered severely in earlier engagements, it was almost impossible to arrive at any reliable conclusion as to its size based on knowledge of the *amabutho* said to have been present.[34] Her reservations seem to have been reinforced by the intelligence that not all the *amabutho* responded fully to the order to muster, and that fewer of the Zulu along the Natal border, for example, took part in the call-up before the battle than for Khambula. In sum, it seems likely that the Zulu army on 4 July was between 15 000 and 20 000 strong, with over 5 000 in reserve. Greater precision is not possible.

Despite reports to the contrary, the king was not in personal command of his army that day. Having instructed his generals, he had left oNdini on the evening of 3 July, and had travelled east with his *isigodlo* to the emLambongwenya *ikhanda* of his father, Mpande. The iNdabakawombe *ibutho* acted as escort. On learning early the next morning that the British were advancing across the river, the king moved further away to his kwaMbonambi *ikhanda*, followed later by his *isigodlo*. He was at kwaMbonambi throughout the battle, and had look-outs posted to give him news of the outcome. Ziwedu kaMpande, his favourite brother, who stood in status among the princes second only to Hamu (who had betrayed them all), watched the battle from the Mcungi Hill in the company of other of the king's brothers and many of the great chiefs. It was Ziwedu's presence which was popularly mistaken for that of the king.[35]

Who were the other commanders present? The British were concerned to establish the presence of Zulu leaders to whom they attached particular notoriety, but the evidence is weak. Dabulamanzi, for example, clearly could not have been at the battle, since he was on the coast under the king's surveillance on account of his intended defection. Mnyamana left the king on the morning of 4 July and rejoined him after the battle, so it is probable but unproven that he was with Ziwedu. It is likely that other close advisers of the king, such as Ntshingwayo, Sihayo and his son Mehlokazulu, Qethuka kaManqondo, Mtuzwa, the brother of Sekethwayo, and Muwundula kaMamba, brother of the eMgazini chief and *induna* of kwaNodwengu – all of whom were reported to have attended what was probably Cetshwayo's last formal meetings with his councillors on 2 July – witnessed the battle.[36] Not one of them, though, came to the fore during its course. Thus besides Ziwedu, whose presence is established, it is impossible to be sure who the other major Zulu commanders were, let alone to identify their subordinate officers.

There is more certainty over the actual Zulu order of battle, though there is nothing comparable to the detailed information available concerning the British dispositions. Ulundi poses special problems, however, because of the numbers of Zulu hanging back as uncommitted reserves. Moreover, as the attack was pressed home, *amabutho* naturally lost formation and became intermingled, making positive identification of their positions even more uncertain. In the end, the most authoritative analysis that survives is that compiled by Captain E. Woodgate, Wood's staff officer, from his own observation and from information gained from prisoners. According to Woodgate, the uDloko *ibutho* came straight at the front of the British square. The encircling left horn consisted of the uThulwana, iNdluyengwe, iSangqu and iMbube, and there is positive reference elsewhere to the uMbonambi. The Zulu right horn was made up of the uMxhapho, iNsukamngeni, uDududu, iQwa, uNokhenke and iNdlondlo *amabutho*. The iNgobamakhosi and uVe attacked the right rear of the square, and the uMcijo the left rear.[37] It seems too, despite the regent Muhena's withdrawal of his support from the Zulu cause, that some Tsonga were also present. Elements of other *amabutho* went unregarded either because they were few in number, or because they made up the uncommitted reserves.

In meeting the imminent Zulu attack the British employed standard tactics. The square is a defensive formation, dependent on a great development of fire which will mow down an enemy charge and bring it to a standstill before getting close enough for hand-to-hand combat. For fire to be effective, it was essential to ensure that it was accurate and well disciplined, and that it was reserved until the enemy were well into range, or no further than about 630 m away.[38] To open fire too early would not only be ineffective, but might have the additional disadvantage of scaring the enemy off before its full effect could be felt. The initial objective, then, was to tempt the Zulu into effective range. The case of Khambula had already demonstrated how effective irregular horse could be in provoking uncoordinated charges that could be dealt with most successfully in turn. They were accordingly sent into action while the regular cavalry of the Second Division (the 17th Lancers and the small detachment of Dragoons), who considered the terrain not suitable and the Zulu line too powerful to be charged, entered the rear of the square.[39]

Buller's irregular horsemen engaged with the Zulu between 8.35 and 8.45 a.m. Baker's Horse first made contact when they advanced towards the left horn of the rapidly closing Zulu formation, which broke up and scattered into skirmishing order when they saw the horsemen coming. Lieutenant Parmenter cantered ahead with about twenty men and at close range poured a volley into the Zulu at about 180 m. Furious at being bearded by so small a body, the Zulu fired at random and rushed forward to try – unsuccessfully – to cut Parmenter off. Even more effective were Captain Cochrane's Natal Native Horse, who were in advance of the right of the square. They conducted a measured withdrawal, pouring volley after volley into the Zulu and hurrying on their advance. Irritated Zulu called tauntingly after them: 'Gallop on, but we will overtake you. We are going to kill every one of those red men!'[40]

All Buller's mounted units were soon heavily engaged on three sides, and retired independently on the square with equal regularity and steadiness, drawing the Zulu behind them. Meanwhile, Shepstone's Horse, who were attached to the Second Division, waited to the left rear of the square for the uMcijo to come on in a great column more than thirty deep, firing wildly, waving their shields and shouting 'uSuthu!' Shepstone's Horse opened fire at the close range of 270 m before retiring slowly into the square before them. As they fell back the artillery opened fire over their heads. Soon all the horsemen were safely back in the square, the front and rear faces of which had wheeled outwards to receive them, before closing again to face the Zulu. The battle was about to begin in earnest.

The nine-pounder guns fired their first shot at 8.45 a.m. when the Zulu were well within range 990 m away. Soon the guns on all four sides of the square, where they were dispersed to meet the Zulu envelopment, were firing away, at this stage from positions just outside the formation. The Zulu, mainly because they were in skirmishing order, suffered little harm at first, though some were staggered by the bursting shells, and a few scattered. Perhaps there is some truth in the observation that the shrapnel eventually 'took the dash' out of the Zulu attack,[41] but this was not immediately apparent. For the Zulu instantly rallied, with the intention of rushing in. Their great circle surrounding the square contracted to within 270 m, or close range for the Martini-Henry rifles and Gatling guns, so that small-arm fire joined that of the guns. At 8.50 a.m. the fire from the square became general, though the right face, where the Natal Native Horse had drawn the Zulu on so effectively, came into action a few moments before the other three.

The Zulu advanced into this terrible fire still in skirmishing order, but with large masses behind in support. They closed in steadily and in silence, and only uttered their war-cry 'uSuthu!' when they were preparing for the final rush.[42] Those who made this desperate charge were stripped for battle of all finery, and were fine, well-built men of the younger *amabutho*. Indeed, the perfect state of their teeth was to be a matter of admiration for the British when they later inspected the dead.[43]

In the main, the attack brought the Zulu no closer than between 63 m and 90 m of the British position, or within point-blank range. There were individual exceptions, like the young warrior who was shot fruitlessly throwing his spear at 18 m. But this failure to reach the laager and engage in hand-to-hand combat (as the Zulu had managed to achieve at Khambula) has encouraged historians like Jeff Guy to assert that the Zulu attack was half-hearted, because the Zulu entertained no hope of success.[44] Certainly, there is some contemporary evidence to support this view. Prisoners were reported to have said that as they were moving to the attack word passed among them: 'What are we marching there for? Only to be killed.' Consequently, there were those who fought without enthusiasm, while others broke away.[45] In this regard, the comments of Wood, the victor of Khambula, have been unduly influential. In his autobiography he unfavourably compared the 'hurried, disorderly manner' in which the *amabutho* came on at Ulundi with their 'methodical, steady order' at Khambula.[46] But Wood was not a disinterested observer. He was not in command at Ulundi, and clearly wished to minimize Chelmsford's success there while emphasizing the magnitude of his earlier victory at Khambula. It cannot be denied, though, that the Zulu must have learned from their experience at both Khambula and Gingindlovu, and were thoroughly aware of the effect of British fire at close and point-blank range. Nor can there be any doubt that their string of defeats had affected their confidence and shaken their earlier sense of invincibility. Mehlokazulu even stated that the Zulu at Ulundi did not fight with 'the same spirit, because [they] were then frightened'.[47]

Yet this is really no more than proof that the Zulu had acquired a better appreciation than before of the effectiveness of close-range and concentrated fire, and thus a more realistic sense of when it was pointless to persist in an attack. As Colonel W. A. Dunne commented, though their bravery was conspicuous, the Zulu were no longer prepared to display the reckless daring so evident in earlier battles.[48] For there is overwhelming evidence to show that in the initial stages of the battle, before the hopelessness of their task overcame them, the Zulu came on with enormous pluck, advancing with the 'same intrepidity' as at Khambula and Gingindlovu.[49] The newspaper artist Melton Prior could only reflect that of all the campaigns in which he had taken part, never before had he come across so courageous a foe, nor one which he had felt more pride in seeing beaten.[50]

The British were confident of their ability to crush the Zulu assault, and the men of the 1/13th Regiment were seen beckoning to the Zulu and shouting, 'Come on, you black devils!'[51] Yet how intense or effective was the British fire? The British infantry – and the following figures exclude the colonial mounted units, for which there is no tally – fired some 35 000 rounds exclusive of artillery fire, which amounted in turn to ninety rounds of artillery ammunition and the three rockets shot at kwaNodwengu. Rounds fired were calculated at between seven and 6.4 per infantryman.[52] From these statistics Frances Colenso concluded – and in this she is followed by Guy – that there was a low rate of fire, which proved how easily the Zulu were repelled.[53] Colonel Callwell, however, pointed out in his official manual on the conduct of 'small wars' that heavy expenditure of ammunition was unusual on such campaigns, and that in a typical battle under ten rounds per man was the norm.[54] Moreover, it should be remembered that it is unrealistic to link ammunition consumption with rate of fire, because none of the men in the square was engaged without pause for the entire battle. Strict fire discipline was practised as the British steadily fired volleys by company, and this would have reduced the rate of fire while increasing its accuracy.[55]

At close range (up to 270 m), it is calculated, fire was 10 per cent effective; while at point blank range (up to 90 m), the figure could go up to 15 per cent. Although casualties per shot seem to have been low, the effect was enough to disable assailants four times the number of those firing. In determining the outcome of a battle, moreover, volume of fire was just as important as the casualties inflicted, for if it could be maintained (which it certainly was by the four-deep British formation at Ulundi), that was sufficient to subdue the fiercest attack.[56] In other words, it is important not simply to judge the effects of fire by the casualties inflicted, but to consider how successful it was in *deterring* the enemy.

The Zulu were a hard target to hit because of their open order and their wonderful use of whatever cover was available. Those advancing were seen running in a crouching position behind their shields, while the masses lay in the high grass (the British had only managed to beat down the grass for a few metres outside their square) and afforded no target to the British except the smoke of their firing. This was probably the reason for much high volley-firing from the square, which saved the Zulu casualties. In addition, the volume of smoke aided the Zulu, as the British could not see many metres to their front because of it. The smoke from their weapons was made worse from the billows given off by kwaNodwengu, which the British had set alight as they passed, and Chelmsford very soon had to order the fire there to be extinguished. Every now and again the bugles had to sound the cease-fire to allow the smoke to clear away, and then the Zulu would take advantage of the lull to creep closer and blaze away at the square.[57] The new British weapon, the Gatling gun, was not as effective as had been hoped, for the pair in operation were capable of causing havoc among the Zulu only for so long as they did not jam, which they did repeatedly. Their effect was certainly initially demoralizing for the Zulu, who suffered heavy casualties before them at point-blank range (Wood counted sixty dead in the long grass 63 m to their front),[58] though some Zulu still managed to get up to within 36 m of them.

In other words, while the Zulu were able to make use of cover to avoid the full effects of British fire at some distance from the square, they were unable to press with any degree of safety or success into the zone within 90 m (or point-blank range) of the British firing-line. It was this impenetrable wall of fire which ultimately deterred the Zulu and persuaded them to give up their assault.

In turn, it may seem extraordinary that the British square was not more vulnerable to the energetic Zulu fire. Most of the Zulu had some form of firearms, and they probably carried more at Ulundi than the British, though the majority were inferior muzzle-loaders of some sort.[59] But there were small numbers of breech-loaders, including Martini-Henry rifles, captured at Isandlwana, Ntombe and Hlobane. And the British square did present an enormous target, with its interior crammed with wagons, draught animals, dismounted cavalry and irregular horse, as well as the NNC. For all that, casualties were very low on account of the usual poor Zulu marksmanship. No sooner had the square taken up its battle position than it had been assailed by a dropping and harmless fire from the distant Zulu who were still out of range, especially those advancing from the direction of oNdini. Yet even when they converged on the square and the range was less, their fire was equally ineffective, despite the heavy fusillade which they maintained for about half an hour from their final position around the square. The fundamental Zulu fault was still that they almost all shot too high. The British supposed they did so because they erroneously believed that by raising their sights so as to fire at long range they would increase the velocity of bullets at short range. Be that as it may, what casualties the British did suffer were mostly in the rear ranks, where the men were wounded in the back as a consequence of Zulu fire coming over the heads of the men on the opposite side of the square.[60] Indeed, there were cases of Zulu being hit by fire from their comrades on the far side of the British square. There were naturally some Zulu snipers who were more accurate than the mass, though the British were generally able to pick them off.

The Zulu came their nearest to breaking through the cordon of British fire and reaching the square at its right rear corner. The angle of a square is its weakest point because less fire can be developed there, and because there is more likelihood of confusion in the ranks. The Zulu instinctively grasped this fact. Thus, when the Zulu advancing against the right face of the square from the kwaNodwengu *ikhanda* were checked by medium-range fire at between 360 m and 450 m, they changed their tactics and made for the right rear corner. (KwaNodwengu, it should be noted, served as a Zulu rallying-point throughout the battle. As it provided good cover close to the British position, crowds of Zulu were constantly rushing into it. Some lined the huts and the stockade facing the square, and kept up a heavy, though inevitably ineffective, fire.)[61] The assault from kwaNodwengu, then, veered left up a depression running along the British rear, which gave the Zulu complete shelter to within 134 m of the right rear corner. Here they rapidly collected, between 2 000 and 3 000 strong and thirty ranks deep. Striking their white shields and shouting 'uSuthu!' they penetrated the cordon of point-blank fire and charged to within 27 m of the corner, while a few corpses were later found only nine paces from the British line. So close did they come that Battery N, 6th Royal Artillery, had to fire seven rounds of case-shot (which is used only at the closest quarters), and several officers drew their swords or revolvers, expecting a hand-to-hand fight.[62] The 5th Company, Royal Engineers, was brought up from its position behind the front face to reinforce the corner, though their help ultimately proved unnecessary. Lord Chelmsford was seriously alarmed, and requested the men of the threatened corner to fire faster. The British infantry were still managing to remain as cool as if on parade, and were obeying their officers' orders on sighting and firing in sections. They responded to Chelmsford by developing such a 'solid and well directed' weight of fire that Captain Slade considered that no troops in the world could have stood up to it, and honestly marvelled at the way the Zulu nevertheless persisted as long as they did.[63]

The determined and nearly successful assault by what were mainly the iNgobamakhosi and uVe on the right rear corner of the square was not fully matched by that of their habitual rivals, the uMcijo, on the left rear corner. Shepstone's Horse had retired before their column of over thirty men deep, which came up in the most determined manner from a hill to the left rear of the British to the cover of a ridge 270 m away. There, almost out of close range, they were checked by the British fire and deterred from advancing any further in force, though daring individuals came dashing down the slope and, concealed in the grass, crept forward to snipe. Meanwhile, the attack against the left side of the square was pushed forward with such vigour that the infantry fixed bayonets in expectation of hand-to-hand fighting. But there too the Zulu were held. At the front face of the square the Zulu developed their attack where a dip in the ground allowed them to form up in comparative safety. Here too they were checked as they appeared at the crest.[64]

At this stage, with the Zulu assault pinned down at every quarter, the main Zulu reserve, a few thousand strong and apparently made up of members of the older *amabutho*, emerged from oNdini. They moved down the slope towards the Mbilini stream in a wide rectangular column fifty deep, beating their shields and shouting their war-cries. The British moved two nine-pounder guns from the left rear to the left front angle (the Gatlings at the front face were jammed), and opened fire at about 2 000 m with shrapnel. The shells burst in front of the Zulu column, which opened out into two wings. When a shell fell on each of the wings they hesitated, then closed. Two more shells falling on the reunited column caused it to turn and leave the field.[65] Other reserves, which were posted to the north on the hills to the British left, as well as between them and the river, with the purpose of cutting off the retreat of the square should it break, were consequently not brought up and never came under fire. Their immobility may also be partially ascribed to the reserves' heeding of the king's warning not to fight the British if they were stationary, as this was presumed to indicate that they were entrenching their position.[66]

The battle in the plain was contested sharply for about half an hour from the time it became general, until at about 9.15 a.m. the Zulu attack began to slacken and then falter. Lieutenant-Colonel Robinson was convinced that this was not from any loss of nerve on the part of the Zulu, but because they were perplexed that they could find no way round or through the British fire. They had doubtless been confident that, working around the faces of the square, they would eventually find some opening to exploit (such as the nearly gained right rear corner), through which to overwhelm the British at close quarters. Yet as success eluded them they began to hesitate: some stopped, while other individuals began to run away. This gradually precipitated a general disorderly withdrawal which was under way by 9.20 a.m., though as yet there was no general rout. For though the Zulu fell back, it was not far, and attempts were made to rally.[67]

When the British realized that the Zulu were retiring they ceased fire. Wood tried to suppress their jubilation, for he believed that the Zulu would make a last stand at oNdini.[68] But it was not to be, and the sound of British cheering only disheartened some of the Zulu further, for it convinced them that the battle was indeed lost.[69] Yet for others the British cease-fire was an encouragement. They paused to look back, clearly hoping to see the British formation breaking in pursuit, and so affording them that long-awaited opportunity to close with the invader in hand-to-hand combat. But they were to be disappointed. The left face of the square greeted the momentary Zulu halt at 9.25 a.m. with a short burst of firing, and artillery-fire broke up every new concentration. Demoralization began inevitably to set in and the Zulu retreat gathered momentum. It was now becoming a question of escaping unscathed from the hopeless field, and as they fled the Zulu felt acutely that their 'fighting strength was sinking like the setting sun'.[70]

This was the moment the cavalry had long awaited. Regular

infantry were unable to deliver an effective counter-thrust against an adversary as mobile as the Zulu, but a well-timed cavalry charge over the open plain was enough to throw the disordered Zulu into a panic, to turn retreat into rout, and to transform a victory into a decisive triumph.

An exultant pursuit was one of the uglier faces of colonial warfare. There is unfortunately no doubt that the British revelled in it. Yet, for all its savagery, the cavalry's counter-attack was a complete success in achieving its objectives. At 9.25 a.m., after hesitating for a few minutes to give the order until the Zulu retreat was general, Chelmsford directed Colonel Drury-Lowe to pursue the Zulu. Five troops of the 17th Lancers, and twenty-four men of the King's Dragoon Guards under Captain Brewster, formed up to the rear of the square, where they were met by heavy fire from a large body of Zulu who had remained hidden in the long grass. Their firing, though, was as ineffective as ever, and the cavalry ignored them, charging initially in the direction of kwaNodwengu.[71] The Lancers, having soon dispersed or killed those Zulu who had been unable to reach the shelter of the *ikhanda*, and discovering that there were too few Zulu in its vicinity to make their presence worthwhile, halted, and then wheeled right about to confront large numbers of Zulu who were again concentrating to the right rear of the square. In a furious charge they pursued the Zulu, who scattered in an attempt to reach the lower slopes of the hills about 3 km away, overtaking and killing the warriors, who were running away nearly as fast as the horses could gallop. By the time the Lancers had driven the Zulu to the hills they began to realize that the ground had become too difficult for cavalry. Moreover, the Zulu were now rallying on the hills to receive them and, reinforced by some of the reserves, were setting up a galling fire on the floundering cavalry, whose horses were in any case quite blown. So recognizing that the pursuit could not be continued, and having no fresh horsemen in support, the cavalry wisely rallied and retired with some loss out of range of the Zulu.

The Lancers felt they had proved their worth that day, and vindicated the use of the lance, which, although as anachronistic as the infantry square in terms of European warfare, was still invaluable in the colonial context against irregular troops scattered in flight. Despite a tendency to stick in the shield it had penetrated, which had persuaded the cavalry to draw their heavy sabres, it was quickly recognized that only the lance was effective when the Zulu flung themselves flat or sheltered in crevasses. Although some of the Zulu avoided the deadly thrusts of the lances in this way, many of the pursued desperately turned and fought for their lives in stubborn knots, never crying for quarter. They dodged among the horses, firing at them, stabbing at their bellies and sometimes seizing a lance in an attempt to drag the horseman from his saddle. The heavy casualties among the cavalry horses – twenty-eight killed and forty-five wounded – attests to Zulu determination.

Meanwhile, Captain Browne and the Mounted Infantry of the Flying Column moved out of the square in support of the Lancers. They fired into the flank of the Zulu retreating before the cavalry, and eventually merged into their line. The rest of Buller's mounted men dashed out of the right front corner of the square a few minutes after the Lancers began their charge. Captain Cochrane and the Natal Native Horse, who were in the lead, chased the Zulu beyond oNdini until they reached the Zulu reserve. The Zulu turned at bay when overtaken by Buller's horsemen, as they had with the Lancers, first firing at them and then using their spears, or crouching down to hide in the long grass. The irregular horse used their carbines pistol-wise, and probably with more deadly effect than the lance or sabre of the cavalry. Like the Lancers, they pursued the Zulu as far as the hills. Once on the hillsides, which were inaccessible to the horses, the Zulu began rallying in groups to fire on Buller's men, who retired in their turn.

It still remained for the British to flush out and kill those Zulu who had succeeded in concealing themselves in dongas and long grass during the pursuit, or who had feigned death, or who had thought the retreat of their comrades only temporary, and had not joined the flight. Yet, whatever their reason for lingering on the fatal plain, they also died hard in the end, fighting to the last and never crying out for mercy. Some of the Natal Native Horse, for example, attacked and killed about seventy Zulu who had been cut off in a donga to the rear of the Lancers as they charged.[72] Others dispatched Zulu who had taken refuge in the pools and under the banks of the Mbilane stream. The regimental mascot of the 17th Lancers, a great cross-bred dog, distinguished himself in his regiment's eyes by running about and barking furiously whenever he came upon a living Zulu in the grass.[73] The Native Horse in particular were both thorough and cruel, under no circumstances sparing an enemy, even if wounded. Hours after the battle was over the firing of their carbines told of their horrible work, from which they were not to be dissuaded. Yet even then the wretched Zulu fugitives, if not too badly wounded, would try to sell their lives dear. They also fell victim to the NNC who emerged from the square to spear disabled Zulu and to plunder the *amakhanda*. As a consequence of this pitiless activity, of which many British officers were heartily ashamed, only two Zulu prisoners were taken alive that day.[74]

As the main body of Zulu retreated in great masses over the hills to the north, the British moved up their six nine-pounder guns to shell them. They opened fire at 9.40 a.m. on the Zulu, who were squatting down in exhausted groups on the hilltops 4 400 m away, and in a kloof near oNdini. Though out of range, and bursting too high to cause much damage,[75] the shrapnel rapidly caused the resting Zulu to scatter,and after a few rounds they had disappeared over the crests of the hills. It seems that the shrapnel bursts may have caused a few casualties among the women who had been watching the battle from what they had supposed was the security of the hills.[76]

Once the British had finished congratulating each other, attending the wounded and burying the dead where they had fallen, the square moved forward at 11.30 a.m. to the banks of the Mbilane stream. There the men rested and had their dinner. Meanwhile, the mounted men continued to scour the surrounding plain. Besides flushing out Zulu fugitives, they engaged in setting all the *amakhanda* in the plain ablaze, or in completing their destruction. Among those burned were oNdini, kwaNodwengu, kwaBulawayo, kwaKhandempemvu, kwaGqikazi, kwaNdabakawombe, kwaMbonambi and emLambo-ngwenya, as well as more distant ones of lesser importance.

In the case of oNdini, the nine-pounders shelled it at 10.07 a.m. and drove out over the hills a large concentration of Zulu who were still sheltering there. Chelmsford then ordered the cavalry and irregular horse, who had returned to the square for a short rest after their pursuit, to go out once more and burn oNdini.[77] So began a race between mounted officers for the honour of being the first at Cetshwayo's 'capital', which was won by Lord Charles Beresford. It was lucky for these single horsemen that in this and other *amakhanda* they encountered no organized resistance.[78] Buller ordered the firing of oNdini at 11.40 a.m., and his men moved from hut to hut with flaming torches of grass. It seems, though, that the Zulu themselves, having stripped the *ikhanda* bare, had set fire to it first, though for lack of wind the huts did not burn freely and the

British effectively completed their work.[79] There is evidence that the Zulu started the firing of the neighbouring *amakhanda* as well, and there was nothing extraordinary in this action. They had as precedent the burning of emGungundlovu, King Dingane's royal homestead, which he had ordered after the defeat of Blood River, administered by the Boers in 1838.[80]

It might have been a 'grand sight' for the victors to see all the *amakhanda* of the plain sending up their columns of smoke. But for the Zulu, either looking down from the surrounding hilltops, or seeing the black haze of smoke covering the country from further afield, it was a clear sign that their kingdom had fallen. It signified the same to Captain Slade, watering his horses in the Mbilane. He voiced the general British sentiment when he wrote to his mother that 'we all felt at last that the power of the Zulus had been destroyed'.[81]

At about 2 p.m. the British began their return march to their camp at the White Mfolozi, reaching it by stages between 3.30 and 5.30 p.m. Considering the scope of their victory, British losses had been light. In all, two officers and ten men were killed, another officer died of his wounds on 14 July, and sixty-nine men were wounded. All the serious or fatal wounds were from bullets.

How many Zulu had died? The official British estimate of Zulu losses was set at 'not less than 1 500',[82] though exaggerated estimates reached 2 500. When on 9 August 1879 a British patrol went over the ground, they found no more than 300 skeletons. But this indicated not that the Zulu had suffered few casualties, but that in the interval they had been able to dispose of many of their dead initially left unburied on the field, and had retrieved their weapons.[83] Furthermore, in the early stages of the battle the Zulu had been able to evacuate many of their casualties. Yet the great problem in trying to reach any accurate assessment of Zulu losses is the fact that the dead lay in twos and threes for kilometres around, on plain and hilltop. Naturally, most of the casualties were concentrated within a 360 m radius of the square – or within close or point-blank range. Where the fight had been hottest, skeletons still lay in August twelve to fifteen deep.[84] Norris-Newman considered that the British left between 500 and 600 Zulu lying dead within close range of the square.[85] Buller himself estimated that his irregular horse had inflicted a loss of at least 450 in pursuit.[86] The regular cavalry took credit for 150 'kills'. In all, it seems that the official figure of 1 500 Zulu dead (or a casualty rate of about 10 per cent) is reasonably accurate, especially when it is remembered that most of the wounded would never have survived, even if they had managed to reach their homes.

The night following their victory the British triumphantly agreed that the Zulu challenge to fight them in the open rather than from behind the protection of their laager had been 'fairly answered'.[87] For a relieved Lord Chelmsford, British arms had at last been vindicated throughout southern Africa.[88]

Notes

1 For a very detailed account of the battle, see Laband, *Battle of Ulundi*, pp. 1–48, passim.

2 Carle Faye Papers 7: 'How we captured Cetywayo' by Martin Oftebro, p. 1.

3 Montague, *Campaigning in South Africa*, p. 311.

4 For the most persuasive expression of this line of argument, see Guy, *Zulu Kingdom*, pp. 58–9. It has since been hallowed by S. Marks in 'Southern Africa 1867–1886' in R. Oliver and G. N. Sanderson (eds.), *The Cambridge History of Africa*, Cambridge, 1985, vol. VI, pp. 392–3. J. Belich is right, however, to warn on p. 332 of his influential *The New Zealand Wars and the Victorian Interpretation of Racial Conflict*, Auckland, 1986, that Guy's case 'is too perfunctory to be entirely convincing'.

5 Laband, 'Border levies', pp. 160–1.

6 For the last-minute Anglo–Zulu negotiations, see Laband, 'Humbugging the general', pp. 58–9.

7 Colenso and Colenso, *Digest*, series 1, part 2, pp. 593a–b. Magema interviewed Mfunzi in October 1879 and was shown the still unopened letter.

8 *Times of Natal*, 13 July 1879: statement of Undungunyanga, son of Umgenane, a prisoner taken at the battle of Ulundi.

9 Mitford, *Zulu Country*, pp. 230–1: eye-witness account in the *Port Elizabeth Telegraph*, 12 August 1879; Vijn, *Cetshwayo's Dutchman*, p. 52.

10 Hotham Papers: H. E. Hotham to his pater, 5 July 1879.

11 *Natal Colonist*, 12 July 1879.

12 Vijn, *Cetshwayo's Dutchman*, pp. 50–1, 144: Colenso's notes; Webb and Wright, *Zulu King Speaks*, p. 58; H. F. Fynn Diary: entry placed between those for 10 and 11 February 1883.

13 *Natal Colonist*, 20 September 1879: Cetshwayo's statement on his march to the coast; *JSA* IV, p. 72: testimony of Mtshapi.

14 *Times of Natal*, 13 July 1879: statement by Undungunyanga; Vijn, *Cetshwayo's Dutchman*, p. 143: Magema's statement.

15 For descriptions of Buller's reconnaissance and the Zulu ambush, see WO 32/7764: Wood to DAG, 5 July 1879; Tomasson, *With the Irregulars*, pp. 157–64; Mossop, *Running the Gauntlet*, pp. 88–9; Molyneux, *Campaigning*, pp. 183–4; and Malet, *Diary*, pp. 25–6.

16 Webb and Wright, *Zulu King Speaks*, p. 58; *JSA* IV, p. 73: testimony

of Mtshapi.

17 *Illustrated London News*, 26 July 1879, p. 78: Archibald Forbes's report, 3 July 1879; Moodie, *British, Boers and Zulus*, p. 355: Melton Prior's account.

18 *Times of Natal*, 13 July 1879: statement by Undungunyanga.

19 Moodie, *British, Boers and Zulus*, p. 355: Melton Prior's account.

20 *BPP* (C. 2482), enc. in no. 32: Chelmsford to Secretary of State for War, 6 July 1879.

21 AC, p. 141: Robinson to Maude Lefroy, 6 July 1879; Commeline Letters: Commeline to his pater, 18 July 1879.

22 WO 32/7764: Glyn to AAG, 5 July 1879.

23 Callwell, *Small Wars*, pp. 190, 256–67, 386–7, 414; Whitehouse, *Battle in Africa*, p. 26.

24 McToy, *13th Regiment*, p. 84.

25 WO 32/7764: Glyn to AAG, 5 July 1879.

26 Moodie, *British, Boers and Zulus*, p. 360: account by Archibald Forbes; Tomasson, *With the Irregulars*, pp. 175–6; *Illustrated London News*, 23 August 1879, p. 182.

27 *Times of Natal*, 13 July 1879: statement by Undungunyanga.

28 WO 32/7767: Newdigate's Diary for the week ending 6 July: 4 July 1879.

29 See *BPP* (C. 2482), enc. in no. 32: Chelmsford to Secretary of State for War, 6 July 1879; TS 41: Offy Shepstone to William, 17 July 1879; and Stabb's Zulu War Diary: 4 July 1879.

30 AC, p. 141: Robinson to Maude Lefroy, 6 July 1879; McToy, *13th Regiment*, p. 89; Malet, *Diary*, p. 27.

31 WO 32/7767: Newdigate's Diary for the week ending 6 July: 4 July 1879; St Vincent Journal: 4 July 1879; AC, p. 141: Robinson to Maude Lefroy, 6 July 1879; C. E. Fripp. 'Reminiscences of the Zulu War', *Pall Mall Magazine*, XX, 1900, pp. 556–7, 561.

32 War Office, *Narrative*, p. 117.

33 Webb and Wright, *Zulu King Speaks*, p. 34.

34 Colenso, *Zulu War*, p. 448.

35 Webb and Wright, *Zulu King Speaks*, pp. 34–5; Vijn, *Cetshwayo's Dutchman*, p. 52; Filter and Bourquin, *Paulina Dlamini*, pp. 70–1.

36 Woodgate's Military Diary: 7 July 1879; *Times of Natal*, 13 July 1879: statement of Undungunyanga.

37 Woodgate's Military Diary: 7 July 1879.

38 At long range, or between 630 m and 1 260 m, fire was only 2 per cent effective; at medium range, or between 270 m and 630 m, it was 5 per cent effective; at close range, or between 90 m and 270 m, it was 10 per cent effective. At point-blank range, or between 0 m and 90 m, it was 15 per cent effective (Whitehouse, *Battle in Africa*, p. 35).

39 WO 32/7764: Col. Drury-Lowe to AAG, 6 July 1879.

40 Tomasson, *With the Irregulars*, pp. 177–9, 183; Stabb's Zulu War Diary: 4 July 1879.

41 Mitford, *Zulu Country*, p. 237: eye-witness in the *Port Elizabeth Telegraph*, 12 August 1879.

42 AC, p. 41, Clery no. 17: confidential, Clery to Alison, 8 July 1879.
43 TS 41: Offy Shepstone to William, 17 July 1879.
44 Guy, *Zulu Kingdom*, pp. 58–9.
45 *Natal Witness*, 15 July 1879: correspondent, Umlalazi Plain, 7 July 1879.
46 Wood, *Midshipman*, vol. II, p. 81.
47 Norris-Newman, *In Zululand*, p. 85: Mehlokazulu's statement.
48 Bennett, *Eyewitness in Zululand*, pp. 104–5.
49 *Illustrated London News*, 23 August 1879, p. 182: account by *Natal Witness* correspondent.
50 Moodie, *British, Boers and Zulus*, p. 356: Melton Prior's account.
51 Ibid., p. 366: account by *Natal Colonist* correspondent.
52 WO 32/7764: Lt.-Col. Tatton Browne to AAG, 5 July 1879; Tomasson, *With the Irregulars*, p. 189; AC, p. 141: Robinson to Maude Lefroy, 6 July 1879.
53 Colenso, *Zulu War*, p. 447; Guy, *Zulu Kingdom*, p. 58. Belich, *New Zealand Wars*, p. 322, agrees with their conclusion.
54 Callwell, *Small Wars*, p. 439.
55 H. Paterson, 'The military organization of the Colony of Natal 1881–1910', unpublished M.A. thesis, University of Natal, 1985, p. 115.
56 Whitehouse, *Battle in Africa*, p. 35.
57 AC, p. 141: Robinson to Maude Lefroy, 6 July 1879; TS 41: Offy Shepstone to William, 17 July 1879; Tomasson, *With the Irregulars*, p. 188; Fripp, 'Zulu War', p. 558.
58 Wood, *Midshipman*, vol. II, p. 81.
59 TS 41: Offy Shepstone to William, 17 July 1879.
60 *Graphic*, 13 September 1879, p. 246.
61 Slade Papers: Slade to his mother, 6 July 1879.
62 AC, p. 141: Robinson to Maude Lefroy, 6 July 1879.
63 Slade Papers: Slade to his mother, 6 July 1879.
64 WO 32/7764: Col. Glyn to AAG, 5 July 1879.
65 Molyneux, *Campaigning*, pp. 187–8.
66 Vijn, *Cetshwayo's Dutchman*, p. 143: Colenso's notes.
67 AC, p. 141: Robinson to Maude Lefroy, 6 July 1879; AC, p. 127, Russell no. 2: Russell to Alison, 6 July 1879; Stabb's Zulu War Diary: 4 July 1879.
68 McToy, *13th Regiment*, p. 90.
69 F. Francis, *Wars, Waves and Wanderings*, London, 1881, p. 68.
70 Carl Faye Papers 7: 'When the English took Cetywayo', told by Mapelu Zungu kaMkhosana, p. 2.
71 For the mounted pursuit, see WO 32/7764: Col. Drury-Lowe to AAG, 6 July 1879; St Vincent Journal: 4 July 1879; WO 32/7764: Buller to Wood, 5 July 1879; Ashe and Wyatt Edgell, *Zulu Campaign*, pp. 348–9.
72 *BPP* (C. 2482), enc. in no. 32: Chelmsford to Secretary of State for War, 6 July 1879.
73 Tommason, *With the Irregulars*, p. 197.
74 AC, p. 141: Robinson to Maude Lefroy, 6 July 1879.
75 The maximum range for a nine-pounder firing shrapnel was about

3 230 m.

76 Tomasson, *With the Irregulars*, p. 206.

77 St Vincent Journal: 4 July 1879; WO 32/7764: Buller to Wood, 5 July 1879.

78 However, the Hon. W. Drummond, Chelmsford's intelligence officer, who participated in the race to oNdini, was killed whilst lost among the huts by some of the few Zulu still lurking there.

79 Colenso Papers 27, no. 224: Colenso to Chesson, 25 July 1879; *BPP* (C. 2482), enc. in no. 51: Fannin to Colonial Secretary, [?] July 1879.

80 See James Stuart Collection 83, KCM 53245: translation by E. R. Dahle of J. Stuart, *uKulumetule* (London, 1925), chap. 4, p. 11.

81 Slade Papers: Slade to his mother, 6 July 1879.

82 War Office, *Narrative*, p. 117.

83 Norris-Newman, *In Zululand*, p. 236.

84 *Natal Witness*, 21 August 1879: correspondent with Clarke's Column, 11 August 1879.

85 Norris-Newman, *In Zululand*, p. 213.

86 WO 32/7764: Buller to Wood, 5 July 1879.

87 Moodie, *British, Boers and Zulus*, p. 358: Melton Prior's account.

88 *BPP* (C. 2482), enc. in no. 32: Chelmsford to Secretary of State for War, 6 July 1879.

12

A king who flees to the mountains is finished

Wars usually end, Blainey theorizes, when one side is forced to admit military inferiority, failure of morale, economic dislocation and political disarray. Then significant elements of the leadership are prepared to consider terms (thought quite unacceptable before the tide of war had irrevocably turned) imposed by their successful opponent.[1] So it was with the Zulu in 1879.

After its defeat at Ulundi, the Zulu army speedily dispersed all over the country, and the British, wherever they were in Zululand, detected no organized forces still in the field, but noticed returning warriors crossing their lines of communication in considerable numbers.[2] For a while the country to the north and east of oNdini was clogged with old men, women, girls, children and cattle fleeing from the Mahlabathini plain, as well as with wounded men from the battle.

Cetshwayo was himself one of this number. When the lookouts he had posted reported that his army was defeated, he immediately retired northwards from kwaMbonambi, crossing the nek of the Ntabankhulu range into the bush beyond, where he was later joined by Mnyamana and the other important chiefs. Men of the uMcijo *ibutho* followed after their king some way as he fled, but he soon sent them back, as he feared their presence would attract attention and alert the British to his whereabouts.[3] Cetshwayo travelled on foot with the women of his *isigodlo* and a number of servants. Weighed down with calamity, he spoke hardly a word. The following day he took up Zibhebhu's offer of shelter, and sent his household (including his eleven-year-old heir, Dinuzulu) and cattle to seek sanctuary with him in the north-eastern reaches of Zululand.[4] The king himself did not head through Zibhebhu's territory for the natural fastnesses of the Lubombo mountains as some supposed he might; nor to the Tsonga chiefdoms beyond (where the chiefs in any case had refused his pleas for succour, and were soon to assure the British Consul at Lourenço Marques that they would never allow the king to take refuge with them).[5] Instead, he moved across the Black Mfolozi to Mnyamana's ekuShumayeleni homestead on the isiKhwebezi River, which he reached the third day after the battle. There he stayed for a month, attempting fruitlessly to negotiate with the British.[6]

By 6 July the victorious British had all returned to Mthonjaneni. A storm of bitterly cold wind, rain and hail began that night, and made all further movement impossible until 9 July. Chelmsford's critics seized on his withdrawal south, which, they contended, by not following up the advantage gained by the victory of Ulundi, unnecessarily prolonged the war. Yet if the shortage of supplies, the encumbrance of the wounded, and the need to get his men under better cover made the withdrawal desirable to Chelmsford, what made it possible and realistic was his knowledge that the Zulu army had dispersed following its defeat.[7] This was recognized even by Wolseley, Chelmsford's highly critical replacement.[8] Like many another serving officer, Wolseley was aware that the Zulu army was highly unlikely to answer any fresh calls to reassemble. It would not do so because Chelmsford's victory was a decisive one. King Dingane, after his defeat at Blood River in 1838, had set out with his army to beyond the Black Mfolozi, where near the Vuna River he re-established his emGungundlovu *ikhanda*. It was very different after Ulundi. King Cetshwayo wished likewise to reassemble the iNgobamakhosi, uMcijo, uMbonambi and uNokhenke *amabutho* to build a new *ikhanda* for him north of the Black Mfolozi. But they ignored his orders and stayed at home, reluctant to continue a hopeless struggle.[9]

Indeed, the effects of the battle of Ulundi were immediately apparent. Wood noted that from the moment the Zulu had dispersed, Wood's Irregulars were willing to travel anywhere in the country with a message, as they no longer feared being attacked.[10] The Zulu everywhere openly acknowledged to the British that their defeat was complete and that the war was over. They were generally confounded at being defeated in the open, and felt that the king's prestige was fatally impaired.[11] In fact, the predominant Zulu attitude was that they had had enough of war, and wanted peace and the withdrawal of the British so that they could go home and resume the normal course of their lives.

Wolseley, confident that organized resistance was over, set about the pacification of Zululand with drastically reduced forces. On 9 July the Flying Column began its march back to kwaMagwaza and St Paul's to link up with Crealock's First Division. It remained for the rest of the month at St Paul's, patrolling the area, and being reduced piecemeal until 1 August. The First Division began to break up from 10 July and to return to Natal. By 23 July it had ceased to exist. On 10 July the Second Division retraced the steps of its earlier advance, and moved back on Fort Marshall, where it was broken up by 27 July. Some troops continued to garrison the line of forts, while the remainder returned to Durban for embarkation.[12]

When Cetshwayo fled north to seek sanctuary with Mnyamana, he ordered his chiefs not to follow, but 'to look out for themselves'.[13] They scarcely needed any such urging. In the wake of Ulundi there was a rash of submissions, a regular *sauve qui peut*. Among the most prominent to 'come in' were Dabulamanzi, who at last surrendered himself on 12 July;[14] and Gawozi kaSilwana, chief of a section of the Mpungose and a great favourite of the king, who surrendered to Wood at St Paul's on 13 July. So when Wolseley, who was determined that not another shot should be fired before peace was achieved, resolved to put the earlier submissions by the coastal chiefs to Crealock on a more formal basis, almost all of them responded to his invitation to meet him at his camp near the destroyed emaNgweni *ikhanda*.

On 19 July Wolseley there addressed some prominent 250 Zulu. He announced the end of the Zulu kingdom and his intention to break it into a number of districts, to be ruled by chiefs whose names he would announce when he reached oNdini. Following Crealock's successful formula, he required of the chiefs only that they hand over their arms and royal cattle. The surrendered chiefs not unnaturally expressed their satisfaction with these easy terms, while some of the young men were heard to state that they never would have fought for Cetshwayo if they had known that this was all the British would have exacted from them.

Despite the very satisfactory coastal submissions, Wolseley was most concerned that more of the great northern chiefs had not as yet sued for peace.[15] He put this down to the fact that Cetshwayo was still at large. The coastal chiefs had assured him that, as long as the king was at liberty, fears of the possibility of his return to power could well impede further submissions, and would unsettle and discourage those who had already given up.[16] Furthermore, Wolseley was convinced that Chelmsford's withdrawal from the Mahlabathini plain had been, if not a military miscalculation, then certainly a political blunder, for it had left the northern Zulu with a false impression of British intentions. To Wolseley's mind, if the rest of Zululand besides the coastal region were finally to be pacified, it was necessary both to reoccupy oNdini and to capture the king. With these intentions, he sent messages to the chiefs to meet him near the burnt-out oNdini on 10 August.

Meanwhile, Wolseley issued instructions on 26 July to all his officers concerning the procedure to be followed in inducing the Zulu to give up and return home. Chiefs and *izinduna* were to submit on Crealock's original terms, which meant surrendering arms and royal cattle.[17] Apprised after his meeting of 19 July with the coastal chiefs of what concerned them most, Wolseley required that not only should they be informed that both the *amabutho* system and the monarchy with which it was interwoven were to be abolished and the kingdom divided into independent chiefdoms, but that no land or cattle were to be transferred to the whites. It was again promised that Wolseley would announce at oNdini who the new independent chiefs were to be. Those chiefs who had not already submitted were invited to do so, and to bring in their arms and cattle. Combining the stick with the carrot, they were also sternly reminded that if they neglected to surrender by 10 August they would then be treated as enemies and punished.[18]

Wolseley's Zululand policy thus defined, he made the practical arrangements necessary for its fulfilment. From the disbanded First Division he created a column under Lieutenant-Colonel C. M. Clarke, which was to reoccupy oNdini, and to send out patrols to capture the king. Wolseley himself was to accompany this column. A second column, made up from Wood's disbanded Flying Column, he put under the command of Lieutenant-Colonel Baker Russell. Russell's objective was the pacification of north-western Zululand, where Wolseley feared the Qulusi and Manyonyoba might attempt a last-ditch resistance.

Wolseley determined that Russell, when operating towards the headwaters of the Black Mfolozi from the south, should be supported by a simultaneous advance from the north across the Phongolo by Swazi forces and by British troops from the Transvaal operating through Luneburg, both of whom would clear his front.[19]

The Transvaal troops were under the command of Lieutenant-General the Hon. G. Villiers, and were to consist of mounted Burghers and of the adherents of Prince Hamu, who had been living comfortably in Utrecht since his defection in March. Wolseley, when he ordered Hamu to collect his warriors for this purpose, added greatly to his readiness to comply by both promises and threats. If he were successful in bringing in the king, a reward of 5 000 cattle and an independent sovereignty over his own district would be his. However, if he did not cooperate fully, his cattle and country would be offered to the Swazi. Hamu's *izinduna* hastily declared themselves willing to turn out their men and capture the king. While the Swazis' specific objective was to ensure that Cetshwayo did not slip across the upper Phongolo into Swaziland, Villiers, as Special Commissioner to Hamu, was to obtain the submission of the turbulent and semi-independent Zulu of the Phongolo frontier.

Besides the north-west, where the royalist Qulusi were concentrated, there was another region where loyalty to the king persisted. This was southern Zululand, along the middle Thukela, a sector the British had never penetrated in any depth.[20] There Godide of the Ntuli, Manqondo and his son Qethuka of the Magwaza, and the blind Sokufa and his son Sigananda of the Cube were loath to submit. During July and August they treated evasively with Natal officials, and stopped short of fulfilling the conditions Wolseley had laid down for submission. It is apparent, though, that their indecision was in part a reflection of divisions among their adherents. While the married men seemed content to accept the British terms, the younger warriors resented having to give up their arms, and were prepared to carry on the struggle.

Upstream of them, it was different.[21] Mbuzo, a minor Ntuli chief at the confluence of the Thukela and Mzinyathi rivers, had put out peace feelers as early as June. After the battle of Ulundi, Natal officials exploited the favourable climate its impact had created to open negotiations with Chief Ndwandwe kaMhlala of the Langa, Chief Matshana kaSitshakuza of the Mchunu (an *isikhulu* with a long tradition of seeking greater autonomy), and Chief Matshana kaMondisa of the Sithole, who, like the other Matshana, officials had hoped before the war might throw in his lot with the British. It took some time for these chiefs to conform with Wolseley's terms, for their adherents had taken refuge during the war in caves and forests – particularly as a result of the Second Division's punitive patrols during May – and it was necessary that they should return to their *imizi* before the requisite guns and royal cattle could be collected. By mid-August it was done, and on 20 August the four chiefs and seven other lesser ones surrendered at Rorke's Drift to H. F. Fynn, the Resident Magistrate of the Umsinga Division. There was no such formal surrender among Sihayo's adherents. He and his son Mehlokazulu were prisoners-of-war, and the Qungebe were in their places of refuge, away from the border and the danger of British raids. Yet by the end of August many were drifting back to their homes, though it was not until October that they were all to return.

When Wolseley set up his camp at oNdini on 10 August, the coastal region had fully submitted, the south-west was well into the process of doing so, and it seemed not unlikely that the south would soon follow suit. In central and even northern Zululand it appeared as if the chiefs were prepared to accept Wolseley's conditions and abandon the king's cause.[22] It is true that none of the important chiefs had assembled at oNdini by 10 August, but Wolseley had received word that they were coming in. Zibhebhu was reported still to be in his district, but Wolseley entertained high hopes of his co-operation. He had noted his 'time-serving disposition', and presumed (correctly as it turned out) that the promise of an independent sovereignty under the British settlement would detach him from the king's cause.[23] By 13 August Zibhebhu had promised to come into Wolseley's camp, as had no less a personage than Mnyamana. To Wolseley, the submissions of Zibhebhu and Mnyamana were of the utmost significance. He was sure they would induce the remainder of the chiefs to follow their lead, and would have the effect of countering messages the king had been sending out, exhorting the chiefs not to give in.

Significantly, the king's messages were in any case largely ignored by chiefs concerned to secure their own future, and he found that few shreds of authority still clung to him. Moreover, with the dispersal of his army and his own flight, he was left with few counters with which to negotiate with an enemy who had already achieved his objectives of destroying Zulu military capability and shattering royal power. All that he could realistically hope to bargain for was his personal safety and future liberty.

The outcome of Wolseley's meeting of 19 July with the coastal chiefs had helped dash Cetshwayo's hopes for continued resistance, and he sent to the southern chiefs urging them to comply with British terms in the hope that his cooperation would soften the British towards him.[24] A suppliant royal messenger duly approached Lieutenant-Colonel Clarke at kwaMagwaza on 26 July. Clarke replied that the king's life would be spared if he surrendered, and directed the envoy to Wolseley.[25] A spate of similar messages and replies were exchanged, until on 7 August Wolseley interviewed an important delegation sent on by Clarke. It was led by the influential Chief Mavumengwana. He had with him yet another letter from the king taken down by Vijn, in which Cetshwayo pathetically declared that he was still collecting cattle which he would send in with Mnyamana, and that he would follow in their wake. Meanwhile, 'the English should take pity on him and leave him the country of his fathers'.[26] But they had already determined on his exile, and Wolseley demanded his immediate surrender.

Mavumengwana and his returning delegation fell in with Mnyamana and the promised cattle, and decided to go back with them to Wolseley instead of reporting to the king. Cetshwayo, meanwhile, learning that British patrols were out seeking him, took fright and fled from ekuShumayeleni to the fastnesses of the Ngome forest. When King Dingane had fled to the Lubombo mountains in 1840 after his defeat at the battle of Maqongqo, the Zulu knew his power was broken, as 'a king who left his home and went to the mountains was finished'.[27] So it was with Cetshwayo, who was now being abandoned by all. Vijn, who had come into Wolseley's camp on 10 August with a last message from the king begging to be allowed to stay in Zululand, agreed, on the promise of a reward, to persuade Cetshwayo to surrender. But he could not overcome the king's dread of being sent into exile, and returned empty-handed to Wolseley on 13 August, while the king pushed on further into the forest.

On 14 August Mnyamana, Ntshingwayo, Mgidlana and Sukani (two uninfluential half-brothers of the king's), Sitshaluza kaMamba (the regent of the eMgazini in the north), Melelesi kaManyosi (chief of the Mbatha in central Zululand) and 150 lesser chiefs and *izinduna* presented themselves at Wolseley's camp. All wore only skins and carried sticks.[28] They had with them the 617 head of cattle which Mnyamana had collected on the king's instructions. These cattle indicated that Mnyamana's overt intention of coming in was not to surrender, but to sue for terms of peace on the king's behalf. At last, as the British had for so long insisted, a major chief was to negotiate direct for the king. Yet was it to negotiate, or simply to beg? As Ntshingwayo later told Magema Fuze, 'We had gone simply to ask for his head, that he might live and not perish.'[29] Yet once assured that the British would not execute Cetshwayo the chiefs' duty was done, and their thoughts turned to their own futures. They soon declared that they had themselves come to surrender, and that they hoped for peace. In which case, they had not met the required terms for submission, and Wolseley ordered that the five principal chiefs, including Mnyamana, be held hostage in camp until the necessary arms and royal cattle had been collected. On 16 August Cetshwayo's favourite brother, Prince Ziwedu, came in and was also detained. Then, on 26 August, Zibhebhu himself appeared. He had with him as tokens of submission a number of guns and cattle, and claimed that he had hesitated for so long primarily for fear that he would be killed for the part he had played in the war.[30]

At the same time as these significant developments at oNdini, the people of central Zululand as far down as the coast, wishing to bring their families back to the shelter of their homes, were surrendering in great numbers at Fort Evelyn, Fort Marshall and kwaMagwaza. Baker Russell was also achieving success in the north-west, despite the failure of Wolseley's overall strategy for the region.[31] The Boers of Wakkerstroom, not the least surprisingly in the light of their recent record, refused to volunteer for Villiers's force, prevented local blacks from acting as auxiliaries, and even helped the Zulu by forwarding them information of British movements. Hamu's men proved initially unwilling to advance further into hostile territory than midway between Utrecht and Luneburg.[32] As for the Swazi, though they were happy to loot Zulu *imizi* along the Phongolo, they were still too afraid of Zulu power to risk their army in Zululand unless heavily supported, and were eventually called back on 24 August. Their ineffectualness did not much concern Wolseley, however, for by this stage he was satisfied that Cetshwayo was not heading in the direction of Swaziland, and he was in any case reluctant to let loose an army in Zululand which he might not be able to control. Besides, he was satisfied that Villiers was in no danger, as the Zulu against whom he was to operate would offer 'no formidable opposition'.[33]

Villiers therefore advanced on the Mkhondo River with the 300 mounted white troops and 700 auxiliaries he had managed to raise. Hamu's men, who had begun to recover their nerve, also started to join him, and wasted no opportunity in looting the countryside as they went. Villiers reached Luneburg on 25 August without meeting any Zulu resistance. On 27 August the mounted men of Baker Russell's Column, who likewise had encountered some unfriendliness on their march, but no outright resistance,[34] pushed ahead and reached eZungwini. The Qulusi *izinduna* and Manyonyoba, situated as they were between Baker Russell and Villiers, were in a vulnerable position and were faced with the dilemma of whether or not to resist. Following the pattern of southern Zululand, it seems the *izinduna* were predisposed to give up, but the young men wished to continue fighting. The Qulusi knew, to their disgust, that many Zulu on Baker Russell's line of march, especially the Mdlalose, had been clearly relieved that they had not been required to fight (though here too a few of the younger men had shown some disposition to resist), and had surrendered both arms and cattle. By the end of August the Mdlalose were all back in their homes from their places of refuge in the hills. On 25 August their chief, Sekethwayo, had himself submitted at Fort Cambridge after the confiscation of 300 of his cattle had helped him make up his mind. Baker Russell had ordered him to oNdini. Significantly for those Zulu of the north-west still contemplating resistance, he had been promised independence in his own district and the restoration of his cattle should he comply, and threatened with the loss of everything if he did not.

The Qulusi seemed at first determined to be more staunch in their loyalty to the royal cause than the Mdlalose. On 22 August Baker Russell's spies reported them to be mustering for war near ebaQulusini under the *induna* Mcwayo kaMangeda. But on 28 August two sons of Msebe, the Qulusi *induna* who had sent out feelers to the British in February and had subsequently been victimized by the other Qulusi, informed Baker Russell that both he and Manyonyoba wished to surrender. Msebe gave himself up the next day and, resentful at his treatment at the hands of the other Qulusi, indicated his desire to join the British in their operations against them.[35] This proved unnecessary. On 28 August Cetshwayo was captured by a patrol in the Ngome forest and this intelligence had an immediate effect on those Qulusi still resisting. At a council held on 30 August they decided to surrender, doubtless influenced by a secret message the captive king is reputed to have sent Mahubulwana kaDumisela (the principal *induna* of the Qulusi and his commander in the field in the north-west), ordering him to disband his men still under arms.[36] On 1 September Mahubulwana submitted on behalf of his people, and Baker Russell resumed his advance on Luneburg.

Manyonyoba, now completely alone in his contemplated resistance and threatened by Villiers's plundering rabble, sent word to Luneburg that he was prepared to lay down his arms on 4 September.[37] This intention, which would have ended the war in the north-west without any further bloodshed – and indeed, concluded the whole post-Ulundi pacification process without a life being lost – was tragically frustrated.

Baker Russell, sceptical of Manyonyoba's intentions and following Wolseley's orders to clear him out, sent a force to the Ntombe valley to ensure his surrender. Many of Manyonyoba's adherents in their caves began to surrender, but the firing of a shot provoked some of Teteleku's Mounted Natives into butchering seven prisoners whom they were guarding. After that act of treachery, Manyonyoba's adherents not unnaturally refused any longer to come out of their caves and give themselves up, while Manyonyoba, his faith in British promises of amnesty dashed, broke off negotiations.

As a consequence, Baker Russell despatched a strong patrol on 5 September to take Manyonyoba's principal cave on the left bank of the Ntombe. Most of his adherents had already slipped away, though the remainder resisted attempts to smoke them out. The next day Manyonyoba's brother and a few adherents were captured, and on 8 September Baker Russell made a determined effort to finish the business. One force proceeded without resistance against the Ntombe caves, which they blew up with dynamite. However, at Mbilini's mountain across the Ntombe, the other force lost two NCOs of the 2/4th Regiment to fire from the caves. The troops in retaliation blew up the caves with at least thirty people still sheltering in their depths. This act of barbarism ended resistance. Manyonyoba's son, an *induna* and a few others were rounded up, though Manyonyoba himself eluded capture up the Ntombe valley. With resistance effectively over, Wolseley sent Villiers's disorderly force home and ordered Russell on 10 September to proceed against the Pedi in the Transvaal. Enough troops were left in Luneburg to control the Ntombe valley, and fear of starvation at length compelled Manyonyoba to give himself up on 22 September with his wife and principal *induna*.[38]

Except for the diehards of the Ntombe valley, the capture of the king was proving, as Wolseley had anticipated, a decisive event, as it took the meaning out of continued resistance.[39] Initially, sheltered by the local population as he moved north from ekuShumayeleni, Cetshwayo had succeeded in evading the patrols sent after him. Wolseley, by increasing pressure on the chiefs in whose districts Cetshwayo was reported to be, succeeded in undercutting this aid. Though he long remained frustrated by the general reluctance of the chiefs to come forward and help in the search, he firmly believed that 'in their hearts' they were anxious for the king to be caught.[40] In the end he was justified in his conviction.

It has been the contention of the apologists of those chiefs who eventually betrayed their king that they had been left no choice. Colenso and Fuze argued that as the country was occupied by the British, and the last harvest destroyed by their patrols, the chiefs' hand was forced by the condition of their adherents, who were threatened by starvation if they could not return to their homes in safety to plant their crops. Jeff Guy in particular has sustained and popularized this line.[41] Certainly, the king's remaining at large could only have hindered the inevitable settlement on terms dictated by the British. Yet by August much of the country directly affected by the war was already pacified, with the people returned to their fields – while vast areas had never seen so much as a British patrol. Moreover, the British conditions for submission were not such as to disrupt the functioning of the ordinary Zulu *umuzi*. This was widely known. Therefore, the chiefs' response must be regarded as realistic. There was little point in persistent loyalty to an already fractured polity, but much to be said for rational calculation on how best to enhance personal power and independence in a Zululand where the centralized royal state was to be replaced by a number of independent sovereignties. Wolseley worked on these obvious perceptions.

On 23 August Lieutenant-Colonel Clarke left with a strong patrol to pressure the neighbourhood where the king was reported to be in hiding. This was a large area that comprised territory which was severally controlled by Mnyamana, Somkhele (the Mphukonyoni chief, who had submitted on 4 July), by Mgojana kaSomaphunga (the Ndwandwe chief and husband of the king's sister, who came into Wolseley's camp the day Clarke left), and by Zibhebhu (who submitted three days later). It is particularly significant that Wolseley intended to make the last three independent chiefs, but only on condition that they 'behaved well'.[42] The chiefs could not have failed to understand this caveat. Wolseley used the same tactics with Mnyamana. In a crucial interview of 26 August between John Shepstone and Mnyamana, Shepstone was empowered to threaten the chief that if he did not cooperate he 'should have nothing'. Mnyamana hastily reassured Shepstone that both he and Mgojana were sending messages to their districts ordering their adherents to take the king captive. The former chief councillor of the king added that since the battle of Ulundi the chiefs had 'lost all regard and interest' in the king, and that, having done all that could be required of them for him, Cetshwayo could have 'no further claims' upon their loyalty. Mnyamana reportedly concluded by pointing out that as the Zulu had been afraid to kill neither Shaka nor Dingane, and had only spared Mpande for fear of his white friends, they now had no reason to be afraid of Cetshwayo.[43] Mnyamana proved as good as his word, as the fugitive Cetshwayo was to discover.

John Shepstone later wrote that Mnyamana came alone to his tent and said merely: 'I have come to tell you that the wind blows from the Ingome forest.'[44] Mnyamana's adherents soon warned the king that their chief had promised Wolseley to assist in his capture, and that he had instructed them to deliver up the king should he seek refuge in any of their homesteads. Cetshwayo was aghast when he heard of what he considered to be Mnyamana's treachery. He was indeed almost immediately tracked down in the Ngome forest and captured on 28 August by Major R. J. C. Marter at the remote kwaDwasa homestead of Mkhosana kaSangqana, one of Mnyamana's adherents.[45] On 31 August the captive Cetshwayo was brought in a cart into Wolseley's camp at kwaSishwili, hard by the burned-out oNdini, where only ten huts remained standing. To the king's humiliation, he was treated not as a defeated monarch, but as a fugitive from justice. Wolseley informed him that since he had broken his 'coronation' pledges he was now deposed in the eyes of the British, that his kingdom would be split up among his chiefs, and that he himself would be kept a prisoner. The next day Cetshwayo set off under escort, not for Natal as he had supposed, but to his dismay for Port Durnford, from whence he was taken off by sea on 4 September for bitter exile at the Cape.[46]

When John Shepstone had told Cetshwayo that there was no possibility of his being allowed to remain in Zululand, the defeated king had at last abandoned all hope, and the tears had run down his cheeks.[47] Never once had his words swayed the British from their purpose, for their demands as expressed in their ultimatum had never been negotiable. Cetshwayo had ever failed to accept that reality, and had always striven for peace on terms acceptable to him and his councillors. Thus his overtures, which had run the gamut from half-hearted fencing, through an attempt to impose a settlement from a position of military advantage, to increasingly desperate efforts to stem the inexorable British advance, and finally to the last, broken pleas for clemency, had consistently bypassed the central reality of Britain's determination to destroy the Zulu kingdom.

With Cetshwayo at last a prisoner, and the chiefs relieved of their increasingly embarrassing moral obligation to stand by their defeated monarch, Wolseley could now proceed to his final settlement of Zululand.[48] This entailed the formal dismemberment of the Zulu polity into thirteen fragments. He signalled his intention to all the great chiefs of holding a meeting on 1 September at oNdini, on which day he announced those chiefs favoured with independent sovereignties. It is not at issue here that the boundaries of the chiefdoms were ill-conceived, nor that the settlement paved the way for disastrous civil war, colonial partition and eventual annexation.[49] Wolseley never disguised that in going for 'an economical and speedy peace [he was] thinking of the immediate effect and not of the unfortunate future'.[50] Consequently, it is more relevant to understand the rationale behind Wolseley's division of the kingdom, and to see how the existing ambitions of the chiefs (which were so well known to him) coupled with the extent of their collaboration during the war, affected his choice of the thirteen 'kinglets'.

Wolseley's settlement – the details of which the British government had left to his discretion, so long as it ensured the peace and security of the neighbouring colonies without involving Britain in any further involvement with Zulu affairs – was consequently dictated by strategic considerations, influenced by the British school of Indian defence, through which his Chief of Staff, Sir G. Pomeroy Colley, had made his reputation.[51] His settlement thus closely resembled that which Lord Lytton had intended to impose on Afghanistan, whereby the North West Frontier would have been secured by breaking Afghanistan into a number of impotent principalities, ruled by chiefs amenable to British control in the form of Residents. So too in South Africa, where Natal and the Transvaal would be made safe through the fragmentation of the unitary Zulu kingdom. Wolseley turned to local advisers when deciding how Zululand should be divided, and who should be set over the pieces. In particular, he accepted the counsel of Sir Theophilus Shepstone, who was a leading proponent of the creation of a number of independent kingdoms. Shepstone argued that the preservation of the Zulu monarchy would prolong the life of the Zulu military system. Royal authority, he claimed, was actually fragile because the chiefs yearned for the independence their predecessors had enjoyed before the rise of Shaka. The appointment of thirteen chiefs – a number he considered manageable – would ensure that royal influence would be stifled. Whether these chiefs were hereditary, with a tradition of independence, or whether they were new men owing their elevation to the British, they would collaborate in ensuring that the Zulu monarchy did not re-emerge. In actually choosing the chiefs, Wolseley felt he had found the perfect adviser in John Dunn.[52]

It went without saying that the reliability of the chiefdoms abutting the Transvaal and Natal borders was the most crucial, for they would act as buffer-zones against the conceivably more volatile chiefdoms created to the north of them. That is why Hlubi of the Tlokoa, whose men had fought for the British during the war, was given the strategic territory at the confluence of the Thukela and Mzinyathi.[53] He was put over the two Matshanas as well as Sihayo. (This erstwhile royal favourite was now destitute, since Mnyamana, in one of his final acts of authority, had confiscated 400 of his cattle and 600 from his people on the grounds that they had been the cause of the war that had destroyed the kingdom and been the death of so many people, including four of Mnyamana's sons.)[54] The two Matshanas had at least shown themselves more amenable than Sihayo by eventually submitting, and Hlubi confirmed them in their chiefdoms. It was because Wolseley considered Hlubi particularly reliable that he decided in October to relocate Manyonyoba and ninety-four of his remaining adherents to his chiefdom.[55]

Hlubi was an alien, one who had never been a person of power and status in Cetshwayo's kingdom, and therefore owed his elevation entirely to the British. John Dunn's position was more ambiguous. He had been a chief and favourite of the Zulu king, yet he had been the first of the leading men of Zululand to desert his cause. He had served the British well during the war and had successfully won Wolseley's confidence. Dunn had no wish to see the king he had betrayed restored, and he possessed a firm power-base in south-eastern Zululand. So it was that Wolseley restored him to his chiefdom, and more besides. Dunn was entrusted with a territory which, running along the Thukela frontier, was the most significant in Zululand in terms of Natal's security. Wolseley saw it as a buffer between the Colony and the possibly less amenable chiefdoms to the north. As such, it was to serve the same function as Lord Lytton had envisaged for Kandahar, which was to have acted as a bulwark against the more rebellious sections of Afghanistan.[56] It included those chiefs along the middle border whose submissions, even by early September, were still half-hearted and unsatisfactory, and of whom Manqondo of the Magwaza was proving the most recalcitrant. To bring them to heel, Wolseley decided on a show of strength, and ordered Clarke's Column to march out of Zululand by way of Middle Drift. Dunn joined the column on 4 September, and patrols were sent out as it advanced, demanding arms and royal cattle, and exacting cattle-fines from those chiefs who did not comply in time. By 20 September all the chiefs of the region had met the conditions for surrender without any attempt at resistance, and Dunn's authority was established. Sensibly he confirmed Godide, Mavumengwana, Qethuka and Sigananda as principal chiefs, so perpetuating their existing local authority.[57]

The area where there was the greatest likelihood of a royalist resurgence was north of the Black Mfolozi, where Cetshwayo's most immediate adherents were settled. There Wolseley ensured that he established chiefs of great status and local power, who could be relied upon to suppress any such aspirations. Wolseley may have asserted in his typically barbed way that Hamu was not a chief whom he himself would have selected, and that he was doing sc only to honour the pledges made to him when he defected.[58] Yet, in reality, there was no one else with the status and hereditary authority capable of controlling the north-west, where, after all, the Qulusi had been among the last to submit. Furthermore, Hamu's long-standing ambitions, which clearly were not satisfied even by the greatly enlarged chiefdom Wolseley awarded him, ensured that he would keep the royalists down. Zibhebhu, thanks to his timely submission, was confirmed in his already quasi-autonomous chiefdom in the north-east, and had his sway extended considerably to take in the homesteads of some of the king's family and closest adherents, known as the uSuthu.[59]

Mgojana had not the ambitious record of these two members of the royal house, but he had cooperated in the hunt for the king and was chief of the Ndwandwe, who, before their defeat by Shaka, had been one of the greatest clans in Zululand. Wolseley hoped that the chiefdom he had created for Mgojaṇa would also serve to keep the royalists in check, as would Mlandlela's, centred as it was on that other great pre-Shakan clan, the Mthethwa. Somkhele, like Mlandlela, had made an opportune submission and had subsequently made explicit his antagonism to the king and his regret that he had sent his people to fight in the war.[60] Besides, he possessed a coherent power-base and was entrusted with the most northerly of the coastal chiefdoms. The only other chiefdom on the periphery of Zululand was that created for Sekethwayo. Wolseley may have characterized him as 'a stupid and infirm old man',[61] but he had early attempted to throw in his lot with the British, and so merited his promised reward.[62]

It is noteworthy that all the chiefs appointed to territories along Zululand's borders or coast had either materially aided the British during the war, shown themselves to have ambitions to independent sovereignty, or had abandoned the royal cause sufficiently early to have at least a degree of trust placed in them by Wolseley. They effectively neutralized the appointed chiefs in the interior of the country, who had not a similar record. Of these, Faku kaZiningo of the Ntombela was a nonentity, though Mfanawendlela kaThanga of the Zungu was an *isikhulu*. Both were likely under the new arrangement to remain under the influence of their more dependable neighbours. Two of the others had been important chiefs, though their submissions had been neither particularly sought nor much noticed. They were Gawozi kaSilwana, the Mpungose chief and an *isikhulu*, who had been a great favourite of the king; and Mgitshwa kaMvundlana, a younger brother of Mkhosana, the Biyela chief, who had been killed at Isandlwana. Although both enjoyed a developed power-base, they were reputed to have been firmly of the peace party before the war, which was a distinct recommendation. Indeed, Mgitshwa was to prove a determined foe of the royal house.

Only one of the great chiefs upon whose co-operation the British had relied, who was sufficiently powerful in his own right to maintain an independent sovereignty, and to whom Wolseley had promised one as a suitable reward, actually declined the offer. This was Mnyamana. The motives for his refusal (which he rapidly came to regret)[63] were apparently mixed. Some of the Zulu ascribed it to his abiding loyalty to the king;[64] while Wolseley supposed it was due to a sense of slight that his designated territory was not as large as he thought his due. Mnyamana himself insisted that it was because he did not wish to be split from the bulk of his adherents, who had been assigned to Hamu's territory.[65] It later came out that another powerful reason for his forgoing an independent chiefdom was to curry favour with Hamu, whom he expected the British to reward by making him king (as the Boers had done with Mpande in 1839), and who he hoped would retain him as chief *induna*.[66] In any event, Wolseley awarded the chiefdom first offered Mnyamana to Ntshingwayo, who, although he had not had a particularly large following in the time of the king, nevertheless had enjoyed a prestige and influence second only to Mnyamana's. Like his old friend, he had submitted in time enough, and the remaindered chiefdom was the reward for his good sense.[67]

In the final analysis, it would appear that the Zulu polity preserved its cohesion under the impact of the invasion of 1879 only so long as the success of British arms did not seem inevitable. Even so, it must not be forgotten that there were some chiefs, most notably John Dunn, Hamu and Sekethwayo, who, more perceptive than their fellows and anticipating the likely outcome of the looming conflict they so wished to avoid, either managed to defect or entered into early negotiations with the British, though their submissions were initially thwarted by the intervention of the king or local loyalists. In regions such as the west and south-east, where the British military presence was effective over a long period, the pattern was an accelerating one of negotiation and submission. (The exception to this generalization was the disputed territory of the north-west, where low-intensity resistance continued over a long period, despite constant British activity.) The southern border, a region of desultory raid and counter-raid, only fully submitted when penetrated in strength by the British in September. On the other hand, great districts in the east, centre and north, although never entered by the British, submitted as soon as the royal cause seemed lost.

This varying pattern of resistance must be explained in terms of the attitude of the Zulu ruling elite. Especially after the repeated defeats of the Zulu armies in the field, and the ever more apparent inability of the Zulu state to continue the struggle at a national level, there was a concerted attempt by the majority of chiefs to preserve or even augment their positions by coming to an arrangement with the

British. The British peace conditions facilitated this process, for, by not disrupting the Zulu homestead economy, they made the fate of the Zulu state as such an irrelevance to the bulk of ordinary Zulu; while by generally recognizing the existing chiefs, and adding appreciably to the powers of a favoured few, they left the influence of the chiefly class undisturbed.[68] Only the king's power was eliminated with the destruction of the *amabutho* system on which it depended, and that of the royal clan curtailed. The fact that the chiefs, almost without exception, accepted this situation cannot be attributed, as Sir Theophilus Shepstone was to maintain until the end of his life, to the yearnings of the incorporated tribes of the kingdom which Shaka had created to throw off the Zulu monarchy and to 're-enter upon their separate existence'.[69] Rather, it was because the chiefs were pragmatic and ambitious men. The Zulu state had never been so monolithic that they, especially those on the margins of the kingdom and in contact with the whites, had not the ambition – and the relative scope – for greater local autonomy. The war gave these men their opportunity, while the others strove to save at least their local positions from out of the debris of the kingdom's collapse. Both these objectives required a degree of co-operation with the British which transcended any urge to self-defeating sacrifice in the ruined cause of a unified Zulu state under its king.

Notes

1 Blainey, *Causes of War*, pp. viii, 82, 122–4, 158–62, 173–4.

2 See, for example, WO 32/7767: Precis of Diaries of Officers Commanding Posts on Frontiers and Lines of Communication: Fort Newdigate, 6–9 July; Fort Evelyn, [?] July; Conference Hill, 7–9 July 1879.

3 Webb and Wright, *Zulu King Speaks*, p. 35; Fuze, *Black People*, pp. 114–15; *JSA* IV, p. 73: testimony of Mtshapi.

4 After the king's capture, his full brother, Ndabuko, insisted that he assume the custody of Dinuzulu. Zibhebhu reluctantly complied, but kept the royal cattle. This dispute was to form one of the roots of the subsequent uSuthu–Mandlakazi feud which was to tear Zululand apart in the 1880s (Filter and Bourquin, *Paulina Dlamini*, pp. 71–2; *JSA* IV, p. 192: testimony of Ndabazezwe kaMfuleni).

5 WO 32/7775: Wolsley to Secretary of State for War, 6 August 1879.

6 Webb and Wright, *Zulu King Speaks*, p. 35.

7 *BPP* (C. 2482), enc. 2 in no. 23: telegram, Chelmsford to Wolseley, 6 July 1879; Harness, 'Zulu campaign', pp. 483–4.

8 Chelmsford resigned his command on 8 July 1879 (Mathews, 'Chelmsford', pp. 336–7).

9 Vijn, *Cetshwayo's Dutchman*, p. 53.

10 Wood, *Midshipman*, vol. II, p. 81.

11 AC, p. 141: Robinson to Maude Lefroy, 6 July 1879; Commeline Papers: Commeline to his father, 18 July 1879.

12 War Office, *Narrative*, pp. 119–25.

13 WO 32/7760: Wolseley to Secretary of State for War, 10 July 1879. See also Webb and Wright, *Zulu King Speaks*, p. 35.

14 For Zulu coastal submissions after the battle of Ulundi, see Laband, 'Zulu polity', p. 15.

15 For Wolseley's negotiations near oNdini, see ibid., p. 16.

16 From the very first Wolseley considered Cetshwayo the chief stumbling-block to his settlement, and wrote candidly to his wife that he 'should be quite happy if some kind friend would but run an Assegai through him' (Wolseley Papers, Letters 2: Wolseley to his wife, 10 July 1879).

17 All the surrendered arms and cattle were to be made over to the military authorities, even if given up to Natal officials (CSO 2631, p. 22: Colonial Secretary to Border Agents, 27 September 1879).

18 WO 32/7786: Brig.-Gen. G. Pomeroy Colley: minute for the guidance of all officers commanding posts and all political officers dealing with the Zulu people, 26 July 1879.

19 For Wolseley's arrangements for the pacification of north-western Zululand, see Laband, 'Mbilini', p. 204.

20 For a general discussion on the state of the middle border between the battle of Ulundi and the advance of Clarke's Column, see Laband and Thompson, *Umvoti*, pp. 79–82.

21 For the pacification of the Mzinyathi frontier, see Laband and Thompson, *Buffalo Border*, pp. 78–81.

22 For the submission of central and southern Zululand, see Laband, 'Zulu polity', pp. 18–19.

23 *BPP* (C. 2482), no. 27: Wolseley to Secretary of State for Colonies, 18 July 1879.

24 Webb and Wright, *Zulu King Speaks*, p. 59.

25 For Cetshwayo's final efforts to negotiate with the British, see Laband, 'Humbugging the general', pp. 59–60.

26 Vijn, *Cetshwayo's Dutchman*, p. 54.

27 *JSA* III, p. 123: testimony of Mgundeni kaMatshekana. See P. Colenbrander, 'The Zulu kingdom, 1828–79', in Duminy and Guest, *Natal and Zululand*, pp. 93–4.

28 Wolseley's Journal: 14 August 1879.

29 Vijn, *Cetshwayo's Dutchman*, p. 160: Colenso's notes.

30 See Laband, 'Zulu polity', pp. 18–19.

31 For the pacification of the Mdlalose and Qulusi, see Laband, 'Mbilini', pp. 204–5.

32 Hamu himself, who was in a 'funk', used stomach pains as an excuse to return to Utrecht (AU 14, no. 391: Rudolph to Commandant Utrecht, 18 August 1879).

33 *BPP* (C. 2482), no. 8: Wolseley to Secretary of State for Colonies, 20 August 1879.

34 Watson Letters, p. 145: 12 August 1879: 'The Zulu were very grave

and appeared as if they felt humiliated . . . rather than angry.'

35 Woodgate's Private Diary: 28 August 1879; WO 32/7782: Diary of Baker Russell's Column, 29 August 1879.

36 Webb and Wright, *Zulu King Speaks*, p. 30.

37 For the final subjugation of Manyonyoba, see Laband, 'Mbilini', pp. 205–7.

38 At the end of September 1879, all Zulu refugees and captives in Natal (except those facing outstanding charges) were sent back to their homes in Zululand.

39 The Zulu near Fort Evelyn, for example, greeted the news of the king's capture with relief, for as they said, 'we may now plough again' (Stabb's Zulu War Diary: 29 August 1879).

40 Wolseley Papers, Letters 2: Wolseley to his wife, 26 August 1879.

41 Colenso Papers 27, no. 230: Colenso to Chesson, 13 September 1879; Fuze, *Black People*, p. 115; Guy, *Zulu Kingdom*, p. 59.

42 Wolseley's Journal: 23 August 1879.

43 Wolseley's Journal: 26 August 1879; *BPP* (C. 2482), no. 82: Wolseley to Secretary of State for Colonies, 27 August 1879.

44 John Shepstone Papers 10: 'Reminiscences', p. 103.

45 For the capture of the king, see War Office, *Narrative*, pp. 132–6; and Carl Faye Papers 7: Oftebro, 'How we captured Cetywayo', passim.

46 C. T. Binns, *The Last Zulu King: The Life and Death of Cetshwayo*, London, 1963, pp. 174–7.

47 John Shepstone Papers 10: 'Reminiscences', p. 104.

48 For the British settlement of Zululand, see Laband, 'Zulu polity', pp. 22–4.

49 E. H. Brookes and C. de B. Webb, *A History of Natal*, Pietermaritzburg, 1965, p. 147; Guy, *Zulu Kingdom*, p. 76. See also, J. Laband and P. Thompson, 'The reduction of Zululand, 1878–1904', in Duminy and Guest, *Natal and Zululand*, pp. 202–24.

50 Littleton Papers, no. 107: Littleton to his mother, 11 July 1879.

51 A. Preston (ed.), *Sir Garnet Wolseley's South African Journal, 1879–1880*, Cape Town, 1973, pp. 2–3; C. Ballard, 'Sir Garnet Wolseley and John Dunn: the architects and agents of the Ulundi settlement', in Duminy and Ballard, *New Perspectives*, pp. 130–1.

52 Ballard, *John Dunn*, pp. 147–8.

53 For the boundaries of the chiefdoms, see ZA 19, enc. in St. L. A. Herbert to Melmoth Osborn, 24 February 1880: report of the Zululand boundary commission by Lt.-Col. G. Villiers, Capt. J. Alleyne and Capt. H. Moore, 5 December 1879.

54 CSO 1927, no. 4162/1879: Robson to Colonial Secretary, 8 September 1879. It seems Mnyamana never made over the confiscated cattle to the king as he ought, but kept them until forced later by the British Resident in Zululand to return them to Sihayo (T. B. Jenkinson, *Amazulu: The Zulus, their Past History, Manners, Customs and Language*, London, 1882, p. 148).

55 Manyonyoba was permitted to build a new homestead near the site of Sihayo's Sokhexe *umuzi*. His notorious reputation as a freebooter went

before him, and his unenthusiastic new neighbours took immediate precautions to safeguard their livestock.

56 Preston, *Wolseley's Journal*, p. 318 (note 53.22).

57 WO 32/7785: Journal of Clarke's Column, 4–5, 8, 11–20 September 1879. All the chiefs who submitted are listed. See also Laband and Thompson, *Umvoti*, pp. 84–6, 89. About 400 guns were surrendered and some 1 000 cattle seized as fines.

58 *BPP* (C. 2482), no. 179: Wolseley to Secretary of State for Colonies, 11 November 1879.

59 From being the distinguishing cry of Cetshwayo's adherents in the civil war of 1856, 'uSuthu' became, on his accession, the Zulu national cry. By the 1880s the term had become particularly associated with the royalist cause (F. E. Colenso, *The Ruin of Zululand*, London, 1884–85, vol. II, pp. 384–5).

60 J. Home Thompson Papers: report by Thompson, 3 September 1879: interview with Somkhele, 20 August 1879.

61 *BPP* (C. 2482), enc. 2 in no. 93: Wolseley to Villiers, 9 September 1879.

62 It is incidentally of note that Wolseley, by making the northern limits of Hamu's territory the Bivane, and that of Sekethwayo's the Phemvana, ceded the entire former Disputed Territory between the confluence of the Phongolo and Phivane (including the Ntombe valley and Luneburg) to the Transvaal. This cession, along with the death of Mbilini and the relocation of Manyonyoba, at last closed that troubled frontier and confirmed the political authority of the settlers in the region.

63 *Times of Natal*, 3 November 1879: *Natal Mercury* correspondent at Ulundi, 18 October 1879.

64 *JSA* IV, p. 300: testimony of Ndukwana.

65 Wolseley's Journal: 1 September 1879. Indeed, more adherents of Mnyamana ended up in Hamu's territory than there were of the Ngenetsheni chief himself.

66 *BPP* (C. 3182), enc. in no. 34: minute, Osborn to Wood, 30 May 1881.

67 Wolseley did not go to the trouble of having the treaty already drawn up for Mnyamana's assent rewritten, but simply scratched out the latter's name and replaced it with Ntshingwayo's (Original Zulu War Treaties: treaty with Tshingwayo, Ulundi, 1 September 1879).

68 As Hart-Synnot wrote on 18 September about the evacuation of Zululand: 'Zulus have no reason to wish to attack us, for the terms of peace are manifestly for the benefit of all Zulus excepting a few great men, whose greatness departs with the fall of Cetywayo' (Hart-Synnot, *Letters*, p. 173).

69 Sir T. Shepstone, *The Native Question: Answer to President Reitz*, reprinted from the *Natal Mercury*, 29 January 1879, p. 6.

Select bibliography

Only documents and works which have been referred to directly in the footnotes, or which are essential reading, have been listed below. For a comprehensive bibliography and an analysis of the sources, reference should be made to my Ph.D. dissertation listed below.

Manuscript sources

Private papers

Great Britain:

The British Library, London

Hutton MSS

The Brynmore Jones Library, University of Hull

Hotham MSS

Hove Central Library

Wolseley MSS

National Army Museum, Chelsea

Anderson MSS
Anstruther MSS
Chelmsford MSS: 7–36
East MSS
Fairlie MSS
MacSwiney MSS
Roe MSS
Slade MSS

National Maritime Museum, Greenwich

Hamilton MSS
Milne MSS
Smith Dorrien MSS

Public Record Office, Kew

Buller MSS: WO 132/1–2
Wolseley MSS: WO 147/7

Rhodes House, Oxford
Anti-Slavery Society MSS: G12
Collection of Dr G. Kemble Woodgate, St Peter's College, Oxford
Woodgate MSS

South Africa:
The Africana Library, Johannesburg
Conductor in the Transport Division MSS
MacLeod MSS
Stabb MSS
The Brenthurst Library, Parktown
Alison MSS
Bulwer MSS
Harness MSS
St Vincent MSS
Killie Campbell Africana Library, Durban
Cato MSS: 1
Clarke MSS
Colenso MSS: 27–9
Commeline MSS
Cramer MSS
H. F. Fynn, Jnr, MSS
Goatham MSS
Hewitt MSS
Lugg MSS: 1–3
Mason MSS
Stainbank MSS
Stuart MSS: 79–88
Watson MSS
Wood MSS: 4–5, 7, 9
Local History Museum, Durban
Turner MSS
Vause MSS
Natal Archives Depot, Pietermaritzburg
Chelmsford MS
Colenso MSS: 2, 8, 73
Fannin MSS: 2/4–6
Faye MSS: 7–8
H. F. Fynn, Snr, MSS: 18
Lugg MSS
J. Shepstone MSS: 1, 9–10
Sir T. Shepstone MSS: 32–42, 68–71, 95
Home Thompson MSS
Wood MSS: II/1–5

William Cullen Library, University of the Witwatersrand, Johannesburg
Booth MSS
Parke Jones MSS
Littleton MSS: 53–116
Original Zulu War Treaties, September–October 1879

Unpublished official papers

Great Britain:

Public Record Office, Kew
Colonial Office: CO 179/126–32
War Office, Papers Relating to the Anglo–Zulu War: WO 32/7708–93

South Africa:

Natal Archives Depot, Pietermaritzburg
Colonial Secretary's Office, Natal: CSO 625–734, 1925–7, 2479, 2629–31
Government House, Natal: GH 500–1, 568–9, 600–2, 1220–1, 1326, 1398–402, 1410–13, 1421–4
Secretary for Native Affairs, Natal: SNA 1/1/30–5, 1/4/1–2, 1/6/3, 11–16, 1/7/11–13, 1/9/6–7
Zululand Archives: ZA 19, 21

Transvaal Archives Depot, Pretoria
Argief Utrecht: 1, 13–14, 25
Argief Wakkerstroom: 4–5, 43–4
Staatsekretaris, Transvaal: SS 236, 281, 283, 286, 291, 292, 295, 298, 306, 314, 316, 318, 346, 348–9, 352, 358

Official printed sources

British Parliamentary Papers: C. 2000, C. 2079, C. 2100, C. 2222, C. 2234, C. 2242, C. 2252, C.2260, C. 2269, C. 2308, C. 2316, C. 2318, C. 2367, C. 2374, C. 2454, C. 2482, C. 2505, C. 2584, C. 3182, C. 4643.
CO 879/14: *African Confidential Print* 158, 162, 164, 168–9
CO 879/15: *African Confidential Print* 170–3, 181a, 187, 190–1, 196
CO 879/16: *African Confidential Print* 202
WO 33/33: *Isandhlwana*, 1879
WO 33/34: *Zulu War, Miscellaneous*, 1878–79
Natal Government Gazette, XXX (1878), XXXI (1879)

Unofficial contemporary printed sources

Newspapers and periodicals

Natal Almanac, Directory and Yearly Register 1879
The Graphic, 1879
The Illustrated London News, 1879

The Natal Colonist, 1878–79
The Natal Mercury, 1878–79, 1929
The Natal Witness, 1878–79
The Times of Natal, 1878–79
Punch, 1879

Articles

Brown, Surgeon D. Blair 'Surgical notes on the Zulu War' *Lancet*, II, 5, July 1879

Forbes, A. 'Lord Chelmsford and the Zulu War', *Nineteenth Century*, February 1880

Fripp, C. E. 'Reminiscences of the Zulu War, 1879', *Pall Mall Magazine*, XX, 1900

Harness, Lt.-Col. A. 'The Zulu campaign from a military point of view', *Fraser's Magazine*, CI, April 1880

Hutton, Lt.-Gen. Sir E. 'Some recollections of the Zulu War', *Army Quarterly*, XVI, April 1921

Montgomery, A. N. 'Isandhlwana: A visit six months after the disaster', *Leisure Hours Magazine*, 1892

Schermbrucker, F. 'Zhlobane and Kambula', *South African Catholic Magazine*, III, 30 and 31, 1893

Pamphlets

Fynney, F. *The Zulu Army and Zulu Headmen. Published by Direction of the Lieut.-General Commanding*, Pietermaritzburg, April 1879

Molyneux, Maj. W. C. F. *Notes on Hasty Defences as Practised in South Africa*, Private circulation of notes made in 1879

Plé, J. *Les Laagers dans la Guerre des Zoulous*, Paris, 1882

Shepstone, Sir T. *The Native Question: Answer to President Reitz*, reprinted from the *Natal Mercury*, 29 January 1892

Books

Ashe, Maj. W. and Wyatt Edgell, Capt. the Hon. E. V. *The Story of the Zulu Campaign*, London, 1880

Blood, Sir B. *Four Score Years and Ten: Bindon Blood's Reminiscences*, London, 1933

Callaway, Rev. Canon *The Religious System of the Amazulu*, Leipzig, reprint, 1884

Callwell, Col. C. E. *Small Wars: Their Principles and Practice*, London, 3rd edit., 1906

Clairemont, E. *The Africander: A Plain Tale of Colonial Life*, London, 1896

Colenso, F. E., assisted by Durnford, Lt.-Col. E. *History of the Zulu War and its Origin*, London, 1880

Colenso, F. E. *The Ruin of Zululand*, London, 1884–85

Colenso, Bishop J. W. and Colenso, H. E. *Digest of Zulu Affairs Compiled by Bishop Colenso and Continued after his Death by his Daughter Harriette Emily Colenso*, Bishopstowe, 1878–88, series no. 1, parts I and II, December 1878–April 1881

Cox, Sir G. W. *The Life of J. W. Colenso*, London, 1888

Dawnay, G. C. *Private Journal of Guy C. Dawnay. Campaigns: Zulu 1879; Egypt 1882; Suakim 1885*, printed for private circulation

Francis, F. *Wars, Waves and Wanderings*, London, 1881

Frere, Sir B. *Afghanistan and South Africa: Letters*, London, 1881

Gibson, J. Y. *The Story of the Zulus*, London, 1911

Haggard, H. Rider *Cetywayo and his White Neighbours; or, Remarks on Recent Events in Zululand, Natal and the Transvaal*, London, 1888

Hallam Parr, Capt. H. *A Sketch of the Kafir and Zulu Wars*, London, 1880

Hamilton-Browne, Col. G. *A Lost Legionary in South Africa*, London, 19[?]

Harrison, Gen. Sir R. *Recollections of a Life in the British Army*, London, 1908

Holt, H. P. *The Mounted Police of Natal*, London, 1913

Intelligence Branch of the War Office, *Narrative of the Field Operations Connected with the Zulu War of 1879*, London, 1881

Intelligence Division of the War Office, *Precis of Information Concerning Zululand*, London, 1895

Jenkinson, T. B. *Amazulu: The Zulus, their Past History, Manners, Customs and Language*, London, 1882

Lucas, T. J. *The Zulus and the British Frontiers*, London, 1879

Ludlow, Capt. W. R. *Zululand and Cetywayo*, London and Birmingham, 1882

Mackinnon, J. P. and Shadbolt, S. (comps.) *The South African Campaign, 1879*, London, 1882

Malet, T. St. L. *Extracts from a Diary in Zululand*, Upper Norwood, 1880

McToy, E. D. *A Brief History of the 13th Regiment (P.A.L.I.) in South Africa during the Transvaal and Zulu Difficulties*, Devonport, 1880

Mitford, B. *Through the Zulu Country: Its Battlefields and its People*, London, 1883

Molyneux, Maj.-Gen. W. C. F. *Campaigning in South Africa and Egypt*, London, 1896

Montague, Capt. W. E. *Campaigning in South Africa: Reminiscences of an Officer in 1879*, Edinburgh and London, 1880

Moodie, D. C. F. (ed.) *The History of the Battles and Adventures of the British, the Boers and the Zulus in Southern Africa, from 1495 to 1879, Including Every Particular of the Zulu War of 1879, with a Chronology*, Sidney, Melbourne and Adelaide, 1879

— *John Dunn, Cetywayo and the Three Generals*, Pietermaritzburg, 1886

Mossop, G. *Running the Gauntlet*, London, 1937

Mynors, A. C. B. *Letters and Diary of the Late Arthur C. B. Mynors, Lieut. 3rd. Batt., 60th Rifles, Who Died at Fort Pearson, Natal, the 25th of April, 1879*, Margate, 1879

Norbury, Fleet-Surgeon H. F. *The Naval Brigade in South Africa during the Years 1877–78–79*, London, 1880

Norris-Newman, C. L. *In Zululand with the British throughout the War of 1879*, London, 1880
Paton, Col. G., Glennie, Col. F. and Penn Symons, W. (eds.) *Historical Records of the 24th Regiment from its Formation, in 1689*, London, 1892
Plant, R. *The Zulu in Three Tenses: Being a Forecast of the Zulu's Future in the Light of his Past*, Pietermaritzburg, 1905
Smith-Dorrien, Gen. Sir H. *Memories of Forty-eight Years' Service* London, 1925
Tomasson, W. H. *With the Irregulars in the Transvaal and Zululand*, London, 1881
Vijn, C. (tr. from the Dutch and edited with preface and notes by the Rt. Rev. J. W. Colenso, D.D., Bishop of Natal) *Cetshwayo's Dutchman: Being the Private Journal of a White Trader in Zululand during the British Invasion*, London, 1880
Wood, Field Marshal Sir E. *From Midshipman to Field Marshal*, London, 1906, vol. II
Wynne, W. R. C. *Memoir of Capt. W. R. C. Wynne, R.E.*, for private circulation, Southampton, n.d.

Later edited, annotated and printed contemporary sources

Bennett, Lt.-Col. I. H. W. *Eywitness in Zululand: The Campaign Reminiscences of Colonel W. A. Dunne, CB: South Africa, 1877–1881*, London, 1989
Butterfield, P. H. (ed.) *War and Peace in South Africa 1879–1881: The Writings of Philip Anstruther and Edward Essex*, Melville, 1987
Child, D. (ed.) *The Zulu War Journal of Colonel Henry Harford, C.B.*, Pietermaritzburg, 1978
— *Portrait of a Pioneer: The Letters of Sidney Turner from South Africa, 1864–1901*, Johannesburg, 1980
Clarke, S. (ed.) *Invasion of Zululand 1879: Anglo–Zulu War Experiences of Arthur Harness; John Jervis, 4th Viscount St Vincent; and Sir Henry Bulwer*, Houghton, 1979
— *Zululand at War 1879: The Conduct of the Anglo–Zulu War*, Houghton, 1984
Emery, F. *The Red Soldier: Letters from the Zulu War, 1879*, London, 1977
— *Marching over Africa: Letters from Victorian Soldiers*, London, 1986
Fannin, N. (ed.) *The Fannin Papers: Pioneer Days in South Africa*, Durban, 1932
Filter, H. (compiler), Bourquin, S. (tr. and ed.) *Paulina Dlamini: Servant of Two Kings*, Durban and Pietermaritzburg, 1986
Fuze, M. M. (Lugg, H. C. (tr.) and Cope, A. T. (ed.)) *The Black People and Whence They Came: A Zulu View*, Pietermaritzburg and Durban, 1979
Hall, H. L. 'With assegai and rifle: reminiscences of a transport conductor in the Zulu War', *Military History Journal*, IV, 5, June 1979, Appendix VIII
Hart-Synnot, B. M. (ed.) *Letters of Major-General Fitzroy Hart-Synnot C.B., C.M.G.*, London, 1912
Hattersley, A. F. *Later Annals of Natal*, London, 1938

Holme, N. (comp.) *The Silver Wreath: Being the 24th Regiment at Isandhlwana and Rorke's Drift*, London, 1979
Jones, L. T. (ed.) *Reminiscences of the Zulu War by John Maxwell*, Cape Town, 1979
Laband, J. *Fight us in the Open: The Anglo–Zulu War through Zulu Eyes*, Pietermaritzburg and Ulundi, 1985
Lloyd, Lt. W. N. 'The defence of Ekowe', *Natalia*, V, December 1975
Preston, A. (ed.) *Sir Garnet Wolseley's South African Journal, 1879–1880*, Cape Town, 1973
Webb, C. de B. and Wright, J. B. (eds.) *A Zulu King Speaks: Statements Made by Cetshwayo kaMpande on the History and Customs of his People*, Pietermaritzburg and Durban, 1978
— *The James Stuart Archive of Recorded Oral Evidence Relating to the History of the Zulu and Neighbouring Peoples*, Pietermaritzburg and Durban, 1976, 1979, 1982, 1986, vols. 1–4
Webb, C. de B. (ed.) 'A Zulu boy's recollections of the Zulu War', *Natalia*, VIII, December 1978

Later printed sources

Articles

(Articles marked with an asterisk are among those collected in Laband and Thompson, *Kingdom and Colony*, listed under *Books* below.)

Atmore, A. and Marks, S. 'The imperial factor in South Africa in the nineteenth century: towards a reassessment', *Journal of Imperial and Commonwealth History*, III, 1, 1974
Bailes, H. 'Technology and imperialism: a case study of the Victorian army in Africa', *Victorian Studies*, XXIV, 1, autumn 1980
Benyon, J. A. 'Isandhlwana and the passing of a proconsul', *Natalia*, VIII, December 1978
Bourquin, S. 'The Zulu military organization and challenge of 1879', *Military History Journal*, IV, 4, January 1979
Burroughs, P. 'Imperial defence and the Victorian army', *Journal of Imperial and Commonwealth History*, XV, 1, October 1986
Cobbing, J. 'The evolution of the Ndebele amabutho', *Journal of African History*, XV, 4, 1974
Cope, R. L. 'Political power within the Zulu kingdom and the "Coronation Laws" of 1873', *Journal of Natal and Zulu History*, VIII, 1985
Emery, F. 'Geography and imperialism: the role of Sir Bartle Frere (1815–84)', *Geographical Journal*, L, 3, November, 1984
Etherington, N. 'Labour supply and the genesis of South African confederation in the 1870s', *Journal of African History*, XX, 3, 1979
Guy, J. 'A note on firearms in the Zulu kingdom with special reference to the Anglo–Zulu War, 1879', *Journal of African History*, XII, 4, 1971
Hall, Maj. D. D. 'Artillery in the Zulu War, 1879', *Military History Journal*, IV, 4, January 1979

Harries, P. 'History, ethnicity and the Ingwavuma land deal: the Zulu northern frontier in the nineteenth century', *Journal of Natal and Zulu History*, VI, 1983

Jackson, F. W. D. 'Isandhlwana, 1879: the sources re-examined', '*Journal of the Society for Army Historical Research*, XLIX, 173, 175, 176, 1965

— 'Isandhlwana revisited: a letter to the editor', *Soldiers of the Queen*, XXXIII, July 1983

Knight, I. J. 'The uniforms and weapons of the Zulu army, 1879', *Soldiers of the Queen*, XVI, February 1979

Koopman, A. 'Zulu place-names in the Drakensberg', in Sinclair, A. J. L. (ed.), *G. S. Nienaber – 'n Huldeblyk*, University of the Western Cape, 1983

Laband, J. P. C. 'The Zulu army in the war of 1879: some cautionary notes', *Journal of Natal and Zulu History*, II, 1979 (*)

— 'Bulwer, Chelmsford and the Border Levies: the dispute over the defence of Natal, 1879', *Theoria*, LVII, October 1981 (*)

— 'British fieldworks of the Zulu campaign of 1879, with special reference to Fort Eshowe', *Military History Journal*, VI, 1, June 1983 (*)

— 'The cohesion of the Zulu polity under the impact of the Anglo-Zulu War: a reassessment', *Journal of Natal and Zulu History*, VIII, 1985 (*)

— 'Humbugging the general? King Cetshwayo's peace overtures during the Anglo–Zulu War', *Theoria*, LXVII, October 1986 (*)

— 'The battle of Khambula, 29 March 1879: a re-examination from the Zulu perspective', in Knight, I. J. (ed.), *There Will Be an Awful Row at Home about This*, Shoreham-by-Sea, 1987 (*)

— 'Mbilini, Manyonyoba and the Phongolo River frontier: a neglected sector of the Anglo–Zulu War of 1879', *Journal of Natal and Zulu History*, X, 1987 (*)

— 'Introduction', *Companion to Narrative of Field Operations Connected with the Zulu War of 1879*, Constantia, 1989

Morris, D. 'Isandhlwana', *Soldiers of the Queen*, XXIX/XXX, summer 1982

Raum, O. F. 'Aspects of Zulu diplomacy in the nineteenth century', *Afrika und Obersee*, LXVI, 1983

Strachan, H. 'The early Victorian army and the nineteenth century revolution in government', *English Historical Review*, XCV, October 1980

Thompson, P. S. 'Captain Lucas and the Border Guard: the war on the lower Tugela, 1879', *Journal of Natal and Zulu History*, III, 1980 (*)

— 'The active defence after Isandlwana: British raids across the Buffalo, March–May 1879', *Military History Journal*, III, June 1981 (*)

Webb, C. de B. 'Lines of power: the High Commissioner, the telegraph and the war of 1879', *Natalia*, VIII, December 1978

Whybra, J. 'Contemporary sources and the composition of the main Zulu impi, January 1879', *Soldiers of the Queen*, LIII, June 1988

Books

Aron, R. *Peace and War: A Theory of International Relations*, London,

1966
Ballard, C. *John Dunn: The White Chief of Zululand*, Craighall, 1985
Barthorp, M. *The Zulu War: A Pictorial History*, Poole, 1980
Belich, J. *The New Zealand Wars and the Victorian Interpretation of Racial Conflict*, Auckland, 1986
Benyon, J. A. *Proconsul and Paramountcy in South Africa: The High Commission, British Supremacy and the Sub-continent, 1806-1910*, Pietermaritzburg, 1980
Binns, C. T. *The Last Zulu King: The Life and Death of Cetshwayo*, London, 1963
Blainey, G. *The Causes of War*, Melbourne, 1977
Booth, A. R. *Swaziland: Tradition and Change in a Southern African Kingdom*, Boulder, Colorado, 1983
Bonner, P. *Kings, Commoners and Concessionaires: The Evolution and Dissolution of the Nineteenth-Century Swazi State*, Johannesburg, 1983
Brodie, B. *War and Politics*, London, 1974
Brookes, E. H. and Webb, C. de B. *A History of Natal*, Pietermaritzburg, 1965
Bryant, A. T. *The Zulu People as They Were before the White Man Came*, Pietermaritzburg, 1949
— *Zulu Medicine and Medicine-Men*, Cape Town, 1966
Delius, P. *The Land Belongs to Us: The Pedi Polity, the Boers and the British in the Nineteenth Century Transvaal*, Johannesburg, 1983
Duminy, A. and Ballard, C. (eds.) *The Anglo–Zulu War: New Perspectives*, Pietermaritzburg, 1981
— and Guest, B. (eds.) *Natal and Zululand from Earliest Times to 1910: A New History*, Pietermaritzburg, 1989
Edgerton, R. B. *Like Lions They Fought: The Zulu War and the Last Black Empire in South Africa*, Bergvlei, 1988
Featherstone, D. *Weapons and Equipment of the Victorian Soldier*, Poole, 1978
Fortes, M. and Evans-Pritchard, E. E. *African Political Systems*, London, 1940
Goodfellow, C. F. *Great Britain and South African Confederation, 1870–1881*, Cape Town, 1966
Guest, B. and Sellers, J. M. (eds.) *Enterprise and Exploitation in a Victorian Colony: Aspects of the Economic and Social History of Colonial Natal*, Pietermaritzburg, 1985
Guy, J. *The Destruction of the Zulu Kingdom: The Civil War in Zululand, 1879–1884*, London, 1979
Howard, M. *The Causes of Wars*, London, 1983
Knight, I. J. (ed.) *There Will Be an Awful Row at Home about This*, Shoreham-by-Sea, 1987
— *The Zulus*, London, 1989
— *Brave Men's Blood: The Epic of the Zulu War, 1879*, London, 1990
Krige, E. *The Social System of the Zulus*, Pietermaritzburg, 1974
Kuper, H. *An African Aristocracy: Rank among the Swazi*, London, 1947
Laband, J. P. C. and Thompson, P. S. *War Comes to Umvoti: The Natal–*

Zululand Border, 1878–9, Durban, 1980
— and Thompson, P. S. with Henderson, S. *The Buffalo Border 1879: The Anglo–Zulu War in Northern Natal*, Durban, 1983
— and Wright, J. *King Cetshwayo kaMpande (c. 1832–1884)*, Pietermaritzburg and Ulundi, 1983
— and Thompson, P. S. *Field Guide to the War in Zululand and the Defence of Natal 1879*, Pietermaritzburg, 2nd revised edition, 1983; reprinted with minor revisions, 1987
— *The Battle of Ulundi*, Pietermaritzburg and Ulundi, 1988
— and P. S. Thompson, *Kingdom and Colony at War: Sixteen Studies on the Anglo–Zulu War of 1879*, Pietermaritzburg and Constantia, 1990
Lamar H. and Thompson, L. (eds.) *The Frontier in History: North America and Southern Africa Compared*, New Haven and London, 1981
Lider, J. *On the Nature of War*, Farnborough, 1979
Lugg, H. C. *Historic Natal and Zululand*, Pietermaritzburg, 1949
— *Life under a Zulu Shield*, Pietermaritzburg, 1975
Mair, L. *African Kingdoms*, Oxford, 1977
Martineau, J. *The Life and Correspondence of the Right Hon. Sir Bartle Frere,Bart., G.C.B., F.R.S., Etc.*, London, 1895, vol. II
Morris, D. R. *The Washing of the Spears: A History of the Rise of the Zulu Nation under Shaka and its Fall in the Zulu War of 1879*, London, 1966
Ngubane, H. *Body and Mind in Zulu Medicine: An Ethnography of Health and Disease in Nyuswa–Zulu Thought and Practice*, London, 1977
Oliver, R. and Sanderson, S. W. (eds.) *The Cambridge History of Africa*, Cambridge, 1985, vol. 6
Peires, J. B. (ed.) *Before and after Shaka: Papers in Nguni History*, Grahamstown, 1981
Samuelson, R. C. A. *Long, Long Ago*, Durban, 1929
Schnackenberg, Pastor J. (ed.) *Geschichte der Freien ev.-luth. Synode in Sudafrika 1892–1932*, Celle, 1933
Smail, J. L. *From the Land of the Zulu Kings*, Durban, 1979
Strachan, H. *European Armies and the Conduct of War*, London, 1983
Summers, R. and Pagden, L. W. *The Warriors*, Cape Town, 1970
Von Clausewitz, C. (Howard, M. and Paret, P., eds.) *On War*, Princeton, 1976
Whitehouse, H. *Battle in Africa, 1879–1914*, Mansfield, 1987
Wilkinson-Latham, C. *Uniforms and Weapons of the Zulu War*, London, 1978

Unpublished Theses and Conference and Seminar Papers

Cobbing, J. R. D. 'The Ndebele under the Khumalos, 1820–1896', unpublished Ph.D. thesis, University of Lancaster, 1976
Cope, R. L. 'Shepstone and Cetshwayo 1873–1879', unpublished M.A. thesis, University of Natal, 1967
Cope, N. L. G. 'The defection of Hamu', unpublished B.A. Hons. thesis, University of Natal, 1980
Dominy, G. A. 'Awarding a "retrospective white hat"? A reconsideration of

the geopolitics of "Frere's War" of 1879', paper presented at a workshop on Natal in the Colonial Period, University of Natal, Pietermaritzburg, October 1984

Harries, P. 'Labour migration from Mozambique to South Africa; with special reference to the Delagoa Bay hinterland, *c.* 1862 to 1897', unpublished Ph.D. thesis, University of London, 1983

Kennedy, P. A. 'Fatal diplomacy: Sir Theophilus Shepstone and the Zulu kings, 1839–1879', unpublished Ph.D. thesis, University of California, 1976

Laband, J. P. C., 'Kingdom in crisis: the response of the Zulu polity to the British invasion of 1879', unpublished Ph.D. thesis, University of Natal, 1990

Mael, R. 'The problem of political integration in the Zulu empire', unpublished Ph.D. thesis, University of California, 1974

Mathews, J. 'Lord Chelmsford and the problems of transport and supply during the Anglo–Zulu War of 1879', unpublished M.A. thesis, University of Natal, 1979

— 'Lord Chelmsford: British general in southern Africa, 1878–1879', unpublished D. Litt. et Phil. thesis, University of South Africa, 1986

Monteith, M. A. 'Cetshwayo and Sekhukhune 1875–1879', unpublished M.A. thesis, University of the Witwatersrand, 1978

Paterson, H. 'The military organization of the Colony of Natal 1881–1910', unpublished M.A. thesis, University of Natal, 1985

Rawlinson, R. 'Ondini: royal military homestead of King Cetshwayo kaMpande, 1872–1879', paper presented at the Conference on Natal and Zulu History, University of Natal, Durban, July 1985

Index

In accordance with modern practice, Zulu words are entered under the stem and not under the prefix.